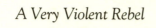

A Very Violent Rebel

A Very Violent Rebel

The Civil War Diary of Ellen Renshaw House

Edited by

Daniel E. Sutherland

Voices of the Civil War

Frank L. Byrne, Series Editor

THE UNIVERSITY OF TENNESSEE PRESS / KNOXVILLE

The Voices of the Civil War series makes available a variety of primary source materials that illuminate issues on the battlefield, the home front, and the western front, as well as other aspects of this historic era. The series contextualizes the personal accounts within the framework of the latest scholarship and expands established knowledge by offering new perspectives, new materials, and new voices.

Library of Congress Cataloging-in-Publication Data

House, Ellen Renshaw, 1843–1907.
    A very violent rebel : the Civil War diary of Ellen Renshaw House / edited by Daniel E. Sutherland. — 1st ed.
            p.   cm. — (Voices of the Civil War)
    Includes bibliographical references and index.
    ISBN 0-87049-944-0 (cloth: alk. paper)
1. House, Ellen Renshaw, 1843–1907—Diaries. 2. Tennessee, East—History—Civil War, 1861–1865. 3. United States—History—Civil War, 1861–1865—Personal narratives, Confederate. 4. Women—Tennessee, East—Diaries.
I. Sutherland, Daniel E. II. Title. III. Series: Voices of the Civil War series.
E605.H83 1996
973.7'82—dc20   96-4455
                                                          CIP

In memory of John Moore House (1844–1865),
as Ellen would want it,
and for Christopher Michael Sutherland,
who is a rebel in his own right

Contents

Illustrations

MAPS

Foreword

A staple of southern historical novels is the Belle, usually portrayed as a planter's daughter. The foremost exemplar of this character is Margaret Mitchell's Scarlett O'Hara. Her family's plantation was a central locale in both the novel and the film in which she figured, causing much of her audience to pay scant attention to the longer part of her life spent in Atlanta. But the Belle could also bloom in an urban setting. Such a city flower was Ellen Renshaw House, whose wartime diary fills this volume. A member of a prominent Knoxville family, her life belied the stereotype that East Tennesseans were all unionists. Like Reuben G. Clark, whose reminiscences comprised one of the first volumes in this series, Ellen House was a fervent Confederate.

As such, she bitterly resented the fall of the metropolis of East Tennessee to the forces of what she viewed as an enemy government. One of the values of her diary is its revelation of the mixed reactions to Federal military rule by the city's inhabitants, white and black. House eagerly followed news of military actions that might portend the recapture of her home and gave an inside view of the siege of the city in 1863 by the army of Confederate General James Longstreet. Despite her own privations, she devoted much attention to providing relief to Confederate prisoners of war in the city. Her open sympathy for them combined with her scorn for the Yankees (together with suspicion that she was spying) finally led the Federals to expel her from Knoxville. After describing in detail the procedure by which this was done, House gave useful information on conditions elsewhere in the South, especially in Georgia during the latter part of the war.

Running through House's diary is a strong current of violence. This might be taken for granted on the nearby battlefields, but political differences and sometimes plain lawlessness led to physical attacks of neighbor on neighbor, even to the extreme of murder. The finish of the formal war did not end the killing. Not long after the advent of peace, House sorrowfully reported the shooting of her beloved brother. Even after the turmoil of Reconstruction was over, one of House's family connections was killed in a street affray that was cited by Mark Twain in a critique of southern society.

Ellen Renshaw House's skillfully edited diary recreates for modern readers a fiery, attractive belle, strong-minded with a faint hint of espionage. The color of her real life challenged that of the fictional Scarlett.

Frank L. Byrne
Kent State University

Acknowledgments

Ellen Renshaw House never intended that anyone should read her wartime diary. At least, she never allowed anyone to do so during her lifetime. A granddaughter, Cynthia Rutledge Barnes, came into possession of the diary after Ellen's death. She guarded it jealously, admitting to other family members that the diary existed, but leading them to believe that only a portion of it—a few months in 1863—had survived the ravages of time. Not until 1992 was the truth discovered and permission gained to present Ellen's story to the world.

The supposedly lost diary was discovered by Ellen Allran and Victoria Guthrie, respectively the great-great-granddaughter and great-granddaughter of Ellen Renshaw House, and publication of Ellen's diary would have been impossible without their cooperation and enthusiasm. They initiated the publication process by offering the manuscript to the University of Tennessee Press. Thereafter, they provided whatever resources the family possessed to ensure the highest possible degree of historical accuracy and completeness, including copies and transcriptions of the original diary, family correspondence and photographs, additional diaries written by Ellen House and her father, and newspaper clippings. Their enthusiasm and total candor eased the often tedious research required to prepare the diary for publication and made the entire project a labor filled with joy and satisfaction.

I also extend thanks to Ann Ellis Pullen of Kennesaw State College, who assisted Ms. Allran and Ms. Guthrie in transcribing the diary and identifying some of the people and places mentioned by Ellen before I became involved in the project. Also in this early stage, Marianna Titus devoted long hours to typing the diary from Ms. Allran's handwritten transcription. Ms. Titus, Garrie P. Landry, and Joyce Simpson undertook the delicate assignment of restoring the only surviving antebellum photograph of Ellen House, which appears in this book. Mary Adair Horde supplied additional information about the House family, and Digby Seymour graciously provided me not only with a copy of his important book about the war in East Tennessee but with permission to reproduce portions of it. Among the many archivists and librarians who assisted me, I am particularly grateful to the staffs of the University of Arkansas Library, University of Tennessee Library, Knoxville Public Library, East Tennessee Historical Society, Georgia Department of Archives and History, Atlanta History Center, Fort Worth Public Library, and the Fort Worth branch of the National Archives. Patricia Singleton and Christopher Battle, graduate students at the University of Arkansas, helped with some of the more tedious facets of the research and editorial process. Suzanne Smith cheerfully assisted in preparing the manuscript for publication, and Karin Kaufman, my copyeditor, did an excellent job of catching those little things.

Editorial Policy

A few fundamental but important rules have been followed in bringing House's diary to print. First, the diary as presented here is actually two diaries: Ellen's regular diary, or "journal" as she called it, for 1863–65, and a pocket diary used from April to August 1864 while she traveled from Tennessee to Virginia to Georgia. The latter has been integrated into the former. Second, the diaries have been published in their entirety. Very few ellipses have been used, and then only to indicate portions of the diary that are completely illegible.

The only inconvenience posed by this latter decision is the presence of occasional repetitions that could have been avoided with the use of ellipses. Editorially, the decision required that I comment on all historical inaccuracies. Ellen occasionally recorded rumors without waiting to have them verified or failed to correct them when she later discovered they were inaccurate. Similarly, she commented on obscure military actions that never found their way into official reports. The heaviest editorial burden was to confirm the authenticity or inaccuracy of those rumors and actions. They have been left in the text, however, to convey a sense of the confusion and chaos inspired by the war.

Nearly as trying was the need to identify the hundreds of people and places, some well known, others obscure, mentioned in the diary. This task was pursued with the utmost diligence and tenacity, but I was not able to identify everyone. Ellen simply mentions too many Captain Smiths and Mr. Hills, too many Emmas and Harolds. However, the most important players—

indeed, the vast majority of the people in her story—have been identified, and nothing of the diary's historical value or human drama has been lost by the occasional gaps.

Like most diarists, Ellen House did not aspire to consistency in spelling, capitalization, punctuation, or usage. She nevertheless was an extremely literate woman. Her diary is readable as originally penned and, therefore, only a few liberties have been taken in the name of consistency and accuracy. Ellen sometimes used a day of the week, sometimes a date, sometimes both day and date to begin her entries—and occasionally one or the other was incorrect. I have used both the correct day and date. Ellen's spelling has been left largely untouched. Where she spelled a person's name differently at different times, I have used the most accurate rendition throughout the manuscript. Misspelled words and place names have been left uncorrected if they are recognizable, although a warning *sic* has been used on a few occasions. Capitalization has been left untouched unless alteration was required by a change in punctuation (most often a period). Finally, Ellen almost invariably used the word sit when she meant sat; the past tense has been used where appropriate.

The biggest liberty has been taken in shaping the contours of the manuscript. Ellen tended to write a single long paragraph for each daily entry. As some of these entries continue for several pages, I have, for the sake of convenience, broken them into paragraphs. Likewise, I have divided the diary into six chapters. Ellen also tended to rely on dashes instead of periods and commas as a primary form of punctuation. I have restored the periods and commas. Frequently Ellen wrote very long sentences that at worst produce muddled thoughts and at the least become tiring to the reader. I have imposed a logical sentence structure where understanding and readability were in jeopardy.

Introduction

In the midst of the Civil War, a rural East Tennessee girl, about eight years old, answered a knock at her father's door. Before her stood a Confederate officer seeking information about local roads. The girl looked him up and down, quite coolly for one her age, and then asked, "What I wants to know is are you a Reb, or a Yank, or a bushwhack?" Such was the condition of East Tennessee between 1861 and 1865, a region of divided loyalties and intense partisanship. "The residents in all that East Tennessee country, at that time, were very much divided in their allegiance to the two contesting parties," observed the Confederate officer, "& we learned that bushwhackers were abundant, & all strangers were regarded with suspicion."[1]

Unhappily for East Tennesseans, it was also a very desirable region. Geographically and strategically, it formed a vital fault line in the Confederacy that ran from Chattanooga northeastward through Knoxville, on to southwestern Virginia, and down the length of the Shenandoah Valley. The region's natural resources included niter and saltpeter. It boasted the only southern blast furnaces outside of Virginia. Branches of the East Tennessee railroad radiated from Knoxville into Virginia, Georgia, and Kentucky. Politically, the region formed one of the largest conclaves of unionist sentiment in the South. The Confederacy needed to hold East Tennessee and to pacify its hostile citizens; the Union wanted to liberate it. Consequently, North and South contended for East Tennessee from the earliest days of the war. Fault line it may have been, but one Richmond newspaper underscored its importance by calling it the "Keystone of the Southern arch."[2]

Ellen Renshaw House knew all about the divided loyalties of East Tennessee. She was born in Savannah, Georgia, on August 10, 1843. Her father, South Carolina-born Samuel Crawford House (1794–1866), moved
to Savannah shortly after marrying Frances Budden Renshaw (1805–92), a
native of Philadelphia, in 1831. Ellen had five siblings, all born in Savannah: Frances (Fannie) Renshaw House (1832–1923), William McLean
House (1834–84), Samuel House (1837–90), John Moore House (1844–
65), and Charles Frank House (1848–54). Her father provided for this brood
by working as a customs collector and trade commissioner until 1848, when
his wife's health forced the family to move to Marietta. Samuel then identified himself as a planter, and in 1850 he owned seven slaves. The family
also employed two white servants.[3]

Around 1857, two of Ellen's brothers, Will and Sam, moved to Knoxville
to engage in business. In 1859, Sam settled in Memphis to work in the cotton
trade. "I like my new business very well," he informed his father. "I like the
City. . . . There is so much life & bustle every one appears to be doing well
& the city is improving very rapidly." Will seemed to be just as pleased with
Knoxville, but the rest of the House family chafed in Marietta. They spoke
of joining either Will or Sam. Both sons recommended Knoxville. Will
wanted his father there to assist him in business, and Sam admitted that
"Knoxville would be the best place." "It is healthier and I expect the society is better," he confided to the family. "Most all here are parvenus. Money
is the standard by which every thing is weighed." So in late 1859 or early
1860, Samuel took his wife and remaining three children—young Charles
having passed away—to Knoxville. They lived in a rented house, probably
on Cumberland Street, and owned no slaves, although they employed an
Irish housemaid, twenty-five-year-old Catherine Owen. Two black
women—Martha and Sidney—eventually replaced Catherine, but it is difficult to say whether they were hired or owned by the House family. Samuel,
listed in the 1860 census as a bookkeeper, and William, identified as a merchant, each owned personal property valued at one thousand dollars.[4]

Then came the war, and the House family did all it could to support
the Confederacy. Poor health prevented Will, who had married Jane
(Jeanie) Strong Hazen of Knoxville, in 1860, from serving in the army. He

did, however, find work as a government clerk. "I am glad Will has got in Employ of Government," Sam told his father. "He could not stand the army and a substitute is too expensive!" Sam, on the other hand, rushed to enlist on April 15, 1861, in Captain T. N. Johnson's company of the First Tennessee Heavy Artillery. By June, his unit had moved to Randolph, Tennessee, and Island No. 10. "We expected Mr. Lincoln and his angels some days ago, but they disappointed us!" he informed his mother. "We would give them a glorious reception—the display of fire works would have been splendid."[5]

Sam offered to find a place for John in his company. They could use more men, he informed his family playfully, for "standing Picket Guard way out in the swamp the Insects nearly eat a man up & you have to stay out all night." But John had already decided to enlist in Company E, Nineteenth Tennessee Infantry, then assembling at Knoxville. The regiment would serve locally at Cumberland Gap and elsewhere in Tennessee and Kentucky under General Felix K. Zollicoffer. Shortly after Zollicoffer's death in October 1861, John joined the staff of General Alexander P. Stewart as a clerk. Meantime, Sam had achieved a less sanguine view of the war. "I have no mercy with the Yankee or their sympathizers," he told his parents from Columbus, Kentucky, in September. "I have seen too much of their Hellish work—burning & Pillaging—ever to give quarter." Sam's regiment moved to Vicksburg in December 1862. "We thought Columbus was bad enough," he sighed, "but this place beats it all hollow." Sergeant House was still there when the Confederate garrison surrendered in July 1863. He spent the next five months in prisons in Mississippi and Alabama. Exchanged, he served at Fort Morgan, Alabama, until that garrison surrendered in August 1864. He then endured imprisonment at Castle William, in New York Harbor, until February 1865, when he was transferred to Elmira, New York. He was finally exchanged and sent home in March 1865, having first spent several days in a Richmond hospital recovering his strength.[6]

John fared just as poorly. Never in robust health, Johnnie, as Ellen called him, returned home at least once on sick leave. "What does he intend doing?" a concerned Sam asked from Mississippi in September 1862. "Of course he wont think of going back to the army for some time to come." Yet back he went, to be praised for his work on Stewart's staff and to be captured at Missionary Ridge in November 1863. He spent the next twenty-two months imprisoned on Johnson's Island in Lake Erie. By the time he left prison, he weighed a mere ninety pounds, less than the petite Ellen.[7]

Ellen House was particularly close to John, just a year younger than herself. She worried about Sam, but she grieved over the confinement of Johnnie. In fact, we may have John's capture and imprisonment to thank for Ellen' diary. She commenced her daily record of events in Knoxville when Federals captured the city in September 1863, nearly three months before John fell captive, but toward the end of her diary, Ellen claims to have maintained it primarily for John's benefit. "Today finishes my journal," she wrote on the last day of December 1865, just five weeks after her brother had been murdered by a highwayman. "I do not think I will keep another. I have no reason for keeping one. This I commenced for Johnnie. I thought he would like to know what was passing while he was far away from me in prison." She named her first child, a daughter, Johnnie.

Another family member to play a military role in the war was Frank Bostick Renshaw (1815–67), a younger brother of Ellen's mother. Renshaw enlisted in the U.S. Navy as a midshipmen in 1828. He was the senior lieutenant at the Pensacola Navy Yard when it surrendered to Confederate forces on January 12, 1861. Although a Pennsylvanian, he had married a southern woman, and so following the surrender, Renshaw resigned his commission to join the Confederate navy. "Is very hard to give it up [his commission]," he confessed to Ellen's parents, "but one must have to decide—either North or South." A month later, he reported, "Officers resigning every day & we are still at the yard. I will remain, Wife & Babes . . . will stay till the Ball commences. Then I will pack them to town." Renshaw served through the war and was paroled at Montgomery, Alabama, in May 1865.[8]

Ellen began her wartime diary in January 1863. She had kept a diary before, at age fourteen, while living in Marietta. Like most adolescents, her attention at that time had focused on social activities. By 1863, at the ripe old age of nineteen, she tried again. She faltered at first. After making a few scattered entries for January and March, she lapsed into silence until September and the arrival of Federal troops under General Ambrose Burnside in Knoxville. But thereafter she kept a remarkable record of life in the occupied city. Another break came between September 1864 and January

1865, when she was a refugee seeking a place to settle in Virginia and Georgia. After several months at Abingdon, Virginia, she finally landed in Eatonton, Putnam County, Georgia. There, resuming her diary, she recorded an insightful view of life in exile until her return to Knoxville in June 1865.

While Ellen continued to comment on the activities of her middle-class social circles in Tennessee and Georgia, she had by 1863 matured into a perceptive, intelligent, and wry observer. Her diary provides a daily account of what she called the "frustrations of war" under Federal rule, during the siege of Knoxville, and as a refugee. It also extends into the months immediately following the war to describe the fate of unionists and returning soldiers in Knoxville, as well as the shooting death of her brother John. Ellen provides direct, often caustic, appraisals of the Federal soldiers—mostly officers—with whom she had contact. Likewise, she is not shy in expressing her opinion about Knoxville neighbors, particularly unionists such as William G. "Parson" Brownlow. Ellen was, in her own words, a "very violent rebel." She worked to secure food, medicine, clothing, and blankets for Confederate prisoners being held in Knoxville. She found homes in which to place prisoners too ill to be cared for in the jails. She and her parents cut up their own living room carpet to provide the shivering men with blankets. Ellen also describes the shortages, insults, and anguish suffered by the city's southern loyalists. And she is a good barometer of how much southern civilians knew about the war. She frequently comments on nearby fighting, and although she repeats many invalid rumors, much of what she reports is accurate.

In spite of herself, Ellen did befriend a few Federal soldiers who sympathized with the House family, but her rebellious streak finally overcame good judgment. Federal authorities asked Ellen to leave Knoxville in April 1864, when she insulted the wife of a Union officer who resided in her parents' house. Federal authorities may also have suspected her of being a spy, although it is unlikely that she played this dangerous game. Certainly Ellen says nothing in her diary to suggest a tendency toward espionage. The suspicion may have arisen from the amount of information she possessed about Union army activities in and around the city. Likely, some of this information—harmless enough in itself—came from her soldier acquaintances. Then, too, one could learn a lot about Union plans and movements from the local newspapers. General William T. Sherman, well known for his contempt for the press, complained to General John Schofield in April 1864, "The papers also contain a message from Knoxville giving my movements . . . from Parson Brownlow. . . . Tell Parson Brownlow that he must leave military matters to us, and that he must not chronicle my movements or those of any military body. If he confines his efforts to his own sphere of action he will do himself more credit and his country more good."[9]

Of course, Ellen can best tell her own story, but a few remarks about secession and the first half of the war in Knoxville and East Tennessee will help set the stage. Tennesseans rejected secession as a solution to national woes in the winter of 1860–61, but that is not to deny they were swept up in the partisan fever of the moment. Only a third of the state's 1,109,801 citizens owned slaves, and only 47 slave owners had more than 100 slaves each. It was a state of small farmers, merchants, and manufacturers. John Bell, Tennessee's native son, won the state's electoral votes in the presidential contest of November 1860, but most people did not feel threatened by the victory of Abraham Lincoln. When South Carolina seceded, most Tennesseans seemed to agree with the *Memphis Enquirer,* which declared, "Let every man put his foot on secession, it is no remedy for Southern wrong." Still, as seven sister states methodically withdrew from the Union between November 1860 and February 1861, Tennesseans could not ignore the debate.[10]

Knoxville and Knox County reacted swiftly. In 1860, 20,020 whites and 2,370 slaves resided in the county. Knoxville, the county seat, had 3,704 citizens. On January 25, 1861, unionists and secessionists held rallies at opposite ends of Gay Street, the city's principal thoroughfare. What drove a person to one end of Gay Street or the other is still a question of dispute among historians, though clearly slave ownership alone was not enough. East Tennessee, if not Knoxville, was strongly unionist in its sympathies, far more so than the western and central portions of the state. The region rejected a call for a state convention to consider secession in February. In fact, East Tennessee tipped the balance in defeating efforts to hold the convention, which was favored elsewhere in the state.[11]

Lincoln's call for troops following Confederate bombardment of Fort Sumter changed the situation in Tennessee dramatically, just as it did in Arkansas, North Carolina, and Virginia. Governor Isham G. Harris and the legislature endorsed secession and called for a popular vote on the referendum on June 8. East Tennessee unionists, hoping that an appeal to reason might deflect the secessionist onslaught, called for a convention in Knoxville on May 30 at which "the conservative element of our whole section may be represented, and that wise, prudent and judicious counsels may prevail, looking to peace and harmony among ourselves." Several hundred delegates from nearly thirty counties attended. They passed a resolution denouncing secession, but by that time few people were listening. Tennesseans voted in favor of disunion 104,913 to 47,238. Unionists met again at Greeneville about a week later to voice their displeasure, but the war had started without them.[12]

East Tennessee had consistently voted against secession. On June 8, East Tennesseans rejected disunion by more than three to one, although Knoxville endorsed southern independence by sixty-eight percent. But Confederate recruitment was already well under way, and Knoxville, awash in mustering troops, became a Confederate bastion. On July 26, the Richmond government, appreciating the strategic importance of the region, assigned General Zollicoffer to command the District of East Tennessee. Zollicoffer's appointment was influenced by his reputation as a popular Whig politician in the state. As someone who had supported John Bell in 1860, he seemed the right person to win the confidence of dissident unionists and guide them into the Confederate fold. But when, in August, the government required a loyalty oath of all East Tennesseans and announced it would confiscate the property of all "alien enemies," it created a bitterness that would mark East Tennessee for the remainder of the war.[13]

Flight and mass arrests of unionists followed. Many sought refuge in neighboring Kentucky. The more defiant, such as Parson Brownlow, editor of the *Knoxville Whig*, were lodged in the Knoxville jail, although Brownlow was eventually released and exiled to the North. "More than one hundred persons have been arrested in East Tennessee," reported one observer, "without warrants in some cases, marching great distances, and carried into court on no other charge than that they were Union men." Unhappily, a good deal of bullying and harassment, mostly by Confederate soldiers, accompanied the purge. Unionists responded with a guerrilla war, characterized by bushwhacking and sabotage. The most famous instance of the latter was the "bridge-burning" incident, in which unionists attempted to destroy the railroad bridges in East Tennessee in conjunction with a proposed Federal invasion. They burned five bridges, but no Union troops moved into the region, and several bridge-burners were hanged.[14]

This unionist-disunionist split is crucial for appreciating the political and military ferocity of the war in East Tennessee. The people feared and despised Federal and Confederate soldiers nearly as much as they did neighbors and political foes who espoused the rival cause. One Knoxville citizen insisted, for example, that unionists were often arrested in the autumn of 1861 "at the instigation of a personal enemy." Others saw the roots of conflict embedded in "party prejudices" and "personal animosities." When the disunionists held power, they took special delight in humbling the likes of Brownlow; when the unionists finally gained control, those who had been oppressed relished the role of oppressor. This strain and antagonism is a constant theme in the diary of Ellen House.[15]

The situation deteriorated further in January 1862. General Zollicoffer, the best hope for moderation in East Tennessee, died in the battle of Mill Springs. General Edmund Kirby Smith replaced him, and he quickly determined that East Tennessee was a land of "unionism and traitordom." Smith declared martial law, stepped up the oath-taking campaign, and arrested all who resisted. More East Tennesseans fled, many to enlist in the Union army. General John P. McGowan, a native of Sevier County, replaced Smith in August, to be followed a month later by General Samuel Jones. Both men attempted to soften occupation policies, but it was too late. Nothing could heal the breach between unionists and Confederates.[16]

Final Confederate military failure to hold East Tennessee came during the tenure of General Simon B. Buckner, who assumed command of the department in May 1863. Buckner, too, hoped to pursue a moderate occupation policy, but he had to cope with a problem not faced by previous Confederate commanders: Federal invasion. Union cavalry had been staging raids into East Tennessee since December 1862. Knoxville saw its first combat on the night of June 19–20. With Buckner and most of his troops away, General William P. Sanders threatened the outskirts of town with fifteen hundred cavalry and two artillery pieces. One Virginia and one Florida regiment, about one thousand men total, literally manned the barricades, for the streets were blocked with bales of cotton, and the hills surrounding the town were fortified for battle. About two hundred private citizens and convalescent soldiers joined in the defense of the city, among them several leading Knoxville secessionists, including Landon C. Haynes, William H. Sneed, John H. Crozier, and Joseph H. Martin. The fight lasted only an hour. Four defenders were killed and four wounded. Among the dead was Captain Pleasant Miller McClung, a friend of Ellen House.[17]

The raid was but prelude to the fall. Burnside's army advanced through Thoroughfare Gap and moved toward Knoxville in August. Buckner, believing himself to be severely outnumbered, evacuated the last of his corps from the city on August 25 and moved north to Virginia. Ellen House never forgave him. The Federals walked into town on September 1. Many Confederates fled, and some prominent absent unionists, including Brownlow, returned home. The game had turned.[18]

The Civil War Diary of Ellen Renshaw House

Chapter 1.
The Yankees Are Here

Jan. 1. Thursday. Clear and cold. Commenced the year finely by mending an old skirt. Father is not very well. He just returned from down the road where he caught cold. In the afternoon sister and I went up to Col Tooles store.[1] Stopped to see Cluss on our way home but she was out.[2] Just after we got in Dr Ramsey came in to vaccinate us.[3] I was very glad as the small pox is spreading here considerably. As soon as he was done we went over to see Miss Kate White.[4] After tea Capt Kain came over to see mother to tell her what she ought to do about the place.[5]

Glorious news today. We have gained another victory at Murfreesboro. Gen Bragg in an official dispatch to Gen Smith says "We assailed the enemy at 7 oclock this morning and after ten hours hard fighting have driven him from his position, except his extreme left which has successfully resisted us. With the exception of this point, we occupy the whole field. Have captured four thousand prisoners, including two Brigadier Gens, thirty one pieces of artillery, and some two hundred wagon and teams. Our loss is heavy but that of the enemy much greater."[6] I am very anxious to hear more of the fight. We have so many friends in the army there. Frank Matthews is in Gen Breckinridge's Signal Corps, so of course must have been in the fight.[7]

Jan. 2. Friday. Clear and Cold.

March. Wednesday. Clear and pleasant. Rose early and practiced [piano] an hour before breakfast. Took a music lesson at nine oclock—my sixth lesson.

Planted out some rose cuttings Johnnie brought up from Marietta yesterday morning.[8] Went over to take some of them to Mrs Kain. Both of the children are sick, though better.[9] When I came home found Mary Francisco and Rach Rogers here.[10] Worked on my collar. In the afternoon the Miss Massells called.[11] No news of any importance from our Army for the last few days.

Thursday. Clear and pleasant. Rose early and worked some on my collar. After breakfast practiced an hour then mended Johnnie's pants. Worked more on my collar. Miss Russell called in the afternoon.[12] At night practiced another hour.

Friday. Rain—cold. Took my music lesson & practiced an hour. Worked on my collar.

Saturday. Rose early practiced as usual before breakfast. Washed and ironed some collars. Worked on my collar. After dinner Johnnie & I went around to Tooles store then to see Mrs. Churchwell.[13] She was out, but we saw Mrs Charlton.[14] After we left there we went round to see Rach Rogers. She seems as happy as can be in her little nut shell. I came home and then went down to see Mr Latta.[15] Vic Vaux is really married to a Col. Jno Gurding.[16]

Sunday. Clear and pleasant. Went to church in the morning. When we came home found the baby had been right sick. Poor little creature. She has the whooping cough and I am afraid it will go hard with her.

July 21. Tuesday. I fully intended—when I commenced to keep this [end].

Sept. 1. Tuesday. I think it is outrageous. The Yankees are here. Just think, here—here in Knoxville. Walked in without the least resistance on our part. Buckner evacuated it last week, took everything.[17] There is one consolation. We lost nothing in the way of eating, clothing, ordanance stores &e. But to let them have the place. I never never could have believed it. Only one regiment of the cavalry has come in yet, a Col Foster I think in command.[18] He has taken up his quarters in Sneeds house and the good for nothing things have such comfortable quarters.[19] How I hate them. Four came here and we had to give them something to eat. That was too much. Thank fortune Sam left last Thursday and took all of his clothes with him. I gave him my watch so in case he should get out of money he can sell it.[20]

Sept. 2. Wednesday. After dreaming of our boys, to wake and find the Yankees here, too bad—too bad. More came in today. I don't know how many there are or care. To know they are here is quite enough and more than enough. This afternoon Sister and I went out to see Mrs McPherson.[21] Did not meet a soul going. Coming back Miss Kate White was at her door and we stopped to talk to her a little while. This morning sister was sitting at her front window reading [when] two men rode by with a flag. She turned her head. One of them said, "Did you see that girl, she would not look at our flag," & they both laughed.

Sept. 3. Thursday. They have been coming in today. They all ride two abreast. I suppose that is to string them out as much as possible. Our friend across the way came home today.[22] Every union man in town I believe has been to see him. All looking perfectly delighted. They think they have every thing their own way now, & I suppose they will for a time. A man came today to buy some bacon. Mother told him she had none to sell, and very little. She could give them a piece, he was very polite. I don't suppose they will molest us if we keep quite. I certainly shall not let them think I am a Lincolnite, but will behave as a lady. Gen Burnside came in this afternoon and has taken up his quarters at Col Croziers house.[23]

Sept. 4. Friday. They keep coming in. They [are] certainly splendidly mounted. Four cannon came in this afternoon, they were right large ones. The caissons are not like ours, having only one box. The cannons were drawn by eight horses. Their wagon train came in today. I wish I had counted them. Also their pack mules, loaded with salt, sugar and coffee. They have from 240 to 300 in the train. Gen Carter has made Col Haynes house his head quarters.[24] His body guard are in the school house. All of them have grey horses.

Three of them came here for supper. Mother told them that supper was not ready. She could give them some if they waited. I did not see them. I have not spoken to one yet and do not intend to as long as I can help it. Father told them that we were secessionists. One replied he did not know that or he should have been afraid of intruding. Father told him he was welcome to his supper but he hoped he would prevent any more from coming as he did not have very much to eat and did not know where he would get more when it was gone. They asked if he had any sons in the "Rebel Army." He said yes—two. One on Gen Stewart's Staff and one who had been taken prisoner at Vicksburg, who only left here Thursday.[25] One said he might have taken the oath. Never—said father.[26]

Mrs Kain was down at Mrs Strongs[27] today when a Capt came down to take an inventory of the furniture she had belonging to Capt Campbell.[28] Said that the property of those who had taken up arms against the government was to be confiscated. Mrs K asked him if she understood him to say that all the property of Rebel Officers was to be confiscated, that if such was the case she would thank them to put her across the lines, as she did not choose to live here if they left her nothing to live on. He told her, "They would not leave her destitute." Some of them are camped over in the lot across from us. We are completely surrounded by them.[29]

Sept. 5. Saturday. Miss Kate White came over early this morning and stayed some time. She says [she] intends to open school on Monday at home. A Regiment of infantry came in this morning with the bands playing & colours flying. Martha asked me if that was not our band.[30] Some time after, Miss Nancy Scott came in.[31] She came to ask us to send something to eat [for] some of our men who were here in jail. They have over a hundred. Among them there are seven who have no friends here. They have issued no rations to them and would have been without any thing to eat had not those who had friends here shared with them what they got. Miss Nancy said she had been to Provost Marshalls and obtained a permit to visit and send them something to eat.

Col Cummings is among them. They have given him a kind of trial and he thinks they will send him north. He told them that his life, liberty and property were in their hands, his Honour in his own, and he would keep it. He would not take the oath.[32]

As soon as she left we went to several places in the neighborhood to ask them to contribute some thing, which they gladly did as they were all good southerners, or as the Yankees are pleased to term us—Rebels. By the time we returned Miss Nancy sent a note from Col C saying twenty-five prisoners had just been brought in who had no breakfast. We then went over to Mrs Kains & from there to Miss Nancy's, who said if we would send the things to her she would send them. There were soldiers camped in the lot adjoining her and they were all spread along the fence—some in the yard. They sent over this morning to ask her how many she could get breakfast for. She sent them back word none. She did not have more than she wanted to eat [than they did] themselves.

Just after dinner Mary Hazen came in and staid some time.[33] The Yankees caught Gid the afternoon they came in, but he succeeded in getting away—though he lost his horse and every thing else.[34] The day after they came in the country people cut down our secession flag staff and danced over it. I suppose they think that they spite us dreadfully, but they are very much mistaken. I had much rather have it cut down than have their old rag flying from it. Dr Jackson's British flag seems to provoke them very much. They think it is a Confederate one. Some of them threatened to tear it down. Mrs J. told them that she dared them to put their fingers on it.[35]

Sept. 6. Sunday. Miss Kate White came over this morning before I was out of bed. She wanted to know if there was to be any church. After a while Miss Nancy Scott came in. She was just from the jail. They keep bringing in our men. I think that they must some of them be Conscripts who allow themselves to be taken.[36] Just after Miss Nancy left, father came in & said Mr Humes was going to preach in our church.[37] I am not going to hear him, that is certain. I hear that Gen Carter sent to him to know if he was not turned out of the church and that if such was the case for him to go back. Mr. H told him he had too much respect for Mr. Vaux to preach there.[38] I knew he would do it the first chance he got. Father went out to hear him to see what he would do. After Church Jeanie came.[39] She went to hear Mr Martin as the lst Church was closed.[40] Cluss came in just before dinner. Yesterday afternoon they sent two cannon across the river to fight the Indians over there. It is my opinion they will get themselves in worse. They have had their Chief killed and are perfectly furious against the Yankees.[41]

In the afternoon Miss Kate came over again. There was a grand funeral that started from Carter's Head Quarters. They say it was one of their men who was killed here during the raid on the 20th of June and just wrapped up in his blanket and buried, a very likely story. I don't believe it. Sister and I walked home with Miss Kate. Mrs W says they have taken Col Cummings and the other prisoners up to the jail. Gen Buckner had not one bit of business leaving that for our men to be put in. It was outrageous.

Three men came to get their suppers. After we were done, sister and I went over to Mrs Kains and left mother to see them. They have been very annoying to her (Mrs K). One went there today and asked if a dozen could get their dinner. She told them no. A little while after one came and asked if five or six men could get their dinner. She told them she did not have dinner enough for so many in the house, that she had done hers and the servants [had] gone out. He said he had not had his, he was hungry and he was going to have it. She told him if he had stayed at home he would have had his dinner. H——l and D——n said he. What did you say? She repeated what she had said. I'll have your case attended to before I leave. Very well she replied. I can hold my own with you any day. After a while father and mother came over. I asked her if she made them [the men] pay. She said they handed her a five dollar bill and she could not change it. But they would want their breakfast next morning. I'll bet she never sees them again. Some more cavalry came in today and some wagons—but they did not seem to have anything to eat in them.

Sept. 7. Monday. Before we were awake this morning Miss Nancy sent sister a note saying that many prisoners had been brought in the night before nearly starved and they were offering $5 for a biscuit. Mother set Sidney to work to get them something and sent the note over to Mrs Kain.[42] There is something in the wind. Last night between 2 & 3 oclock I was waked by the bugal call—then I heard the long roll and men racing up and down on the street. My heart was in my mouth. Miss Nancy stopped on her way from the jail. She had just been to get another pass from the Provost. He dated it *Knocksville*, smart fellow. He is the second one who has spelled it so. She said that she found Lt Hobb writing her a note asking her please to send himself and some others some breakfast. She was going right home to do it. Mother told her she had sent a quantity round to her—but she had just gone out.

She said she was very glad to hear it. I told her I thought Mrs Sam Boyd would send [something] if she knew it and I would ask her.[43] So off I started to see her. She said certainly she would divide the last she had with our soldiers.

Gen Burnside left this morning with almost his entire force. It is rumored that Gen Longstreets Corps is up above here and he has gone to meet them.[44] I hope it is true, that was what all the fuss in the night [was] about. Old Mrs Boyd has had a brother-in-law staying there, Cliff the renegade. He told her that Ky was completely cleared out. They had plenty provisions on the other side of the Ohio, and as soon as we got Chattanooga they would have no trouble in getting it here. He says the Yanks suffered a good deal in crossing the mountains. They did not have enough to eat. Good for them. I then went to tell Miss N that Mrs Boyd would send the things to her and she could send them to the jail.

There I met Mrs Cocke, Ella Cocke, Miss Kate White and Mrs Morgan.[45] The latter had been ordered to leave her house. She sent to Gen Carter about it. He gave her an order to stay in it. His A[dj] Gen told her it would do for the present, but she would not be allowed to remain long. That all those ladies who had Fathers, Husbands, sons and brothers in the Rebel army would be sent across the lines, that they had found from experience they were the worst enemies the Union cause had. I think that was a compliment. I heard there that Capt H. L. McClung had fired into the train at Watauga Bridge and torn up the track. Hurrah for him I say.[46]

The man who they buried yesterday turns out to be one of their men who was shot between Loudon and here by one of our men, bushwacked. They did not want the Rebels to know—so they tried to palm him off on them for one killed during the raid. Murder will out. When I got home mother told me they had been to Mrs Kains to tell her they were going to take her house— at least the lower part of it. One man a Dr told her she had best consent willing for those men round her would not hesitate to burn her house down and cut her throat. She told them she would not assent to any thing that she knew her husband would disapprove of so strongly. She sent for Dr Jackson and he said he [would] see what he could do for her. Some of the men at the school house told Old Buck that nothing belonged to her and they would not be satisfied till they had him waiting on them, every servant off the lot and she doing her own work and bringing her water from the Spring.[47]

In the afternoon sister & I started over to see Miss Kate and met her going out, so we turned back and went over to Mrs Kains. Dr Jackson had got it all fixed for her. I hope she will not be troubled any more. If she is she intends to take two officers to board for protection.

Sept. 8. Tuesday. It is awfully hot and dusty. I wish it would rain. The constant passing up and down fills the house. Every breth you draw about a peck of dust goes into your throat and you feel it down to the end of your toes. If it was Confederate dust I would not care half as much, but Yankee dust and I dont agree at all.

There are rumors in town today of a fight at the Gap. An officer was heard to say that the 2nd Ten (U.S.) had been cut to pieces there. Some say that we have been whipped and three thousand men taken prisoners besides several hundred killed. Of course we will not hear the truth for some time if ever.[48]

In the afternoon sister and I walked out to Mrs McPherson. She was out but Mr McP was home. Mr & Mrs Sam Wallace are staying out here.[49] They have paroled him. I understand Gen Carter says he intends to send all the run-a-way negroes back to their masters, whether Union or Rebel, that he has nothing to feed them with and does not want them. Rumors of a fight below. Some say that Bragg has fallen back to Dalton. I don't believe it.[50] If we could only hear from the boys. I don't feel as anxious to hear from Sam for he has not been exchanged yet and is not in as much danger as Johnnie. I hope we will hear before very long. Two hundred and forty wagons came in today.

Sept. 9. Wednesday. It is dreadfully hot and dusty. I went over and sat the morning with Mrs Kain. Mrs Strong came in while I was there and stayed a little while. She looks like she was worried almost to death. I would not be fretted so by the servants. We have not been at all troubled with ours. They have been perfectly quiet and polite. I do not think they will leave if left to themselves, though they may be enticed off. There was another man buried this afternoon. He was killed ninety miles above here. They say he was the only one killed, but I don't believe it. I hear that the Indians have killed about thirty of those sent out after them.

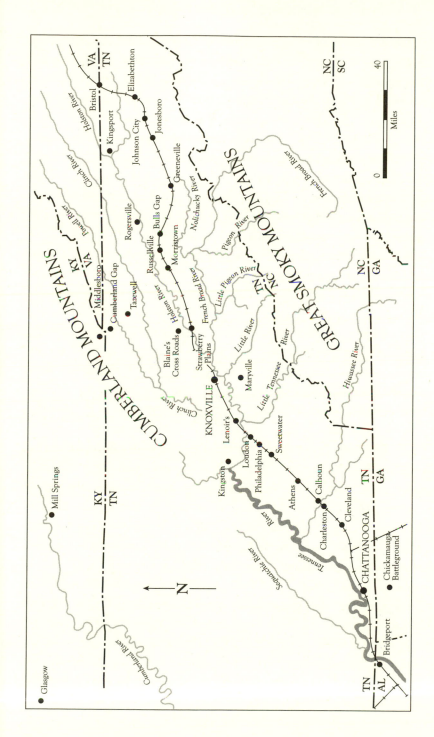

East Tennessee and vicinity, 1863–64.

Sept. 10. Thursday. I tried to sew a little this morning. Did not succeed in doing much. I have been all this week trying to make a shirt for father and have not finished it yet. They have taken Mr Powells store.[51] They have been after it for several days and he has got them two or three others that were empty, but that did not satisfy them. There has been a fight up at Limestone on the Rail road The Yankees acknowledge that they had two hundred and fifty men taken prisoners. They say that they had but two hundred and fifty of Fosters men there and they kept five thousand of our men at bay for I dont know how many hours, and the only man they had killed was the one they buried yesterday. A very likely story. Some of their men were brought in wounded. I dont know how many. They have my best wishes to die.[52]

After dinner Mrs Kain came over and sat some time. She has a Capt boarding there, has taken him for protection. The men over at the school house are stealing her wood so and annoying her in other ways. He is Captain of the Provost guards who are camped back of Miss White's and has his office next door to us where Miss Catherine and Joanne used to live.[53] He asked her what she would charge. She replied she did not know. Then he told her the price had not been regulated yet. Later in the afternoon sister and I went over to see Miss Kate. She was out but we saw her mother. She had several of the animals boarding there.

Sept. 11. Friday. Father says that the Yankees have Cumberland Gap and they say that they are in Dalton and Bragg has fallen back to Rome, some say Atlanta. I dont believe it but there is no accounting for what he does. At the Gap they say they have taken two thousand prisoners and fifteen pieces of cannon. I wonder if Lt Wilkins was among those taken.[54] What a pity for that new coat to go to prison. The Report says that Gen Gracie was in command now.[55] I know that he is down the road. Mrs Kains Capt says the war will be over by Christmas. What a fool. He does not know that every advantage they gain lengthens it instead of shortening it. He will find himself mistaken when the time comes. God grant they may not be here. Mr Hendricks has taken the Oath.[56] Poor old man, he is not in his right mind. More prisoners were brought in last night and today. No gas tonight. I hope we wont be long without it. I hear the Yankees have sent fifty wagons over to Anderson Co for coal to light the city. I wonder if they are afraid of the dark, wicked people always are.[57]

I took my sewing and went over to sit with Mrs Kain after dinner. That Capt asked Nonnie today at dinner to kiss him. She told him "she would not kiss a Yankee."[58] Two or three nights ago we were sitting out at the front door after supper when two Yankee soldiers came riding along. When they saw us they stopped and one says, "Want to buy a pair of shoes, ladies?" Father told him no. I wonder what they will do next. I don't see any of our men doing such a thing. Yesterday two of the blue devils were out at Mr George Mabry's—in his parlour when they got to high words, when one drew a pistol and shot the other.[59] Good. I was very much in hopes we would have some rain as it was thundering at one time this afternoon, but it all passed off. I wonder if we are ever going to have any more.

Sept. 12. Saturday. I finished fathers shirt today for a wonder. I really must try and do some sewing next week. I made a white body today too. Dr. J. G. M. Ramsey's house out at Mecklenburg was burnt last night and Mr McNutt plundered.[60] It is supposed it was done by some of the Union men. The Yankees have been looking for them all day though they do not seem as though they were very anxious to find them. Some of them arrested John Williams on suspicion but let him go.[61] I hear that Col Wolford has three men who have been arrested for doing it.[62]

Jeanie came in before dinner. After dinner Mary came for her to pay some visits. She says she sent word to some officers, who said they were going to call on her. She would most certainly insult them if they did. Mother, sister and I walked out to Mrs McPhersons. She told us that four men (soldiers) had been out there two or three days before and arrested Mr. McP but did not prove anything against him so they let him go. One of the charges were that he had men and arms concealed in his house. Some one stole Wallies pony last Sunday night.[63]

Tonight it rained a little. I was very much in hopes from the way it started it was going to rain all night.

Sept. 13. Sunday. This morning Jeanie, sister and myself went to the Second Church to hear Mr Martin. There were quite a number of blue coats there. I wonder how much good going to church does them. Some more of our men were brought in last night, poor fellows. The Yankees who went to the Gap came back today. I heard one say that they had taken ten thousand prisoners. He certainly has a very fertile imagination and draws on it considerably. The negroes are getting pretty high. Mrs Strongs man threatened last night to shoot her. In the afternoon we went over to Mrs Kains. She has a Lt boarding there too. They say that they will soon have Jeff Davis, and they intend to hang him.

It is quite amusing to see the soldiers. They go about all the time as if they were on a march. Yesterday afternoon some men were sent out from the Provost Guard to cut poles for their tents. They went with all their equipment just as though expected a fight on the way. Oh! if Bragg would only whip them. It would be perfectly glorious. I wonder where the boys are now, and what they are doing, thinking of home I expect. If we could only hear from them some times I would not mind the Yankees so much. Capt Kains company was at the Gap. I am very sorry that they did not get away. The Capt was not with it. He is down below here attending to some ordanance stores. Lt O'Conner was in command.[64] He turned a cannon over after they had taken the Gap and they threatened to shoot him for doing it. Cooke Danner, Charley King and Green McClannahan were all in the Co.[65] They say they intend sending them all to Camp Chase.[66]

How dark every thing seems just now. I don't think it can last much longer without a ray of light for our cause. Oh! there has been so many mistakes— fatal mistakes [have] been made by those in authority. I cannot see why they gave up Knoxville. I am very thankful we live in town. They are taking every thing from secessionists in the country. Out at Lona's they went as far as to take an axe and chop up her bureau. They have not troubled us at all as yet. Whenever they have come to the house they have been very respectful.

Sept. 14. Monday. A good many Yankees have passed today. I dont know whether they were new ones just come or the same that were here before. There are all sorts of reports on the Lt [Wilkins?], but of course none can be believed as they all originate with the Yankees. I wish that we could hear something that we could believe. Late this evening I went over to Mrs Kains. Did not hear anything. Tonight as father, mother, sister and I were in the sitting room playing whist, we were all started from our seats by what I thought the report of a pistol directly under the window. Sister thought that it was a stone thrown at the window. Whatever it was it put an end to the game and sent all to bed.

Sept. 15. Tuesday. Two weeks today since the Federals came in. It seems more like two months. I never heard such a racket as they kept up last night. Cavalry and infantry coming in, it seemed that there was no end of them, and their men racing backwards and forwards as fast as they could go. More cavalry came by this morning and two Companies of Artillery—one four guns and the other six. Byrd's Tenn Reg came in yesterday,[67] so I suppose Jim Brownlow and Ed Maynard are both along.[68] It makes me heart sick to see so many blue coats. Oh! why did Buckner evacuate East Tenn, give it up without a single blow struck for its defense. He will never find a place that will be easier to hold. He ought to be turned out [of] the army. He was completely under the influence of the Union men while he was here. They all think him something extraordinary because he let them do and say what they pleased.

Mrs Kain came over this morning to tell us the good news. That Capt told her that Longstreet was reported at Greenville with twenty-five thousand men.[69] She asked him if they had that many. He said no, that he believed they would be whipped. Oh! if they only are how happy I would be. Father came in after a little while and said he had heard that Gen Ewell was along and we had twelve thousand Cavalry.[70] There is some trouble down the road too. The cars went down this morning as far as Concord and came back in a hurry. They acknowledge that they were whipped at Jonesboro.[71] Three regiments of infantry passed—very small ones. They looked as though they were going to certain death. Not a smile on one single face.

After they passed, Mother, Sister and I went out to pay some visits. First to see Mrs Jim Cooke.[72] I would not like to live where she does now, right next to head quarters. She told us what I did not know before. Gens Burnside and Buckner are intimate friends. Burnside is Mrs Buckner's trustee. She is a millionairess. That accounts for Buckner acting as he did.[73] From there we went to Mrs McClannahan's, Mrs Jackson's and Mrs Frank McClung's.[74] When we came home I asked father if he had heard anything more. He said only that we were getting a heavy force at Morristown.[75] After dinner Cluss come over for a little while.

Troops were passing all the afternoon, some going one way and some another. Some of them across the river. I suppose they have gone down toward Loudon.[76] After they all passed, came the wagons. I thought they never would get past. They have the greatest fancy for stopping in front of our door. Sometimes they stand still for an hour at a time.

Sept. 16. Wednesday. Men and wagons were passing almost all night and more this morning with two batteries. I believe they are the same two that went across the river yesterday. It is really very amusing to see the way they spread themselves. They make a hundred men look like two or three. Two of the Regiments that passed this morning only had a hundred and ninety-five men each, and if I had not counted them I should have thought there were at least four hundred in each. There was only one that came up to that many. There has not been over fifteen hundred in all that have passed to-day, and Oh! what long faces they all had. Rumors say that A. P. Hill is with Longstreet.[77] I hope he is. I ripped up my old brown dress today, intend trying to fix it tomorrow. I must see if I can't do some sewing now for I shall not feel like doing much for some time after our army gets here. I will be too happy and frisky to sit down quietly and sew.

In the evening I went over to see Miss Kate White. She is quite sick, though I hope she will be well again in a day or two. The Yankees seem to be burning fortifications. There are several fires over in the direction of them and I dont know what else it can be. Buckner ought to have burnt them before he left. The Cannon that they have brought here is splendid, all brass pieces. If our boys can only take them and turn them on the vile Yankees it will be splendid. I feel very hopeful. I dont think they can retain possession much longer. Ten officers met Sidney as she was going to the Spring. One said to her, "Old woman I'll tell you what. We Yankees feel might proud walking these streets." Truly something to feel proud of, to come in and take quick possession of a town where there was nothing in the world to oppose them. A valiant set who will boast of such an achievement.

Sept. 17. Thursday. The town is rather quiet today though Burnside left this morning, as did Carter's Body Guard.[78] Three teams and two men were drowned in attempting to cross the river. The best of it is that the teams were loaded with ammunition. In the afternoon sister and I went round to see Rach Rogers. While we were there two tory neighbors rode past with two Yankee Officers.[79] The dust was awful. I would not have been riding in such weather for any thing—even with one of Our officers. One of the girls said that she supposed they thought that they were so much more fascinat-ing than we, was the reason that they had beaux and we didnt. I dont think a Yankee would make much in calling on any one of us.

Sept. 18. Friday. It rained in the night and is quite cool this morning. I took my sewing and spent the morning at Mrs Kains. Her boarder has left, told her that the board was so very high the Lt and himself thought they could mess cheaper. He came to settle with her while I was there. He owed her ninety-six cents and because she had not the change for $1.00—five cents, he said he would not do it then, but would call in some time. I dont believe the meanest, lowest soldier in our army would have done such a thing, and that was after cheating her out of a day. A five cents looks as big to them as five dollars does to a southerner. I am very glad that the Provost Guard have moved from the corner lot. Mrs Kain came over and sat the evening. I finished my old Brown dress. No news today that I can hear of except that the cars did not go any farther up the road than Strawberry Plains.[80]

Sept. 19. Saturday. It is cold enough this morning to make [a] fire very comfortable. Miss Nancy Scott came in as she was going home from the Jail. She said that they were going to send our fellows to Camp Chase on Wednesday. Our Cavalry dashed into Kingston and captured the Yankee force there with the ammunition they had, which is said to have [been] considerable.[81] At two oclock I went in with her to the Jail. Lt Hobb is quite sick, poor fellow. It is a most miserable place to be sick in. They told us there that they were to be sent off Monday, perhaps tomorrow. I suppose they are afraid of our men making a dash in and taking them back. Some of them are very much in need of drawers and socks, so after we left them we went around begging for them. Mr Charles McGhee gave me a piece of domestic to make the drawers out of.[82] Sister cut them out and we got them all made, that is we sent them around to the girls near us. I never knew a dozen pair could be made in so short a time.

Sept. 20. Sunday. This morning Miss Nancy went around to the Jail. She stopped in as she came back to say that the prisoners were to be sent off at twelve, and she would stop for me. Lt. Hobb was so sick that he was in hopes they would not send him. Mrs McPherson sent two pair of socks. She stopped for sister when she was going to church and I told her they were much needed. They were sent off at eleven. We went around to see them go, poor fellows. There were not more than fifty who had had the courage to go. The others—poor miserable creatures—had all taken the Oath, over three hundred of them. At the last moment Gen Carter sent an order for Capt MacHand not to go, and none of the commissioned officers.[83] There is a report in town today that there are six thousand Confederates between here and Loudon. There was not a camp fire to be seen any where last night. That is a good sign for us.

In the afternoon I went over to see Mrs Kain for a little while. It is really amusing to think that the Yankee Officers are so mad with the Rebel girls here because they dont take any notice of them whatever. They would much rather be insulted by us for then they would have a chance for re-venge. As it is they cant help seeing what a contempt we all have for them—and yet no chance for resenting it. They say the ladies go to the jail and brush past without noticing them in the least—and go in and talk to all the prisoners. The Doctors at the Hospital too say that the Rebel ladies do not treat their sick in the same manner the Union ladies do their friends—the Secesh are so kind and attentive to their soldiers.

Today when we were standing waiting to see our poor fellows go off, John Brownlow came along and stopped within ten steps of me.[84] I dont think he took his eyes off my face for five minutes the whole time I was there. I looked at him just as I would at any stranger. If he thought I would speak to him, he was very much mistaken. I had not spoken to him for months before he went north, when we were in power here. I most certainly shall not now when he is. It would look entirely too much like cowardice.[85]

Sept. 21. Monday. While we were at breakfast Miss Nancy sent a note around saying that Lt Hobb had accepted my invitation and Gen Carter had promised to parole him, that he would be around between nine and ten oclock. So we went to work and fixed our room for him, and went in Johnnies room. Miss Nannie went round to the jail to bring him round but the Dr had not been there yet so he could not come. She went back after him and he was gone. Before dinner she wrote mother a note saying that she would keep him to dine with her and bring him around in the after-noon, but they did not come. I dont know what to make of it. Father came home this morning to tell us that the Yankees said there had been a fight at Cleveland and we had taken two hundred of their men prisoners.[86] If they acknowledge to two hundred I know we took more. I went over to tell Mrs

Kain the news. In the afternoon I went to see Miss Kate White. When I came home I heard that there had been a fight down at Kingston Ga. which the Yankees said was a drawn battle, in which they were very much cut up.[87]

Sept. 22. Tuesday. The weather is much pleasanter today. I hope we will have a good deal more warm weather before winter sets in for good. Miss Nannie came around this morning for a little while. I made my light domestic skirt, or rather dress skirt. After dinner read "Dollars and Cents" till Miss Kate White came in.[88] After she went I ran over to Mrs Kains for a short time. After tea Miss Nannie came again. She said that she had seen a gentleman who told her he had seen a Cincinatti paper which said Charleston had not fallen, (I knew if it had there would be a big fuss made over it) and that Bragg had over a hundred and twenty thousand men.[89] (I knew that before). They commenced fighting four days ago. (I wish I knew where Stewart was, in Atlanta, I hope. I am not anxious to have Johnnie more exposed than can be helped. Most of the forces we had here have been sent down to Rosecrans. I hope Bragg will be able to completely annihilate his whole army). Lee has fallen back within his entrenchments and sent Longstreet to reinforce Bragg. She asked father to go to the Lamar House with her to see after the Lt [Hobb], but they did not find him.[90] I suppose he will make his appearance some time. It is reported that Our Carter had a skirmish with the enemy at Bristol in which he killed six, took thirty prisoners, and dispersed the rest.[91]

Sept. 23. Wednesday. It is perfectly delightful today. This morning I amused myself mending the carpet for the sitting room, such nice—light— fancy work, and father put it down. After I finished that I finished "Dollars and Cents." The town is very quiet today, nothing to be heard or seen ex- cept these abominable flags, stretched across the streets or hung from the windows of every house that holds a vile Yankee soldier. The sight of them has the same effect on me as the blue jackets, it completely nauseates me. I have been sick to my stomach ever since the creatures have been here. Wont I be happy when they go. I am afraid I shall go crazy. They are ship- ping ammunition to Loudon as fast as they can. The Lt passed this after- noon and I was at the front door and did not recognize him till he had passed. I am so sorry. I hope though it will all be right tomorrow.

Sept. 24. Thursday. Clear and pleasant. No news today.

Oct 8. Thursday. I have been in such a state for the last two weeks that I could not compose myself to write or do anything else. The day after I last wrote we heard Gen Bragg had whipped Rosecrans (the day after the Yankees said that they had taken Bragg prisoner with one hundred thousand men and forty pieces of artillery, very probable). Then there has been fighting above and below all the time. We fought them five days at Limestone, and they say they had one man killed. Bluntsville has been burnt. So has Athens. They fought right in the town in the latter place.[92] Report says that we burnt Chattanooga before we evacuated it. I heard today that Longstreet was on Lookout Mountain and that Rosecrans was evacuating Chattanooga, and that we have possession of the rail-road both above and below him, and he has to wagon all his supplies across Cumberland Mountain. I hear also that Gen Lee is with Bragg, but it is not generally known, with very heavy reinforcements. The Yankees say that Rosecrans had been reinforced by forty thousand. I only hope there wont one be left.

A gentleman who has come through the lines within the last few days says that in the late battle Bragg lost two thousand men and the Yankees twenty thousand. Capt Lackey (of the Knoxville Guards) was killed, as were Bob Crozier & Jim King.[93] I would give anything if we could only hear from Johnnie. He is on General Stewarts staff and of course was in the fight. One day last week the Confederates were over at Maryville. The Yankees on the other side of the river were drawn up in line of battle all day.[94] It is astonishing what reports they start and they make their men believe. Two weeks ago Richmond was in ashes, today Meade has taken it, and they have burnt and captured Charleston half a dozen times.[95] There was a rumor on the st several days ago that France has recognized the South. I am afraid it is too good to be true. The Confederates are below Greenville and reported thirty thousand strong. The Yankees are sending up the road every man they possibly can. I do not know which of our Generals are in command there. I only hope he will whip them well and retake Knoxville.

It is miserable living in the same place with them, and they have not been acting up to their principle in full, by any means. Today a circular came out of Carters [office] "That for every prominent union man taken up by

the rebels or molested by them, a prominent Rebel or active Rebel sympathizer shall be arrested by them, that he will put an end to such barbarous
treatment by retaliating." The Union men are coming in from above here.
They say that they are compelled to leave, that our forces are sweeping every thing before them. It is just what they ought to do. The tories have always had the upper hand here. Even with our Generals they have been believed sooner than Southern men. It is time they were suffering a little. I
suppose our men have heard the way that some of the Southern people have
been treated here and think they will retaliate.[96]

A good many houses have been searched.[97] They went to Mrs Parmers
and took everything she had, did not leave her anything in the house to get
supper with or even a candle. Said they were commissary stores.[98] Went to
Dr Ramseys for Hospital medicines, searched the house. Mrs Jennings was
absent at the time.[99] When they came to her room they wanted to open a
camp chest that she keeps her clothes in. Mrs Ramsey sent for her.[100] When
she came she offered the key to the Officer who refused to take it. She then
handed it to Mr Humes who took it, opened her chest and took every thing
out. A nice business for a minister to be in. I think he must have felt rather
small when he got through. When they went to Mr Gammons for commissary stores, they even looked in the drawers and wardrobes for them.[101] The
impudent creatures.

Yesterday I went up to the jail after dinner with Miss Nannie. There
were only fourteen of our men there, seventy-one had taken the oath the
day before. There is a Lt Spencer from Lexington Ky. He knows Uncle John
very well.[102] He was taken two or three days ago. I took him up some thing
to read. He told me that the Vicksburg prisoners had been exchanged, but
that they were still at Demopolis.[103] There is a young man there too from
Memphis. He knows Sam very well. It was very unexpected to meet any
one who knows him. After dinner I went down to Mrs Strongs to see if I
could get any thing for our prisoners to read from her. Afterwards I went to
Tooles store with Nina Danner, and then to Mrs John Whites.[104] She is
breaking up housekeeping. Col Cummings has taken her house and she will
board with him. After tea Miss Kate came over and sat till bed time.

I hear that twenty prisoners were brought down yesterday, and several
Yankee dead and wounded. Burnside has resigned. The Officers here say it

is because he is to be the next president. I suppose he is very popular now from his taking East Tenn and is afraid to losing it by waiting here a little longer and being whipped by the rebels.[105] Capt Morrow has gone to Cincinatti, as have several of the prominent Union men here.[106] I wonder if it is because they think our forces will get possession here and they want to be out of harms way. I hope so. Mr Powell left today for the same place. I dont know which hold their heads the highest since the Yankees have been here, the negro girls or the tory girls. Such grand times as the latter have been having, such famous riding partners, so much high life below stairs. I expect they think we rebels fret very badly. I get so sickened out with Blue that I am compelled to go to the Jail to see a grey Jacket.

Oct. 9. *Friday*. Clear and pleasant. I took my sewing over to Mrs Kains this morning and sit some time. Did not accomplish much, as Proff Strong was there and I was too mad to sew, the old Union thing.[107] In the afternoon she came over and stayed all the afternoon. There was quite an extensive funeral. It must have at least been a Maj. I hope it was a Col, the higher the better. Gen Burnside went up the road yesterday on a tender. Rumor says we have quite a heavy force there. Col Toole was ordered to shut his store. I have not heard for what.

Oct. 10. *Saturday*. Clear and pleasant. Finished making a shirt for father. Miss Nannie sent over three pair of drawers and asked us to have them made for our prisoners. I took one pair over to Mrs Kain and two pair down to Mrs McCullough and Miss Lile. Then sister and I walked out to see Mrs McPherson.

I hear that we whipped them yesterday up at Bull's Springs—fifteen miles this side of Greenville. One of their officers said that they "were cut to pieces." Longstreet is on Lookout Mountain—and has command of the railroad and river, so Rosecrans has to wagon all his supplies across Cumberland Mountain. Nineteen days ago he had twenty-eight days provisions.

Gen Shackleford left today. I am so glad. I do think he is a most disgusting looking man, and he passes the house so often. He has his Head Quarters down at Mr Latta's. It is perfectly disgusting to see a man touch his hat to every negro he meets as he does. I suppose it is done to irritate the white rebels.[108]

Oct. 11. Sunday. Clear and pleasant. Sister and I went to the 2nd Presbyterian Church this morning. I wish there was some place one could go
without seeing Yankees, and such an abnominable looking set they are,
none look like Gentlemen. They have pulled the fence down between us
and the next lot. Mother sent word to Mr Humes, and yesterday he gave
father protection for his property and ours too besides for the family. So
much for living in a Union mans house. In the afternoon Father, sister and
I walked out to the Grave Yard. Nothing has been done to the babys grave,
not even the dirt cleared away, and she has been dead over three months.[109]
When we came back we went to Mrs Kain's. She told us that some of
Carter's Staff had given Lizzie Campbell's piano to the Boyds.[110] I guess when
our boys get back they will have to give it up. Nothing from above. I hear
that Lt Luttrell has written one of the Paroled prisoners that they would be
here in a month at farthest.[111] I hope they will, and if Johnnie comes back
with them safe and sound how happy I shall be. If they only bring word that
he is well. I shall be more than satisfied. Oh! so thankful. I hear that some
of the prisoners have been sent off today.

Oct. 12. Monday. Cold and cloudy. Several rumors on the street today,
among them that we have captured a whole regiment at Blue Springs, that
Rosecrans had been again defeated, that Forrest and Wheeler had taken
Nashville, that our forces are at Bluntsville and that we have a strong force
at Athens.[112] I went over and sat with Mrs Kain in the morning. After dinner I went over to see Miss Nannie Scott to ask her if she knew who it was
that had been brought in wounded from above. She did not, but was going
out to the Hospital to see. When she came back we went to the jail and
took some clothes & books. The Officer who they had captured was a Lt
Chapman from Georgia, shot in the mouth. Cant speak, poor fellow.

Oct. 13. Tuesday. Raining all day. We have captured fifty wagons this
side of the Gap, loaded with provisions and Suttlers stores. I am so glad.[113]

Oct. 14. Wednesday. Raining off and on all day. Mrs Kain came over to
sit some time this morning. She has Capt Pike, Capt of Gen Carters "Body
Guard" rooming there. Does not like it much, but could not help it.

Oct. 15. Thursday. Raining still in the morning. After dinner the sun came out for a little while and Sister and I went to see Mrs McClannahan. Just got home in time to save ourselves from being soaked. Our forces have captured and destroyed eight hundred of the Yankees wagons between Chattanooga and the mountains, seventy-five of them were loaded with ammunition. One of the Cincinatti papers says that Rosecrans lost 75,000 men in the late fight near Chattanooga.[114] Gen Longstreet has been shelling the place and he has been compelled to change his position. Mr Helms came back day before yesterday, said Johnnie was well five weeks ago, but that was before all the fight.[115] All we can do is hope for the best. I hear the Confederates are coming up to Loudon as fast as they can. Col Foster has been badly whipped up above here, and he is under arrest.[116] It was only two or three days ago that they were bragging about sending him up there to flank our men and take them all. They sing a different song now.

Oct. 16. Friday. More rain. One good thing. The more it rains the worse the roads will be, and the harder for the Yankees to haul over. Longstreet has left Lookout Mountain, so says madam rumor. We have confirmation of the capture of the wagons. I forgot to mention yesterday that I received two letters from cousin Annie making inquires respecting Capt Ford.[117] I answered them at once. Mother also heard from Aunt Mary. She is in Philadelphia.[118]

Oct. 17. Saturday. Clear and warm. I did a good many little odd jobs that have been hanging over me for some time. While we were eating dinner Miss Nannie came over for me to go around to the jail. There is a Capt McLean confined in one of the cages.[119] He was captured near Dandridge. He says he cannot find out what the charges are against him, but he thinks bushwacking is one of them. Miss Nannie says she heard that he was thought to be a spy. I hope he will be able to clear himself of whatever they are. Brownlow and Maynard are back with their families.[120] The latter is staying at Dickinsons.[121] Mrs Sanborn offered Maynard her house till he could get his own fixed, but he refused to take it. Said he would cover no rebel property.

Oct. 18. Sunday. Raining most of the day. Brownlow and Maynard each made speeches this last night, the latter spoke from Dickinsons. Said that when he left here some said he was an abolitionist, but that he was not, but he would tell them that he had come back one. He spoke of the ladies as "She Rebels." He said they would find out that they would be obliged to have Yankee Officers for beaux, or do without. I am sure I would rather go without. He spoke of the McClungs, Ramseys and Dr Strong in a very contemptuous manner. Capt Kain was the only one he spoke of with respect. That we were fighting for Southern rights and Southern Independence and some had gotten a little more of the Southern Rights than he had bargained for, meaning those of our men who had been killed. That the Yankee Army had never wanted to come to East Tenn, he had never wanted them to come. The Rebels had invited them in and now it was as little as they could do to feed them. Meaning that we had brought on the war.

All that I heard of Brownlow was that one of the common Yankee soldiers said "Any man who could make such a speech had not respect for his wife and daughters," and that he said Lincoln was the best president they ever had. The Rebellion must and should be crushed. If there were not men enough in the North to crush it, the women must be armed, and if they were not enough the negroes and beast of the forest, and if it could be effected in no other way the whole population of these states must be exterminated, men, women, and children. I sent the Capt, Lieut and Mr. Spicer breakfast and some apples this morning.[122] No news today.

Oct. 19. Monday. Clear and pleasant. Good news today. Meade has been whipped by Lee. He thought Lee only had A. P. Hills Corp and found out too late that Ewell had been sent round to flank him. He is to be superceeded by Sickles.[123] Just after dinner a couple of men came to the door. One was dressed in Yankee uniform and was armed. The other was in grey (but we did not notice it at the time), had some flour which he asked to have cooked for him. Mother told him yes and after he had gone Sidney told us he was one of our men. She had seen him at the Jail. When he came back to get it, Mrs Kain and Mary Hazen were both here. I went out to meet him at the door [and] asked him to sit down, and commenced talking to him and told him I did not know he was one of our men &e when out came Mrs K and Mary to see a "Grey Jacket" and Mary just commenced. Told him John Morgan was her cousin and all his men were kin to her (he was one) that our boys would be back in ten weeks &e. The guard became very angry, and answered her back. I was very much annoyed. She ought to have had more consideration than to have gone on so. The guard will not be willing to go out with him again if he is subject to insult.

Seventy-five of our men have been brought in since last night. Among them three Lieuts, one of them a member of Jacksons Staff. As Mrs Kain and Mary went out the gate Capt Pike came out of hers, and what did Mary do but wait at the corner just to be introduced. She told him she was a union girl and all sorts of things. He admires her very much and she has heard it. She will get herself in to trouble if she goes on at the rate she has been for the last day or two. More good news. Rosecrans has been whipped again and he is to be superceeded by either Grant or Thomas.[124]

Oct. 20. Tuesday. Clear and pleasant. I went round to Mrs A. Frenches to see if Miss Nannie would go over to the jail after dinner.[125] Dined there. Capt Pike went out to Mrs Coffins yesterday and Captured! several trunks of officers clothing that had been left there, and has been sporting one of the coats today.[126] After dinner Mary Hazen came in, said she had just walked round the flag that hung at the State Bank, Carters Head Quarters, and said that there were a great many officers standing there some of who were making remarks about it. After I came home I went over to see Mrs Kain and Kate and her were there. Mrs Kain says that just after we left Capt Pike came in and commenced about the flag business. As soon as he had gone Col Lunt came in and started the same subject. Said if he had been there he would have taken hold of her and made her walk under it, that he had written a piece on the subject which was to come out in tomorrows papers &e &e.[127] I am very much afraid that she will get herself in trouble.

Maynard met father on the street today when he was talking to Mr Humes. He says they looked at each other and Mr Humes introduced them. M—— said he had known Mr House before but that he like some other of his friends had failed to recognize him, that they would not look him in the eye. Father says he looked him straight in the eye and told him he was waiting for him to make the first advance. M—— then said he understood that Mr House and his family said he ought to be hung. Father told him he had not said so. M—— replied Maybe not. Brownlow and he are to speak next

Saturday at the Court House. It is thought they intend to invite a mob, and Mr Martins name has been mentioned in connection with it. I dont think the Military will allow them to take matters into their own hands.

Oct. 21. Wednesday. There is report that we have whipped Wolford, completely surrounded him and he cut his way through at or near Loudon.[128] Cluss came around after dinner and stayed some time. She said she heard that Maynard is insulting everyone he meets. I suppose that was what he was after, but father was too much for him. The prominent Union men here are very much incensed at the manner in which he and Brownlow are act-ing. They say that if they expect them to uphold them in the course that they are pursuing, they are very much mistaken. Sister and I went over to Mrs Kains in the afternoon.

Oct. 22. Thursday. Clear and pleasant. There is a report today that we have twenty five thousand men at Mr Charles McGhees. I hope and trust it is so. After dinner Miss Nannie came for me to go around to the jail. Sister said she would go too. So we went round to Lt. Shaws office to get a permit, and the clerk there refused to give her one, said he had been ordered not to and refused to tell her why.[129] We then went up to the jail, but the guard refused to let us speak to the prisoners without a permit. That is something entirely new. There is good news for us and they are afraid that someone will tell the prisoners. Miss Nancy says she is going to see Gen Carter about it.

Mrs McPherson came in after we got home. She says she has sent her cook off, she was so impudent. So she has only one servant now. We have been so fortunate with ours. Both of them seem to hate the Yankees as much as we do, and Sidney is never so well pleased as when she is cooking for our prisoners. There was a little fellow who came here yesterday and asked for his dinner. They both seemed very much interested in him. He came from Jefferson Co. to see his brother—a member of Capt Kain's Co. who he had heard was here in Jail. Poor little fellow. When he got here he found he had been sent to Camp Chase three weeks ago. Father told him to come back at night so he came and stayed all night. He went off after breakfast and has not been back since. I suppose he has got some work to do.

There is a report that Wolford has been very badly whipped at Loudon, some say he was taken prisoner. I doubt that though. The Yankees say that the Rebels were completely whipped and eighteen hundred of them taken prisoner and the rest of them were running South as fast as possible. Of course I believe it. A Regiment of Cavalry, four pieces of cannon, and a great many wagons went down the road this evening. Capt Pike told Mrs Kain they expected to have a fight six miles below here.

Oct. 23. Friday. Rained most of the day. No news of anything. One hundred and eight of our men were brought up today caught tearing up the railroad track between here and Loudon. I sent Sidney around to the Jail this evening with something to eat for Lt Spencer, Capt McLean and Mr Spicer. She came home with some corn meal to cook for some of them and said one had asked her to ask her Mistress to please fix him some corn bread, and a Mr McLowry[130] asked her if she had a young mistress. She said yes, two. He told her to ask one of them please to send him something to eat in the morning, he did not care what, that he was so wet and hungry.

Oct. 24. Saturday. I got up right early to see about sending the prisoners their breakfast. Sidney took the cornbread she had baked, and I fixed up some thing (I should have been ashamed two months ago to serve it to the meanest soldier in our army) and sent to the other two and told her to tell them I would send some hot bread as soon as it was done. Mr McLowry said he was ten thousand times obliged. He hoped to be able to do the same for me some day, and he would pray for me every day as long as he lived the same as he would pray for Jeff Davis. The Guard said that was the D——l of a message to send a young lady. I suppose he only sent it to vex them. He must be a queer sort of fellow.

When she went back one begged her to bring some thing to eat and insisted upon her bringing a dollar home with her to pay for it. So we set her to work to make some biscuits and boil some middling and sent it to him with the money. She says that the Guards all look surprised enough at her refusing to take it, but when she took it back they thought she surely was crazy, and tried every way to make her keep it. She says she felt so grand when she was refusing it. They told her she was such a D——d Rebel. The poor fellow who she had taken it to—Johnson—sent me word that he would pray for me while he lived and hoped to meet me in Heaven. S. says she never saw so many starving men in her life. There were three hundred there and the last time she went after eleven oclock they were just taking them something to eat. Poor fellows. They had not had anything since the day before.

I went down to Mrs McCallas to ask her to have something cooked for them.[131] She told me the reason they would not give Miss Nannie a pass was because they said she had taken a flag and flaunted [it] in the guards face. It is not so, though I was glad I knew the reason. So I went round and told her. She said she was very glad she knew the charge against her. She had not been able to see Gen Carter yet, but she was going right off.

Oct. 25. Sunday. I went round breakfast to the jail this morning. Mrs McPherson called by to see if we were going to church. Sister went. Miss Nannie came in just after dinner and sat some time. Has not seen the Gen yet. No news at all from any quarter. It is my opinion that we have whipped Rosecrans again, and the Yankees are keeping [it] quiet.

Oct. 26. Monday. Clear and cold. Col Cummings told mother that he had seen one of the prisoners that he knew who told him Gen Joe Johnston had been suspended from charges brought against him by Pemberton, who was in command of Gen Polk's Army Corps, the latter having resigned.[132] There has been a fight down in Loudon and we have whipped them again. They expect to fight again tomorrow.[133] I went over to see Cluss in the afternoon. Fifty ambulances went down the road. They must expect to have a great many wounded.

Oct. 27. Tuesday. Nothing today. The very durth [dearth] of news is in our favor, for if the Yankees had any good for them they would tell it soon enough. Sister and I walked out to Mrs McPhersons in the afternoon. It rained in the morning.

Oct. 28. Wednesday. Just before dinner someone rang the front door bell and I went to the door. A Yankee soldier handed me a note. I was kinder surprised and felt a little uneasy till I opened it and saw who it was from. It proved to be a note from Capt McLean, asking for some milk for Lt Thomas,[134] who was sick—and if Mrs Morgan had gone to Ky yet & whether she had heard from Col Garrard.[135] (Poor fellow. I am afraid it will go hard with him [McLean]. I hear that the Yankees intend to shoot him. I only hope our boys will come in time to save him.) I invited the Yank to come in, and talked to him while I fixed a basket of things to send. I was killing polite to him, asked if I wrote a note to Capt McLean if he would get it. He said if I would have it ready by half past four he would call for it. So as soon as I ate my dinner I went round to see Mrs Morgan, and she wrote a note for me to send him. Then I went to see Miss Nannie and told her we had eleven men sick at the Jail who needed light bread, milk &e. Then I came home and wrote my note. The Yankee came for it as he had promised, and I made myself as pleasing as possible, for I thought that he would be willing to do any thing for our prisoners again if I treated [him] like a gentleman. I wanted to knock him down and take his boots and gloves all the time.

Mrs Morgan says one of the Officers told her yesterday that the roads were in such a condition that they would not be able to haul over them more than two weeks longer, and if they did not get the railroad they would have to leave. They wont get it certain and sure. Oh! [How] delighted I will be to see Grey Jackets once more.

Oct. 29. *Thursday*. Clear and pleasant. Sent breakfast round to the jail. Just as we were sitting down to breakfast, Sissie Kain came in to tell us the Yankees had evacuated Loudon and were coming this way as fast as they could. The Confederates were twenty thousand strong under Gen Stevenson at Lenoir coming after them, that one of the Officers there said he was going to get his horse and go to Ky.[136] Another told him that would do no good for the Rebels would get him there. Pegram has taken Glasgow and Danville.[137] Father went to town and came back and told us Gen Bragg had demanded the surrender of East Tenn. The Yankees have brought their pontoons here from Loudon and are measuring the river here. Four hundred wagons are expected here from Ky today.

About eleven I went over to Mrs Kains. She says that she asked one of the Yanks there if there would be any fighting here. He said he thought not, and nowhere in East Tenn. The Rebels have too heavy a force for that. I hope he is not mistaken. He told her too that we had captured a train this side of Loudon, set it on fire and ran it into the river. Hurrah for the Rebels. They haven't quiet played out yet. The wagons came in this evening without a guard from the Gap. Sidney came home from the jail in fine spirits, said that they had just brought in a Capt who said our forces were sixteen miles from here and coming here. Miss Kate stopped a little while in passing. It is amusing to see the long faces of the blue jackets. Some are cursing dreadfully, say Rosey has been whipped again, and they had been whipped alive here and now they had left Loudon because they had been whipped there and had to leave.[138]

Oct. 30. Friday. It rained in the morning, but the sun came out by dinner time. A little while after Col Cummings came around to say he would go to the jail with us. So we got up some clothes and a bag of smoking tobacco, which I intended to take Capt Mclean, and went over to Col Cummings, where he was to meet us. By the time he came with the pass it was raining so that we concluded we better put it off to another time, and send the things by him.

Oct. 31. Saturday. Disagreeable. I commenced fixing my black silk dress this morning. Just before dinner Col Cummings came over. He said he had not succeeded very well in begging, thought we could do better and handed us the six dollars he had collected. So Sister and I started right out, begged some and bought a piece of cotton to make some shirts. Then we came home to dinner. After we had finished, sister cut out the shirts and I went round to see who I could get to make them. The town is in a considerable state of excitement. It is reported that our forces are within a few miles of here on all sides. Some think they will be in tonight, though I dont believe we will see them for several weeks. They are taking their time. Mary and Jeanie Ramsey came in and sat some time. It is amusing to hear them talk of Uncle Thomas.[139]

Nov. 1. Sunday. I was awoke this morning by the front door bell. Col Cummings was sent over to say that our prisoners were to be sent off very soon, and to ask if any of the shirts were done. I jumped up in a hurry and dressed, [and] started Martha round to see if any of them were done. She came back with one, and some other clothes Miss Nancy sent. Then father came and I went over to Col Cummings, met him, and walked up to the jail where I saw Lt Spencer and Mr Spicer. Asked how the Capt was and if I could get a pass to see him. They said yes, and the Col proposed I should return in an hour. So I came home and went to work sewing trying to finish another shirt, and mother went over to ask Mrs Kain for some clothes she had. Miss Nannie came around to go with us, and just after she came in Mrs White sent us word that they were taking the prisoners out.

So we started off. Stopped for the Col. When we got to the jail we found them all drawn up in marching order, and wonderful to relate were allowed to speak to them. Sidney was standing there with a basket of breakfast which we had sent her with half an hour before, and the Guard would not let her pass. We took it from her and gave it to them with some Miss Nannie had sent round, and gave them some clothes we had for them. I saw the Lt and Mr Spicer. I asked if Capt McLean was going with them. They did not know, said he had been taken out just after I left to the Court House. Mr Spicer asked me if I had not received a note from the Capt the evening before. I told him no. He said that he had written one and he had sent me some money to ask me to get him a pair of gloves, and sent it by the Yankee Lieut. I'll do my best to find him out. We stood and talked to them about an hour, when they were faced about so we had to leave.

Just before they left Mr Spicer told me that there was a friend of his in Jail very sick, and he asked me to do whatever I could for him. Of course I promised. Capt Rivers asked Miss Nannie about him too. She said he was a very particular friend of his, and he felt very uneasy about him, so we concluded we had better try to get him out.[140]

When I came home and dressed I went over to Mrs Kains. As I went out their front gate I saw Mrs White standing by hers looking toward the Jail. I thought probably the prisoners were still there, and walked up to see, but they had gone. A man passed while I was standing there who Mrs White spoke to. I asked him if Capt McLean had gone. He said one went of that name, so it must have been he. I never thought that I would feel so delighted to hear of one of our men being sent to Camp Chase, but I knew he would be shot if he was left here.

At dinner time father went to the Jail with Sidney. He found Mr Hill lying on the floor on the same blanket with a cousin of Mr Humes and both were very sick, as were several others. He came home and told mother, and we went to work and cut up the dining room carpet into blankets, and got three pillows and took them round to them. (There had been an order issued about a week since to take their blankets because they were U.S. ones. The guards had sold them to our boys and then took them away.) By the time he got back Church was out so he went round to see Mr Humes and tell him about his cousin. They went to the jail together and fortunately found the Yankee Dr there, who gave them a certificate of disability for the two. Then Mr H went round to Gen Carters with father, but he was out so they had to go again after supper, when they found him and they went to the jail—where father stayed while Mr Humes took his cousin round to Mr Martins. Then he brought Mr Hill here. Sister and I have given up our room to him. Dr Rogers came to see him. Mother wanted him to blister him but he would not. Said he would do very well without, but if he had been left another night in Jail he would have died.[141]

Just after dinner the Yankee Cavalry came in from below where we had whipped them. They stopped about a mile out of town and they sent out to them arms and clothing—so to make out they had not been whipped. There is so much humbug about the Yankee Nation. I saw one of the Jail guards this afternoon who I told about the note Capt McLean had sent me and he promised to try and get it for me.

Nov. 2. Monday. Mr Hill was right sick all night, though the Dr says he is doing very well. Mother still wants the blister, but he objects. Miss Nannie came round this morning to see him. The Yankee Dr came this morning, and recommended more prisoners to be moved. (I told him about Capt McLean's note too.) I took one of them to Miss Nancy, as she said this morning she was going round to try and get families to take them. She said she had not succeeded. So I took and went to Mrs George White—but she could not—then I went to Mrs McKinny.[142] She would give me an answer in the morning, so the poor fellow has to stay in jail another night. Mr Walker will take the other.[143] Dr Rogers put a blister on Mr Hill tonight.[144] Miss Nannie and I will sit up with him.

Nov. 3. Tuesday. He was right sick all night. This morning I started out to see if I could get any place for Mr Roberts. Mrs Crocket said she would take him. Mr. Walker was so sick last night he could not take Mr Parsons, so Mrs Hugh McClung took him and had a man paroled to nurse him. Mr Orr and a non Commissioned officer with him brought Mr Hill his parole of honor to sign, and I told him about the note.[145]

Nov. 4. Wednesday. Mr Hill is worse this morning. Miss Nannie and I went round to a good many places this morning to see if we could get someone to take any more of our sick. Mrs Drake will take one, Mr Horn one to board, and Col Cummings another.[146] The one he had is better. That was all we could do.

Nov. 5. Thursday. Mr Hill is no better. I wish Dr Paxton was attending him instead of Dr Rogers.[147] Miss Nannie came over this morning and again this evening. There is a report in town that Capt Plumlee escaped and took five Yankees with him.[148] Some say all of our men have escaped. I hope it is so. There were between two hundred and fifty and three hundred with a guard of only sixty, green men at that, and Pegram and Wheeler are in Ky cutting up generally.[149]

Nov. 6. Friday. Mr Hill was much worse this morning, and Dr Rogers threatened to throw up the case because mother made so [many] suggestions and [he] was very impudent to her. She sent round for Miss Nannie, and it was unanimously agreed to call in Dr Paxton and let him walk, which was done immediately. Dr Paxton said when he saw him the chances were very much against him, but tonight he thinks him a little better. I went to Mrs Ramsey's this afternoon. Mary and Bettie are both quite sick.[150]

Nov. 7. Saturday. Miss Nannie came over early this morning to see how Mr Hill was (he is much better) and get me to go out to the Hospital with her. We stopped on our way out to see our sick soldiers at Mr Horns, but did not see him. We got Mrs Newman to go to the Hospital with us.[151] We have about a dozen there, sick and wounded. One poor fellow was burnt last Summer by a caissons exploding. He belonged to Huwalds Company.[152] His back was dreadfully burnt, and he had to lie on his face all the time poor fellow. I am afraid he will die. The Yankees neglect our sick.

Nov. 8. Sunday. Sister and I went to church this morning. I am getting to like Mr Martin very much, but I shall be delighted to get back to my own church again. After dinner father and I went over to see Mr Roberts. He is improving slowly. After I came home, sister and I walked out to Mrs McPherson. We have whipped the Yankees well up at Rogersville. Report says they have lost thirteen hundred. Gen Burnside says that it was a disgrace to their army. Their men ran like frightened sheep. They brought in two or three prisoners taken over at Maryville last night.[153]

Nov. 9. Monday. When Sidney came home from the Jail at dinner time, she said that they were going to send our prisoners off this afternoon. So I took what I had over to Col Cummings, and then went round to Miss Nannies to get what she had. Came home and sewed up a jacket that Mrs Kain had sent over, then took them over to the Col's.

Nov. 10. Tuesday. Sam's birthday. I wonder where he is. How I would love to see him and Johnnie. I hope to before long. Miss Nannie sent over before Sunrise this morning to say she would be round directly, as our boys were going to start at seven. So up I got and dressed in a hurry, and had just got down stairs when she came. So off we went. Stopped for Col Cummings but he was not up, so we went up and gave them the basket full of bread we had for them and came home. About an hour after Col Cummings came over and said that Mr Powell, Mr McGhee &e were out in the street ready to start. (The Yankees say they are going to take them to Ky and try them for Cattle stealing.)[154] So I sent round for Miss Nannie and off we went again. Mother sent the hat Sam wore from Vicksburg to a poor fellow who Col said had none, and no shoes.

When we got there the guard would not allow us to speak to the prisoners. Lt Shaw was there, but we would not ask permission of him. The Col did and went in. They have had no fire there for two days and the weather is bitter cold, and some of our men sick with pneumonia. They will be paid for it some of these days. They did not know when they would start so we came home again, and I went to work about eleven oclock. Mrs Cummings came over and said they were about to start so we tried it a third time. We gave them the clothes we had and talked to them till the guard made us stop. One of them told me that Capt McLean was taken off in irons. How it made my blood boil. These outrageous creatures—devils if I must use the word—to treat our officers in such a way. God will punish them for it in his own good time. Capt Rivers escaped from them, as did several others. They kept the poor fellows standing there for several hours, and did not send them off today. There are several sick still in jail.

Nov. 11. Wednesday. Col Cummings came over just after breakfast to say that the prisoners were about to start. Miss Nannie came along just at the moment with Ellen McClung, and they went round to see them off.[155] I did not go as I told them goodbye yesterday. A Sutler came in yesterday afternoon with a wagon full of goods, which he sold immediately to Mrs Van Gilder.[156] He said that the rebels had captured thirty-nine wagons at Morristown. He was just an hour too soon for them so was fortunate enough to escape, but he was too badly frightened to wait to retail his things, wanted to get them off as soon as possible. That was the reason that our prisoners were not sent off yesterday. Mrs Kain came over about eleven oclock and we went up to the stores. Did not see any thing that I wanted or rather needed. Mrs McPherson came in just after dinner. After she went, I went up town again with Mrs Kain. When I came home I found father had been round to the jail. There was a wounded man and two very sick men there without covering so I went down to Mrs Jones to beg some. Got a pillow and two pieces of carpet. Mother sent a piece and Mrs French sent a quilt.

Nov. 12. Thursday. Clear and pleasant. In the afternoon, I went over to Mrs Kains. When I came home I found Cluss here. She stayed to supper. We were all up in Mr Hills room laughing & talking when mother came up and said the Yankee Dr had come to see him, and there was a "Paroled Confederate prisoner" with him—a Captain Phillips who would like to see her daughters. I got downstairs in a hurry, and found an old Yankee sitting up there as large as life. I was mad. He was captain of the Battery that was captured up at Rogersville the other day. He said he had lost all of his guns and everything else. I told him I was glad to hear it, and I hoped the Rebels would make good use of them particularly the guns. If he comes again, I'll give him a dose certain.[157]

Nov. 13. Friday. Clear and pleasant. I finished Allie McPhersons cloak this morning.[158] I am going to try and do something for myself next week. No news that I can hear of. Went over to see Mrs Kain a little while in the afternoon.

Nov. 14. Saturday. I fussed about generally this morning with my flowers, changing some of the pots, and trimming them up. It rained all the morning very heavily. After dinner Miss Nannie came for me to go round to the jail. While we were there a Yankee came riding up—said that there had been a fight over near Maryville in which they had the worst of it. Wolford was cut up again very badly.[159] The Yankee said he believed that Bragg's whole army were over in South America. I heard cannon several times this morning that must of been ours, for they had none. The pontoon bridge was crowded with people coming over. They say the Confederates are all round. The Yanks have driven the hogs they had out of town. Wagons and Cavalry have been going all the evening. Gen Shackleford & body guard, Gen Carter and his escort left this evening. Father says there is a great deal of excitement on Gay St. We have news today of another Victory at Chattanooga.[160] If we only knew that Johnnie was not hurt in the fight, how happy I would be. I suppose our boys will be here before much longer. I hope so. I hate the Yankees more every day I live. They would like to exterminate the whole Rebel population of the South.

Chapter 2.
A Leaden Cloud
Hangs Over Our Spirits

Nov. 15. Sunday. A very disagreeable day. Miss Nannie came in this morning just after breakfast. She says that the Secretary of War had commanded the evacuation of Knoxville immediately.[1] Maynard and Dickinson left yesterday morning for Yankeedom. They were packing up and fixing to leave all last night.[2] I went over to tell Mrs Kain. She said that her Yanks told her goodbye last night expected to leave at two oclock, but they did not go. Said that they had better news this morning. They had been wagoning ammunition & stores to the depot, I suppose to burn. If our boys would only come in time enough to get them.

Nov. 16. Monday. Just as I sat down to breakfast this morning, Sissie Kain came over to say that the Sutlers were selling out for any thing they could get—and packing up what they could not sell, for me to hurry and meet her and go with her to see if we could get any shoes. So I swallowed my breakfast and set out. Every body was out. I mean all the rebel Ladies looking as smiling as possible. We whipped them twice below here today, terribly down at Campbell's station. Longstreet is down there. They are fighting over the river and up at Bull's Gap this side of Greenville. Such running and racing never was seen.[3]

This morning a Major Haggerty called, bringing a letter of introduction from Isiah Davenport[4] to father. Mr D—— had not heard from his family in Sav[annah] for three years, and asked father for some information respecting them. After sitting and talking some time, he said he was Pay Master—

had only arrived Saturday, did not think he would be able to stay many days. The men were very much in need of money but he could not pay them off now—there was too much excitement. I told him I hoped our boys would catch him. He said they would get a pretty good haul if they did. I understand that he had $2,800,000 with him. Late this afternoon I went over to see Miss Kate White. Her mother is quite sick. Mary Ramsey came over while I was there. She said she had heard that the Pay Master had left town. It is too bad.

Nov. 17. Tuesday. Last night at about half past two the wagons came pouring in. A great many went past. Both the vacant lots were full, and our garden. They unfastened their horses and brought them in the yard. One man insisted on coming in the house, said he had been fighting all day and was hungry and tired, and would come in. Tried to make mother think they were rebels. Could'nt cover it though. They forced open the kitchen door and went in. They did not stay long before their order came to hitch up. Of all the cursing and swearing I ever heard they did the most. One of them said they had been badly whipped. Some few stayed in the woodshed all night. They told father that they had whipped the rebels all to pieces, that it was Burnsides policy to draw them on to Knoxville if possible.

Miss Nannie came in about 9 1/2. She had been round to the jail. They had all of our well men out, ready to start off. There is one very sick there with pneumonia. She said that the Yankees say that Longstreet is four miles out of town and Hooker in his rear,[5] that there will be terrible fight here today, that Grant had telegraphed to Burnside if he could hold out till Thursday he would relieve him. I believe it is all a pack of lies. After she went sister went over to Mrs Kains.

All of her men left [at] three oclock last night. Now as I am writing, the excitement and commotion beat any thing I ever saw: Cavalry and footmen running backwards and forwards, 4 regiments of infantry is passing now with their old rags and music. Their Flags tell a tale of rebel bullets.[6] The men are the most diabolical faces I ever saw. They say they are arming the negroes.[7] Baxter,[8] Temple[9] and Brownlow left night before last. Old Sam Morrow was so drunk his wife wanted him to go and they could not. Cavalry are racing in Main and out Cumberland—in Cumberland and out Main. None seem to know what they are after, or where they are going.

Such a flurry as they all are in, and such long faces! They are planting canon all around town, but I dont think they will save them. Picket firing can be heard in several directions, they are fighting out at Reese's on this road,[10] and out by John Moses.[11] Gen Burnside went out with his staff and body guard to the University, to take a look I suppose. He likes to keep in a safe place.

A Yankee soldier came and asked for something to eat. Mother went out to give it to him. She says she was sorry for him. He had been sick, and looked so dreadfully. Just as he went out the gate another came in. He wanted to buy some thing. Mother gave him some bread and meat, but refused to take his money thinking it the safer plan just now. I went out to see if I could get any thing out of him. He said it was only picket fighting, did not know who was in command of the Rebels. He said camp life was very hard. I said it must be on both sides. He said that they had had awful hard times already but he thought the war would be a long one and the hardest was yet to come. I said I thought so that the South and North were both very determined. He said yes it was. They expect a general attack at daylight in the morning.

Nov. 18. Wednesday. The fogg was so dense this morning there had been no fighting of any consequence up to this time, 9 1/2 oclock. The blue jackets are passing back and forth—foot and horse—the same as yesterday. Some with a leg of beef under their arms—or beef put on bread stuck on the ends of their bayonets, the horsemen with bushels of hay or oats strapped on behind or carrying it in their arms. Forage is about the most difficult thing to be had at the present. The Yankees say that Lee has been completely routed and Richmond evacuated. Charleston has been taken at last.[12] I cant tell how many times they have reported the same thing since they have been here. They must get some thing of the kind out to encourage their Soldiers. Whenever they are defeated at any one point they claim a decided victory at another. They insist now that Bragg was completely whipped the other day at Chattanooga, and the men fool like believe it.

About ten the firing commenced and has kept up pretty much all day. Men racing to and from the fortifications. Ambulances going out and coming in. We have taken a regiment and two guns. Sanders (who had command of the raid here last summer) and Fry (who said he had killed General Zollicoffer) were both killed.[13] I heard one man say the Rebels were shooting them down like hot cakes, that the battle ground is strewn with firearms. I was looking out my room window and saw the first gun fired. From the same window I can see two other fortifications. It commands a very fine view. Gen Burnside and staff went out again this afternoon. The fighting today has been mostly out this side, about a mile and a half near Armstrongs and on the Clinton road, some say Reeses. Our house is in exact range of the fortifications on Loudon Hill.[14]

They have taken the 1st and 2nd Presbyterian Churches and Mr Sam Boyds house for a Hospital.[15] Mr Rayal has come in town and gone to Jeanies.[16] They had planted canon right at his house, as they have on every hill round town. They talk of tearing down Staubs house and putting one there.[17] Three men came tonight for our axe but didn't get it. They said they had orders from Gen Burnside to take all they could find. I suppose to cut the trees down, to enable them to see our boys better. I heard a Yankee Officer say tonight that he had just come in and heard firing distinctly about five miles out, but did not say in what direction. There was an order issued this evening that every Southern man who was seen on the St would be arrested and thrown in prison. Capt Lunt told Mrs Kain this morning that the rebels had them just so.[18] She asked him where the opening was but of course he would not tell her. He said they would be captured certain. There would be a desperate engagement for if they escaped they would have to cut their way out.

This morning at about twelve father and I were standing at the front door when Maj Haggerty rode up. After talking some time he informed me that the Rebels could not take the place. I asked him if they could starve it out. He looked at me very hard and says, Yes they could do that. I wonder how long before our boys will take the place. I am almost on my head to see them, and if I can hear certainly when they come in that Sam and Johnnie are safe, I shall be perfectly happy.

Nov. 19. Thursday. Foggy again this morning. The firing began quite early, more in the direction of the Round House, though still some more to the right.[19] Our guns sound very close. The first thing I saw when I looked out this morning was a telegraph wire stretched along right in front of the house. I suppose it goes up to the fortifications. I wish I could cut it or put acid on it to stop its working. I heard a great hammering in the night and could not imagine what they were doing. They must have been putting up the wire.

Before I was dressed this morning Martha came and told me that Miss Peed[20] told her to tell me that one of the Yankees told her that the rebels had caught Brownlow, Baxter Temple and Fleming.[21] I hope it is so, but I had rather catch Maynard then either of them. Lt Shaw met father this morning and told him that we had two very sick men at the jail, and he would have them moved to the Hospital but there was no room for them, every place was filled with their wounded. So he sent to Miss Nannie to come and go with him to see what they could do for them. After making them as comfortable as possible father went for Dr Paxton to go and see them.

They have been firing from College Hill and Temperance Hill.[22] The firing has not been as constant as yesterday, but heavier. The Yankees have sacked Reeses house. I hear that our boys have Robb. Armstrongs for a hospital and the Yankees Jim Armstrong's.[23] Fry was not killed. Sanders was mortally wounded, died this evening.

Miss Kate White came over and sat some time. While she was here a wagon drove up to the door and a Lt rang the bell and asked for Mr House. When father went out he told him he came after that barrel of sugar. Cool impudence. Of course he had to give it up, but he made the fellow let him have twenty-five pounds. (He was the same one who came this morning and asked for liquor.) He looked in all the barrels in the closet and asked what was in them. The whole Morrow family were at the front door looking and laughing. So Ladylike.[24] From here the Yank went down to Mrs Kains. Asked first for liquor then for sugar. She told him she had none. He said he would like to take her word for it, but his orders were to search, so she told him to go ahead. He would not go down to the celler, said it was too low. I expect he was afraid he would get another knock on the head like he did in our closet. But turned and asked Mary if she had any liquor. Took a negro girls word before a lady's. They burnt Mr John Moses house and barn. A Yankee Officer came in town and said he set it on fire.

This afternoon they buried the Adjutant of the 100th Ohio regiment in the 2nd Church yard. They are burying their men just across from Mr McGhees. I understand fifty were buried last night. Dr Borders and Capt Phillips called again tonight.[25] The latter is chief of Artillery here now. He was not taken with his Battery at Rogersville. He said he felt perfectly safe. The Rebels would not attack the place. They were only passing by on their way to Virginia. I asked him why they came this way instead of going by rail. He said they did not think Burnside would fight. They could not take the place. He had twenty-three guns the other side of town. He doubted if there would be one Rebel to be seen any where's around here this morning. Of course I believe it all. They have not taken one of our men so far. They said this morning that last night they had charged the Rebels and taken a hill, but the Rebels had retaken it this morning. They do wonders Charging. One of the shots went through Renshaw's cabinet shop.[26] They have taken the [Deaf and Dumb] Institute for quarters.[27] There is fire somewhere out the other side of the rail road now. Some poor family are houseless.

Nov 20. Friday. I had just got to sleep last night when the Band struck up and woke me. I think they must have been burying General Sanders. They must have been short of ammunition or they would have fired a rally over his grave. Burying him last night looks very much like they expected to have hot times today. The first guns fired this morning at Sunrise. I hear that Dr Croziers[28] and Mrs Deadricks houses have been burnt.[29] They have no idea where the body of our army is. Gen Burnside was up in the Cupulo of the University yesterday, giving orders and countermanding them as soon as given. He don't know what to do. He says this morning he don't feel at all uneasy. Grant is in the rear of Longstreet, was fighting him all day yesterday. Of course it must be true, they never lie.

Just about five oclock this afternoon our forces threw some shells in town. One fell just back of Burnsides quarters. I suppose that was intended to go through the house. Since dark, the whole county the other side of the rail-road appears to be on fire. So many families made houseless. While the fire was raging the two Yankee bands in town struck up. One would play a tune, and then the other. It made me perfectly furious. I could have seen every Yankee here murdered and not shuddered.

A little before nine our Cannons commenced firing. We went to the front door to listen and saw that some house was burning out this road, it must have been Reeses. The cannon-ading was kept up for about twenty minutes. Oh! It was grand, awfully grand. Sidney says three men came to the kitchen about dark and one asked if we had not been making cakes and pies ever since the firing commenced firing for the Rebels, and would not believe her when she said we had not. She said he was right pretty and dressed fine, but he talked so foolish.

Today about eleven oclock two or three Regiments of infantry stopped just in front of the door, one on each side of the St and sat down to rest. One seemed to be dismounted cavalry. They were armed with Breech loading carbines, perfect little beauties. I wanted one so badly. They had ammunition given them while they were here, three rounds to a man. Mr Hill says they always give twenty. The officers came and seated themselves on the front porch, and made themselves comfortable. Had their dinner brought to them and eat it there. The men kept coming in the yard for water and some thing to eat. Mother told them she had nothing. At last one poor young fellow came and begged so hard—said he had nothing to eat for four days except a few dry hard biscuits—she gave him a piece of dry bread, and he eat it as if it were pound cake. I went out and talked to him. He seemed a right decent kind of Yankee. He told me he set fire to the Moses House, that he never hated anything so bad in his life, but his officers ordered him to do it and he had to obey. He said he never saw men fight so since the war as the Rebels did.

While they were waiting an officer walked up to the front door, and rang the bell. Mother went to the door. He said they were establishing a hospital over at the academy for the wounded men & wanted to know if she had any extra bedding &e. She said she had not. He walked past her and said he supposed she would not object to his looking for himself. She drew her protection out of her pocket and handed it to him. She says she never saw a man more taken by surprise in her life than he was. Of course it put an end to his searching. Then he wanted to know if she had any knives &e—cooking utensils. She answered no. He went from here over to Mrs Kains. Took two beds from her, said there were a hundred wounded over at the academy. Miss Nannie came over this evening. She says she hears that Longstreet had demanded the surrender of the place. I doubt it. Col Wolford told Mr Powell he never saw men fight like the rebels did last Saturday across the river. He says our infantry charged their Cavalry—took the horses by the bridle and pulled the men off and bayoneted them.

Nov. 21. Saturday. Cloudy early in the Morning—rained nearly all day. I thought I would try and do some sewing, so I got my black silk sleeves and made them. Started to do it three weeks ago. Mrs Kain could not tell me any news when I went over there for a little while this evening. Capt Phillips called again this evening. He seemed very positive about holding to [the] place, says they have plenty [of] provisions. Thought it was dreadful, our boys throwing those two or three shells in town yesterday afternoon. I got up and told him about Sanders shelling the town on the 20th of last June without a moments warning. He thought that outrageous, at least he said he did. He told us two of our men had been brought in that day or the one before, taken across the river. Mrs Kain told those Yanks over at her house that she thought it was cowardly in Gen Burnside staying in town and hiding behind women, children and old men.

Mr Martin, Mr Charles McClung, Mr James Cowan Jr,[30] Mr Rogan,[31] Mr McClannahan, and Dr Jackson have been ordered to stay in their houses. I think old Mr George White has too. No one has said a word to father. He goes out when he feels inclined. Men are camped all the way down Church St. in Mr McClannahans yard, all in Mrs Alexanders porches and everywhere through the city.[32] There has not been much firing today. I hear some of our men have crossed up at the falks and are building a bridge there. I doubt that part of it, but they captured a team of wagons up there. Some of the drivers were so much frightened they drove right into the river and a good many were lost.

There are a lot of men under our woodshed. Father told them he had no objection to their staying there, but they must not burn the fences or bring their wagons in the lot. They said they would not. They are Capt Lunts wagoners. I suppose it is just as well to let them stay as they seem to be a quiet set, for if they went we might have much worse.[33]

Nov. 22. Sunday. Clear and pleasant. Miss Kate White came over just after breakfast to ask if we would cook for a mess of five round at the Jail. Mother said certainly, and set Sidney right to work. Just as soon as she got something cooked. Father went round with her. Found our two sick improving and four or five new ones, two Lts and the others privates. Could not get the chance to talk to them as the Guard went in with him. Soon after he started Col Cummings came in. He said it was a mess at the Guard house that he wanted us to cook for. They had the provisions and only wanted some one to cook for them. Of course mother was willing, but Mrs George White is going to do it, so we can do something else. The same two regiments that were here on Friday were here resting again today, and the same set of men on our front porch, [to] eat their dinners there again. The men had theirs brought there too, bread and a kind of soup, not ten pounds of meat in the whole of it.

I went to see Mrs Kain a little while. She says that our men up at the falk made a raft and set it on fire and sent it down the river to destroy their pontoon, but the Yankees saw it in time and divided the bridge. I am very sorry for it. The officers vow that they have sixty days full rations. But one was over heard to say that they have five days quarter rations, a very considerable difference, and I should judge much nearer the truth.[34] They have made a fort of Mr Barnes house, taken the window out and fixed it up.[35] Mrs Coffin, Mr Deadrick and Mr William Branner were all burnt out the other night.[36] Mrs Coffin saved a good many things. Mr Deadrick only a very few. The soldiers are stealing everything they can. Some of them took dresses and cups and saucers to Mrs Frank Scott to sell which she recognized as her mother's, reported on them and got them back.

About three, sister and I walked up to Mrs McPherson's. Her beautiful yard is completely ruined. There is a Battalion of Cavalry camped in it. Her grass which was growing so beautifully looks like the middle of the Street. They are all over her piazzas. She says she has the house and thats all. We found her seated at the back door with the baby in her arms. What a time she has had. Allie has been very sick. Wallie is still, and she [with] no servant. I don't see how in the world she has been able to get along at all. She said she was so glad to see us, had been wishing every day we would come. She told us there were two Companies of Sharp Shooters camped in the yard first, and they were the most villianous looking set she ever saw. They did every thing they could to make her leave the house, said it was so exposed, exactly in the range of the Guns &e, but she would not. They only wanted to make her leave so they could sack it. She said it made her blood boil to have them hiding behind her house to shoot at our men and so the Rebels could not see them—and not one in sight. She saw them distribute their rations this morning, each man received a small loaf of bread and a strip of pork about 2 inches by six for two days. One of the men said they had not had as much as one good feed for their horses in three days. They look dreadfully, poor things. I feel so sorry for them. I can hear them crying almost all day long. They seem most starved. I never saw finer mules and horses than they were when they first came in.

Mrs McPherson told us that the Yankees had a hospital flag flying on the side of the observatory of the University towards our forces and a signal flag flying the other. They have two guns planted right in front of the main building.[37] Mrs Sanborn has been notified to leave her house. They have brush pilled up round it ready to burn it. A ball went through Mr Powells kitchen two or three days since. They have rifle pits and fortifications all round his house. White's place on the hill has not a panel of fence left round it. There has not been much firing today, and that more to the east.

Nov. 23. Monday. Not much firing this morning. I went over to Mrs Kains and spent some time. When I came home went to work and made me a pair of hoops. Sister and Mrs Kain went to several places this afternoon, Mrs Jackson's among others. She says that one of Gen Wheelers men was in town last week. She saw him. I wish I could have. I am very much afraid that I shall go crazy when our boys get back. The Yankee officers at Rogan's house say that they had seen a great rejoicing among our men, and a deal of shaking hands—that Buckner has reinforced Longstreet, Pegram and Scott are with him.[38] I hope Stewart is along. Oh! how delightful it would be if Johnnie and Sam could only come with them. I hear we have siege guns along—so it is not impossible.

I am just boiling over again tonight, more Southern property destroyed, first a fire over by the river the other side of the University. I think it must be the Moffets. I dont care so much for that, he is a union man. Before that was half done burning, the round house was in a blaze. I never saw any thing like it. It was terrifically grand—the whole country north of the rail road seemed to be in a blaze. Our boys must be furious to see such destruction of property. Dr Croziers was burnt. I know for I could see it distinctly from my room window.[39] The Yankees buried sixty-one of their men yesterday.

Nov. 24. Tuesday. Rained off and on all day. Last night our boys charged their rifle pits and took them, but retired. I suppose they did not think [it] prudent to stay directly under the Enemies Guns. This morning our boys charged them again, and killed and captured a great many [in a] Michigan Reg. Up to ten oclock this morning they had brought in eighty-seven of their wounded. There has been firing today more to the East. Tonight Capt Phillips came to say that two of our men, Artillerists, were in jail here and were very much in need of blankets. He had been round to see them that afternoon. (They are the same ones who father went to see Sunday. One is Moore from Baltimore, the other Tucker from Richmond). He said that Gen Shackleford went out yesterday with eight thousand men and they had not returned yet. I doubt if they went. If he did I hope they were all caught.[40]

Nov. 25. Wednesday. I went round to Mrs French's to see what could be done in the way of getting blankets for the boys round at the jail. Mrs Eliza McClung was there. She gave me Hugh's blanket for one of them. Poor old Lady. I felt so much for her. When I took it up to bring it off, the tears just rolled down her cheeks. Miss Nannie wrote a note to Mrs Charles Alexander—and she sent one, so father, sister and I went round to the jail to take them.[41] One sick man there is getting better, the others are doing pretty well. One of our men was lying down in one corner when we asked if he was sick. He said no, he had been fighting three Yankees and gotten a black eye. One man was eating raw corn. He seemed to have been grating it on a piece of tin he had punched holes through with nails. There was bread hung up on the wall and such bread, black as could be. Mr Moore & Tucker said they were taken just as they were, and of course needed clothes badly. We promised to send them some. They said they did not get near enough to eat. The Guard told him they got the same as they did. I doubt that, though I know they are on quarter rations.

When we came home sister and I went to work to make a shirt. We made two. After we got it done we thought we might make two pairs of drawers if we had the cotton. So I started to Col Cummings. Mrs Cummings let me have six yards and I am to pay her back tomorrow. So we each made a pair by candle light, tallow candles at that. Heavy firing today.

Nov. 26. Thursday. Yankee thanksgiving day. Kingdom only knows what they have to give thanks for in this part of the world. Ella Cocke came over this morning to see if we were going to the jail today. She said she would go up town and buy some towels and take them to the jail. So we went up but the store was closed, so we did not get any thing. I went to Mrs McClannahan's to beg for some clothes and blankets. Mrs Cocke and herself both promised and have sent some. After I came home I went over to see Col Cummings. He said he would like to go round to the jail. So I told him we would stop for him when we went. Mother sent some dinner round to them. In the afternoon Ella came for me and we went over for the Col, so he went with us. The poor fellows were all so eager for the few clothes we took them. Some six or eight are still without blankets. I hope we will be able to get more tomorrow.

I hear they brought in four hundred wounded yesterday, also that we captured one of Shacklefords regiments. The cannonading has been slight today. Jeanie came up this morning to ask father to go round to the jail with her. She had been told that Gid had been taken prisoner and brought in last night. It proved to be young Glenn from this place.[42]

Dr Borders and Capt Phillips called this evening. When they came sister and I were sewing a blanket or rather sewing a carpet to make a blanket of it for one of our men at the jail. They say they have a good many wounded. They have four churches and two lecture rooms besides all the hospitals full. They still insist they have plenty to eat for a month or two. They do lie so. The men are begging all round town, say that they dont get quarter rations. They are burying the Yankees right fast back of Columbus Powell's. They plant them in rows just like peas or potatoes. There was another officer buried this evening in the 2nd Church yard. One of the prisoners says that we have communication direct with Atlanta, that our men have plenty to eat, are well clothed and in fine spirits. That Longstreet is across the river with thirty-thousand men, besides what they have on this side.

Nov. 27. Friday. Clear and Cold. As soon as I ate my breakfast I wrote a note to Nina Danner asking her to beg some clothes &e in her neighborhood for the men in the jail. Then I started off. Went to Mrs McKinny's. She was out, but I left word [with] the Judge. She sent me round two pieces of carpet and a blanket. Just after I came home Ella Cocke came in to say she was going up town to buy some socks, and I went round to Miss Nannie to see her a little while. Mr Craighead was there and gave me three dollars.[43] From there I went to Mrs McGhees, Mrs Powell, and Mrs Sedgwick— they each promised something. Mrs Powell sent a basket full. Mrs Sedgwick said that Mrs Horn had never been paid any board for the sick soldiers she has boarding there and they were about destitute.[44] So when I came back I stopped and told Miss Nannie. She had never seen Mr James Moses who was to pay his board, and now we cannot see him. Miss Nannie said she would try and get some somewhere.

After I came home Col Cummings came in. He said the boys at the jail needed socks and Plumlee said he had seven pr he could have for cover. He wanted me to beg it. He gave me a dollar. While he was here and I was fussing about Mrs Horn not being paid, Mr Powell came in. When he heard about it he gave me $20. Oh! How glad I was to get it! Sister and I started right off to pay her. As we were coming back we met Ella Cocke, Blannie McClung and Annie Brinkly in front of Mr Cockes gate, and Miss Nannie came along while we were standing there.[45] I told her I had paid Mrs Horn $23. Ella said that Ellen McClung and herself would be round in half an hour to go to the jail, so when they came we filled the clothes basket with the things we had and started off.

Stopped for Col Cummings. He had quite a lot himself. The guard would not let us in. So we had to call the men to the gate and distribute the clothes as well as we could. The boys seemed perfectly delighted to see us, begged us to call again. When we came home I went over to Mrs Kains and begged a hat for one that had none. When I returned I found Nina Danner here and Miss Fletcher.[46] They had brought up two large baskets full of clothes. I think we have enough to make them comfortable. Late in the evening Mrs Smith came in from the jail, said that the man who was sick at the jail had never had his blister dressed, and it was in a dreadful state. She is going round tomorrow morning to dress it. We gave her a quilt for him which she said she would send round tonight.

There has been very little firing today, several [shots] were fired while we were round at the jail. Mr Craighead says that our sharpshooters picked the yanks off a thousand yards without any trouble. It is rather dangerous to walk across the lawn at Mr Barnes. One man was shot standing in the kitchen. Our men have a small gun with a telescope at the end—it extends beyond the barrel of the gun. I suppose they are just such as the Yankee Sharp Shooters had at Vicksburg. Mr Powell says they have cut a hundred holes in his house to shoot at our boys.

The Yankees said yesterday the Rebels were all gone, today they say they were mistaken. The Yankees say that they had fifteen hundred bushels of corn come down the river this afternoon. I don't believe it. Our pickets have been calling to theirs to put a double load in their guns—the shot did not reach but half way to them, that they need not think Sherman was coming to help them, that he is in the same fix Burnside is. He sent to have the wounded Rebel that was brought in a day or two since brought to to him, and asked him how many men Longstreet had. He told him one hundred and seventy-five thousand. Old Burnside told him that would do.

Nov. 28. Saturday. There was firing off and on all night. Just before daylight it was quite heavy. Cannon and musketry both. Sister and I mended up the clothes that had been brought home from the jail to wash. Mrs Smith came in on her way to the jail. The sick man is better. She says there are a great many Confederates up at Bean Station, and I know that they are all round here.[47] Mr Branners little boy came to bring some things and go to the jail with father. He says they tried to burn their house but did not succeed. The Yanks tore up his, his mothers and sisters clothes and piled them up in the middle of a room with a lot of hay, and set it on fire. It all burnt but left the house. It wont burn, but it is ruined. He says three Yankees got upon the house the other day, and three Indians picked them off. They took three cannons out to batter down the walls of Reeses house, but did not succeed in doing it. One of our Batteries threw so many shot and shell they had to leave. Our Sharp Shooters get up on the walls and pick them off every day.[48]

When father went round to the jail they would not let him in. Lt Shaw says that he has had orders to let no one enter, and the sergeant that went with him to the gate did not want him to say any thing to the prisoners, said they were allowed too much liberty. The good for nothing thing. I'll make him pay for it. He is the same one who stopped my talking to the prisoners when they were starting for Camp Chase. One of the men cursed

Mr Hill. He says he has his eyes on him. He wont be a prisoner much longer, [and] the tables will be turned then. There has been some cannonading late this afternoon (It rained heavily this morning held up this afternoon). Mr Hill says they are fighting all round. He can hear them. Gen Burnside was over heard to say to one of his officers two days ago, that he could not hold out more than three days longer. Then it would be one of three things, raise the white flag, fight or run. I dont know where they will run to. Oh! how I do long to see our boys back here. A good many ambulances came in this afternoon, and all seemed to have at least two wounded men [in] them. I wish they had all been killed.

Nov. 29. Sunday. They were fighting all night. I could not sleep. I would doze a little while when bang would go two or three guns and of course I was wide awake. I could see the flash of the cannons where I was in bed, since during the night there was very heavy firing of musketry, and I could hear our boys cheering distinctly.[49] They stormed the brestworks and were repulsed. They got inside the first ditch and thought they had possession at the place when they were all taken. They had another trench to cross. When our men were in the trench the Yankees lighted the fuses to the shells and threw them at them. They say that we had six hundred men killed, and they seven, that all our dead and wounded were in their hands, and three hundred prisoners. One hundred were brought in this morning, and about fifty were brought past here afterwards. They seemed to all have blankets and be in fine spirits. I think there were eleven officers, mostly Georgian and Mississippians.[50]

At about two they all commenced bringing in the wounded. They say that they have none at all, they were all ours. I dont believe it. If none of theirs had been wounded they would not have gone out in such a hurry this morning with a flag of truce to bury the dead and bring away the wounded. They claim a great victory, think it was very smart to stretch wire about a foot above the ground to trip our men when they got inside the trenches.

Mrs Smith came here for some Brandy for one of our men, and I went back with her. We stopped for Cluss. When we went into the store where they had our poor fellows lying on the floor Ellen McClung and Blanch were there. Ellen said to me just to look at two or three that were there. They had each lost either a leg or an arm, some without even a blanket over them and one saying that he was freezing, and he looked as if he were. I told her if she would come with me, I would go round to Miss Nannie's. I knew she had several pieces of carpet.

The Dr said we could not come. If we left we should not come back. Ellen told him she had a written permit from Gen Carter to come. He said when Gen Carter gave it, he did not know that they were to be exchanged. She begged him, told him she would not do or say any thing. Her word was passed and of course she would not violate it. Nothing could move him. He even went so far as to make some insulting remarks [about] a Southern Congressman who told a lie in Congress. He would let our poor fellows lie there without any covering, the coldest day we have had this winter, not a spark of fire, let us see them so, and would not let us relieve them. It is the most brutal thing I have ever heard of. His name is May. I'll have him dealt with when our boys get in. God grant that may be soon.

I told Ellen I would come and get the carpets and she could receive them at the door. So I came out and run almost every step of the way home. By the time I got back with the blankets, he had made the girls leave, and they had to give them to one of the Yankees and trust to their giving them to our men. One of the noble men who was lying there, without any covering, had lost his left leg, was a Capt Bell from Baker Co. Geo.[51] I met Duff Rice in one of the ambulances.[52] He was slightly wounded in the foot. I asked him if he would like any thing. He said something to eat, so I stayed there to watch the ambulance that it did not get out of sight, and sent Sidney home for a bucket of biscuits we had made this morning. They had started when she got back, but I made the driver stop and gave them to him. He said he thought there were about one hundred wounded. The Yanks brought in 63. He promised to write Johnnie as soon as he got in our lines. Said A. P. Stewart was in front of Chattanooga, so if Johnnie's life has been spared he is there.

All our wounded have been exchanged but two, who were too badly injured to stand it. Lt Shaw said that about 250 prisoners [had] been brought in. He did not have the list finished, but if I went down to Mrs McCalla's tonight he would let me see it. So down I went, and saw it. There were none I know. He said it was not complete. There are three from Marietta. I never heard their names before. I am going up there tomorrow to see them all. Lt Col O'Brien—Mrs Brownlows brother—is among them.[53] I think it is rather singular if all the dead and wounded were left in the hands of the yankees, and they had none wounded, that they should exchange the wounded. They expect an attack tonight. The arms are stacked half way between the two armies, and they are to contend for them. There was a truce till five this evening, which was extended till two tomorrow. The vile old Yankees have taken advantage of it to make shells. The foundery is so much exposed they cannot make them except during an armistice.

Nov. 30. Monday. Very cold. This morning mother and I went round to the jail, and took some things. Miss Nannie went too. Ford under old Shaw let us in.[54] The Georgia Adjutant I was so anxious to know the name of from Augusta is Tom Cummings.[55] He said he got along very well except that he wanted something to read. So I sent him up some books. He told me Mr Tom Bones has lost one of his legs.[56] I am so sorry. I like him, and it seems such a pity for so fine a fellow to be mained for life, but he lost it in a glorious cause fighting for his Country. No one else that I know from Augusta has been killed or wounded. After I came home I wrote a note to Capt Phillips requesting him to get me a permit from Gen Burnside to visit the jail. (Ellen McClung and I went around begging clothes &e) which he was kind enough to do. So Ellen and I went round and took the clothes and eatables we had. Mr Tucker wrote to me begging me to get his mess something to eat. I received the note too late this afternoon to do any thing.

Just after dark some one rang the bell. A Yankee Lt came in, said he had called to see if he could buy a blanket—that someone had stolen both his, and he could not buy one in town. Mother told him she had none, that all that she could possibly do without she had sent round to the jail. Sister said that Miss McClung had taken three very nice ones around this afternoon. Then I put in that she gave them to three of the poorest, dirtiest Confederates soldiers he ever saw, and it did my heart good to see them get them. He came in and sit down, regularly spent the evening.

I peppered him well, told him the idea of their talking of reconstruction of the Union was simply ridiculous. Southern children hated the Yankee nation from the time they were born, and the hatred grew with their

growth and strengthened with their strength. Gave him a dose of the slavery
question then we touched upon the news today that Grant had whipped Bragg
all to pieces. I asked him how he would account for the difference of their
report and what one of our prisoners told me today that A. P. Stewart was
in front of Chattanooga. He said that the dispatch they had received was
that Bragg had been whipped, and had fifteen thousand men taken prisoners.
I told him certainly I believe it all. Then he said divide all we heard by 20
and we would about get the truth. I told him that would suit me exactly.
Bragg had whipped Grant and taken five thousand prisoners.

When he left he told Mother he had passed the most pleasant evening
he had had since he had been in Knoxville. He must like being abused, for I
told him all sorts of things. He said something about the Rebels. I told him
it was the proudest name I ever bore. His name is Torr. He says Gen Lee is
his Cousin. I doubt if the Gen knows it. He is attached to Gen Shacklefords
staff.[57] There was a fight across the river night before last, where we took
fifteen hundred prisoners. Today I hear that we captured a wagon train over
there in sight of the Yankee pickets.

Dec. 1. Tuesday. Still very cold. Ellen McClung, Ella Cocke & I went
all over town to see if we could get any thing for our prisoners to eat. We
did not succeed very well. We bought four pounds of rice, and that was all
we could get. Mother went up to Gen Burnsides yesterday afternoon to see
if she could get Mr Cummings paroled. Mrs Brinkley went with her, but
they could not do anything. He said he could not do it. He had paroled Col
O'Brien. Then she asked for permission for father to go out. He said Gen
Carter would attend to all such matters. There were one or two guns fired
about two oclock yesterday. There does not appear to be much fighting today.

While I was sitting down sewing (Mary Hill Alexander came to bring
her shirt and some socks)[58] Carter Cummings came over to tell me his father
wanted to see me quick. So I went right over, found Ellen & Ella there.[59]
He said that so many men wanted shoes, he thought we had better beg some
money. So we went right to work and begged about fifty dollars, and after
getting it found there were no shoes to be had. The Yankees had pressed all
in town. So they bought some domestic to make shirts with.

Sister and I went around to the jail about four oclock and took a large basket of clothes another of Provisions. A great many have been there to-day with clothes and something to eat. Marg Aults youngest sister and Miss O'Conner went round with us this evening.[60] Lt Shaw only let them go to the gate. He did not want to let us go in but I was determined he should. Lt. Cummings said that two of the men were sick, and he was very much afraid they were getting Pneumonia. So when I came home I went round to Dr. Paxton to try and get him to go, but found him sick in bed.

When I came home I found Mrs Vanuxum and Mrs Dr Crozier with some clothes, so I went round with them to the gate.[61] As I was coming away I met Mr Mike Branner going there with some carpets.[62] I was very glad to see them going. He said that he hoped to get Mr Cummings paroled. I had not been in the house but a little while when an ambulance drove up and two Yankees came up and rang the bell. I went to the door. They wanted to know who lived here. I told them. They said they had come to get any extra bedding we might have. I told them we had none & that we had protection. Just then mother came to the door, and told him she had nothing. They said her protection was worth nothing, as they had orders from Gen Carter to search the house. Mother told him she could pledge her word of honor as a lady she had nothing but what she needed. One of the imps said "a rebel had no honor." I was just blazing, and said I would go to Gen Carter and went but he was out, and I was silly enough to say so when I came back.

They were standing at the front door, had been in the two front rooms and come down, and when I came in they turned around and came back again even went in the servants rooms. I told one that we were Rebels. He said that did not matter. I said it did. We were too good rebels to have bedding hid away when our boys were needing it so much round at the jail. I just gave it to him. He said he had taken fifteen ambulance loads of blankets and quilts from houses where the ladies said they had nothing. They belonged to people who lived the other side of the rail road, and a little bedding was all they saved when they were burnt out, and now they have had that little stolen from them. One of them was the same man who insulted Ellen McClung Sunday. I'll fix him. They did not get any thing for there was nothing to get. They have a list of the Rebel families here, and they are going to all of them. They went to Mrs Crockets yesterday and asked who those young ladies were who were offering blankets to the wounded Rebels Sunday. They were going to them to get them for their sick. I'd burn any thing I had before they should have it. Some of our men said this morning, they had not had any thing to eat since they had been taken.

Gen Burnside issued a congratulatory order today to his men, on the great victory Grant had gained. I believe it originated in his fertile imagination. The men don't all believe it true. Mr Humes says that Grants center & right whipped Bragg badly, but that his left wing under Sherman has been cut to pieces. If he says so its so. I mean Sherman has been defeated.[63]

I declare it is distressing to go to the jail. So many poor fellows want things that can't be had for love or money, so many begging for something to eat. They are on less than quarter rations. Oh! If Longstreet would only come. The city is completely ruined, scarcely a fence standing. The side walks are like a stable yard, and the stench is horrible, particularly from the hospitals, and there are one hundred and fifty of them. I understand Gen Burnside says that Sherman is within striking distance (He sleeps at present in Mrs Temples cellar—a brave general truly), and that if Longstreet does not attack the place before twelve tomorrow he will be taken prisoner. Mrs Baxter says she has received a dispatch from her husband from up the road, that Brownlow and he are within 20 miles of Knoxville with ten thousand reinforcements. How they all lie.

Dec. 2. Wednesday. I went over to Mr Brinkleys this morning and got Blannie McClung to go with me to Gen Carter. I wanted to get a permit for father to leave the house, and tell him the way those impudent creatures did last night. When we got there he was engaged. I stated my errand to one of his staff, told him some one had been kind enough to break into our store room and smoke house two nights before and taken every thing that was there, and there was no one but father to get any thing. He said he would have it attended to and went out [of] the room. In a few minutes he returned saying he was sorry but Gen Carter said he had received positive orders from Gen Burnside to give no one a permit. I told him I thought it very strange. Mother had been to Gen Burnside and he had sent her to Carter. He said that was a way Burnside had of getting rid of unpleasant business. I asked if we were to starve. He presumed we young ladies could attend to all such matters. We generally carried all before us. I replied judging from the success we had met with this morning I thought we [would] not be able to do much. They think a little flattery will smooth it over, and I understand they are in the habit of using it perfusely.

Then we went to Mrs French's. Miss Nannie and Mary Hill were mending old clothes. After staying there a little while we left and separated at Dickinsons corner.[64] I had promised one of the prisoners to go to Mr Parmer's and take a message for him, so I went down there. As I was coming back up Main Street, I met Sister and Ella Cocke going over to East Knoxville, so I turned round and went with them. When we came from there we stopped at Mrs Hugh McClung's. After I came home Miss Nannie, Ella Cocke, and Mary Hill came round with Dr Levine to go to the jail.[65] When we went, Lt Shaw said he had positive orders from Gen Burnside not to allow any one to speak to the prisoners or go in. Everything that goes is to be sent through Lt Shaw. There was no use talking. He said he could not do it. So we had to send the things by him.

Not long after we got home Lt Shaw came to say that Adjutant Cummings had been paroled. He did not know with what restrictions. Mr Branner had taken him from the jail, so sister and I went round to see him. He is confined to the bank building. There has been some fighting across the river. I dont know with what result. Late this afternoon I was at Mrs Kains when a Yankee came to beg some bread for a sick comrade. I went and talked to him, made out that I was dreadfully sorry for him &e. He said that they had been kept in readiness for an attack for the last three days, expecting it every hour. They have scarcely any thing to eat, and that is of the coarsest kind, and so many are sick that every man has extra duty to do. Mrs K——— had not a piece of bread in the house. I sent him over to Morrow's, but he did not get any there. Such people. Gen Burnsides official report sent north is that we lost thirteen hundred killed, wounded and prisoners.

Dec. 3. Thursday. The first thing I saw this morning was an officer and three of Pikes men go into Mrs Kains. As soon as they left I posted over there to see what it was for. She says he searched her house from cellar to garret for a reason. I told her I hope he found it. She thinks perhaps it was for Mr Kain. After I left there sister and I went to the stores to find some things we needed if possible. Did not succeed. I should not wonder if they made some fuss about so many people coming to our house. Not a day passes but ladies are coming and going all hours. They call it rebel head quarters. Mrs McCaffrey says she has seen Gen Longstreet with her own eyes.[66] She can see the Rebels rifle pits from her window. Mrs Jackson says they have planted another Battery across the river, and a Yankee Officer was over heard to say that we had received fifteen thousand Mississippi Cavalry reinforcements. I hope and pray it is true, and yet they insist that the Rebels are all gone. They have said that every day for the last week.[67]

Just about dark some one rang the bell, sister answered it. The same officer who was at Mrs Kains this morning said he had orders to search the house. Fannie asked him in and called up to mother. He had a guard stationed at the front and back doors and one with him. He asked for Mr Humes key so I sent Martha for it. He would not tell what he was hunting for. I suppose they have heard Johnnie is outside & are after him. The Lt was very gentlemanly, said he regretted it &e. If he had not been I'd have give it to him in style. The two Chaplains who searched our house two days since searched Mrs Frenches yesterday evening. Miss Nannie came over to tell us about it. She said she tongue lashed them good. They threatened to have her arrested. She dared them to do it. They told her the same thing they told mother, that a rebel had no honor.

There has been firing to the north east today. The soldiers are still begging for some thing to eat. One told me today they did not get sixth rations. They stay in the Rifle pits forty-eight hours. They don't dare to raise their heads above the trenches for fear a sharp shooter will take it off. One of ours has fixed himself in the walls of Mr Deadricks house, and they say he has killed nearly a regiment. They have sent out after him, but cant catch him. Father over heard some Yanks say that Rebels had whipped them out of their Rifle pits. They say that Wheeler has been taken prisoner with all his staff.

Dec. 4. Friday. I hear this morning as usual all the rebels have gone. What the firing was for then I can't imagine. Mr P. Williams told father our forces had captured a quantity of flour coming down the river. I hear too that they captured a wagon train of three hundred wagons coming in from Ky yesterday. A Yankee soldier who came here to get board said that all who are able to walk have been sent out of the hospitals to make room for the wounded, that there was a fight across the river day before yesterday in which they had three thousand killed and wounded. Sherman was in command of their forces. In the evening I went over to Mrs Kains. Her Yankees insist on it that Longstreet has left, that they have plenty [of] forage. It looks very much like it when they went down to the Bell house the other day and ripped up the shuck mattress to feed their horses. The kitchen has been full of yankee soldiers all day, most begging something to eat. One of them told father Morrow sent them here.

Dec. 5. Saturday. Raining and disagreeable. Every body says this morning that Longstreet has left. I dont and wont believe it, though the thought that it might be true almost kills me. If they have gone, I dont know what in the world they sit down out side here so long for. God grant it is not so. It is so. When I first knew it to be true I felt as though I was choking. I could scarcely breathe. It was just the way I felt one night last Summer when I thought I was dying.[68]

They have brought in a good many prisoners today. I think they must be deserters. I saw Lt Shaw this morning and told him I was sorry but I would have to turn Mr Lemstraw over to him. Mrs. Horn says she has not enough to feed her own family. Mrs Smith came over after dinner to say that our wounded had been left out at Armstrongs. Gen Shackleford has gone after Longstreet. I hope he may catch him. I don't think he will find it very pleasant. They say that Bragg has been whipped all to pieces, and is in full retreat to Atlanta. Lee has been completely routed in Virginia and now they will have Longstreet in a very few days. The Rebellion is played out entirely. Longstreet they think has gone towards Virgina, and intends making a stand at Bristol. They know a heap about it.[69]

I sent Sidney round to the jail with something to eat this evening. When she came back she brought me a note from one Alexander Lovett, asking for a pair of pants, some tobacco and something to eat. As I had no pants I went over to get a pair from Ellen McClung. There I met Blannie. She says a lady who came in town today and has been with our army ever since it has been round here told her that during the attack last Sunday morning Longstreet received a dispatch for Gen Bragg saying that after four days hard fighting he had gained a more brilliant victory than at Chickamauga, but as Grant has received very heavy reinforcements, he had thought best to fall back to Dalton. So he thought best not to follow up the charge. He commenced leaving Tuesday. The last went [at] twelve oclock last night. He is going to reinforce Bragg, but says he will be back in two months and take the place. What an age it seems. What may not happen before that time. I may be in eternity. If I could know that at that time he would come and Sam and Johnnie would be safe and well I could stand it easily, but the thought that they may be dead or lying in some hospital, mutilated and uncared for almost crazes me. God guide and protect them from all dangers.

Gen Burnside has resigned and Foster from North Carolina is to superseed him.[70] He is almost as bad as Butler. One thing puzzles me and that the officers here all wear such long faces. They dont look as one would suppose they would. One thing is certain they are very short of provisions. Mrs Brinkley went to Burnside day before yesterday to ask if she could get a peck of meal and she could not. One of the officers down at Mrs Strongs said before her, in speaking of our dead who were not buried last Sunday night, "Let them lie there, and let the hogs fatten on them, and we will eat the hogs." They went up to Mrs McPhersons yesterday and demanded her two rooms for a hospital. She gave them her out house. After that some Gen went there and wanted to take it for head Quarters. I think it is Ferrero, the one who has been up at Barnes.[71]

Dec. 6. Sunday. Cold and unpleasant. The Yankee officers here wear very long faces for men who ought to feel very much relieved. Report says two of Shermans Brigades came in yesterday. I suppose it is what is left of his command. I hear that we had a fight up at Strawberry plains day before yesterday, and Gen Sam Jones took five thousand of Wilcox men prisoners, whipped him completely.[72] They say they are fighting there today. Gen Longstreet fooled these Yankees good. They were looking for an attack for four days and nights, and all our men gone. They were up in line of battle all Friday night, and the last of our men left at twelve oclock that night.

The two Yankee Chaplains who searched our house for extra bedding went down to Mrs Mitchells to search.[73] Miss McCaffrey was there very ill, and one of them said she was not sick, only making believe, and they [said she] had bed clothes hid under her. They went so far as to have her turned over to examine. One of them told Miss Harriet Park she had hid [bedding] from her threshold to her garret, and the Rascal who told mother a Rebel had no honor preached in our Church last Sunday.[74] I think that it has been as much dissecrated as the others, if not more. Mrs Smith came over this afternoon to say that a Maj Smith has been captured, a member of Gen Wheeler's staff.[75] He was sick has the rheumatiz I think, and suffering from a wound besides. He was at a house some nine miles out and did not know Longstreet had left.

Reported fighting today some twenty miles above here. I hope we are peppering them well. I believe Longstreet knows what he is doing, and am perfectly satisfied to trust all to him. Tonight just about dusk a Yankee Officer, came here, said he had orders for a room in our house from Gen Carter for a Major on Gen Blairs Staff.[76] The Gen was to stop at Mrs Frank McClungs, some of his Staff at Miss Harriet Parks, and the rest wanted a room near, and he must have it here. Mother told him we occupied all the rooms in the house, and sent him over to Morrows. He came right from Memphis, by way of Tuscumbia, Lafayette, Chattanooga. They had marched all the way, about fifteen miles a day. The Yankees here insist that they have the rail-road from here to Dalton. If they had they would not have marched from Chattanooga here. There were two Brigades came in yesterday. I suppose they are all that are left of Shermans Division. It is just too bad that they had to come here tonight when we wanted to get Maj Smith Paroled and sent here, and now we will have to wait a day or two. If they had got one man here they would have taken the house.

Dec. 7. Monday. This morning I saw baggage going from Mrs Kains, and I went to see what was up. It was only old Winslow going away, and Yankee like went without paying his board.[77] Said he would settle when he returned—ten chances to one if he ever comes back. As I was going over I met Annie McFarlane.[78] She says that Longstreet has made a stand twelve miles above here, and is expecting reinforcements from Virginia. One can hear any thing they want to on the street today, both sides. The Yankees say that we are completely used up and still all are leaving and going home that can, and wear the longest faces imaginable. I went up to the stores this afternoon with Mrs Kain to get some thing for Nonnie for a birthday present. She could not get any thing but candy and there was not but half a pound of that in the city.

Dec. 8. Tuesday. Nothing of any importance today. Gen Carter played into our hands most beautifully. Mr Hill went up to Lt Shaws office this morning to report as usual. When he returned he said Gen Carter had paroled Maj Smith and we sent him right back after him. When they brought him his parole to sign, we found that he was paroled to this house. Ten chances to one if we had applied for him, that he [Carter] would have refused. I think it such a pity his being so badly wounded as to make him a cripple for life. Mr McClung says that instead of a general going to Mrs Frank McClungs night before last she had fifteen, and such a house as they left. Gen Blair said he was just from Vicksburg, and going direct to St. Louis. I understand that the men he brought with him here are all ordered back to Chattanooga. Ella Cocke came over this afternoon and stayed a little while. She is coming tomorrow morning to go to the stores with me, and to get some shoes for some of our poor fellows in jail. Fighting is reported up the road.

Dec. 9. Wednesday. Ella came this morning and we went to the stores, but did not succeed. After that we went down to Mrs Hugh McClungs after Ellen. Miss Nannie came in while we were there. She had just come in from Mr James Parks.[79] She went out yesterday to see our men who were left sick and wounded. She says they need something to eat badly. I think there are about one hundred and eighty all together, poor fellows. Mary Hazen says she asked Dr Strong after Sam and John.[80] Sam is in Atlanta, part of the time in Marietta. Very well. Johnnie [is] well too. At the fight of Chickamauga his horse was killed, shot just behind the saddle, a right narrow escape. I have felt perfectly happy since I have heard they were both safe.

I hear that we captured a wagon train coming here from Ky. The number I have not heard. Gen Burnside was reported captured, but he was sick in bed. I understand he did not resign, but has been superceeded because he was too lenient toward Southern people. Mr Brinkley says he was told today that Carter had resigned, and Granger was to take his place.[81] Gen Foster is a second Butler, a little worse if anything.[82] I expect we'll see sights now. Mr Brinkley is going back to Memphis if he can get a pass from Gen Burnside. I'd rather risk the chance of the Confederates taking this place.

Dec. 10. Thursday. I hear that there has been a fight up above here, and two Yankee regiments very badly cut to pieces. There is a rumor that Gen Wheeler with all Gen Braggs Cavalry has crossed the river above here and joined Gen Longstreet.[83] The Yankees say that all the officers who left here yesterday have been captured. I hope it is true. Capt Phillips went with them. It will be fun if our boys have caught him. Tonight after supper Carter Cummings came over and asked sister to cut out a couple of shirts for two of his old regiment who were going off tomorrow and needed them. Of course she did it. We sent one to her and went to work and made the other. While we were making it, the two men came here after some clothes. Said Ellen McClung sent them so of course I gave them some. When we asked them how they got out of jail, they said Dr Levine [was] their security. They vowed they would never take the oath. They know Johnnie.

Dec. 11. Friday. This morning one of the 19th came in before breakfast. He was the brother of one of the men who was here last night. His name is Russell.[84] We asked him in to breakfast. After he was done, gave him some clothes and some thing to take with him to eat. He said that Gen Carter sent them and they were to be sent to Camp Chase today. After he was gone four or five others came, one with a guard, and mother gave them each some thing.

After they were gone Lt Shaw came to bring some books home, that I had lent an officer, with a very pretty note from Capt Dumas thanking me for them, and to bring a list of the officers who needed any thing.[85] Told mother they were all deserters. I hope it is not true. I should hate very much the idea of giving them any thing when our true men are needing them. The list he brought were those taken at the attack on Fort Sanders, fourteen of them all wanting socks, shirts, and drawers but two that only [want] socks. So I had to go round begging, and buying what I could not beg. I succeeded in getting enough except the socks. Those it is impossible to get one pair of.

As I was coming home I stopped to ask Lizzie Walker to make a shirt. She told me Andy White had just told her there had been a fight across the river.[86] Gen Wheelers men, and of course we whipped them. I hope it is true. I dont think the Yankees are at all satisfied here, all that can get away are leaving for Ky. They say Longstreet is fortifying forty-five miles above here at Morristown. Gen Bragg at Ringgold. Gen Joe Johnston between Bridgeport and Chattanooga. If that is all true, Grant must be in a tight place. Bragg has been very heavily reinforced from Charleston and Mobile.[87]

Dec. 12. Saturday. I rose early this morning to see about sending the clothes to the jail. Before I was dressed Mrs Humphreys sent over four shirts and a coat.[88] Just after I came down, Nina Danner and Miss Fletcher came to bring home the drawers they had taken last night to make and four pairs of socks with them. After they left I went over to Col Cummings to get Carter to go and ask Shaw when the prisoners were to be sent off. Then I came home and fixed up the things to send, for though the Lt says he did not think they would go today, we thought they had better send them at once. Just as we had sent them Mrs Smith came in. She says the Yankees were expecting an attack last night. The men were all in the trenches ready for it, that they had taken all the cannons off the fortifications, and that Gen Wheeler says these prisoners shall not go to Camp Chase. I hope he did say so. I sent Capt Dumas a copy of Shakespeare. This morning when father came back from Gay St. he brought two letters from Johnnie, one written in Sept, the other the 16 of Oct. He said he was well, and so was Sam. Ruth Bostwick is dead, and Mary Brumby and Annie Glover are both married. Such is life.[89]

Dec. 13. Sunday. Raining most of the day. Rumors of fighting above here. Gen Hascall has been killed.[90] The Capt came over this evening to tell the Maj a Lady had received a letter from Cleveland saying Gen Bragg was there on his way here. Gen Beauregard at Chattanooga watching Grant. Joe Johnston at Bridgeport. I hope it is all true.

Dec. 14. Monday. Yesterday about two oclock a Yankee Doctor came to borrow a bucket. He said he was establishing a hospital for our sick. One of our prisoners died in Jail Saturday night from want of attention, some say starved to death. His name was Hall from Georgia.[91] I suppose they thought it would never do to get out, so they are fixing up a hospital in Wayne Wallace's house.[92] One of our men who is detailed as nurse came later in the evening to borrow a tin pan to make some bread. I told him if he would bring the flour here we would have it made. He brought a little flour in a bag, five days rations for twelve men—eight sick and four nurses. Two of them are very ill. They keep a guard of 6 Yankees there all the time. The Dr will go round with any one when he is there, but allows no one to enter in his absence. This morning I received a note from Mr Tucker begging for some thing to eat. They have not drawn any thing for two days. No news today except confirmation of the fight above here.

Dec. 15. Tuesday. The prisoners were sent off today, some five hundred of them. They had those that had taken [the oath] guarding them, and they looked ashamed of them selves. They were standing in the street several hours before they started. Some wagons came in filled with Commissary stores, and they gave them all something to eat. I am glad the poor fellows did not have to leave hungry. They were in fine spirits. Said they would be back in a few days. I hope they may. Jeanie and Mrs Rayal came in the morning, as did Lt Hobb to see the Maj.[93] I asked him how he managed to stay here. He said he had several Yankee Officers on his hands. Some times Carter will send him an order to keep his room, and twice he has been sent back to jail. In the afternoon, sister and I walked out to Mrs McPherson's. Mrs Smith came over tonight. She says Bragg has been whipped and superseeded by Gen Hardee. I dont believe he has been whipped. Tonight a little boy brought me a note from Duff Rice asking for some thing to eat, and some bandages. He says they have suffered terribly for the past few days. I thought he had been taken off with the army. Poor fellow. I'll send him some thing tomorrow.

Dec. 16. Wednesday. I got up right early this morning to see about sending Duff something. As Miss Nannie had said yesterday she was going out today, I went over to ask her if she would take them for me. She said she would, so I came over & fixed something to eat, and some raw rice and took them over. Reported fighting today up at Beans Station. Longstreet has the best of it, and is driving them down this way. He has been reinforced since he left here.[94] We have captured a long wagon train, quantities of coffee and sugar. They brought in a long string of ambulances filled with their wounded. Some were taken to the Lamar House and some to the Deaf & Dumb Asylum.

Lizzie Walker came over a little while this morning. She says they searched their house for fire-arms two or three days ago. In the afternoon mother and I went over to Mrs French's. Mrs Eliza McClung and Ellen were there. Mr. Kain's Yankee came back last night. They say the war will be over by spring. They can't crush the rebellion, but are going to starve it out. They will find out when the spring comes.[95] Lt Shaw told Mr Hill he must report tomorrow morning to go either to Jail [or] to the Hospital as nurse. He says he is going to the latter place.

Dec. 17. Thursday. Glorious news. Longstreet has driven the Yankees like chaff before the wind, is now within eighteen miles of here. The Yankees acknowledge a very heavy loss. Miss Nannie came this morning. She says she found Duff, the dirtiest most ragged fellow she ever saw. They have suffered very much. Ten days since they had not one mouth full to eat at Woffords Hospital, the one where he is.[96] After she got through talking about him, she started on Lt Shaw and because the Maj said he would do any thing he could for him, if he were in his power, she pitched into him. I never heard any thing to equal it since I was born, particularly from a Lady. He kept his temper remarkably I think, much better than I could have done. He said after she left he wished she had been a man, he would have knocked her down.

Mr Hill has been in several times today. Two of our poor fellows are dead and ten more very ill. He says the Dr does all he can, but he has not sense enough to do much. I went over to Mrs Kains to borrow a head dress to make one by, and tell her the good news. She had not heard a word of it. Young man named Beauchamp, shot in the arm, came in for Woffords Hospital today, and we sent Duff out some clothes by him.[97] Col Gilbert the Military Governor has been killed.[98]

Dec. 18. Friday. The Yankees acknowledged a loss of 70 Officers, and one thousand men wounded. Wednesdays fight they say their loss was fifteen hundred, and that they whipped Longstreet, a very likely story. There is a report pretty well authenticated that Gen Wheeler has recaptured our prisoners that were sent off Tuesday. Joe Parsons Regiment was sent to guard them because they were deserting so fast.[99] They say that the officers told them they were coming to East Tenn to protect them and their families, and some of their best friends have suffered most from them. Good for them, I say. There were three hundred wagons in the train captured up above here, sixty of them sutlers.

Dr Piggott came in this morning and two of our men.[100] One lost his right armed named Cox, and a brother of Beauchamp who was here yesterday. One of them brought me a very pretty note from Duff Rice thanking me for my kindness to him. I wish I had had it in my power to do more. Dr Piggott is very much of a gentlemen, a Virginian, and seems to try to do all he can for his men. He has his Hospital in tents, and is very much in need of blankets, clothes &e. Mr Hill went down to the hospital yesterday. He was in several times during the day. Two of our men died yesterday. I can't help thinking of the poor fellows dying away from all they love for want of attention.

Cluss and I went down to Jeanies this morning, the first time I have been there since she has been keeping house. After we went all round to the stores, there were some five or six sutlers who have brought stocks of goods, and dont ask any thing for them. Tom Van Gilder has opened his in Nelsons store.[101] Will is staying in there. The Yankees said yesterday that Longstreet would be here in a day or two at farthest and they would have to stand another siege. He has captured eighteen of their guns. Today they say he is retreating. I don't believe one word of it.

I had my hair shingled yesterday. It had been dropping so much for the last three months that I had scarcely any left and that perfectly dead, so I thought I'd have it off. I knew I could never muster courage enough to do it if the "Rebels" got in. I received a letter today from Cousin Annie. She says they are suffering very much. The week before she wrote she had nothing to eat in the house except what some neighbor sent them, and not a stick of wood in the yard. She has sold all her handsome furniture and Jewelry, says that Mr Ford must be dead, she has not heard from him for so long a time. Aunty is very well. I had a letter from Aunt Mary also. She says every one at the north feels the war except the Army contractors &e, who are filling their pockets well. I wish they were all starving, as I think will be the case here if the Yankees keep possession much longer. I have a very bad sick head ache tonight.

Dec 19. Saturday. Cold. I went up town just after breakfast with Mrs Kain, found it most too cool for comfort. The capture of our men by Wheeler is contradicted. I believe it not withstanding. There has been a fight at Louisville between Thomas' Indians and the Home Guard and Yankees. The former were all captured or killed, a great many skalped. Two Yankees Capts were badly wounded. We hear nothing of Longstreets movements today. Our Gurrillas captured a train of sixty sutlers wagons, with a lot of medical stores, and clothing for a Brigade. There were three hundred captured by Longstreet. The Yankees have the face to say they have recaptured all but ten wagons and those we burnt. How they lie.[102]

One of our men was in from Dr Piggotts Hospital today who has lost an arm. I forget his name. He is a cousin of Billy Graves, and one of the nurses. Duff Rice wrote me quite a long note, telling me the Marietta news. Bolan Glover was deranged after the death of his wife for some time. Annie was married three weeks after that sad event. Peter Cox is married, so is Willie Hansell. Judge Rice is Capt of a six month cavalry service. Gen Hansell, Mr Howell and all the old folks have turned out.[103] Hurrah for them I say. Another of our men died down at the Hospital today and Mr Hill says one or two will before long. None of them have been blistered. It is terrible for them to die so. The way that the Yankees happened to say Longstreet [lost] seems to be this. After the cavalry captured a train of wagons, they threw out two divisions to protect them. After the wagons were safe of course they fell back to where he was fortified.

Dec. 20. Sunday. Intensely Cold. I have scarcely been comfortable today, for all I have not moved ten steps from the fire. Madam rumor says that we have Lookout Mountain and Missionary Ridge again, that Hardee is in command. Some say Joe Johnston. Oh! if our army could only retake East Tenn, it would be glorious.

Dec. 21. Monday. Very cold still. The Yankees are in trouble again today. They are planting cannon over to the North and East. They say they cant find Longstreet. It is my opinion they dont want to find him, or they could do it. They are pressing all the negro men to work on the pontoon bridge. If they dont succeed in rebuilding it, our boys can take the hill on the other side of [the] river. The boats are scattered all along the river. I dont believe they will be able to find many of them.

Maj Smith went to Shaws office today and from there up to see Gen Carter to ask for a parole to the streets. He gets so tired of the house. Carter gave the desired permission, but the Maj had a fracus with his [Carter's] Inspector Gen, who saw him on a parole of honor. He [Smith] cursed him up and down for it, and the Gen said he was right. He went up to the jail to see the prisoners, who were brought in a day or so since. One of them, Capt Lytle, is a friend of his. He is the only officer there. There are about thirty privates. The poor fellows are very much in need of some thing to eat. They were broken down when Longstreet drew back his forces, so of course were captured. Dr Piggott, Dr Cotton, and two or three others were here today.[104] Duff Rice has been quite sick with chills and fever.

Dec. 22. Tuesday. Milder today than yesterday, in fact perfectly delightful. Sister and I walked out to tell Miss O'Conner if she sent the prisoners at the jail something to eat, I knew they would get it. Then we walked over to see Mrs McPherson. After we came home I went over to Mrs Kains for some time. The Yankees over there say that Longstreet is completely surrounded and himself captured. Of course it is true. Mr Humes came to see father today to tell him he must have the rent for next year, half in Tenn and half in Greenbacks, whatever party is in here, and wants his notes to that effect. He wont get them. For a minister he is the grandest old rascal that ever was. We will have to get another house some where, thats certain.

Dec. 23. Wednesday. Very disagreeable. Mother and I went up to Mrs McPhersons this morning, to see if we could get part of her house. She wanted us to do it about a month since. She said we could have her sitting room and the one joining, and as many up stairs as we wanted. We had not been home very long when she came in saying that the Yankees had taken two rooms up stairs and threatened to take the house. A Capt some body had come and brought his baggage, and asked to see the rooms, and had his things taken up. I went round with her to Gen Carter. He was busy. His Adjutant said that the Gen had nothing to do with any thing of the kind. Capt Whitman attended to every thing of the kind.[105] So over we went to

Capt Whitmans office in the Ocoee Bank. After waiting some time for him to come in, he said he had sent this Capt there at the written suggestion of Gen Carter. He wanted the rooms for Gen ———, the sitting room and those opening out of it, because they were furnished, but he presumed the Gen would be satisfied if she furnished the up stairs rooms.

I came home just as mad as could be, and not made any the more pleasant by the Maj's saying, as soon as I came in, that Gen Carter had told him to be ready to start north by day light Christmas morning. It is abominable. He shant go. Wallie McPherson says he heard this morning that Longstreet was coming this way in three columns. One had crossed the river. I hope it is true, and that he will get here before they finish the pontoon, for they cant get the men across fast enough to do much good without it.[106] Some of our cavalry are reported at Clinton, and Breckinridge at Sweetwater. I hope it is true.[107]

Dec. 24. Thursday. Christmas Eve. What a dull, sad one it will be to many a poor family, dreary enough for us, but we are infinitely better off than many, many others. God grant the time may come when we will rejoice once more, as we did before the war. Just as soon as I ate my breakfast I went round to Lt. Shaws office to ask him to try and use his influence to keep the Maj from going off tomorrow. He said he had heard nothing of it. When the Maj came in at one oclock he said Carter had told him he did not know when he would send him off. Dr Piggott came in this morning with Mr Beauchamp. The latters brother has gone. It is some days since he left. I expect he is safe in the Confederate lines. The Dr says one of his men will die before tomorrow night, and two more before very long, poor fellows. It is hard for them to die here, with no comforts around him, far away from home, and all he loves. Oh! the horrors of war.

One report today is that Longstreet has sent half his men to Virginia and the other to reinforce Gen Bragg. The Maj says a Yankee told him that they expected a big fight up the road at Blains Cross Roads today, and the Rebels he thought would whip them. Col Cummings says he heard the 9th Army Corps was up there. It had gone out to find Longstreet, had found him and come back five miles much faster then it went. Mrs McPherson came round this morning to tell us to move up just as soon as we possibly can come. To get there and get fixed before the Yankee Generals gets there.

Dec. 25. Friday. Christmas day with the Yankees, but I should not complain. We are so much better off than many. Wallace McPherson came to say that the Yankee Capt there said he would let her know tomorrow whether we could have the house or not. I dont know where we will get one if we cant have that. We have passed a very pleasant Christmas, considering all things. Gen Carter paroled Capt Lytle to eat dinner with the Maj, poor fellow. I hated so to see him go back to jail. Father went down to the Hospital to ask Mr Hill to come around too. He said that he did not think he could come. There were two men that he thought would die during the day, one man they thought was taking the Small Pox. I hope not. It is scattered all through the town. There is a case up at Mrs George Whites, one at Dickinsons, one at Lees and a half dozen other places, at most among the negroes. The Yankees are keeping them in town instead of sending every one out to the pest house as fast as taken as the Confederates did last year.[108]

While we were eating dinner, Ella Cocke came in to ask me to take a short walk with her. She said she had been so much confined to the house she needed it. So sister and I went. As we were coming back we met Ellen McClung and Allen French coming to meet her. Miss Nannie Scott sent for her to come home at once. She did not think her aunt would live through the night. Poor woman, how she has suffered. A rumor of fighting above here.

Dec. 26. Saturday. A report today that we have whipped them at Dandridge very badly. I hope and pray it is true.[109] Mrs Cocke is alive this morning and that is all. Father heard an Officer say that there was fighting going on at Strawberry Plains. I hope we are making them fly before us. A man named Ludwick, a cousin of Miss Lizzie Lyles, came here this afternoon, told mother he had taken the oath.[110] It was either that or die. She asked him where he was staying. He said he had come to see if he could not stay all night with the Maj. She told him he could not possibly as she had been obliged to put him on the bed in the Parlor. I did not like him at all. He asked the Maj if we were Rebels or just said so. He knew very well we were. One of the nurses from the Main St. hospital came tonight to ask for some eggs, to make some egg nogg for one of the sick. He says four died there today. The one they thought had Small pox had Typhoid fever. He died today. They seem to take them from the jail to die. The Small Pox is spreading every day. I am thankful I do not dread it like some do.

Dec. 27. Sunday. Raining almost all day. Will came around in the morning. I knew he had heard some bad news as soon as I saw him, and was afraid to ask what it was. I heard soon enough. Johnnie, our darling Johnnie, is a prisoner at Camp Douglass.[111] He was taken near Chattanooga. When I first heard it I was wretched, but when I thought how fortunate he has been so far, and now is well, I felt thankful it was no worse. If he had been wounded, and fallen into their hands, it would have been terrible. Park Baker wrote to Mr Stephenson.[112] He was a prisoner there, and some one said they saw among the list of prisoners in a Nashville paper the name of Lt John M House, Maj Gen A. P. Stewarts staff. That certainly must be him. I have always dreaded either of the boys being a prisoner so much. Now both are. Sam of course as a paroled one is having a delightful time, but I hate to think when every man is needed, as they are now in the hour of darkness, both my brothers are unable to lift their hands in defense of their Country. The Maj says Johnnie will fare much better for being a staff officer. He always said when he was taken he wanted buff facings. I little thought how soon it would be.

Mr Hill came round this afternoon for a little time. He has had so much walking to do lately that he is quite lame. The rumor of our whipping the Yankees up at Dandridge is confirmed. The Yankees say that we whipped them first, then they drove us fifteen miles and recaptured the two pieces we had taken and others besides. That is always the way. They never acknowledge to being whipped. They are fighting above here today.

Dec. 28th. Monday. Raining morning and evening. Stopped during the middle of the day. We received a letter from Uncle John this morning saying he had received a letter from a Miss Lila V. Johnston of Louisville, who wrote she had seen in one of the papers a list of Confederate prisoners, singled out the name of John M. House, Lieut on Maj Gen Stewarts Staff, and went to see him, furnish him with what he needed—clothes, shoes and a carpet sack. God bless her. She will have the prayers and deepest gratitude as long as we live. He had requested her to write for him that he was there a prisoner. Frank Matthews was well the day he was taken, and Sam had not been exchanged. Uncle John seems to think he is in Prison north, instead of enjoying himself as he is down home. After Mrs Newman and Mattie came to tell us that she, Mrs Newman, had just received a letter from her husband at Johnsons Island in which he says "John House was brought here several days ago, he was quite unwell at the time but is better now. He rooms with me."[113] So he must be there. I think it was very kind in her coming to tell us at once.

Sister and I commenced making a pr of pants for the Maj today. They will be very fancy, buttons down the side, and open from the knee down & laced across with yellow. Mrs Kain came over for a little while. She says she is going South in the Spring if the Rebels do not retake the place. Mrs James Cocke died last night, poor woman.[114] She suffered dreadfully, was sick eleven weeks and the saddest part of all has left a blind baby seven or eight months old. Reported fighting up the road, we cant hear any particulars. One report is that the Yankees attempted to cross the river above here and were repulsed. Another that John Morgan with three hundred of his men crossed the Tennessee sixty miles above Chattanooga, and is now in Blount [County]. I hope it is true.[115] The Yanks say Longstreet is killed and his army completely surrounded. I wrote to Aunt Mary today, also to Mrs Whaling telling them Johnnie was a prisoner. The Small pox is spreading all over the city. There is a case down at Mr George Whites, one at the Dickinsons, one at Lees—and I dont know how many other places. The Yankees are losing a good many men with it.

Dec. 29. Tuesday. Rumor says still fighting above here. If the Yanks had the best of it they would let it be known, and they are keeping very quiet. Mrs Cummings came over in the afternoon and sat some time. Mrs McPherson stopped to see if we would go over to Mrs Cockes funeral. We thought best not to venture into a crowd at the present time. There is a case of Small Pox in the little wooden house next door, and old man Lea is dead.[116] In the afternoon I went up to Van Gilders to see if I could get the puncher to put the islets in the Maj's pants. Will Rogers said he could not find them. He says tomorrow will be a year since John was captured.[117] Oh! how I wish they could hear something reliable of him that he is alive and well. An Officer told Will he was at Johnsons Island, held as a hostage, and not allowed to write home, poor fellow. I cant bring myself to think he is dead and I will never see him again.

Mr Hill went into the baker's this evening to get bread for the hospital when a Yankee soldier asked him if he was a Rebel. He said yes. Then the Yank told him he should not say so in there. He told him he had as much right to his opinion as he had when one that was standing behind him knocked him down and another kicked him and blacked up his eye. It is perfectly outrageous treating a prisoner so. Lt Shaw said if he could find out who the men were he would have them punished. Gen Foster has been in-jured in some way, thrown from his horse I think and broken his leg. Pity it had not been his neck instead.[118]

Dec. 30. Wednesday. I have been boiling over all day. The Maj went up town as usual this morning after breakfast. He came back in a very little while and told us he was ordered off at half past eleven, an hour and a half notice. It was too bad. Sister and I went to work and finished his pants, and made a nap sack. I hated to see him go. He was going right to Johnsons Island and will see John, but I cannot be selfish enough to want him there because my darling is there. Mr Hill asked them to send him too. He says he is tired of Knoxville. I dont wonder. Father went up to Gen Carter with the Maj. He was to go on horse back and start from there. After some time he came home and said that they would not go today. I was so glad. In the afternoon I went to see Mrs Kain, amused myself making a doll for Nonnie. The Yanks over there are scared to death about the Small Pox. They put Mr Hill in jail with the others. His eye is so blacked I would scarcely have known him. He says he is glad they did it. Three men died at the Rebel hospital last night—one was only taken there from the Jail yesterday morn-ing. It is terrible.

Dec. 31. Thursday. The last day of 63. How differently the year has ended to what I had anticipated, how differently from the last. Then all was life and gaiety. Now a leaden cloud hangs over our spirits, and try as we may, the gloom will gather around us and darken many an hour. It is wrong—sinful I know, this repining, this wishing for things that may not be, but we are but weak and erring creatures, prone to sin. This time last year Johnnie was here, home, the light and life of the house. Now he is in a distant Northern prison, a stranger among a strange people, far from all who love him. Who could have thought how differently we would be situated in a short twelve months.

Col Cummings came over this morning before breakfast to see the Maj. He met Lt Shaw as he was coming, who told him he did not think the prisoners would be sent off today. It has been raining off and on all day. Our hearts were made to beat faster this morning by the report of several guns from Summit Battery.[119] For a moment we hoped the Rebels might be the cause of it, but the hope did not last long. When father came home, he said Gen Grant had arrived, and he supposed it was to salute him. Some say he has come to take command, and Gen Foster is to be sent to Chattanooga. I should like the exchange, as I understand Grant is a gentleman. Others say he is only here for a day or two.[120]

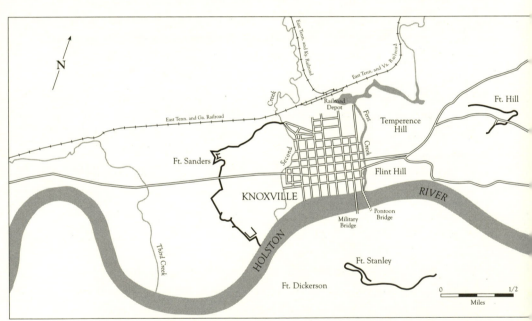

Knoxville and vicinity with principal fortifications, roads, and railroads, 1863–64.

Late this afternoon two Yankees—Capt —— and another came to take the house for Gen some body's head Quarters. He wanted the furniture too, said if we went to Mrs McPherson's we would need very little of it as her rooms were furnished. Mother told him we were not going to leave the house. He said too he supposed if we went to McP's we would not object to moving before our time was out, so that Mr Humes could get a tenant. I do think those Yankees take the lead of any thing I ever saw or heard of. He has had a guard here for the last few days, watching his fences to keep our servants from burning them. The Guard told the soldiers over at the school house they could have as many of the boards as they want, and helped to pull some off for them. Our day will come some time. I wrote a long letter to Johnnie today and gave it to Lt Shaw—asking him to give it to Capt Lytle. He said he would do so, so I hope it will go. It would be too bad for them all to go, and none take a letter for him. God grant the next year may end more pleasantly, more hopefully to us, that long ere that time he may have been exchanged and with those who love him once more.

Chapter 3.
I Am Determined Not to Be Blue

January 1, 1864, Friday. The sun rose in unclouded splendor after a night of rain. Sister, Major Smith and I sat up to see the Year in, or the old one out. How dark and gloomy things look for our cause. The Yankees have completely over run Tennessee, and are tightening the cords on the Rebels every day. Southern men are allowed to do nothing. The consequence is as the season advances the suffering of their families increases. Today is the coldest we have had this winter, and yet they sent off our prisoners, many of them without blankets or even shoes or coats. They seemed glad to go. They cannot well be worse off than in the Jail here, such a horrid place as it is. The poor fellows have taken up some of the flooring to burn. They get no wood half the time, and such weather as this it is perfectly outrageous. When the Maj went up to Gen Carters to report as usual this morning, the Gen told him he could go either today or tomorrow just as he pleased, as some of the prisoners were going each day. He preferred waiting. Col Cummings had invited father and him over to drink egg nogg. Mrs Cummings sent over after Sister and I, so we went. They wanted us to stay to dinner, but we thought we had better come home, where we had not been ten minutes when Lt Shaw came to tell the Maj he had received orders for him to leave immediately as they found that they could get transportation for all today. So he had to start right off. I was so provoked, but that was no use. It did not do me one bit of good. They are to go by rail to Strawberry Plains, and from there they have to march.[1] After he left Sister and I went over to Mrs Kains. We had been there only a little while when he sent for us. Lt. Shaw kept him till the train had gone. I think it was real good in him.

Capt Moody called after tea.[2] He is the finest looking man I have ever seen, very tall, but so well formed that his full height does not show unless he is standing by some one else. Gen Carter says he is to go North tomorrow with Maj Smith by way of Nashville. The Capt told him it would be perfect murder to send him there, the condition he is in now. He was shot through the lungs not long since and left sick out at Mr. Hazens. When Gen. Longstreet left Gen Carter told him it would be no worse than our starving their officers to death in Richmond. What abominable lies they do tell. There were about a hundred and fifty sent off today. I hear that fifty were brought in yesterday, stragglers, a good many without shoes. If they have deserted they dont deserve any.

There are daily reports of fighting up the road. The fight on Tuesday was quite an affair. They acknowledge four hundred killed. Mr Dodd of the 8th Texas Cavly who had been tried as a spy and acquitted, was not sent off with the others.[3] Lt Shaw says because the result of the trial has not been made public yet, and they want to frighten him as much as possible. Parson Brownlow has kept very quiet since his return from Yankeedom, have not seen or heard anything of him.[4] Gen Grant has issued an order for every one to have their yards cleaned up, and for the soldiers to clean the streets. It will be a good move, the city is in a dreadful condition. I hope he will send out to the Battle field & have the men they pretended to bury covered over. I am told that there are any amount of arms and legs sticking out, and there was one whose face was uncovered. A Yankee officer says he took his stick and put some dirt over it. If that is the way they do their own men, how must they do ours who are unfortunate enough to fall into their hands.

Jan. 2. Saturday. Intensely cold. The Maj went up [to] report as usual, and see when he is to leave. Gen Carter told him he might leave any day or not for some time. Lt Shaw says he will try and get leave and go on with him. Father heard in town today that the Yankees were falling back here and intended making a stand at this point. I dont suppose it is any thing but a report. They intend pulling down three more houses on Summit Hill to make room for more guns. Capt Moody has been confined to the house. The pontoon has been washed away again. On the day the other was taken down by the current the guards sent to ask Gen Foster if they should cut it loose, as the river was rising very fast. He sent word back that when he wanted the bridge cut loose he would order it done. Not two hours after, away it went. I only wish Gen Longstreet could come down on the other side now. He could take the place easily. We received a short letter from Dear Johnnie today from Johnsons Island. He says he is well, was captured on the 25th of November at Missionary Ridge. Sam was well the day before. All the Knoxville boys are well. Our city is well represented there. There are two cases of Small Pox in the old Swann house. As yet there are none between us and the creek.[5]

Jan. 3. Sunday. Still very cold. Gen Grant has gone up the road. I understand he says either they or the Rebels must leave East Tenn and that soon. He is fortifying very strongly at Blains Cross road and Strawberry Plains. I have felt miserably all day. Had a sick headache. One of our men died at the Hospital last night.

Jan. 4. Monday. Still very cold and raining. Gen Grant is making preparations for a big fight up the road. I hope and pray Longstreet will whip him and retake Knoxville. It is dreadful living as we do, as if it last much longer. Heaven only knows what is to be done. Some of the wealthiest people are trying to sell their parlour furniture. Mr Columbus Powell and Mr McGhee have come back. I wonder what they did with them in Ky. Mr George White has [illegible]. A man died in the old Swann house today, Small pox. Mrs Kain came over this morning for a little while.

Jan. 5. Tuesday. It is not so cold today and still raining. Dr. Piggott sent in this morning for some liquor &c. The Yankee papers say that Kirby Smith and Taylor have whipped Banks all to pieces, taken all his guns, captured most of his wagons and run him into New Orleans.[6] The papers call it a disgraceful affair. I received a note this evening from Mr Dodd thanking me for some things I had sent him, and asking me to send him a piece of soap, towel, needles, thread &e. He expects to leave tomorrow morning for Camp Chase. It was after dark when I got it, so I will have to wait till tomorrow morning. Mr Humes came round this afternoon to tell father Gen Tillson wanted the house, and he had told him he might have it.[7] That we would receive notice from the military to leave. Mother told him she would not leave. He certainly could not turn women into the street. He had always been paid regularly, and she was good for the rent.

Jan. 6. Wednesday. Snowing slightly. I sent the things round to Mr Dodd before breakfast. I was very much afraid he would be gone before I sent them. Had I known then what I do now, I should have prayed instead that he had gone. The Maj came in about eleven and told us his sentence had been read to him that morning. He is to be hung on Friday. Oh! it is terrible, terrible, so totally unexpected. If I only could do some thing for him. Were he a spy, badly as I would feel about it, I know it would be perfectly useless to do any thing. But for an innocent man to die such a death is awful beyond conception. The Maj obtained permission to visit him with a guard. He is in the Citizens prison.[8] He feels dreadfully about it. He says Mr Dodd saved him from being taken prisoner once, and is as noble a fellow as ever lived. I started over to Mrs Kains to see if I could get any liquor. As I went out the gate, I met Mr Martin and told him about it. He said he would go and see him. She did not have any so all hope is over in that direction. We have not a drop in the house. Oh! if we only had some that was drank like water here last week. Oh! I cannot, cannot believe that they will hang him. Something must stop it.

Jan 7. Thursday. Snowing today a little. This morning the Corp[oral] guarding Mr Dodd brought me a note from him written this morning, enclosing one he wrote yesterday but had no chance of sending, asking me to send three members of the 9th Tenn Cavly two blankets. How thoughtful of the comfort of others when the poor fellow is so near such a dreadful death. He says he is prepared to meet any fate in store for him, as becomes a Texan and a Ranger. I wish he had said Christian too. I took the note over to Miss Nannie to see if she had any blankets and if we could do any thing for him. She proposed getting Mrs H. L. McClung and Mrs. Gillespie to intercede with Gen. Carter for him.[9]

I left her and came back home. The Maj had gone to try for a new trial for him. The principal witness who could have cleared him took the oath some days ago and was sent off immediately. When he came home I saw from his face he had not succeeded. He said his only hope for him now [was] that his being a Mason might save him. Miss Nannie came in to say she had written John Williams a note that she wanted to see him immediately. She thought if she could get him interested he might do something. Later she came back to say she had not been able to see him, but she had got the Masons interested, and some of them said he should have justice done him.[10] God grant he may, but there is little dependence to be put in what a Yankee says. Late this afternoon as the Maj was reading to sister and I, Lt Shaws clerk came for him to go to the office. Not long after I saw him pass with Capt Moody and a Sergeant going towards Gay St.

I went over to Mrs Kains and stayed some time. She says that at Head Quarters they have an inventory of all her furniture and one of the officers told her it would be sold very soon. An order came out yesterday forbidding any one from buying any thing except those who take the oath as Loyal citizens, not even a dose of medicine or a spool of thread. Brownlow is at the bottom of this. Capt Lunt says it is too arbitrary an order to last long.[11] Mrs Kain says she had a Capt Dodd there to tea last night. She spoke of Mr. Dodds being convicted as a spy. He says when Gen Longstreet left, he left two Yankees hanging with their names & spy pinned to them. It never ought to have been done. They ought to have been quietly buried and not left hanging to taunt the Yankees. Since I have heard it, I feel less hopeful for Mr Dodd.[12]

Gen Wheeler made a raid into Sweetwater night before last.[13] Captured thirty-five wagons and fifty [men], so the Yankees say. If they acknowledge to that many of course there must have been more. They are frightened here. Last night after dark Capt Lunt had his safe taken from his office down to Mrs Kains. I think they are expecting him in here and that is one reason that Mr Dodds sentence is to be carried into execution so soon. They are afraid of his being resqued. The Maj did not return till after dark, when Capt Moody and the Sgt came with him. (Gen Foster had ordered that their paroles be taken from them and they put in jail, together with Lt Col O'Brien. His excuse [was that] some of the men paroled at the hospitals out of town had broken theirs and gone off. That was the fault of the paroling officer (Lieut Cowdry).[14] No limits were assigned to them and the guards passed them). The idea of making that an excuse for putting sick officers in such a place as that jail is ridiculous. Gen Carter had gone to see Gen Foster about it, and I was very much in hopes that their paroles would be returned to them.

After eating dinner they went up to Shaws office again. After he had gone Miss Nannie came in again to say she was very much in hopes some thing could be done for Mr Dodd. Maj Smith did not return till ten oclock, when he said he had to go right back. He had only come for his blanket. They have orders to stay in the office tonight, and tomorrow he would get a room for them where they should be well treated, because the Confederates had treated their officers well when here. He wanted a pack of cards and chess board. Says they intend to sit up all night. He seems to think there is some hopes for Mr Dodd being saved. God grant he may be.

Jan. 8. Friday. The snow is several inches deep this morning. I could scarcely sleep all night. I never felt as miserable in my life before, could think of nothing all night long but Mr Dodd. Before breakfast Corp Connerly[15] came to bring some papers to the Maj and a few lines to me. Poor fellow. I asked if the Masons had not been able to do any thing for him. He said nothing. They had been with him two hours last night, but they said the proof was so strong, nothing could be done. Unfortunately he had a note book with him when captured in which he speack of going to certain houses and passing himself off for a federal, and was dressed at that time in Yankee Overcoat and pants, but had on his Texan hat & star.[16] He is very much composed. Says he is not afraid to meet his God, and he can die like a soldier and he hopes a christian trusting in the mercy of his Savior. Mr Martin was with him last night.

Later, at eleven oclock I heard a gun fire. At the sound my blood seemed to freeze in my veins. A short time after I heard another. Oh! my God it was terrible, an innocent man to die such a death. It will, it must be revenged a hundred fold. It will not bring him back to life, but the Yankees must suffer for it. Mr Martin came to see us this afternoon. He went out with him this morning. The first time they hung him the rope broke, and he lay about fifteen minutes when they hung him again. What torture. I hear too that when he fell he broke his thigh bone. Was such brutality ever heard of before. A federal officer says he was the most astonishing man he ever saw. Last night he obtained permission to visit him. When he went in the room he was sitting at a table writing. He got up and offered him a seat by the fire. The officer said to him he had permission to visit a man under sentence of death, would he be kind enough to tell him where he could find him. He replied he was the man. He then asked him if he was innocent. He said he was perfectly. The officer says he was so much impressed by his manner that he went out to the execution, and only a minute before the rope was put round his neck he asked again if he was innocent. His reply was "I die innocent of the charge against me."[17]

When we sent the Maj his breakfast this morning he was up at the jail. An order came last night for them to go there. It appears since it was caused by a misunderstanding on the part of Lt Shaw. Gen Carter and Col Rily[18] are at dagers points and they sent over contradictory orders that Lt thought the only thing he could do would be to send them to the Jail. It was so cold they nearly froze to death. The consequence is the Maj is right sick today and had to send for a doctor. I went round to Mrs Frenches to see if she had any old clothes, as I received a note from Mr Dodds friends saying they needed some. There I met Ella Cocke and made her go with me begging down Main Street. We succeeded in getting a few things.

When we came back we stopped at Lt Shaws office on pretense of seeing when the prisoners were to leave, but in fact I wanted to see the Maj and Ella [wanted to see] Capt Moody. The Maj looks right badly. He says he hopes to get home again in a few days. I hope he will for we miss him dreadfully. It is the first time since the first of November we have been alone. We sent them their dinners to them and father went about eight oclock to see if they would be sent back to the jail, and found they had all three been sent to Dr Currey's with a guard.[19] I am very glad they will be comfortable. I hear that Gen Longstreet has been very heavily reinforced and that Gen Grant is coming this way with forty thousand men. They have seven thousand sick here now.

Jan. 9. Saturday. We were just starting out this morning when Miss Nannie came in. We talked to her a little while and then left. Went first to Mattie Luttrells. Her mother is very sick.[20] Then to Ella Cockes, Miss O'Conner, Mrs Goodlin[21] and then over to see the Maj. He said he was very comfortable, but hoped to be home again in a day or two. We succeeded in getting a few clothes and Mrs McPherson sent an old carpet which made fine blankets, and an old quilt. I have been working and running about all day, sent the things round to the jail. They leave early in the morning. Father came home at dark and said the Maj was ordered off in the morning too, but would try and get down to see us if he possibly could. I am not sorry he is going for he says he will be uneasy while he is here, afraid of being sent back to jail, and the sooner he gets to Johnsons Island, the sooner he will be exchanged. Then he will go by Nashville and see his wife and mother, probably get a parole from Andy Johnson for a few days.

I wrote to Miss Lila V. Johnston today thanking her for her kindness to Johnnie while he was in Louisville, and took it over to Mrs. Kains to get Capt Colby to mail it for me across the mountains. Mrs. Currey[22] says she hears that our front extends from State Line to Rome, & that Gen Grant has torn up the rail-road from Cleveland to Bridgeport. He must intend leaving from that. They are fixing up for a big fight above here. A good many men have gone home on leave, have reinlisted. They get eight hundred bounty, two hundred from State, two hundred from Co. and four hundred from US Government. I hear too that there are seventy-five thousand negros at Nashville ready to march on & take Richmond.[23]

Jan. 10. Sunday. Intensely cold. Miss Nannie woke us up before day. Father went down and opened the door & made a fire in the sitting room. As soon as Martha made our fire we got up and dressed. Miss Nannie thought the prisoners were to leave at daylight, was the reason she came so soon. Father and her went round to take them some clothes & bread. I did not go as I wanted to go up to Mrs Currey's to tell the Maj Good by. When they came back they said they thought the men were all right comfortable, thanks to the rebel ladies of Knoxville. They said before the guards if it had not been for the Southern ladies of Knoxville they would have frozen stiff. Mr Baird said he had Mr Dodd's hat to take to a friend of his at Camp Chase.[24] The Yankees have taken the star off.

It was bitter cold going up to Mrs Currey's. We found them at breakfast. Cordie Fletcher was there to tell Col O'Brien good bye. We all kissed the Maj. As we were standing on the front door the prisoners passed on their way to the depot, over a hundred of them and on the impulse of the moment I said "girls shake your handkerchiefs to them" and we all did it, at least the others did. I could not very well as I left mine at home, as I started off in a hurry, but I shook my gloves. Thought that better than nothing.

After we came home, we went out to see Mrs McPherson, & then to see Cluss. Later in the evening I went over to Mrs Kains. Capt Lunt came in while I was there. He is quite handsome and has the prettiest foot I have ever seen on a Yankee. But the vainest creature I have ever seen. Told me his wife was coming and he wanted me to call on her. I believe he has some good in him, for he started to tell some one he had seen Mr Dodd on his way to execution, and the tears rolled down his face & he stopped, turned and walked off. He gave me two Cincinnati papers to read, the one of the 30th Dec says Averells raid could not have accomplished as much as had been supposed, as the rail-road is in running order again.[25]

Jan. 11. Monday. Still very cold. We moved into the back room and almost froze doing it. Mrs. Hamilton, Miss Fletcher and Mary Eastin came to see us.[26] Mary says not half an hour after we left Sunday morning Adj Thomas came there and asked what young ladies had been there that morning.[27] Mrs Currey told him and he took our names, also Lizzie Weltker's who was there when he went. Said we had made some very impudent demonstration when the prisoners were passing. Mary is very much distressed that her aunt had not given her name too. I suppose we will flourish in Brownlow's next. It was in his last he said in speaking of Mr Dodd, "He met his fate with perfect composure, and seemed indifferent to the dreadful end before him. Men going into this Rebellion become hardened by sin, and lost to all sense of honor or shame. Our idea is that they expect after death to wake up in one of the Cotton States." He is the vilest thing that ever lived. Mary Eastin says she heard there was to be another man hung on Friday. It is reputed that Gen Hardee has his head quarters at Cleveland.[28]

Jan. 12. Tuesday. Very cold this morning, and only moderated enough to make walking very bad. I went over to Mrs Cummings for a little while. When I came back found Mrs Kain & Mrs Strong. Mrs K. had come over to tell us that Gen Tillson was to take the house for head quarters tomorrow, and I suppose we were to be turned into the street. Mother said one of his Staff had been here and wanted to see father. When she told him he was out, he said Gen Tillson wanted to see him as soon as he came home. When father went the Gen was out and the ape with speckticles told him that we had to move, and immediately, the Gen had not come yet (a lie). Mr Humes, that piece of perfection, who is so awfully [*illegible*] said he had rented the house to Gen Tillson & had not rented it to father. I dont wonder that sinners lie when ministers set the example. Then Mr ape made a great talk about the extensive demonstrations his [Mr. House's] daughters had made on Sunday, that if he had his way we should have been ordered South immediately. Said he would give father an order on Mr. Joe Walker, Mrs Hamilton or Mrs Currey's, in fact to any of those Rebel's houses.

As soon as he came home and told us, I went with him up to Mr Walkers. He was out, and there are two families besides his in the house. Then we went to Mrs Currey's. She said she had no place but the School room. Mr Gammons's family had occupied that last winter. I suppose it will be the best we can do. What a walk I had, mud five inches deep I do believe. About every five steps my rubbers would come off, and I would have to stop, and pull them on. Capt Whitman says we can have Latta's house but we wont go there after it had been four months in the hands of Yankees and free Negroes. I think this turning us out is perfectly outrageous, and for a set of men too. Our day will come some time, it must. God grant it may come soon. We have packed a good many things since dark ready to move. I hope we will be able to get wagons tomorrow, as we have to go. I had rather move and be done with it at once. No army news today.

Jan. 13. Wednesday. This morning we got to work right early, but then there are so many things to move, and so much to do, one does not know where to commence. Miss Nannie came and sat a while. Mrs McPherson came to tell sister and I good bye. Mrs Martin had just told her two young ladies were to be sent South immediately, for waving their handkerchiefs to the prisoners on Sunday morning, and as she knew we were the ones, she thought we were to start right off. No such good luck for us. I wish to heaven they would send me. They could not possibly please me better. Father went out this morning to get the order so they could not turn us out here. He saw the Gen, who told him he had rented the house in good faith. Mr Humes had offered it to him, he gives $35.00 a month. That is more than we give.

Father says he told him they were making a great fuss about the demonstrations made by us when the prisoners left, that we had no reference to the Government, only waved to our friends who were going. (I would not have said any thing about it, it was none of his business). He said we did nothing wrong. If he had not said so it would not have made a bit of difference to me. About one oclock sister and I walked up to the room. The walking was fully as bad as yesterday. We found Dick [Currey?] scrubbing the floor, he says he never saw as dirty a place except a stable. They sent one load up. I dont think I ever saw such skirts as ours were when we got home.

Jan. 14. Thursday. I came up right after breakfast and tried to pile up the things same way as they were sent up. I think we will be quite comfortable if we can get the petitions [*sic*] put up, and one of the little back rooms for a kitchen. We will have to give Sidney up, as there is no place to put her, and do with only one servant. We must try and live as cheap as possible as long as the Yankees are here, for father is doing nothing, and of course we have very few Green backs.

Mother & sister came up tonight. They say Mrs Kain has been over to tell them that the Yankees had told her our names were on the list of those to be sent off by the 20th at an hours notice, and that Col John Williams told Will there was a list a yard long of our misdoings at Gen Carter's. I was bragging only a day or two since of behaving so well since the miserable creatures have been here, and here some one had been reporting me. I don't more than half believe it. John Williams wants to frighten us. He has mistaken his coustomer if he thinks I am afraid of the Yankees for I aint one bit. He has been advising Will to take the oath. Says it is the only thing to do to keep from being sent to Camp Chase, that all would be obliged to take it, it does not amount to any thing, and is only binding while they are here. Both the Branners and Dr Paxton have taken it and Dr Rogers intends doing it. They are not allowed to practice if they dont. Mother and sister are for father taking it. I am very much opposed to it, any thing rather than that. There is a report in town that there are thirty thousand Confederates at little Charleston.[29]

Jan. 15. Friday. Colder this morning than yesterday. As soon as I dressed I went down to the house. I felt worried about Leo, found him safe and perfectly delighted to see me. I worked right hard for some time, when I went over to Mrs Kains and begged some thing to eat. After I went back I wrote sister a note begging her to come down, which she did. After we made a clearance we went over to Mrs Kains, found her at dinner, and dined with her. After dinner Capt Lunt came in. Sister said she rode down Gay St in a wagon with three negro men, and was going back in it when he offered to bring us home in his ambulance. Sister accepted, and as I thought it much better than walking in the mud [I joined them]. He came up too.

This morning I went round to Mr Shepherds to ask him to put up the petitions [sic] for us, did not see him.[30] Emma said she would tell him. I saw the Sgt at the Jail and asked him if Maj Martin was in jail. I heard last night that he was. He went and looked over the books and said he was not. As I was coming back met Lt Shaw. He said there are one hundred and ten prisoners, some officers, most pretty well clad, some very needy. Ten were brought in last night without a whole garment. I told him we were moving, and it was impossible for me to do any thing, but just as soon as I possibly can I will try and get something for them. Among the officers is a Capt Correnth. I want to see him very much. Intend going to the jail just as soon as the walking will permit.

I have been mad as a hornet all day. Father went and took the oath, and what is the worst took Mr Humes with him as his friend to vouch for him. It is not going to do one bit of good, and I would have done any thing rather then have had him do it. I know it dont change his feelings one bit, but it is so humiliating. It mortified me to death. What is the use of fussing though, it wont do any good.[31]

Mr. Humes is trying to exonerate himself from blame. He went to Will today and told him if he had not rented his house, the Military would have taken it any how. That does not mend the matter one bit. Will came round tonight for a little while. He looks miserably. Says he went in Gen Carters office today to take the oath but could not. It made him sick to think of it, so he turned round and came out. Mother and sister advise him to do it. I dont. I cant. I wish he was in our army where he ought to have been long ago.

Jan. 16. Saturday. Still very muddy. We have fixed things a little better than yesterday, but it is regular pigging it yet. Mrs Currey was sick today, so we have not been able to fix the kitchen. The Yankees say that our boys captured a wagon train. They recaptured it, and took Gen Vance and three hundred men prisoners.[32] They are to be brought in tomorrow. I hear Brownlow gave it to Mr. Craig in his paper of today. I would like to see it.[33]

Jan. 17. Sunday. Clear and pleasant, in fact perfectly delightful, like Spring. I saw Brownlow's paper this morning. He says on Sunday morning Mr Currey's piazza was crowded with she-rebels, who as the prisoners passed waved their handkerchiefs, and made such bold, impudent flirting demonstrations as only she rebels know how to make, and we ought to be sent South immediately. For a wonder he did not publish our names.[34] Gen Vance and fifty men were brought in today. I am very sorry that he has been taken. They said yesterday that there were two hundred to be brought in today. Dr Piggott sent a note in today to father, saying Duff Rice had broken his parole and gone. He Dr P. was uneasy lest it might get father into trouble, as he understood he had given his name as a reference to some of the Guards. Father says it cant possibly hurt him. I am glad he is gone.

Jan. 18. Monday. The Yankees have an excitement of some kind on hand. The walking is so bad we found it would be impossible to go down to the Jail as we wanted to. We have the room we intend for a kitchen cleaned out, will get it quite comfortably fixed by tomorrow. We received a long letter from Johnnie today, the first he wrote after he arrived at Johnsons Island. He writes in good spirits. Says he was captured at Missionary Ridge on the 25th of Nov. and all owing to his own carelessness in riding. He rode right into a whole brigade of Yankees before he knew it. They fired upon him killing his horse, and of course he was obliged to surrender. Having on thin clothes when captured and no blanket, he contracted a violent cold which turned into putred sore throat, but he was well again when he wrote. He says there are fifteen there from Knoxville. I cant count more than six.

Jan. 19. Tuesday. The Yankees are badly frightened, one who is just in from the front says. That at New Market, on Sunday, the Rebels attacked them. After four hours hard fighting gained certain positions which they wanted intending to have the big fight next day. When courier after courier came dashing into their (The Yankee's) camp, with dispatches that Gen

Hardee had whipped Thomas badly, and taken all the heights around Chat-tanooga, which caused them to fall back immediately. He says their army is completely demoralized, and in full retreat with Gen Longstreet after them, that he is coming in three columns, one on the other side of the river. Wheeler is reported to have had a fight above and whipped them.[35]

The military here seem to be anticipating another siege. I hope there will be one, if they will only come. They brought two guns this evening and mounted them just before the house. We have a full view of Temperance Hill from Mrs Currey's front door. Gen John Morgan is reported near Maryville with three hundred men.[36] Cavalry have been coming in all day. They say that their horses cant hold out three days longer on a march, that they cant go to Chattanooga, and of course the sick cant cross the moun-tains. I never saw any thing so thin and looking so miserably as the poor creatures do. Many seem to have scarcely life enough to carry themselves, much less their riders.[37]

Jan. 20. Wednesday. Gen Vance and all the prisoners were sent off this morning. That looks as if they expected the Rebels. Mary Polk and I went round to Mrs Kains this afternoon.[38] She says her Yanks say they expect a siege, and have not a weeks rations. The Cavalry who crossed the river yesterday are reported to have all come back today. While they were crossing the pon-toon gave way and twenty-five were ducked. Pity they had not been drowned.

Dr Piggott came in today, found us all in confusion. He says he thinks Duff Rice got off safe. I gave him a copy of Mr Dodds letter to Col Cook and the other papers in case he had a chance of sending them through. I was afraid to trust the original. I should dislike so much for it to be lost. He says his men who recover do it from force of nature, that he can get neither medicines or liquor for them. Many of them have died from want of it. He said too that they were very much in need of tobacco, so Mary Polk and I went over to Mr Sedgwicks store and begged some for them.[39] There is a report today that Gens Morgan and Forrest have taken Loudon, also that Longstreet is four miles this side of the plains, and the bridge was not burnt. I doubt both.

Jan. 21. Thursday. The blue coats say today that the cars came through from New Market, and there are no Rebels to be seen, that it was only a raid they were so much frightened at. They captured 6000 bushels of corn, which Capt Lunt had bought and paid for. In the afternoon Mark Polk & I went to see Mrs Kain, then out to Mrs McP. Capt Whitman was there Saturday, and threatened to take her house for a hospital. When she asked him where she and her children were to go if he did, he said if he compelled her to give up her house, he could compel some rebel family to take her in. The town is full of Union men from above. Many are going to Ky.

Jan. 22. Friday. Considerable excitement in town today. Father heard a Yankee officer say he was shot at by the Rebels only three miles from town. There is quite a force four miles above, & the report says Gen Hardee is coming up, and they will be completely surrounded. Many are expecting another siege. I would not care. Any thing for a little excitement.

Jan. 23. Saturday. Sister, Mary Polk and I went on Gay St to get some things. Mary & I went to Mrs Kains, where I heard some of the Yankee officers say that they believed they were evacuating. It looks like it. Troops and wagons have been going down all day. Others says Knoxville, Loudon and Kingston are to be garrisoned for five thousand men each. I bought some things for Mrs Kain at one or two stores. If they find it out at Head Quarters I suppose there will be a fuss made. I'll risk it though. Rumored fighting all round. Of course they had the best of it.

Jan. 24. Sunday. Another May Sunday in January. Jeanie and Will came round in the morning. He looks very badly. The Officers here say the Rebels have all fallen back, none are to be seen or heard of. I expect they will hear from them when they least expect it. Gen Longstreet is worrying them a great deal and has been ever since he left here in Nov. The small pox is still spreading. Many are very much frightened. I am very thankful I do not fear it.[40]

Jan. 25. Monday. One of the men from our Hospital came to get a bottle of wine for a friend. He said they needed many things. I told him I would make some corn starch and take them in the morning. His name is Griffin from Mississippi.[41] I made it this afternoon. Had a time doing it, did not cook it enough the first time and had to try again. I will know better next

time. I hear eighty prisoners were brought in today, but dont believe it. Kate
Crozier is at Mr Currey's today. She says a Negro woman of Dr Baker's had
three babies on Friday and another on Saturday, three are alive.[42]

Jan. 26. Tuesday. Mary Eliza, Mary Polk and I went down to the Hospital this morning. We saw a good many of the men. There is one there from
Marietta named Newton—from Marietta—and a number of Georgians.
One I was very much pleased with, Pate. He had lost one eye at the storming of Fort Sanders. He seems to be a very intelligent fellow.[43] After we left
the hospital, we went round to the Jail. They were issuing the rations when
we went. They get half a loaf of bread each, & such looking stuff. I dont see
how they can eat it.[44]

There are one hundred and twenty prisoners there, among them four
commissioned officers. Capt Bennett of Gen Bennings Staff, very talkative,
takes things very cooly. He is from Columbus Geo.[45] Says he saw Johnnie
several days after the fight at Chickamaga. He was Inspector Gen on Gen
Stewarts Staff and at the time he saw him was inspecting their brigade. He
says he was looking very well. He did not know him, but thought he was a very
young looking man for the position he occupied. Was very much surprised
to hear he was at Johnsons Island. Capt. Robards of Gen Price's army was
sent to Richmond on detail business, and was captured with the others near
Dandridge, & Lts Welch and Nicholson.[46] I did not see the two last named.

Capt Bennett came round to see us this evening with a guard, Corp
Evans. He saw Dr Ramsey about ten days ago. He was well. I should like so
much to see him. Our forces captured a hundred men within a few miles of
town last night.

Jan. 27. Wednesday. It was such a beautiful day sister and I concluded
we could not stay in the house, so we went down to Jeanies. Mary and Kate
were in, and we stayed there some time. When we came home mother said
Wallie McPherson had just left. They have received orders to leave Saturday morning, as have also Mr Martin, Mr Harrison, Mrs Wilson, Dr
Goodlin, [and] Mrs Echels, and Mrs McP sent to ask sister and I if we were
not among the number if we would help her.[47] Of course we will do every
thing we can for her, the way my fingers have been flying. They are allowed

to take only their clothes—and they must all be made—blankets enough to keep them warm on the way and four days rations.

Mrs Hamilton came over this morning. She says Maj Gratz sent her word with the order that she could avoid being sent off by coming up and taking the oath.[48] We advised her to do it. She says she knows no one south. Every thing she has is here, and she dont know how she could take her two little children and go among entire strangers. I asked her tonight what she was going to do. She said put on two veils in the morning and go take the oath.

Mrs Goodlin came over this afternoon. She says she had just come from Gen Carter's office. He said she could take the oath any time between noon and Saturday morning. She says she cant go south. Mr Columbus Powell, Mr McGhee, and Will Rogers have been taken up today and put in Jail, also Mr Sam Atkins, as hostages, I think.[49] I hope they will get out before long.

Jan. 28. Thursday. We went up to Mrs McPherson's this morning. She went up to Gen Carter's office to see what she would be allowed to take, if Stonewall could go and if she could buy her baby a cloak. The little crea-ture has none. Gen Carter left this morning and Maj Gratz replied to the first, only her wearing apparel, to the second if he was a good rebel of course he must go, and to the last No Madam, as if she had asked permission to spend a thousand dollars. Miss Nannie came among others to see her. She has cooled down considerably, says now she will go when she is ordered. Mrs. McPherson gave us a carpet for the jail, and we cut it into four pieces & sent one to each of the officers there. We stopped at Mrs Kains for a little while, to see if she would let me have her hat for Mrs McPherson, as she wants one and of course can buy nothing from the stores. When Mrs Goodlin and Mrs Hamilton went up this morning to take the oath, Col Keith,[50] who is acting in Gen Carters place during his absence, would not let them do it, said they should go South. Mr Humes tried to get Mr Martin's time extended, but did not succeed, but they gave him permission to sell any thing he wanted to.

Jan. 29. Friday. When we went out to Mrs McPhersons this morning found she had received several orders in regard to selling her things. Early this morning when the house was full of persons wanting to buy, one came that if she sold any thing at all she would be severely punished. After all the people had gone another came that she could sell any thing to any body. The same were sent to Mrs Hamilton. The last I suppose was caused by a Mrs Fletcher, a union woman who came from Greenville yesterday. She says Gen Longstreet allowed her to sell her house and lot and every thing she wanted to for Green backs, and bring out what ever she wished. Before Mrs McP trunks were packed a wagon came for them, said they could not wait, so some things were just put in any way. Sister went up with them to the Provost Marshals to have them examined. Jeanie came out in the evening and we went home with her & stayed all night. Mary and Kate were in and Cluss & Tom Van Gilder were there to spend the evening. It is Jeanies birthday and she had a oyster supper for us.

Jan. 30. Saturday. We had not got in the house this morning when Sam told me that they had received orders to leave, though no day specified, and by the time we were seated Sissie Kain came in to say her mother had received her walking papers, and sent her to ask us to come and help her.[51] So we started right off in the rain. After we got there we sent for Mary & Kate Hazen. Mrs Haire[52] and Alice Helms[53] came too and we all worked with a will and accomplished a great deal. Mrs Ramsey, Mrs Weltker, Miss Nannie Scott, Dr Jackson and several others have received orders too. I dont see why Mrs Weltker should have been among the number. She has never done any thing that I have heard of. I suppose they want her big house. Mrs Kain sent for Capt Lunt to see if she could go north. He came back and told her she could by taking the oath, which of course she refused to do.

Jan. 31. Sunday. I went to see Miss Nannie to say good bye. I wanted to see her before she left and dont think I will have time again before she goes. Old Mr McFarlane was buried this afternoon.[54] I met Mrs McClung and Ellen going. Ellen goes to Nashville on Tuesday, of course has to take the oath first. I met Miss Nannie just coming out of her gate, going to the funeral too, so I told her I would come again and went on to Mrs Kains. Mary Hazen came in not long after and after talking a while, we went over to see Miss Nannie again and then to see Ella Cocke. Mary is considerably excited. Capt Lunt told Mrs K he heard she was on the list to be sent out. She wants to go, but is afraid her father will make such a fuss, and compel her to take the oath. She says one consolation if she is sent out I'll be too, for she has not done half that I have. I wish they would send me.

When we went back to Mrs Kains found sister there sewing. Mrs K. said she had been all the morning, and Sissie fussing about it all the time. I told her it was old Keiths sin and no one else's. Mary went over to Ellen McClungs, and not long after I started home as I wanted to write Johnnie tonight. I stopped to have a confab with Mary White. She says her father came home last night and told Moody & her if they had any thing to do they had better do it, as he had been told their names were on the list. Citizens were given till twelve oclock yesterday to take the oath. Mr White went at half past eleven with Mrs Hu[gh] McClung and some others.[55] While we were standing there talking Mary Hazen came along and we walked together some distance. When I started to come home, she begged me so to go and spend the night or a little while any how that I went, and as Will did not feel well spent the night.

Feb. 1. Monday. Last night after we had all gone to bed, father came down to know if I was there. I was so sorry he had such a walk for nothing. The first thing I knew Jeanie came up stairs to tell us Madam Millie had taken herself off.[56] So up we jumped and dressed as fast as we could to go down and help Jeanie. When I went down she had made the coffee and was mixing up some batter cakes—afterward it appeared without sifting the meal. The breakfast was very good considering all things. Jeanie said something was the matter with the coffee. She did not know what. Will discovered there was too much water in it.

I came home before going to Mrs Kains. It rained in the night and the walking was very bad. When I got here, Oh! what a peppering I did catch. I said I expected I would be ordered south among the next set and they opened on me. Fannie said she had no doubt that the order which was sent down to Jeanies on Saturday and found to be a mistake was intended for her and I. I said I did not care. Mother said I had better go and take the oath. I told her I could not for any thing short of saving the life of a member of the family. Sister said of course I was better than any body else, and mother that I would give up my family and go among strangers, who she supposed I cared more for than I did for them. I just boiled over. I said I would not take the oath, I wish they would send me south and walked off. I never was so taken by surprise in my life. It was only yesterday afternoon sister and I were talking about it and she was as anxious to go as I was.

A few minutes after I got to Mrs K, Mary came in, and then Capt Lunt with an ambulance. He had been for both of us, and was only a few minutes too late at each place. We told him we regretted it so much, losing both the ride & the escort, just poured on the flattery. He is so vain. While we were sitting there sewing Mr Butterworth came in, and we got at him. Talked as savory as you please, and when Mrs K asked us if we were not afraid he would report us, smoothed it over by saying before him, Oh! no: we knew [we] were talking to a gentleman. Mary received a letter from Adjt Cummings at Camp Chase He said they had a very hard time on the road. Some were frozen to death and some died of fatigue.

I went up to the stores with Mary after dinner to get some things for Mrs K. As we were passing the Post Office thought we would go in though several yankees standing at the door. I was amply repaid for doing so, as there was a letter from Aunt Mary enclosing one from Johnnie thanking her for a box she had sent him of clothes, goodies, &e. He said there was some talk of moving them. He hoped it would not be done, as they were very comfortable on the Island, more so he supposed than they would be in any other Northern prison. Aunt Mary writes that the reason for moving them is that the Canadians are attempting to liberate them, and not as some said as a step towards an exchange. She said should he be sent to Fort Delaware she would go to see him. She says there are a good many ladies in Philadelphia who devote their whole time to Southern prisoners, and money has been sent to aid them in the noble work from Europe.[57]

I did not go back to Mrs K, but went to work to make some cake without butter or eggs for her to take. There was a rumor today that the cars did not or could not go down to Loudon. I expect it was a mistake.

Feb. 2. Tuesday. I made some more cake this morning. Finished about twelve oclock, when I started with them in a basket for Mrs K. As I passed Dr Jackson's there were three Confederates standing at the gate. I walked passed some little distance, but I could not go on, so I turned and walked back and spoke to them. It proved to be Dr North, from the Paper Mill Hospital, and two of the nurses, Burnside & ——.[58] I told them I was going down to Mrs Kains would be gone all day, but to go up to Dr Currey's and ask for Mrs House & she would give them a lunch. He hesitated at first, but when I told him I had a brother a prisoner, and it would afford her pleasure I knew to see them, they said they would go. Sister and I went to see Miss Nannie a little while, to say good bye, then went back & Capt Lunt brought us home in an Ambulance. He says he will stop with her in the morning to say good bye. We had just got in the house when it commenced raining.

Feb. 3. Wednesday. I was very much afraid they would have an unpleasant day, but it cleared up this morning. Capt Lunt stopped with Mrs Kain & the Children. I hated so much to see them go, and wished I was going with them. (Mrs Weltker & Lizzie have been allowed to take the oath and remain. Mrs Curreys time has been indefinitely extended on account of her bad health. And Mrs Dr Ramseys until she can hear from the Dr. Prudence dictates that she goes to Ky, and Mr Humes advises it. Inclination leads her South to her husband.) Some little while after Mrs Kain passed Miss Nannie came along, walking as slowly as possible. Mrs French told her she would be left behind. She said she knew they were not going without her, and she did keep the train waiting some time.

Just as sister and I were starting out Doctors Piggott and Spinks came in.[59] They are consolidating the hospitals. Dr Piggott is to take charge and the others be sent South, they hope next week. After they left sister and I went up to the stores, and I did the most abominably absurd thing I ever did. Started up into Meeks store, did not look what I was doing. The step was broken and I fell. I dont believe I could [have] possibly picked myself up any where else but on Gay St, and if there had been Confederates all round instead of Yankees I should have been mortified to death. As it was I was considerably more hurt than mortified. I scraped my left arm badly and it is very painful. I heard the prisoners were to leave in the morning and as I had some clothes to send them which needed mending came home and went to work. It almost killed me, but that made no difference. I did it, and sent them to Capt Bennett with some Miss Nannie had left, for him to distribute them. I wanted to go myself, but mother was so much opposed to my going to the jail today, I did not.

Father has spoken to Capt Whitman about the house Dr Goodlin occupied. He said he will let him know. He came today to say Col Barriger, Chief Com, wanted it,[60] but was willing for us to have it if we would board him, and requested that father would call on him, which he did. He objected to $1.00 a day. Said it was too much, his clerks could not afford to pay it. He had no servant, would expect father to furnish him with wood and have his boots blacked. Wanted to know if he was Loyal, as if he was not it would be a very great objection. The impudent rascal requested father to see him again. There are several negro women & children over at the house. Mother told Capt Whitman she could not have them there. He said they were good girls & he could not think of turning them out, so I suppose there is an end to that.

Feb. 4. Thursday. The prisoners left this morning. I wish I could have seen them again.[61] I went to work on my new calico this morning, and have made considerable headway, though frequently called off. There has been quite an excitement on the street today, but I have not been able to learn the cause. Gen Schofield and not McPherson as was supposed is to be Fosters successor.[62] I never heard of him before, suppose he is some dutch rascal. One thing is certain he cant be worse then Foster. Mrs Newman and Mattie Luttrell came in the afternoon. Mattie says Brownlow is sick—paralised—either his tongue or his hands. She dont know which, but thinks it ought to be both. She says she heard several days ago that sister and I were to be sent south, and father & mother kept here to punish us. If they did but know it, it would punish them considerably the most of the two. We received a letter from Johnnie today. He was well, so he said were all the K boys.

Feb. 5. Friday. Finished my calico. Nothing of any kind today. There seems to be a perfect stagnation.

Feb. 6. Saturday. Fussed round generally this morning. Lincoln has called out a hundred thousand men to take Richmond. I think he will have to call more than once before he gets them, and a few more thousand before he gets Richmond, as I dont think Jeff [Davis] has any idea of letting him have possession there.

Feb. 7. Sunday. I went to see Miss White this morning, found her in bed. As I went in I saw quite a crowd standing in front of Lt Shaws office. Mrs Cummings said there had been some prisoners brought in this morning from North Carolina belonging to Thomas' Legion, 16 of them Indians.[63] The Yankees say they have captured two hundred of them and Thomas with them. Of course it is true. I dined with Mrs Cummings. Stopped to see Cluss on my way home. She was out, but I stopped and chatted with her mother a few moments, poor old lady. I feel right sorry for her. She has lost every thing and is so perfectly helpless. As I was coming out I met Cluss, made her turn and walk part of the way home with me. As we passed the Citizen prison Will Rogers called to us & we stopped for a few minutes to talk to him. Col Hugh McClung & Mr Sam Boyd sent in for their families today.

Feb. 8. Monday. Clear and cold. While we were eating breakfast this morning father came in and said he had just seen Capt Whitman. He was coming up to tell us we could have the house Dr Goodlin lived in, wanted us to move at once. He would send some of his men to move us. There were some things in the house that he wanted to move in to the schoolroom. In twenty minutes after he came in the men came & brought every thing over. The house is filthy and it would have been much pleasanter to have had time to clean it first, but we were glad to get it any how. There is a Yankee Lt named Holbrook who has been boarding at Dr Goodlins.[64] He came in while we were in the midst of moving and the way he was mad it amused me not a little. He went [on] storming about being put out of his room without a moments warning &e. I did not take any notice of him, neither did sister. He cooled down enough to know if he could stay up stairs till tomorrow with his clerk. We said yes and he left. One of the men who helped to move us over told me that the war was nearly over. Jeff Davis had sent to Washington offering to make peace if the north would receive the Southern states back in the Union. I told him Pres. Davis never did any thing of the kind. He said it was official. I replied so were a great many other reports which had not one bit of truth in them, that the officers were fooling them.

Feb. 9. Tuesday. Clear and pleasant. Yankee Lt left today. Gen Schofield arrived this morning to take Fosters place. I suppose from his name he is a Dutchman. Miss Kate White came to see us. I went to the stores with

Mary Polk to get her a dress but it was gone. I received a note from Lt Manning saying he understood I might be ordered south any day and wanted to know if I would exchange some Confederate money for Green backs. He would soon be sent north to prison, and disliked going without a cent. I sent him word I did not have any Greenbacks myself, but would try and get him some.

Feb. 10. *Wednesday*. Clear and pleasant. Dr Piggott came in this morning. He bought me one hundred dollars from Lt Manning, which Mary Polk and I went all over town to exchange, but without success. Col Eastin let me have five in Greenbacks for fifty, and that is the best I can do.[65] Mrs McClung, Mrs Gillespie and Mrs Sam Boyd left this morning. Their husbands met them at Strawberry Plains. They seemed to be posted as to all that is going on here. Asked how Gen Schofield was liked, and how Parson Brownlow was, and informed the Yankee officers who went with them that Gen Longstreet intended to take Knoxville.

Feb. 11. *Thursday*. A fight is reported to have taken place at Maryville, in which the Yankees were whipped, and last night the pickets were run in across the river.[66] Ella Cocke came and spent the morning with us.

Feb. 12. *Friday*. The fight &e of yesterday is confirmed today. I see Will Rogers is out of jail this evening, but I dont know how he got out, whether he has taken the oath or not. I hope not.

Feb. 13. *Saturday*. Dr Piggott came in this morning, and according to promise I went after Ella Cocke. She wanted to know him, and he wanted to know her, so I thought it a pity they should not have their wishes gratified. So when he came back as usual here Ella was. Will Rogers came to see us. He says he is out on bail, as the man for who he was held as hostage has been released so in Richmond. I received a letter from Mr Spicer of Memphis from Camp Chase. He says he is very comfortable—for a prisoner, more so than he had expected. They had a very unpleasant time crossing the mountains. One died, and Mr Spencer was quite sick. He was sent to Johnsons Island. Two more have died since their arrival at Camp Chase. Rumor says that the rebels are two miles out of town.

Feb. 14. Sunday. Cloudy. Mary Polk and I went to the Jail this after-noon. As we passed our Church they were singing the first chant. It made me feel oh! so badly to think I could not go to church. How much I shall enjoy it when I have an opportunity. There are four Commissioned officers there, Lts Buchanan, Henderson and two Colberts.[67] I think I saw one of them. Did not like him at all for several reasons. The other two seem to be gentle-men although dirty & ragged. We came home & I sent them some shirts &e, also to the other Lt that I saw, and got some tracts and took down to the Rebel Hospital. I did not go in, as there has been several cases of Small Pox there lately. One of the men told me that the Mr Griffin had taken the oath some time since, the rascal. I saw some of the Indians too at the Jail. One of them is a preacher, has prayer night and morning. They call him Old Smoke. I stopped in to see Cluss coming home. Mary White was there. She says she saw in a northern paper an account of Capt Moody's being sick at Camp Chase. I am so sorry to hear it. They had no business to send him north. I suppose Maj Smith is there too. Dr Ramsey has sent in for his family. They expect to leave tomorrow. Tonight I wrote to Mrs Whaling and Mr Spicer.

Feb. 15. Monday. I have had a sick headache all today, suffered a good deal. The Yankees would not let Mrs Ramsey go today. The Rebels are re-ported at George Mabry's below and above too.[68]

Feb. 16. Tuesday. This morning I received a note from Lt Buchanan ask-ing me please to send him something to eat. I sent all that was in the house, and I was very sorry it was so little, and sent him word I would send more this afternoon or tomorrow morning. Mrs Renshaw promised to send me something to send but has not done it. Mrs Snap—a union woman—has been sent in from above, she says. Capt Kain is Provost Marshall at Bristol and sent her in. Tells all sorts of stories about the way that she has been treated.

Capt Whitman went over to Brownlows to know who were Capt Kains relations here. He intends making them support them, so he says, and went to Will first one. Will told him it would not begin to do, got rid of it some how. The woman only has nine children. He has been to Mr Rayal and Mrs Strongs too. Mrs Strong was here this evening. She says the Yankees stay-ing at her house say no more Southern families are to be sent out, for fear

Gen Longstreet will shell the place if only Union people are here. We received a letter from Uncle John, also one from Johnnie. He is well, says he does not expose himself at all, for he knows if he should be sick mother would worry herself to death.

Feb. 17. Wednesday. Very cold. I got up early and made some biscuits to take to the Jail. My sending any thing there now is entirely different to what it has been before. Until now, I had only to give my orders and the things were made and taken. Now I have to make and take myself, but I believe it affords me more real pleasure than it did then. I found it extremely cold. That only made me walk faster. Capt Whitman came in this morning to see if the rooms up stairs were fixed. I was frightened, thought he was going to put some union family on us—as there were two pay masters just come in who wanted them. I felt very much relieved. I told him yes. Not long afterwards they came with their clerks. Maj Price is the name of one, dont know what the others are. Jeanie came round for a little while.

Feb. 18. Thursday. Still very cold. Nothing today. I took some bread & Biscuits round to the jail this evening and almost froze. Went over to see Cluss for a little while. Two of the Indians were sent off about a week ago on a scout. The Yankees say they have promised to bring in Thomas' scalp.

Feb. 19. Friday. Dr Piggott came in this morning as usual, wanted me to get him some tobacco. He says Mr Cox and Sergt Hicks have left. There was a fight four miles above town this afternoon, do not suppose it amounted to much. Maj Price told mother he left Maryville very unexpectly at midnight Tuesday night. The Ky train was run in today too. I am not going to get excited and hopeful like I did during the siege. The reaction is too great.[69]

Feb. 20. Saturday. Ella Cocke came this morning & we made her stay to dinner. I received a very pretty note from Lieut Buchanan thanking me for my kindness to him. He must be a relation of President Buchanan's. He says he is from Baltimore Maryland. His father was Minister to Denmark during Buchanans term, and is now in Paris with his mother and sister. He cannot return home on account of his Southern feelings. I am so glad I have been able to do any thing for him little as it has been. Poor fellow, how completely isolated he is. Mrs French and Mary Alexander came after Ella, but we would not let her go. They stayed some time.

After dinner, Sister, Ella & I went to the jail to take Lt B. something to eat. We were not allowed to talk to any of the prisoners. All the convalescents have been brought in from the hospitals. That looks more like they were expecting another siege than any thing else. There is a great deal of excitement in town. They say the Rebels are advancing and some say there will probably be a fight here tomorrow. I hope there will be. Any thing is better than being here with Yankees. Yet I should not say that, for I do not altogether mean it. An attack on Knoxville would cause the death of too many of our brave and noble soldiers for me to wish it. Someone must suffer, and we might as well as any others. It cannot last forever. Gen Longstreet will have the place some time.

Feb. 21. Sunday. The Yankees expected an attack last night, but were disappointed. One of the Pay masters & his clerk left this morning. I did not see him once. Drs Piggott and North came to see us. They are at the Lamar House. They dont know what is to be done with them. Dr P. says they watch him very closely, told him he had better not go out much. They dined with us. I promised to go down to the Hospital next day to see the two-story Miss[issippi] Capt. Dr. P has been talking so much about tomorrow afternoon.

About two weeks ago either some soldiers or union men went to a man's house a few miles out of town, I think his name was Duncan, at night and called him out & killed him (his wife was very sick, had a young infant only a few days old, and it excited her so much she has been at the point of death almost ever since) & then went and burnt his mother's house.[70] A night or two afterwards they went to old Mr Staubs in the country. He was sick in bed. Made them all leave the house at midnight & set fire to the house, rolled the old man off the bed his wife had brought him out on & threw it into the fire. Fired on his two sons, wounded one of them. It is perfectly dreadful. The military take no notice of it at all.

Feb. 22. Monday. This afternoon sister and I went down to the Rebel Hospital. Saw a good many of the poor fellows, several very young, who have lost a leg. The commissioned officers have all been sent to the General hospital, so I did not see the Capt. Four of the Indians are there, Old Smoke among them. The steward told me Mr Pate was dead, poor fellow. He died of Small Pox. Coming past Lt Shaws office I asked the Sgt if any prisoners had been brought in. He said several, among them Adjt Smallman of the 8th Tenn Cavly.[71] We went to see Miss Kate. She has been quite sick. Stopped to see Ella Cocke. She was out. Report says a negro was arrested a day or two since as a spy. He had implicated two white men, and one of them is to be hung on Friday. He is a very trifling fellow, yet if he is at heart a Southerner and has been trying to do any thing for the cause, I am truly sorry for him.

Feb. 23. Tuesday. I got up and dressed very early, as I understood the prisoners might leave this morning & I had some clothes I wanted to take to Lieut Buchanan & Adjt Smallman. Mary Eliza went with me. As we were passing Mr George Whites she called to me to tell me she had seen a note for me the evening before from Lt. B. at Mrs McClungs, and she went over after it. Mrs McClung said Mrs French had taken it the evening before & promised to send it to me, so we went round to Mrs Frenches. The little negro boy said he had given it to mother. It certainly seemed very strange. So I just wrote on the top of the note I had pinned to his bundle, "I was very sorry I had not received a note I understood he had written me," and took the things round to the office.

When I knocked who should come out of the inner room but Lieut Shaw. He came up & held out his hand & I shook it, one would have thought to see me, very cordially. Asked him if he had heard any thing of the Maj. He said only that he was well at Camp Chase. He had not had time to go & see him. After talking a little while to him, I left. A few months since how I should have been insulted if any one had told me I should have done such a thing, but I find that it is decidedly the best plan to treat those I come in contact with, especially those connected with the jail, as if I thought them perfect gentleman, but I cant let them think for one moment I am any thing but a Rebel, heart & soul. When I came home I asked mother if she had a note for me. She said she had entirely forgotten it, entirely, and handed it to me. He asked me to get him a hat, cravat & several other things which were in the bundle I sent him this morning. I went to Van Gilders to ask

Will for a hat. Dr Piggott met me there. He says they watch him very closely, as though they suspected him. When I told Will what I wanted he said he (Lt) had applied to take the oath, he had seen the application. I was thunderstruck. Did not say a word more, but came home and sat down to sew, but I could not. I felt so worried. At last I put my work away in disgust, and went after Ella Cocke. I thought I could get her to go with me to the office, and ask to be allowed to see the list of prisoners, as she thought she had friends among them, and I could ask if Lt B had taken the oath or wanted to take it without his knowing that was what took me there.

I found Ella at Mrs Frenches, also Mary and Kate Hazen. Kate leaves in the morning for Lexington Ky, where she is going to school.[72] Her father has been appointed to go North and collect and invest the donations of the Northern States to East Tenn, and will take her on.[73] I gave her cousin Mills two rings, which I had been wearing for a day or two to have them when I should see her, to take to Uncle John. When I told Ella what I had come for, she said of course she would go, so we went, and when I asked the Sgt about Lt. B. taking the oath, he said he had not applied to take it. He did not think any in jail would take it. Oh! I felt so much relieved. The idea of one of our officers—particularly one belonging to a prominent family doing such a thing—distressed me beyond measure. We went back to Mrs Frenches to tell her as I knew she wanted to know what we had learned.

So then I came home for sister and we went to tell Will he was mistaken (met Dr Piggott there again, he expects to go out to the Paper Mill tomorrow) but he said he was not, he had seen it himself in Dr Cardwells office.[74] The application said he was tired of rebellion and wanted to take the oath &e. It made me angry for him to insist on it, yet I must believe him that he saw it when he says he did. I did not know what to do. If it is true (which I dont believe) of course I dont want to give a deserter any thing. If false I would not have him think for a moment I suspicioned such a thing. I believe Dr Cardwell made the application without his knowledge. It makes me feel much better to think so, and poor fellow if he is innocent he will think I never received his note. The Yankees say that Longstreet has gone and the whole of their army after him. I hope they will find him. Mrs French and Ella are so blue. I am determined not to be blue, and have come to the conclusion "Whatever is, is right" and will believe all will end well.

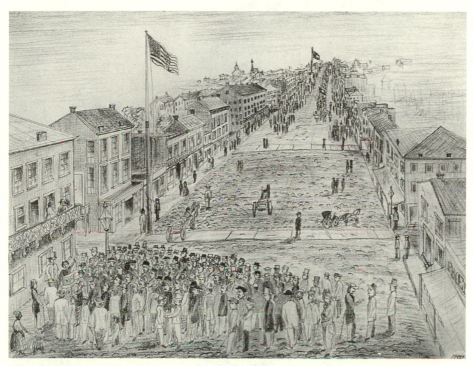

The war begins in Knoxville, as groups of Union and Confederate supporters meet at opposite ends of Gay Street. From Seymour, *Divided Loyalties* (1982). Collection of Richard P. W. Williams.

The front page of *Harper's Weekly*, March 29, 1862, carried this sketch of a clandestine meeting of East Tennessee unionists, among them Col. David Fry.

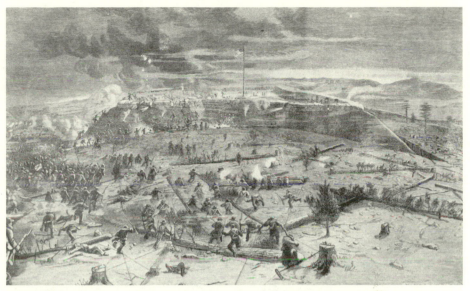

The defense of Fort Sanders in November 1863 marks the military high tide of the Federal occupation of Knoxville. From Humes, *Loyal Mountaineers of Tennessee* (1888).

The Cumberland Gap was one of the main avenues of invasion from Kentucky into East Tennessee. Gen. John W. Frazer's failure to hold the gap allowed Gen. Ambrose Burnside's army to flood East Tennessee and occupy Knoxville. From *Leslie's Illustrated Newspaper*.

William G. "Parson" Brownlow had no sympathy for Confederate rebels. He was a neighbor of Ellen House but may have been responsible for her exile to Georgia. From Humes, *Loyal Mountaineers of Tennessee* (1888).

Horace Maynard was one of Knoxville's leading unionists. From Humes, *Loyal Mountaineers of Tennessee* (1888).

Gen. Samuel P. Carter served as provost marshal in Knoxville during most of the Federal occupation. From Humes, *Loyal Mountaineers of Tennessee* (1888).

Ellen Renshaw House in a photograph taken shortly before the war. Photograph courtesy of Ellen Allran and Victoria Guthrie.

A youthful portrait of Ellen's South Carolina–born father, Samuel Crawford House. Photograph courtesy of Ellen Allran and Victoria Guthrie.

A youthful portrait of Ellen's Pennsylvania-born mother, Frances Budden (Renshaw) House. Photograph courtesy of Ellen Allran and Victoria Guthrie.

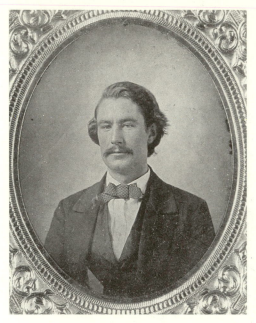

Samuel House, Ellen's second eldest brother, served through the war and was twice captured. Photograph courtesy of Ellen Allran and Victoria Guthrie.

Frances "Fannie" Renshaw House, Ellen's elder sister. Photograph courtesy of Ellen Allran and Victoria Guthrie.

John Moore House, Ellen's beloved younger brother, in Confederate uniform. Photograph courtesy of Ellen Allran and Victoria Guthrie.

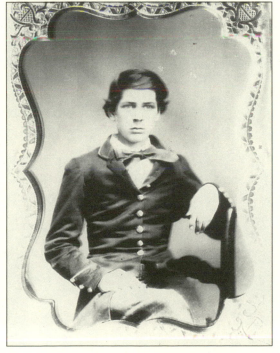

John Moore House was a delicate youth who survived imprisonment on Johnson's Island only to be murdered near Nashville six months after the war. Photograph courtesy of Ellen Allran and Victoria Guthrie.

Frank Bostick Renshaw, Ellen's uncle and a Confederate naval officer. Photograph courtesy of Ellen Allran and Victoria Guthrie.

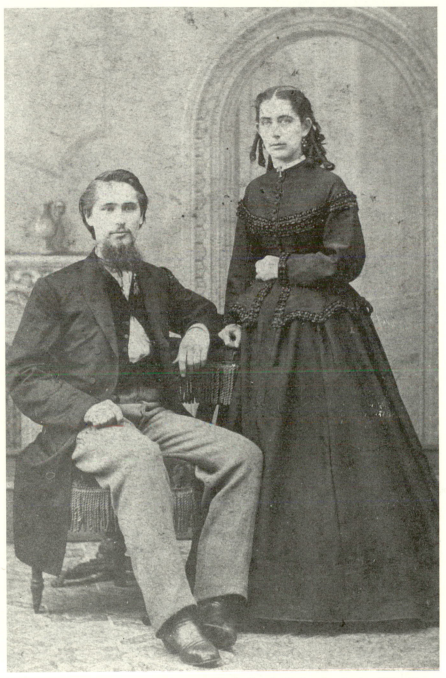

James and Ellen Fletcher. James became Ellen's "brother" after the death of John House. They married in 1868. Photograph courtesy of Ellen Allran and Victoria Guthrie.

Ellen Renshaw House, probably at about the time of her marriage. The years had taken their toll. Photograph courtesy of Ellen Allran and Victoria Guthrie.

Three sisters entering middle age. Left to right are sister-in-law Jeanie Hazen House, Ellen, and Fannie. Photograph courtesy of Ellen Allran and Victoria Guthrie.

Ellen Renshaw House after the war. The melancholy eyes reflect her sense of loss following the defeat of the Confederacy and the loss of her brother and father. Photograph courtesy of Ellen Allran and Victoria Guthrie.

Chapter 4.
I Am Ordered to Leave on Monday

Feb. 24. Wednesday. Ella Cocke came this morning to know why I had not come for her in the evening as I promised. I told her all about it and she thought as I did. I received a note from Adjt Smallman thanking me for the things I had sent him, and asking for a haver sack. I did not have one, but Mary Currey gave me one,[1] and I had it boiled for hours, but I could not make it look clean. I was ashamed to send it, but thinking that perhaps it might be better than nothing sent it with an apology—and some tobacco Mr Peter Recardi gave me.[2]

Coming home I met Mattie Luttrell and made her turn and walk with me. We went to tell Mrs Rayal good bye. She leaves in the morning for Ky, to remain during the war. Mat says she offended Lt Shaw dreadfully by taking the clerk for him. Tom Lewis, Jim Jones and John Miller have come in and taken the oath.[3] I do not wonder at the first. He has never been in the army, his health is bad, he had heard of his father's death and did not know how his mother & sisters could get along, and he has not said one word that I can hear of against our cause. The others are no loss to our side. Jones was disgraced two years ago, and both are drunken fellows. They tell all sorts of tales, say that eleven hundred men are coming in to take the oath, that the Confederacy cannot last three months longer, Longstreets men are starving and without shoes &e &e. Thank God I have no relation mean and low enough to turn traitor to his Country. Letter from Johnnie, Sam was well 20 of Jany.

Feb. 25. Thursday. I received a note from Lt Buchanan this morning very early thanking me & he also said he had written to ask me for a hat & cravat but it made no difference now. Oh! I felt when I read it that I had wronged him, in thinking for one moment he could prove false to every feeling of honor and take the oath to the vilest government that ever disgraced a civilized world. I sent him a hat of dear Johnnies and a cravat with something to eat, which I hope he got. The prisoners left this morning. Report says some were brought in this evening. I doubt it.

Feb. 26. Friday. Maj Price went up to Strawberry plains this morning to pay the troops there. As there was no one left but Gen Beatty, sister and I thought we would go to the table.[4] He is large, rather good looking, somewhere between thirty & forty I should think, is not an abolitionist so he says, and pleasant enough for a Yankee. Certainly would not set the river on fire with his intellect. I gave it to Brownlow, Baxter and Fleming. He said he had thought Baxter had always been a Union man. Was very much surprised when I told him he run for Southern Congress last Summer.

I saw in Louisville Journal a copy of the letter written by Mr Dodd to his father after he was condemned & a sketch of his life.[5] They murder a man & then cry over him. It has made me feel so miserably. I try not to think of him and his cruel fate. It makes me not only unhappy, but I feel perfectly fiendish. I believe I would kill a Yankee and not a muscle quiver. Oh! the intensity with which I hate them. I know it is wicked, but I have become so bad in the last few months, bad as I was before I was good. Oh! so good to what I am now. When I see a yankee going along with one leg or one arm I really feel glad, and wish it was the whole Yankee nation instead. I went down to Jeanies for a little while this afternoon.

Feb. 27. Saturday. Clear and pleasant. Reported fighting at Ringgold. Yanks say Dalton.[6] The Maj Price came back this evening. Gen Schofield is at the front two miles from Strawberry plains. Part of his army have crossed to follow Gen Longstreet. They are moving the pontoon from here [to] there. The bridge across the river here is finished. It is not very substantial. I wish it would be washed away. A Lt Bice is here tonight, he has been sent from Gen Schofield to Gen Granger[7] at Loudon with dispatches. Is to go down on the morning train & return as soon as possible.

Feb. 28. Sunday. Clear and pleasant. Stayed at home all day except late
in the evening went over to Mrs Currey's. Will & Jeanie came up this morning. I hear that a Confederate soldier has been shot in attempting to make
his escape, poor fellow. I hope it is not so. There must have been a mistake
about hanging a man Friday as there certainly was none hung.

Feb. 29. Monday. Raining all day. I commenced making my other calico
dress. I received a letter from Johnnie. He says he received a letter from
Maj Hatcher, Gen Stewarts A.A.G.[8] Sam was well on the 20th of Jany, stationed at Mobile. So I suppose he must have been exchanged. He says he
has sent mother a ring by Marsh Plumlee, who has been on to Johnsons
Island to see his brother, some say to try to get him to take the oath. He
said there that Knoxville was uninjured.[9]

March 1. Tuesday. Wrote to Johnnie this morning. Reports of a fight up
the road. Gen Beatty says all of Gen Wheeler's Cavalry have gone down
the road. They were passing through Maryville all last Tuesday & Wednesday. I hope soon to hear that the railroad has been cut below, or some other
mischief done by them. The bridge at Strawberry Plains has been washed
away. I hear there has been a reverse of the Federal arms in Florida. What I
have not been able to learn.[10]

March 2. Wednesday. I went up on Gay Street this morning. There seems
to be some excitement on hand, men hurrying back and forth. Several almost ran over me.

March 3. Thursday. Gen Longstreet is reported this side of Morristown,
within fifteen miles of Strawberry Plains.[11] Schofield is said to have crossed
all his force before the bridge was washed away, and now is considered is a
very close place, and making strenuous efforts to cross his men.

March 4. Friday. Sister & I dressed & went the rounds this morning to
see Mrs Newman, Ella Cocke, Mrs French, Miss Kate White & Cluss. Poor
Cluss. I feel sorry for her, but she is very careless. I dont see how in the
world a girl can get her own consent to be so slovenly. I would feel so much
more for her if she only would keep herself clean & whole, but dirt and rags

are my abomination and I cant see why she should be so forlorn because she has lost every thing & her mother is worse than she is. Miss Kate said that "Uncle Thomas" said there had been no mails for three days on account of the high water. Cluss [said] that Mary Craig told her they would have to stop on the road for Morgan had torn up the track (they left yesterday morning) and at Dinner Gen Beatty said he understood the bridge over the Hiwassie had been burnt. I hope it is true.

March 5. Saturday. Gen Schofield has come down from the front. Says Gen Longstreet has left (gone up a tree I guess, the Yankees never can find him) & all is quiet in front. Reported fighting at Dalton. I dont believe they have got to Dalton, and I hope we will whip them well. Also rumor of Gen Polk having whipped Sherman badly in Mississippi at Okolona (among the Rebels—the Yankees have it the other way).[12]

March 6. Sunday. Clear and Pleasant. I went round for Ella Cocke to go with me to the Confederate hospital to take some bandages & tracts. When we got to the house they have been using for the purpose for some time a Yankee told us they had been moved up to the Academy, and so we went up there. Did not go in as we were by ourselves. As we were coming past Mrs Cummings, we stopped and had a confab with her. She said she had been up there the day before and one poor fellow said that he did wish the ladies would come to see him, it did him so much good. I asked her if she would go with us some day if we stopped for her. She said certainly. As it was such a beautiful day, we did not want to come home yet. We went down to Jeanies and sat some time. When I came home I found they had been done [with] dinner a long time.

The Federals acknowledge to have lost from twelve hundred to two thousand men in Florida. All the papers speak of it as a disaster, complete failure &e. The fight below here was not quite such a victory as at first they wanted to make out. They did not take Dalton, though from their own account they certainly must have had men enough. I saw Mrs French this morning. She had just received a letter from Mrs Alex Morgan. Sallie died on the 20th of last month very suddenly. Mrs. Charles Alexander's baby is dead too. She has heard of Miss Nannie at Saltville.

Mr Joe King came in last night.[13] He has been over at Maryville about a month, ever since he left Mt Vale. While at the latter place a band of robbers with their faces masked came and took him off. His wife did not know but they had hung him, & threatened to shoot her, stole about fifteen thousand dollars worth from them. I would not live in the country now for any thing. A man named —— was killed a night or two since a few miles out of town. No Southern man's life is safe, even if he has taken the abominable oath, if he has any old personal enemies among the Union men or Renegades.

March 7. Monday. Last night we were woke up by some one pounding at the front door. It proved to be that Lt Bice, who was here before, & a Telegraph operator. Mother asked him this morning if all was quiet at Chattanooga. He said Yes. They had had quite a fight at Dalton, but they did not take the town, and had fallen back to Chattanooga. Rumor says Wheeler is after them too. I hope he is.

March 8. Tuesday. Gen Beatty left this morning at four oclock. I wish he had never come to the house for if he had not poor Leo would not have been hurt.[14] When the Gen went out this morning he got out. Not long after I heard some dogs fighting and then Leo came to the door. I did not let him in. A few minutes after I heard him in the celler and went down found he was badly hurt. After breakfast I went for Will to come & see him. He said he did not think he was badly hurt, he would be well in a week. He seemed very weak today, and tonight I felt so uneasy about him, I went over to get Col Eastin to come to see him. He said he thought he would be well in a few days. Still I do not feel satisfied. He says too one of Capt Whitman's clerks shot a dog last night. He thought probably it was Leo. I would not lose him for any thing. I have had him four years nearly, and he was only a month old. I have become so much attached to him, he is my shadow, follows me every where and seems to love me so much.

The Snap family are over in Mrs Hamilton's house, intend taking Yanks to board I hear.[15] Sherman has been whipped by our forces, and from Northern accounts badly. Rumor says Lee has whipped Meade in Virginia, and they have failed in their attempt on Richmond.[16] Longstreet is—they dont know where. I think they will find out some time. And the army (his) is represented to be in fine spirits, well clothed and fed.

March 9. Wednesday. I felt so worried all night about poor Leo, I could not sleep, and got up before daylight, and went down to see him, poor dog. He did not know me, he was dying. Oh! I felt so badly about it [I] got father to go for Dr Rogers. He could not come, then for Will. By the time he got here he was dead. It seems more like a human being had died than a dog. It even bought tears to Will's eyes. I expect it made him think of the baby, & he used to be so fond of him. I have been crying nearly the whole day. I cant help it. My heart aches when I think of his being dead. Will sent a man round to bury him. Dr R. came after he was dead. Said he thought he had probably been shot.

This afternoon father said Lieut Shaw had told him there were sixty prisoners in the jail, and sister & I thought we would go see them. When we went to the office the clerk Jim said there was only one man besides the Indians. I dont know why they have not been sent north with the other prisoners. While I was standing by the door talking, an Officer came up with a Confederate Lieut. I asked Lieut Shaw if I could speak to him. He said certainly. The officers who came with him very pertly said Oh! yes you can look at & talk to him as much as you like. I turned to him and asked in my very pleasantest manner, Where were you captured Lt. He looked slightly sneaking & replied "I was not captured at all." (I know my face was in a blaze. I would [have] liked to see some one slap his face) "You came in" I asked. He said "yes" the contemptable rascal. I turned round as fast and walked off in a hurry. The Yankee Officers laughed. I know Lt Shaw told him that I was the D——t rebel he ever saw.

From there we went to see Mrs French & Mrs McClannahan. Not long after we came home Capt Whitman came with a Capt McAlister to get board for himself, wife & child.[17] Of course mother had to say they could come. I hate the idea of Yankee woman & children in the house. We have whipped them above here at Panther Springs.[18] Letter from Johnnie & I answered it.

March 10. Thursday. It rained heavily last night. Capt McAlister came this morning. He is the nephew of old Col McAlister of Sav.[19] and studied law there. Knows a great many of fathers friends as does his wife, who seems very much of a Lady. They arrived two days since & have been staying at Gen Carters. The Capt & I got at it tonight. He said he heard of me before he came here. Father, he says, is considered a good Union man, Mother a very proper person, but one of the daughters was an outrageous rebel. I told him I was perfectly willing for them to consider me so, and if I thought there was any chance of them sending me South I would cut up some anticks most certainly. I am glad to hear they consider father a good Union man, as long as he has taken the oath, for that being the case they will not make him responsible for any thing I may do, and I expect sometime I will do something devilish—that is just the word, though not a lady like one.

Poor Leo. I miss him so much, turn round expecting to see him every time I hear a noise. I did not think any one could love a dumb animal as much as I did him, and miss him as sadly. Mrs. Currey came over this morning & took tea. I hear that there is a report in town that Mrs Kain went to head Quarters after she had received her orders and begged to be allowed to take the oath. Said she was a northern woman & had always been a Union woman but had never dared to say so. How on earth such a thing could have been started I cant imagine, at least could not till I heard the fountain from which it emanated was Mrs Longward. Of course I wondered no longer. She like her father needs not the slightest foundation for any structure, however elaborate or gigantic. I wonder what Mrs K could say if she could hear it.

March 11. Friday. No news of any importance today. I am told the pickets were run in last night two miles above here.[20] Some say our saints were that near to Knoxville. Capt McAlister told me tonight that he had seen Gen Carter and had quite a long talk with him, during which he (Gen C) had requested him to caution me, as I would certainly be sent South if I were not more prudent. That I had been very active &e, and the military here had from my actions and conversations been led to believe me a very violent rebel, one who would sell her soul and body for the benefit of the Confederates. I told him I certainly would lay down my life willingly did I know by so doing I would do the Confederacy the least good. That I had never done any thing I would not do again or said any thing I would not say over under the same circumstances. The only thing I have ever done was to wave to our poor fellows as they were going north to prison, and there I forgot for the moment I was not free but was living under a despotism. That if they sent me south they would not punish me very much. I'd have been there long ago if father & mother had not been so much opposed to it &e &e. Gen Carter is foolish if he thinks he is going to frighten me. I am not afraid of him or any other Yankee living or dead. The Capt says Capt Whitman told him the same thing about me.

One of his clerks named Price told Lusie he shot my dog, the triffling rascal.[21] Oh! wont I have an opportunity some time to pay off a few of the debts I owe to the miserable wretches, and wont I do it with a good will. Capt McA told mother Gen Carter was very much surprised to hear she was a relation of Admiral Renshaw. I suppose she should have gone and informed him of the fact on his first arrival in Knoxville. He (Gen C) is an old navy officer.[22]

March 12. Saturday. Clear and Pleasant. Some regiments left for the front this morning. There are pickets on the road again two miles out. This afternoon sister told me Will said Mrs Smith told him this morning there was a Lieut here looking for me, as he had a letter from either Camp Chase or Johnson Island for me. So I posted down to see her about it. She does not know his name. It was the first of last week he was hunting for me, so I dont suppose I will ever get it. How stupid of him not to drop it in the office, and for people not to know where Miss Ellen House lives, particularly when she had moved twice within three weeks lately. I wish I knew who it was from.

I went down to Mrs Frenches for a few minutes with Ella Cocke. She says Gen Longstreet sent in a flag of truce to Gen Schofield requesting him not to destroy [the] bridges and rail-road as he intended to occupy the country. Gen S. replied he expected to hold the country therefore he certainly should not destroy them.[23]

March 13. Sunday. Clear and pleasant. Jeanie & Will came round this morning. Mr Helms came home yesterday. He says "France has recognized

the South, and it is in the northern papers which came yesterday." I hope it
is so. I am sure it will shorten the war. Capt McAlister says the North will
subjugate the South—if she wont submit she will be exterminated. I told
him I had rather see both my brothers dead than take the oath to any such
government as his. Mr Abner Jackson had quite a little fracus on the street
yesterday with Col Barriger.[24] It seems a day or two ago the Col ordered him
out of his office. Yesterday they met. Mr Jackson denounced him as a cow-
ard & infamous villain &e. Gen Carter advised Mr J. to go home & stay
there. Will and Jeanie came around this morning for a little while. No army
news today. Wrote to Mr Spicer & Aunt Mary.

March 14. Monday. Clear and pleasant. I went to every store in town
this morning to try to get some blk trimming for a dress for mother & had
my trouble for my pains. The Military here are expecting a fight above here
in a few days. I hope Longstreet will not disappoint them. I have no fears of
the result. Will & Jeanie came round to tea this evening.

March 15. Tuesday. Clear and cold. The Northern papers say that Gen
Grant has received his commission as Lt. Gen of the U.S. Army and has
gone to see after Meade.[25] If Gen Lee should give him a slight whipping
while he is there, his head will be off too. Schofield is at the front. A great
battle is expected to come off very soon, one which the Yankees say will
determine the fate of East Tenn. Rumors of a skirmish above here today. I
do not suppose it amounted to any thing. Some more Indians were brought
in on Saturday. I hear that the two which were sent out on a scout brought
them in. They had them up on Gay Street having their likenesses taken. I
have not been out of the house today.

March 16. Wednesday. Clear and very cold. Mary White came round
this morning to bring a ring which Johnnie had sent in a bundle to her
from Hugh by M. Plumlee. It is very pretty. She brought a necklace and
ring which her brother sent. They are beautiful. Northern papers say that
Grant says the capture of Richmond is of much more importance than
Georgia and Alabama or both, and his plan will be to mass his men there. I
hope he will. Gen Lee is fully able to cope with him. There is a rumor on

the street today that "France & England will put an end to the war if the South will abolish slavery, and that Pres. Davis thinks favorably of it." I dont believe any thing of the kind. It would be disgraceful in my opinion.

There has been a fight up the road, and the Yankees [have] been driven back six miles.[26] Gen Schofields commission as Maj Gen has not been confirmed yet. If he is whipped of course it never will be, so I do not suppose he is very anxious to fight. The papers say Sherman has returned to Vicksburg and gone down the river to see Banks, but nothing is said of the army, or the manner of its return. I hear from a Yank who ought to know that it returned to Vicksburg in small squads, completely whipped. There was a report here a day or two since that Gen Johnson had Tyners station. It seems to have been without foundation, as the cars still come through from Chattanooga.

I went over to Mrs Currey's a little while this evening. There I heard that Mrs Vicks is to have a concert tomorrow night in the Episcopal Church & decorate the building with flags.[27] She says "the Rebels had flags hung in the church and they had not as much right to put them there as she had to hang the Stars & Stripes. (It is true we did hang two flags in the church Christmas year, and it had the desired effect—it kept all the tories away.) The Chancel is to be used as a stage. I really think that church has been desecrated more than any of the others have been in using them as hospitals. She has been writing for Sue Boyd to return, that young lady arrived today.[28] She says she has been north to purchase her summer wardrobe. She had free transportation there and back.

March 17. Thursday. Cold and windy. The people here say that President Davis has issued a proclamation freeing all the slaves. I dont believe it. They say too Gen Longstreet is retreating and burning the bridges after him. True of course. This afternoon Sister & I went to see Mary & Fannie Alexander and sit most of the afternoon. Fannie was out. We then went to see Mattie Luttrell. She says she is going to school to Mrs Haire.[29] It was either that or go north, and so she chose that. I saw Mrs French & Ella Cocke for a few minutes. They say a flag of truce was sent in a few days since to Morristown, conducted by Gen Buckner's Staff.[30] A Union woman who came in last night says Gen Longstreet had received orders to leave East Tenn and go to the aid of Gen Polk, but since Shermans defeat and return to Vicksburg the order had been countermanded. Thank Heaven for that. I would feel dreadfully if he should leave.

Oh! how I do wish I was in Dixie. I feel sometimes as if I would suffocate, these Yankee's Devils—there thats beautiful [language] for a young lady—but the vile creatures have contaminated the morals of the whole place. Capt McAlister & I have it hot and heavy every day. In my opinion he thinks he has been treated badly by the government. His clerk came tonight, his name Wilson. Capt McA says he is a very nice gentleman. I think he is a very great fool. We never have a moments privacy now. They come walking into the sitting room at any and all times, never think of knocking. I hope they wont stay long. I venture to bet no other Yankees have free access to it. One comfort [is] no tory women have been here to see her. I expect they are half way afraid to come to the house. They had better be, for I will most certainly insult them if they do & give me half a chance. Perhaps if I did Carter would send me my orders to leave. That would be glorious indeed. Mrs Currey came over and stayed to tea.

March 18. Friday. Very windy. Nothing of any importance from the front today. The Capt says Schofield will not move very fast. He is taking his time. I doubt if he takes his own time when he returns to Knoxville. Grant is to make a tour of all the different points of importance. He has made Sherman take his command. Col Wolford has made a speech in Lexington Ky. denouncing Lincoln as a usurper &e. The consequence is, he is in prison. I expect there will be stirring times there very soon.[31] I see in one of the papers an account of the plans &e of the Dahlgren attempt to take Richmond. It was the most most infamous thing that ever was contrived. Thank God it did not succeed.[32] Received a letter today from Mr Spicer. He with a number of others has been moved to Rock Island, Ill.[33] He says he is much more comfortable than at Camp Chase. We have not heard from Johnnie this week. I hope we may tomorrow.

March 19. Saturday. I felt so badly this morning I did not get up till after breakfast. There has been a fight up the road in which the Yanks did not whip and they have fallen back twenty five miles. Yankee rumor says to that there has been an attack made on the train below in which the Rebels were driven back. Dr. Piggott was in this morning. He says all the sick are getting along very well with one exception. He does not know when he will be sent out, says he is afraid he will take root in East Tenn. Capt McAlister and himself had quite an argument in which the Capt did not get much the best. He is so abominably self-opinionated, so fond of talking about his family being a ruling one for so many years, and about his loving the Southern people so, and his being a christian—and having his hands clean, that he used all his influence to prevent the war and all that kind of stuff—and the next minute says the Southern people must & will be exterminated rather than the Union be destroyed. I do believe it would afford him sincere pleasure to see the whole scale lynching of the rebels which he advocated so strongly carried into execution before his own eyes.

Oh! I do get furious to hear him talk. It seems to me sometimes that I feel perfectly reckless of what I say or do. It is growing on me every day. As long as I could keep out of the way of the vile creatures I did it, and got along very well, but since I cant turn round without seeing one, and have them eternally in our sitting room, always introducing the subject, I cant contain myself. I say all sorts of things about all their officers & men, abuse Carter or any of them, and say every thing impudent that comes into my head. If Gen Longstreet dont come soon goodness only knows where it will end.

I hear that Gen Carter says Col Keith ought to have put Mrs Hamilton in prison because she said she gloried in being a Rebel, and if he had her in his power again he would certainly do it. Maj Gratz says Mrs Hamilton told him the reason she did not want to go south was that Sam H. and herself were to be married as soon as he returned from the North. This afternoon what did Capt & Mrs McA. have to do but go to see Mrs Brownlow—rather reversing the order of things. She told them that she never had done any work in her life and it came very hard now, as she has lost a servant and had to do it. Nothing like telling a good one, and she also said that there were many ladies here who would do themselves the pleasure of calling on her as soon as they knew she was here, was sorry she had not known it sooner. If the tory women come here I'll insult them certain and sure.

March 20. Sunday. Cold and gloomy. I passed a miserable night, suffered intensely with my head. The consequence was I did not get up till near dinner time. Will came up this morning. He says Col [Capt?] Wolford is here, he came up last night. Says there had been no attack made on the cars. I suppose it was to cover the fight above, and the men they brought here wounded which they made out were on the train at the time of the attack were in reality wounded in the fight above. They lost three regiments captured in it. Some say the army is being pressed back to Strawberry plains by our noble Gen Longstreet. A man who came in from his lines last night says Our Gallant Gen Breckinridge is in Command, Gen L. having gone to Richmond.[34]

The Ninth Army Corps came in yesterday from above. They say there that there is a raid to be made into Ky and the troops have been ordered back on that account. They are going to make a grand stratagetic movement and prevent it. Grant is to do wonders. He has risen very fast. He used to haul wood in St. Louis by the load himself and all that kind of thing, fit companion for the rail-splitter. This man Crocket who came in last night says Our army has been very heavily reinforced, and is in splendid condition, that they are conscripting every one. That is exactly right. If a man has not spirit enough to fight for liberty, he ought to be made to do it or leave. At the present state of affairs every man is needed, and every one should do his duty.

Dr Piggott said yesterday that President Davis had issued a proclamation—that France had made an offer of assistance if we would abolish slavery, and he left it to the vote of the Army.[35] They are doing the fighting, and they have the right to determine it. Mrs Dr Frank Ramsey is drawing rations from government. I wish her family was twice as large as it is so they would have to give her twice as much, particularly if they are short of supplies. Mrs Currey came over this evening. That little ape Wilson was in the room and as we were talking he must put his tongue in—these Yankees have more impudence—and commenced about the South &e.[36] He made me so mad. Sister got up and went out of the room & banged the door after her. A little while after I did the same thing. Lady like—very—but people are not responsible for what they do while living among such creatures.

March 21. Monday. Cold. Sister & I went to see Cluss, poor girl. I do feel so sorry for her, but if she only would be more particular about her appearance, I would feel so much more for her. Her mother has been very sick for three weeks. She looks dreadfully. Rach Rogers came in while I was there. She says she received a letter this morning from her father by a flag of truce. (Mary Francisco has a son. I expect she is perfectly delighted). She says she knows there is some splendid news for us from the way he wrote, but of course he could not mention it. When we went in Mrs Baxter [was there], but I commenced talking about the prisoners at Camp Chase &e and run her off very soon.

When we came from there home we found Jeanie and Mary Hazen here. As she was going out Capt Lunt came in to see Capt McA. He says he thinks Capt Colby has an album for me. I hope so. I want so much to have one. I told him I wanted it to put Grey coats in. The cotton that had been hauled out to the Depot to send North caught fire in some way this after-noon—and a good deal of it was burned. Good. I wish all had been.

March 22. Tuesday. Snowing all day. This morning I received a letter from dear Johnnie, also one from Lieut Buchanan from Camp Chase. Johnnie is very well, wrote in very good spirits. I had written to him that Maj Price told mother she might rest assured he was going to the Island to see him & added as a matter of course he was a gentleman &e. Johnnie says he may be, but he is inclined to doubt it from the Company he keeps, and I read it out before that little fool Wilson. He by the way told father yesterday he was afraid that he had made himself obnoxious to the ladies by some thing he had said. He hoped they would not [think] the worse of him for it &e. I let him see very plainly that I did not like the way he talked several times.

By the way, yesterday afternoon someone knocked and like a fool I went to the door. Who should it prove [to be] but a Yankee Gen to see Capt McA. I told him to walk in and I'd send a servant to call him, and was not overly polite to him. Who should it prove to be but his majesty Gen Carter. I dont expect his opinion of me improved very much. I hope it did not. Maybe he will send me out yet. I see in one of the Northern papers that President Davis has appointed the 9th day of April as a day of Fasting & prayer.[37]

March 23. Wednesday. The walking has been miserable today—from the snow melting, and I have had to stay in the house all day. It frets me to death, these everlasting Yankees.

March 24. Thursday. Cold. Sister and I went down this morning to see Jeanie. She was out. We then walked over to see Miss Harriet Rogers. Mrs. R has returned from Athens. They still think John is alive. I hope he is. Oh! how I should love to see him. It is now fifteen months since he has been heard from. When we came home we found Dr Piggott here. He dined with us. In the afternoon I went over to Mrs Currey's and sat till dark. I cant stand it in the house with the Yankees all the time. There is a rumor today that there has been a fight above here in which the Yankees had the worst of it. Some say it was at Rutledge, others at Mossy Creek. The Yanks in the house deny it of course.[38]

March 25. Friday. It snowed again last night, and has been raining off and on all day. I wrote a long long letter today to Emily and requested her to send it to Sam. I do not know his direction. If the Yankees were to get hold of it and find out who wrote it, there would be a fuss, and no mistake. The best of it is that I wrote it here in the sitting room right before Capt McAlister and he kept asking me who I was writing such a long letter to. I do not suppose he thought for a moment it was to go to Dixie without Gen Carters approval.

No news today. They deny there having been a fight up the road. I see by the Northern papers that President Davis has appointed the 9th of April as a day of fasting and prayer, also that on the first of next month the present Confederate money is to be taken up at two thirds it value. I think if it is so, it is a very good thing.[39]

March 26. Saturday. Pleasant. This afternoon I went over to take my letter to Mrs Mitchell. She says she has no doubt but that she can send it through. I hope she may be able to, as I am very anxious to have it go. I stopped at Jeanies on my way home. Mary is in town. I asked them to come round to dinner tomorrow. They said they would. Mary says she hears Will Rogers is going to marry Centhy Brooks.[40] I have heard that for some time.

March 27. Sunday. Clear and pleasant. Will, Jeanie and Mary Hazen dined with us today. After dinner Mary, sister & I started down to see Mrs French, stopped to have a talk with Rach Rogers. She told us Mrs F was out, so we thought we would go and see Cluss. Stopped at Mr Whites gate and had a talk with Mrs Maud Mordic.[41] Stayed there till church was out to see the Yanks come out. Oh! how different looking from Dixies noble sons. It makes me sick to look at them. Mrs McClusky is better, but she looks dreadfully.[42] I dont believe she will live through the coming summer, and what will become of poor Cluss. She is so perfectly helpless. I do pity her. The old lady was lying on the bare mattress, not a sheet on the bed. As we were coming back we met Mat Luttrell. She says Gen Carter says he intends sending all the Rebel ladies out. How I do hope it will [happen]. I'll go gladly. Sister went home with Mary tonight after tea.

March 28. Monday. Just after breakfast I went down to Jeanies, and Sister, Mary, Will Hazen and I went to the gallery for Mary to have [her] Photograph taken where we regularly spent the morning. Mary succeeded in getting a good one after many failures. When I came home I found a letter from Lt Manning. I think it was right impudent of him to write me and ask me to answer very soon. I have never seen him, and because I felt sorry for him on account of his being a Confederate soldier & having lost a leg, was no reason why he should presume upon it and write me as if it was a matter of course I would answer it.

Dr Piggott dined with us today. He says he does not see that there is any chance for him to get through the lines, thinks it very probable he will have to go by Fortress Monroe.[43] He had ordered a uniform coat and goodness knows he needs it bad enough. Maj Gratz told him today he could not get it, his clothes were as good as their officers in the Libby Prison. Dr. told him he had nothing to do with Libby prison.[44] After some time the dutch Maj told him he would go and see it, and if it was not too fine he could have it. He said also he had heard three days ago that he had ordered it. How these Yankees do pry into every little thing, things that a Gentleman and Confederate would never think of, or if they did would never stoop to.

I went over to Mrs Curreys and spent the afternoon. These Yankees here expect to leave next week. I hope and trust they will, and let us have a little quiet and privacy once more. They say there are no Rebels any where in front. They certainly have gone to Virginia. Some say Gen Longstreet had mounted some of his men and sent them to Ky on a raid. Whether there are any Rebels in East Tenn or not there was a raid made on Louisville (ten miles from here) when they captured the Provost Marshall among other goods, cattle &e.[45] I wish they would come here & capture me.

Gen Carter has told several that he intends to send all the Rebel girls South. He could not please them better. If I only could get clothes enough made to last me two or three years, I would like to start tomorrow. The widow Fatio has married a Yankee Capt. They say she is crazy.[46]

March 29. Tuesday. It rained very heavily last night, and has been cold, damp and disagreeable all day. Gens Thomas & Sherman arrived here to day.[47] Capt McAlister says Sherman will go on from here and take Richmond. I expect so. No news of any kind today. There was a hundred bales of cotton burnt out at the depot the other day. I wish it had been twice as much. Some children playing out there set it on fire by accident. Mr Peeds son was among them.[48] They were taken up to head Quarters, and they were frightened about to death. I was mistaken, only Sherman came today.

March 30. Wednesday. It has been a very unpleasant day, a little rain, an attempt at snow, with a good deal of wind. Nothing of any kind today. I received a letter from Cousin Annie. Auntie is well.

March 31. Thursday. Clear and pleasant. Sister and I intended going down to Wills quite early this morning. But Cordie Fletcher came in and sat quite a long time. I like her very much. She is very lady like, very well educated and a thorough going Rebel for all she has taken the oath. After she left we went down to Jeanies. Mary had left two April fools for Tom Van Gilder. One sister was to copy and the other Jeanie, and I sent him one beside, which I think pretty good considering I wrote it. I enclosed it to Mr Will Rogers, and requested him to hand it to that little Turncoat. Here it is.

> Oh! Tommy dear, you used to talk
> E'er Blue coats came this way
> As if you were the best of Rebs
> Why are you Yank today?
> You used to say you had no use
> For this same Yankee nation
> But now after the shoulder straps

You run like all creation.
And you were always wont to say
You loved the Rebels dearly.
So a man may change his politics
As he does his dress coat—yearly.
I think that all you want just now
Is to make plenty money.
Whichever army should be here
You'd call them dearest honey.
A storehouse you have rented here
Brought good from Cincinatti.
The clerks you have are gentlemen
I don't mean to flatter.
But Tom it is ridiculous
The way you strut around.
The clerks have all the work to do
While you parade the town.
And then you're always talking of
My show case and my store.
What folks of any sense must think
I cannot tell I'm sure.
Now that you own the drug store too
(Beside that one at first)
Your friends are very much afraid
Your little head will burst.
It is not the variety
Of ideas you have there
That causes any one to think
Reason there is for fear.
But it is the enormous size
(Who all with eyes must see)
Of the only idea you possess
And that is Myself—ME.
Now Tom my dear, do simmer down
I think t'would be but civil
And not be troubling me to write
You, every first of April.

I gave them all three to Mr. Wilson tonight and got him to drop them in the office for me.[49] Maj Huwald was taken today.[50] I cant understand it at all. He says he did not desert, did not come in to take the oath, he came to see his wife. He was taken at her house, in broad daylight, dressed in a full Artillery Maj's Uniform (Confederate). So they cannot hang him as a spy, as some say they will. I expect they would like to. I hope they wont do any thing with him. Five of his men are in jail here too. Ella Cocke came to see us today, but we were out. I am sorry that we missed her.

April 1. Friday. Raining and gloomy. Ella Cocke came round this morning to spend the day with us, and as it was so unpleasant we made her stay tonight. It has been right amusing to see that little fool Wilson. He has been afraid to move or speak, lest some one should make an April fool of him. I wonder [if] master Tommy liked his. I expect he was slightly angry.

April 2. Saturday. Ella insisted on going home this morning, much against my will. I was quite busy till four oclock, when I went over to Mrs Currey's. Mary Polk says there has been some fifty prisoners been brought in. Mrs Gates came in while I was there. She says thirty were brought in today. They say Gen Longstreet has gone to Va. Gen Forrest has made a raid into Western Ky. He has taken Paducah, captured a large amount of Government stores &e.[51] Good for him. They are very much afraid of one [a raid] into Eastern Ky. Hope they wont be disappointed. Rumor says Gen Buell is to supercede Schofield.[52]

April 3. Sunday. Clear and pleasant. I intended going round to the jail today, but Jeanie sent up this morning to ask sister and I to come down and stay with her. Mary was quite sick, and Will had gone out to the Brook.[53] So of course we went down. When Will came in late this evening he said Mary was really quite sick, but he thought if she had a Dr attending her, she would be well in a few days. Dr Rogers is attending her. A Lt. Col. Pierson told Mr. Branner this morning that there had been a raid into Cleveland in which the 4th Army Corps had been whiped out.[54] Capt McAlister says it is not so. He denied every thing.

April 4. Monday. Very unpleasant, raining most of the day. Capt McAlister received a letter from his son this morning—he is [an] Ensign in the Navy—in which he says in the late raid on Paducah by Forrest he lost three hundred men, the Yankees fourteen. Cant they tell the truth sometimes? No news to-day. Another man has been murdered a few miles from town, still nothing is done. I hope it will clear up tomorrow for I am very anxious to go to the Jail.

April 5. Tuesday. Clear and Pleasant. Sister and I went down to Jeanies this morning after going to some of the stores. She is very well. About four oclock this afternoon father came home and told us that the families who had been expecting to leave for so long a time had just been notified that they would leave tomorrow morning at eight oclock. So I went right down to Mrs Strongs to see Nina Danner. I gave her a copy of Mr Dodds letter to Col Gustave Cook of the 8th Texas[55] (I was afraid to send the original. I should dislike very much to have it lost), also the Members of the Court Martial, Witnesses &e. I hope he will get them. She promised to send them, also to write to Emily Howell for me.

When I came home I went over to see if I could help Mrs Currey she said she was so unwell. Gen Carter had given her permission to stay till Friday, when others would be sent. Mr Rayal came last night.

April 6. Wednesday. Clear and pleasant. That old Rascal Capt McAlister went off today, owing mother $8.00. He has acted the rascal to perfection, would not even pay for wood and lights. I told mother all along he would cheat her, but she would not believe me. Sister and I went down to Jeanies for a little while. She says Robt Strong is very ill.[56] As we were coming from there we met Mr Rayal and Will Hazen going down. Mr R says he saw Uncle John just before starting. He was not well. Neither was his wife Lizzie, [who] had not entirely recovered from the attack of fever she had last fall. He says Uncle John is a very good Union man, but he never prays for the President of the United States. Old Dr Paxton died last night and was buried this afternoon by the Masons.

After dinner sister and I went to see Ella Cocke, but she was out, then to see Miss Kate White & Cluss. Old Mrs McClusky is still very sick. I am afraid she will not live long. Poor Cluss. As we were passing Mr Alexanders Mary Hill stopped us, and we had quite a little confab in the street.

Wilson said this morning that there were a great many to be sent out. He had just come from Head Quarters. Asked me if I wanted go, said sister would not be sent out, she stood very differently to what I did. They may send me out soon as they please. Mrs Ramsey, Mr Strong, Mrs Dr Crozier, Mrs Gates, Miss Rogan and others left this morning. I believe I will die if I stay here much longer. I never felt in my life as I have lately. Oh! how delighted I would be to be free once more.

April 7. Thursday. Cloudy. Before we were dressed this morning mother came in and said Robt Strong was dead, and had been carried down to Wills. She wanted me to go right down and bring Jeanie up with me to stay till after he was buried. So I went but she said she could not leave till her mother came in. As all his family were there, she was expecting her any minute. She did not come though as Mary was not well enough for her to leave her. I am very sorry, for I fear the excitement will make Jeanie sick. Mrs Currey was notified today that she would not leave before Monday. She came over tonight to stay till she starts. I begged father for a long time to go to head Quarters tomorrow and apply for permisson for me to go with her, but he refused to do it. Says he wants to keep the family together as long as he can.

April 8. Friday. Well it has come at last. I am ordered to leave on Monday for the South. My orders came about ten. Mother is perfectly furious about it. At first she said she would come too, but we told her that would never do, so she said sister should come with me. I declare she thinks I am a baby and not fit to take care of myself. She went with sister to ask permission for her to come too. Old Gratz objected, said they did want to send her. She had been very prudent. Said he would have to see Schofield about it &e. Mother told him she would like to know why I had been sent out. He would not tell her for some time. At last he said they had a great many charges against me and they had been thinking of sending me South for some time, but the immediate cause was my insulting Mrs McAlister. It is about the only thing they could accuse me of that I have never done & I never have done that. I almost wish I had now. He said it was reported by a third person, and when Capt McA was asked about it he was a gentleman and was obliged to acknowledge it. Also that Parson Brownlow heard it and urged the matter till Gen Carter ordered me out, that they would have the charges written out by afternoon & I could have them.[57] I wish I could get them but no one would go for them for me. I have a great mind to go after them myself.

Some time after Sister came home, her permission came too. Father takes it very quietly. When I told him all he asked was if I was well supplied with thick shoes. He thinks them essential to my health. When Mr Wilson came home I opened on him. Told him I had received my orders to go South thanks to him. I suppose the charge was my insulting Mrs McA, and reported by a third person, that third person must be him & he had reported what he knew to be false. He said I was very much mistaken. He was very sorry I had been ordered out and had never said anything about me. I replied I was not sorry to go, but glad to find out he was more of a gentleman than I had taken him to be. Cordie Fletcher came over and offered to help me. I have a great many things to get, & am very much afraid I will forget many things I need. One thing is certain. I am going to take my derringer and Johnnies's Uniform &e to a dead most certainty. Reported fight down at Cleveland. The Yankees here say that Joe Johnson is nothing for miles of that place.

April 9. Saturday. Reported fighting at Cleveland today, and Madam rumor says we have Missionary Ridge again. We have been in confusion all day, mother just as excited as she could be. A good many persons have been in today. They keep me from doing any thing, and yet if they did not come I would feel slighted. I went up to the stores this afternoon to get some little nic nacs and another trunk. As I was passing a number of soldiers, I heard one say there she is now. Really for a poor little insignificant woman the Yankees all seem to concern them selves very much about me. Gen Carter says he has had me watched for a month. He need not to have taken the trouble to do that. Not that I would not do any thing but because I had not the power. Met Drs North & Piggott. They are both going. It is funny that I should be going at the same time. I have said all along I was going when they did, but had no idea that I would.

April 10. Sunday. I have had a dreadful headache almost all day, caused I suppose by excitement. The Alexanders, Mattie Luttrell, Mrs French, Miss Kate White, Cordie Fletcher, Miss O'Conner, Will Hazen, Dr Piggott and a number of others have been here today. Capt Riddle came to examine our trunks. As he came in Will introduced him to us. I said "I am glad you have come to examine our trunks because I have heard you were such a perfect gentleman." The bait took. He never looked at a single thing, and the little fellow he had with him was just as polite as possible. I only wish I had known who was coming. I would have had a lot of contraband packed away. After he left we went down to Jeanies.[58]

[Ellen's entries for the remainder of 1864 become much briefer at this point, as she was forced to record events in a pocket diary while enduring life as a refugee in Bristol, Tennessee, and Abingdon, Virginia.]

April 11. Monday. Left Knoxville this morning. Arrived at Bulls Gap at 2 oclock and will have to remain all night. There is but one house here & all that mostly occupied by the Military. I dont know how we will do.

April 12. Tuesday. Left Bulls Gap this morning about ten, did not get to Blue Springs till about four. The roads are in a dreadful state. The nine miles seemed like nineteen. Will have to stay tonight.

April 13. Wednesday. We heard this morning that the train would be down today but it has not come. We will have to spend another night here.

April 14. Thursday. Mrs Currey came today. There is no knowing how long we will have to stay.

April 15. Friday. Dr North went up to Greenville with a flag of truce to see if there is any chance of our leaving this place.

April 16. Saturday. The Yankees here with the flag of truce say if the cars do not come down for us soon we will all be sent back to Knoxville, Sue Ramsey & I put under guard and sent to Montreal.

April 17. Sunday. Spent the day as usual wandering over the country. Our provisions are getting very low. Hope the train will come tomorrow.

April 18. Monday. Train came about eleven oclock. Left immediately. Arrived at Bristol at about eight. Kirby Smith has gained a brilliant victory in Louisiana. Captured fifteen hundred prisoners.[59] Capt Ford met us at the train.

April 19. Tuesday. Dr Morrow came up to the Hotel and invited us to come down to his house.[60] We have seen a great many Knoxville people. The troops are all going from here to Gen Lee.

April 20. Wednesday. Commenced writing Sam but have been interrupted about a dozen times. I wish I knew where he was and how he is.

April 21. Thursday. Spent the day with Mrs Kain. Thinly missed seeing Col Ashby, Maj Watts and Capt Hayes.[61] We have gained a victory in N.C. 2000 Y[ankee] prisoners, 30 guns taken, 150,000 pounds bacon, &e &e.[62]

April 22. Friday. General Forrest has taken Fort Pillow, put most of the garrison out of harm's way, killed every officer there. Good for him. I think he did exactly right.[63]

April 24. Sunday. Capt Ford came for me and I went to our church the first time since the lst of Sept. Walked out to see Mrs K in the afternoon.

April 25. Monday. Fight today at Carters Station. Reports says there are four hundred Yankees. We repulsed them. Gen Jackson sent up for a battery which has been sent to him. He killed the Yank commanding.[64] We leave at 12 1/2 tonight for Abingdon.[65]

April 26. Tuesday. Arrived at Abingdon at 2 1/2 this morning. Dr Currey met us at the train, and brought us to his house. Wants us to stay with them. Met Floyd King this evening in the St. He is Lt [Col] of Artillery.[66]

April 27. Wednesday. A fight expected at Zollicoffer.[67] They are sending troops down. Wrote Capt. Ford.

April 28. Thursday. Nothing of importance today.

April 29. Friday. Men coming back. Yanks gone back towards Knoxville then up the railroad after them.

April 30. Saturday. Cloudy. Maj Watts called this afternoon with Dr Ramsey & Lieut McGuire.[68]

May 1. Sunday. Went to church and heard the same sermon that I heard last Sunday. Gen Buckner ordered to the Trans-Mississippi Dept. Gen Kirby Smith reported killed.[69]

May 2. Monday. Walked out to see Mrs Morgan found her gone to Saltville.[70] I stopped to see Mrs Ramsey. Got caught in the rain & ruined my new purple dress.

May 3. Tuesday. Rumors of a Yankee raid here. Most of the military have left for Eastern Va. Wrote Capt Ford asking him to look out for an opportunity for us to go South.

May 4. Wednesday. Clear and cold. Another victory in La. Banks whipped again.[71] In the evening Lt McGuire and Lt Brown called.

May 5. Thursday. This afternoon we all walked up to the hill overlooking the city. Dr [Currey] took his spy glass along with him. When we came home the three Miss Johnsons called at night [with?] Lt McGuire & little Riddle.

May 6. Friday. Clear and pleasant. Tom Wallace and Will Armstrong called this morning & Capts Wallace and Maynard in the afternoon.[72] Went to Soldiers prayer meeting this afternoon. A telegram that the Yanks attacked Ewells & Hill & Heaths commands yesterday & were repulsed with heavy loss. A thousand prisoners. Our loss heavy.[73] Letter from Capt Ford.

May 7. Saturday. Clear & pleasant. Confirmation of the news we received yesterday. Yankees reported coming on a raid from various points. Sending men to Saltville for the defense.

[At his point, Ellen reports many military actions, most of them rumors. Only those with some foundation have been commented on in the notes.]

May 8. *Sunday*. Many rumors none very pleasant. Raiders said to have Dublin, but doubtful.[74] Gen Lee reputed to be following up the Yankees, and Burnside whipped by Bushrod Johnson.[75]

May 9. *Monday*. Considerable excitement. Capt Martin went up to Saltville with his guard and all the men from the hospitals well enough to go.[76]

May 10. *Tuesday*. Yankee Raiders at Dublin. Cavalry & infantry both: some ten thousand. Yankee reported below here at Kingsport coming here.[77] Yellow flags flying.[78]

May 11. *Wednesday*. Some say Morgan has whipped the Yanks & they are retreating. Others [say] they are still in Dublin. Killed everybody there, some 300. Burnt New River bridges, &e.

May 12. *Thursday*. Conflicting rumors from the soldiers. Some say they killed three hundred of our men at Dublin. Confirmation of Lee capturing 3 thousand yankees. Johnston whipped Thomas.

May 13. *Friday*. Rain & cloudy. Johnston reported to have gained a decided victory over Thomas at Charleston. White & negro soldiers fighting at Kingsport. Nothing definite from the raiders. Lee says he has captured one wing of Grants army.

May 14. *Saturday*. Raiders left Dublin. Lee reported to have captured, killed & wounded 30,000. General Stewart Killed. Hardee not Johnston at Cleveland. Total sur[render] 8000 to Price. Taylor demanded the surrender of Banks.[79]

May 15. *Sunday*. Nothing authentic from Lee & Richmond. Johnston reported to have whipped the right wing of Thomas & have possession of Cleveland. Morgan sent 150 prisoners into Saltville, two hundred more to be brought in.

May 16. Monday. Lee still repulsing the Yankees. The last fight we heard of was on the 14th. Our loss 1000 Yanks 20,000. Yankee raiders within five miles of Richmond. Bitter fighting between there & Fredericksburg. All railroads torn up leading to R[ichmond]. Capt Martin returned 10,000. T[homas] reported at Resaca in Johnston's rear.[80]

May 17. Tuesday. Gen Breckinridge had a fight with Averell and whipped him. Beauregard captured four thousand of Butlers men and up to the time the last dispatch left had killed, wounded and captured 60,000.[81]

June 2. Thursday. Dr Currey says that General Johnston has not whipped Thomas, the latter is being reinforced by troops from Ala. Miss Nannie Martin arrived.[82]

June 3. Friday. Our reports today are that Gen Johnston has defeated Thomas and he is going back to Chattanooga fast as possible with very heavy losses. 30,000 from death & desertion mostly.

June 4. Saturday. Some of Gen Vaughn's men passed through from South Carolina and Tenn.[83] Annie Law has been arrested at Knoxville and imprisoned.[84]

June 6. Monday. Report of a fight near Staunton in which Gen William E Jones was killed and our forces compelled to fall back with heavy loss. Johnston at New Hope and Lee's repulse of the Yankees comfirmed.[85]

June 7. Tuesday. Gen Vaughn reported wounded & Gen Imboden taken prisoner. Speak of evacuating to Abingdon. Dr Currey ordered to report to Richmond. Letters from Mrs Kain & Mrs Morrow.

June 8. Wednesday. The rumors of yesterday in regard to Gens Vaughn & Imboden lack confirmation. Merely a sensation story. The Yanks have Staunton & reported coming down the Valley.[86]

June 9. Thursday. The Yankees refuse to give up Gen Jones' body. Grant reported to be attempting to cross James River. The 60th Va men at

Staunton caused the defeat.[87] Capt Ford came up today. Thinking we had better stay here for the present.

June 10. Friday. The Yankees made an attempt to take Petersburg but were repulsed.[88] Wrote Sam and Mary.

June 12. Sunday. No communication either way. The cars have been stopped.

June 13. Monday. The Yankees reported to be coming down the valley very fast, also that they have Liberty.[89]

June 16. Thursday. Yankees reported within eight miles of Bristow in force. Col Fry brought up handcuffed. Capt Osborne captured him. Great excitement in town.[90]

June 17. Friday. Mrs Kain and children came up last night. Brought on the train a woman arrested as a spy. Went back this afternoon. The Yanks reported retreating. Several ladies in Knoxville under arrest.

June 18. Saturday. Lee & Forrest gained a victory in Miss. John Morgan very successful in Ky. A general engagement going on between Johntson & Sherman. We have the advantage. Grant fallen back to West now. Gen Polk reported killed, Ewells corps moving north.[91]

June 19. Sunday. The Yankees reported retreating from Lynchburg. Morgan sent in for five thousand rations this morning. Came in himself this afternoon.

June 20. Monday. We expected to leave this morning but Dr Currey did not get off. Have concluded to remain. Morgan lost all of Gen Giltners men but Lee says he stopped five thousand Yanks on their way here. Hunter defeated by B[reckinridge] on his way here.[92]

June 21. Tuesday. The Yankees reported to have Petersburg & Johnston to have gained a glorious victory over Sherman. Run him 11 miles.[93] Gen Early & Gen Breckinridge have Hunter completely surrounded above and below here.

June 22. Wednesday. General Lee defeated Grant near Petersburg. Dr Currey left yesterday, Gid Hazen missing. Some think dead, poor fellow. His death has come nearer home to me than any since the war.

June 23. Thursday. The Yankees have escaped from Breckinridge and Early.

June 24. Friday. Beauregard still holds Petersburg. The enemy crossing in heavy force on the South side of the Appomattox. Rumor that the Yanks are coming in round [*illegible*] which proves to be as usual only rumors.

June 25. Saturday. Report that Lee has driven Grant to old Point [*illegible*] completely whipped. Johnston gained a splendid victory, and the attack on Lynchburg successfully repulsed & enemy [*illegible*].

June 26. Sunday. No news today. Capt Martin says they have called for more troops in the East. Cant hear any thing definite of Gid. Some say killed, others wounded mortally, some slightly.

June 27. Monday. Received a note late last night from Mr Ingles too late to go this morning.[94] I suppose we will stay here all summer. Rumors that Wheeler has Knoxville, nothing reliable.

June 28. Tuesday. Reported capture of several wagon trains & four hundred negroes.

June 29. Wednesday. Telegram that Johnston had repulsed the enemy on the 25. They have been badly defeated at Petersburg, repulsed in two raids on the railroad near there. Hunter in his retreat compelled to burn wagons &e.[95]

June 30. Thursday. Wrote Mother & sent by one of Morgan's men. The Yankees are getting up a strong force to come to this part of Va.

July 1. Friday. Gen Wheeler reported to have captured a wagon train between Dalton and Kingston.[96]

July 2. Saturday. Gen Johnston attacked and repulsed the enemy with great slaughter.[97]

July 4. Monday. Gen Early surprised the enemy at Martinsburg on 3rd, completely undid them. Captured a number & a fourth of July dinner.[98]

July 9. Saturday. Letter from father. All well. The baby named after mother. Johnnie [torn page]

July 17. Sunday. Gen Early has captured large store of corn &e with a great many losses. Says Breckinridge had no idea of taking W[ashington] City, only went there as a blind while he collected what he wanted.[99]

July 18. Monday. Letter from Mrs Kain. Gen Stewart made Lt Gen in the place of Gen Polk.[100]

July 20. Wednesday. Gen Joe Johnston superceeded by Gen Hood.[101] Kirby Smith reported to be on the march to meet him. Gen Grant reported dead. Letters from Mrs McPherson & father.

July 21. Thursday. Mobile threatened again.

July 22. Friday. Hunter defeated.[102]

July 23. Saturday. Gen Hood whipping the Yankees. Has killed four Gens, captured 23 pieces [of] Artillery & the fight still going on.[103]

July 26. Tuesday. Report this evening that our forces have been whipped and fallen back before Atlanta.

July 27. Wednesday. It proved false. Hood whipped the Yanks in one of their grand flank movements.[104]

July 28. Thursday. Letters from mother, Emily [Howell], Mrs McPherson, & from Sam and Maj Dewar.

July 29. Friday. Grand Picknic at Mangel's Spring. Went & was sick all day.

July 30. Saturday. Report that the Yankees have cut the railroad between W Point [Mississippi] & Montgomery.[105]

July 31. Sunday. Telegram that Grant attempted to take a part of our fortifications at Richmond by storm after effecting a break by mining. Was repulsed with the loss of Prisoners, 1 Gen, 75 officers, 800 Privates. Has fallen back leaving 500 dead [in] our hands, also 4 genls.[106] All the roads from Abingdon cut.

August 6. Saturday. Picnic to Vance's Mill.

August 8. Monday. Left Abingdon under the charge of Capt Alex Morgan. Spent the night at central depot.

August 9. Tuesday. Left central depot this morning and arrived at Lynchburg about 8 oclock.

August 10. Wednesday. Left Lynchburg this morning. Lost my pocketbook.

August 12. Friday. Arrived at Augusta [Georgia] this afternoon at 5 oclock.

August 13. Saturday. Came out to Maj Wallaces this morning.[107]

August 31. Wednesday. Left Augusta this morning and reached Madison at above five in the afternoon.[108]

Sept. 1. Thursday. Arrived at Eatonton about four oclock.[109]

Chapter 5.
Cut Off from Knoxville

[Ellen resumed her diary in January 1865 after having failed to make an entry since September 1, 1864. Early entries for 1865 recount events during Ellen's early months in Putnam County. Her arrival in September was fortuitous in that she escaped the presence of Federal troops that had swarmed through the county in August as Gen. William T. Sherman invested Atlanta. Federal troops burned the Eatonton railroad depot and committed "some other depredations" on August 1. Public buildings around the town square were converted to military hospitals.

Then, on September 2, Gen. John Bell Hood evacuated Atlanta and the fury of war ebbed away from Putnam County. The army returned briefly in November as Sherman's army embarked on its march to the sea. A near neighbor of Ellen during those tense days, living some ten miles from Eatonton, was a youthful Joel Chandler Harris.][1]

Jan. 1 Sunday. Eatonton Ga. Clear and very cold. Went to church this morning. Not to our church, we have none here, but to the Methodist, which is used by Presbyterians and Baptists too. (The Baptist was taken for a hospital last summer and has never been used since). It is the only church I ever saw that is not heated in some way. Whenever it is very cold, as today, they use the basement.

Last New Year's day I was at home, though in the Yankees lines. It is almost nine months since I was ordered to leave Knoxville by Gen Carter, and sister came out with me. We spent three months in Abingdon Va. had a very pleasant time. I like the place very much, and received kindness from

Tenn refugees there that I will never forget. We left in Aug and came round to Geo. Spent two weeks out on the Sand hills near Augusta at Maj Wallace's and then came on here, which we reached the first day of Sept.[2]

I hoped Johnnie would have been exchanged before this. He is now at Johnsons Island where he has been for thirteen months. Was captured at Missionary Ridge on the 25th of Nov/63. Sam was at Fort Morgan when it surrendered, and now is at Castle William, New York Harbor.[3] I thought I would have seen him so soon when he was captured. It was such a disappointment to me, but far more for him. Father and mother are still in Knoxville. I would give worlds to see them. It makes me so home sick to think of them that I try not to do it. I might as well try to turn the earth from her course. Will and Jeanie are there too, and a little niece nine months old named for mother. They write she is a perfect little beauty.[4]

Our cause looks rather gloomy at present, and some of our people here are very blue. They acknowledge themselves to be whipped. They ought to be ashamed of themselves. What if Sherman has Savannah. We will gain our independence yet. I know it. We have good news from Wilmington. The enemy have been defeated there[5] and Gen Johnston is to take Command of the army of Tenn once more.[6] Sister, Miss Annie and Sue Reid and I walked out to the grave yard.[7] They have a brother buried there who was killed in Va. It is a miserable looking place, not even laid off. I do not think it looks well for a place to have no care taken of the last resting place of the dead. They say the war is the cause of this one being so neglected.

Jan. 2. Monday. Clear and cold. Mrs McP and Mrs Rogan[8] went out to Mrs Dennis[9] after breakfast to see Alice McClung and her son.[10] They say he is a very large baby, but by no means beautiful. Sister and I spent the morning over at Mrs Harwells.[11] In the afternoon Mary and I took a walk. Received a letter from Lieut Terry Cahal, dated Nov 17th saying he would do every thing he could for the exchange of dear Johnnie.[12] Confederate money has gone down very fast since the fall of Sav[annah]. It is said gold is selling in Augusta for $55.00 per ounce. Sherman says he made Lincoln a Christmas present of Sav.[13]

Jan. 4. Wednesday. Today is perfectly lovely, not a cloud in the sky. Report says Gen Hood certainly died of pneumonia. After dinner, Mary Rogan, sister and I walked out to see Mr Pleas McClung. He is the largest baby I ever saw, has red hair like his father. Today there was an election for Judges of the Inferior Court. There are only twenty candidates who want to stay home, instead of going to fight the Yankees as they ought to.

Jan. 5. Thursday. Cloudy most of the day, but pleasant. Mrs Lawson came over and sat the morning.[14] In the afternoon sister and I went up to the stores. After we came home Sue Lou and I took a long walk.[15] We have had no mail since Monday. Old Fen brings it over whenever it suits him. I think it is abominable. He ought to be made to bring it regularly.[16]

Jan. 6. Friday. It rained heavily last night after the moon went down. We cannot hear any thing positive but rumors still that Gens Price and Forrest are dead. I cannot believe it true. Mrs McP. received a letter from her father today. He is dreadfully blue.

Jan. 7. Saturday. Clear and windy. Wallie came home this morning, brings no good news. The Yankees have been at Saltville and the Lead mines in Va. Gen Vaughn ran from them at the latter place when they only had three hundred and fifty men.[17] He says there is a report that Thomas has been whipped in Middle Tenn. He brought me two letters from Maj Hatcher of Dec 27 & 29th saying he would make application to the Yankee Col Mulford in my name to have Johnnie exchanged.[18] He has been very, very kind and I shall always feel very grateful to him. Wallie also brought me a letter from Fannie Wallace.[19] She says Augusta is being fortified, but whether for ourselves or the Yankees she cant say. There is a rumor that Charleston is being evacuated. Carrie[20] spent the morning with us. After dinner Mary Rogan, sister and I walked out to see Alice. She is not so well today, but Mrs Harwell thinks it is nothing serious. Mr McPherson says it is perfectly disgusting the way some of the men here are talking. They are nothing but Union men. They think the meeting held and the resolutions passed by the people of Savannah very sensible. I think they have disgraced themselves.[21]

Jan. 8. Sunday. Clear and cold. I did not go to church this morning. Wrote to Ellen Clapp[22] and to Maj Smith asking him to send me sisters and my ambrotypes he took to Johnnie but never had an opportunity to give them to him.

Jan. 10. Tuesday. Yesterday it was cloudy & raining all day. In the morning I went over to Mrs Harwells and did not come home till this morning. We had a violent storm last night and this morning. I never heard it pour as it did and it has been raining almost all day. No mail and no news. The Gov. is going to build a rail-road from here to Madison and repair the one from Milledgeville at once.[23] I crocheted a cape for Mrs Harwell and sent it home this evening. She is so good it gives me real pleasure to do any thing for her. I wish mother knew her. I know she would love her for her kindness to sister and myself. I think Carrie is one of the sweetest creatures I ever saw. She is a little deaf, but instead of its making her appear awkward, it only makes her more interesting. I have used my eyes too much and they have troubled me a great deal lately. Sometimes I cannot see to read or write a word. I am going to be more careful of them in future. I am knitting some yarn undershirts for myself. If mother knew it she would think I was getting prudent.

Jan. 11. Wednesday. The wind was very high last night and the moon light very bright, but it is cloudy again this morning, clear and windy this afternoon. Mary Rogan[24] came over after dinner, and as we heard Alice McClung was much worse we walked out to see her. Found her asleep and better. After tea Mr & Mrs Harwell came over and sat till ten oclock. I have had a real bad headache all day. Nothing inferred by the report that Gen Hood is falling back towards Montgomery Ala. and that the Yankees are at Millen, and some have crossed the Savannah river and gone towards Branchville.[25]

Jan 12. Thursday. Clear and cold. Ice in our room this morning but moderated by afternoon, when Mrs McP, sister and I went to return Mrs Davis[26] and Miss Hardins[27] visits.

Jan. 14. Saturday. Clear and pleasant in the morning, very windy this afternoon. Mrs Cross called this morning. She is very interesting. After dinner sister, Mary Rogan and I walked out to see Alice, who is better, but has still some fever. I finished my first knit shirt this evening and am very much pleased with it. Old Fen came this evening. I was very much disappointed I did not receive a letter from Maj Hatcher saying Johnnie would soon be exchanged. Oh I do want to see him so much. Augusta is under water. The canals broke loose, and they say on Broad St. the water is a foot deep. Several persons have lost their lives.[28] I received a letter from Mrs Dr Morrow. They are keeping house in Montgomery. She says she has only seen Mrs Wallace at church, she is most of the time confined to her bed. I am glad to hear she is still alive. I think her one of the liveliest beings I ever knew.

Jan. 15. Sunday. Clear and pleasant. I went to church this morning, heard a Methodist preacher hold forth. I do wish we had a church here. I would enjoy it so much. When I came home I wrote to father, mother, Sam and Johnnie. In the afternoon sister and I walked out to see Alice. Found her better. When we came [back] found Mary Rogan and Mrs Lawson here. Some cavalry passed through town this morning under Gen Smith.[29]

Jan. 16. Monday. Clear and pleasant. In the afternoon Sue Lou Harwell and I walked out to see Alice. Found her better. There are a number of reports on the street today, none good for our cause, and I dont believe them.

Jan. 17. Tuesday. Clear and pleasant.

Jan. 29. Sunday. It has been very cold for the last week. Every one says this has been an unusually cold winter. Some the coldest they ever remember. I have been real lazy for the last two weeks not to have written a line, but that is nothing unusual for me, I am sorry to say.

We have some news and a thousand rumors. Fort Fisher has fallen.[30] Blair has been to Richmond on a mission of peace.[31] His offer was that we should go back into the Union as we were before except that all rebel property should be confiscated, slavery abolished, &e &e. We could have had that four years ago, without so much bloodshed. Lincoln is an old fool. Gen Hood at his own request has been relieved from command of the army of Tenn, and Gen Dick Taylor assumes temporary command. Gen Smiths corps passed through Milledgeville last week. We are to have a Commander-in-chief of our army. I hope Gen Lee will be he, and Gen Johnston is to take the field again.

There is a report that England, France and Spain, have notified Lincoln that unless peace be declared before the fourth of March, they will recognize the Confederate States, as his last election was sectional and therefore illegal. I believe we will have peace before much longer. There was a report yesterday that an armistice of ninety days had been declared. I hope it is not true, for when ever there is an armistice there will be no more fighting and we certainly could not have our own terms now, and I want them or none.

We have not heard from home or the boys either since I last wrote here. Oh! how I do want to see them all. I think of scarcely any thing else. This afternoon Mr & Mrs McP, Carrie, Mrs McClung and I walked out to old Mrs Pikes[32] to get Mr Pleas some Catnip. Then Carrie and I walked out to Mrs Lee Dennis for sister who spent the day there. Mr McP says that the report of an armistice is without foundation.

Jan 30. Monday. Clear and pleasant. After dinner Mrs McP, Mary Rogan, sister and I walked out to see Alice. While we were there Mrs Clayborne and the Misses Thomas called.[33] I felt real sorry for Alice. The servant brought them right in. She says she felt like she would give any thing to be under the bed. I should judge from Mrs Claybornes appearance that she was something of a tarter. The Misses T. I was very much pleased with. They appear to be very pleasant and intelligent young ladies.

Jan. 31. Tuesday. Today has been perfectly delightful. This morning sister and I went to return Misses Wingfield, Adams and Rossers visits.[34] After dinner Sue Lou went with us to see Alice. We received five letters from home and one from Johnnie, all been some time on the road. All the dear ones are well. Aunt Mary had been on to New York to see Sam, but Gen. Dix would not allow her to see him, the vile old Yankee.[35]

Mrs McP received letters from her father and Fannie. Fan has been quite sick for which I am very sorry. I greatly fear she is predisposed to consumption. Capt Wallace is at home and his sister is looking for him every day. Mr McP went to Greensboro this morning to be absent several days.[36] Blairs errand to Richmond was to offer a safe conduct to our peace commissioners to Washington. Vice Pres Stevens, Mr Hunter of Va. and Judge Campbell have gone. I do hope they will be able to do some thing, but I doubt it.[37]

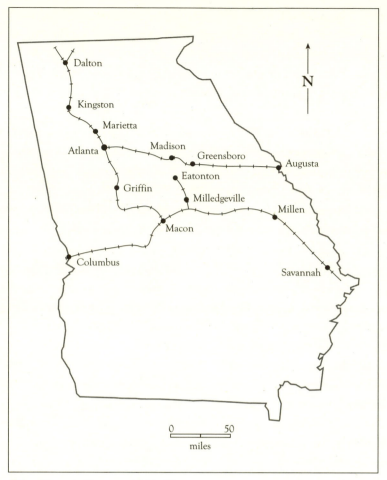

Ellen House's Georgia, 1864–65.

Feb. 1. Wednesday. Mary Rogan came over this morning. She had a letter from her cousin in Bluntsville who says Dr Ramsey, Crow Ramsey, Mr Sam Boyd, Sam McKinney and Sperry were all captured at Bristol during Shermans late raid.[38] I am very sorry to hear it. In the afternoon Carrie and I walked up to see Alice. Just as we got to Mr Dennis' gate we met sister and Wallie in the buggy. They had been out after chickens and eggs. We got in and went home with them. After we came home I went to walk with Mrs Lawson.

Feb. 2. Thursday. Cloudy this morning and raining a little in the afternoon. All three of us went over and spent the afternoon with Carrie and Sue Lou. Mr McPherson returned this evening.

Feb. 3. Friday. Raining almost all day. No news.

Feb. 4. Saturday. Clear and pleasant. Mrs McP and sister went out to see Alice just after dinner, and Carrie & I walked out later. We received a letter from Aunt Mary dated Philadephia Jany 18th. She had been on to New York to see dear Sam, but was not allowed by Gen Dix to see him, the hateful Yankee rascal. Mrs McP received one from mother. Lizzie Bearden[39] is engaged to My particular friend? Maj Gratz. How a Southern girl can marry a Yankee I cannot see, and she has lost a lover and a brother in this war, and has three more brothers in our army now. She must be hard up for a husband to marry Gratz, a little fat Dutchman, who says he came to America just to kill Rebels but whose ardor seems to have abated some what as he always takes good care to keep out of harms way. All at home are well. I can be contented now for some time with that knowledge.

Feb. 5. Sunday. I did not go to church although it has been very pleasant all day. I have not felt very well. I wrote to father, Sam, Ella Cocke and Mrs Morrow. Dr Ramsey is to be sent through the lines to Richmond. Sperry and Maj Crow Ramsey were sent to Brownlow for a Christmas present. Capt Clarke is in a cage in Knoxville, to be tried for the murder of an old Union man.[40] The Marietta Hotel was destroyed by fire a short time since.[41]

Feb. 6. Monday. Clear and pleasant in the morning, raw and unpleasant in the afternoon when sister and I walked out to see Alice. After we came home I went over to Harwells for a little while. I made Sallie a pair of shoes for this morning.

Feb. 7. Tuesday. Raining all day and cold. The gentlemen on the square say they have heard heavy firing from one to four oclock in the direction of Macon. I would like to know what it means.

Feb. 8. Wednesday. Alternate shade and sunshine all day with high winds. No news. Spent the afternoon at Harwells.

Feb. 9. Thursday. Like yesterday. Went over to Reids for a little while this morning. Tonight Sue Lou has a party out at Mr Lee Dennis[42] but neither sister or I care to go although Carrie and her both insist. Sherman has cut the roads between Branchville and Aiken.[43] Our Peace Commissioners have been sent back. Lincoln says nothing but entire submission will do. The Union as it is. I had wished that there might be peace, but am not surprised at the result. If it will only unite the South more, it will be a great thing, and I cannot see how any one can be so base now as to desire reunion. Oh! when will I see my mother. I would give worlds for one kiss from her and father. As things are now I fear I did very wrong to leave them, but I could not foresee the future. God grant it may all come out right in the end.

Feb. 10. Friday. Pleasant, no mail and no news. As usual sister and I walked out to see Alice.

Feb. 11. Saturday. Clear and pleasant. Mrs Harwell came home from Monticello last night, and I took her after breakfast a cape I had crocheted for her while she was away. Alice spent the day with us. Carrie came over in the afternoon, and after Alice left she and I went to walk. She is going to Monticello tomorrow.[44] I am so sorry. I shall miss her so much. Lieut Thomas called this morning. He was with Johnnie on Gen Crittendens staff, and thinks a great deal of Johnnie, so of course I like him. He has not long been exchanged. Is very pleasant and has one of the finest faces I ever saw. He is very tall and loosely put together.

Feb. 12. Sunday. Clear but rather windy. Went to the Presbyterian church this morning. Mr Smith preached from 17th Ps last verse.[45] I am afraid I did not hear much of the sermon and what I did hear did not do much good I was so cold all the time.

Feb. 18. Saturday. Today has been delightful. Miss Kate Thomas and Miss Addie Reid called this morning.[46] What the latter came for I cant imagine—made her first call after we have been here six months—unless it is she thinks it will please Adjt Thomas. Report says she is trying very hard to catch him. In the afternoon Mrs Dr Nisbeth[47] and her sister Miss Lou Dennis[48] called. After they left Mary Rogan, sister and I took a walk, stopped to see Alice.

We had a letter from father today dated Dec 20th. They were all well, so were Sam and Johnnie. Johnnie had just received a barrel of provisions and that day for the first time for more than a month he had had enough to eat. Sam does better, as where he is they are allowed to buy some few things.[49] Oh! how happy I will be when I see them again. The papers state there is to be a general exchange very soon. I hope and pray it may be true.

Feb. 19. Sunday. Clear and pleasant. Went to church this morning and to walk this afternoon, stopped to see Alice. Had another letter from home. I always feel so much better after receiving one from my dear parents.

Feb. 20. Monday. Delightful. I have stopped drinking coffee this morning, and was very much afraid I would have a violent headache by night to pay for it, but find I was mistaken, for which I am very glad. Went over to Mrs Harwells to get some thing to read. When I came back found Mrs Rogan, Mary and Miss Annie Reid here. I have fooled away today—as I did all last week, but am going to try and do better in future, but I [have] made so many good resolves which never amount to any thing else. Mamie & I took a long walk and we wound up the day as usual with a game of Euchre after tea.[50]

Feb. 21. Thursday. Pleasant but cloudy. This morning I commenced working a handkerchief for Mrs McPherson. Capt Wallace has come at last, & Mr Sam Wallace with him. In the afternoon Sue Lou and I walked out to Mrs Dennis. Mr Irby Morgan and Lt Thomas took tea with us. The former is a cousin of Jeanies. Report says the Yankees have Charleston and Columbia.[51] I fear it is true. Every thing looks gloomy now, but there is a better time coming.

Feb. 22. Wednesday. Same as yesterday. I have done nothing worth recording, but still intend to try and write every day, to see if I can be regular about any thing. Capt Wallace and I took a game of chess this morning, the first I have played for a long time. I wish I was a good player but doubt if I ever will be. I dont believe I have sense enough, or I am too absent minded one or the other. I took a buggy ride this afternoon with Tom [Wallace], the first I have taken since I came to Eatonton and of course I enjoyed it very much. Old Fen came today but brought no news but what we heard yesterday. Gov Foote has gone to Europe. Dixie has lost nothing by his leaving.[52]

Feb. 23. Thursday. Raining almost all day and warm. Played chess and cards all day and Chess at night.

Feb. 24. Friday. Spent the day about the same as yesterday. It seems very wrong to waste time so, and yet I might as well play chess & cards as well as any thing else. I lead a very useless life any how, or least it appears so to me. It is almost without aim or object. I seem to do myself or no one else any good. I have heard that [is] the chief and highest source of happiness and I believe it. If I could only act so how much better it would be not only for others but for myself too. I am afraid I am very selfish. I often dislike to leave off any thing I am doing when one of the children ask me to do any thing for them. But if I make an effort & do it, I am always glad that I did. But still it does require an effort. And then when any little thing annoys me, I find it hard to keep my temper, and I am sorry that I dont always succeed. All my life long to keep it has been hard work. Father has naturally (he says) a very violent one, and yet he has it under such perfect control. I never should have thought so. If I could only do it I would be so thankful. It always lessens my self respect for a time, when I give way and say some bitter thing, which I am sorry for as soon as said.

Feb. 25. Saturday. Raining again today, and such a gloomy rain too. The state of the weather corresponds with my feelings. I have been so blue. Capt Wallace's coming, and his sisters happiness at seeing him, makes one think so much of my darling brothers, who are so far, far away in Northern prisons. I seem to realize more and more every day the distance and barriers that separate me from all I love best, father, mother and brothers.[53] I have felt all day that I would give worlds to have mother press a kiss upon my brow, and hear father once more call me his darling daughter. Shall I ever have that happiness again is the thought that is ever present in my mind.

And to make matters worse this morning I said a real unkind of a person who never did me any harm, who I only had reason to like. It was uncalled for on my part, and I said it to that persons friend. I was sorry for it the next moment, but then it was too late. Why cannot I keep my tongue? Mrs McP often tells Mary, she will have to cut a piece of her tongue off. I think mine needs it more than hers. She is a child, but I have not that excuse. I am too sensitive to things [that] are said which without being intended wound me to the quick, and I feel my face burn like fire.

Mamie came in just here and asked me to go in to the other room and dance. Of course I went, a great dance we had. Mr. and Mrs McP hummed for music, and Aunt Becky drummed on the window by way of an accompaniment. The richest music any of us ever danced by. My spirits rose for the time, but as I come back to write I feel bluer than before. I some times wonder if I can be the same girl who used to be always singing and laughing all over the house, with never a care or sorrow. It seems so many years ago. I wonder too if any friends notice any change in me. They never mention it. It is not always [that] I am so low spirited, and when I am I try not to show it. Capt Wallace says Capt. Rumbough was killed at Bulls Gap some time since. He was a brother of the Mrs Williams who is thought to have betrayed Gen Morgan.[54]

Feb. 26. Sunday. Beautiful overhead, the walking rather muddy. Went to church in the morning. Mr Rogers preached, made quite a number of grammatical mistakes, and he set up for some thing extra. After dinner I went over to Reids for a little while. After I came home, Sue Lou, Capt Wallace, sister and I went out to see Alice. Sue Lou came home and took tea. Fannie Wallace gave her brother to her for a sweetheart when she was down here, and I expect to see a near flirtation while he is here. They are both good at it. In Columbia the Yankees have blown up the State house and left the city a mass of ruins.[55] Oh! when will they be checked in their work of destroying Southern property and taking Southern lifes. Surely this state of things cannot last much longer. God will not permit it.

Feb. 27. Monday. Cloudy in the afternoon later it rained. Spent most of the day playing cards & chess. In the afternoon Sue Lou and I went to walk, came very near being caught in the rain, just reached home in time to escape a through wetting. I do think these people in Eatonton are the greatest fools I ever saw or head of. Because I went to ride with Capt Wallace the day after he came, they say we are to be married. I was real mad when I heard it, but we laughed at the idea. It is the most absurd thing I ever heard.

The Telegraph says there are about thirty-five miles of rail-road stock, making nearly three thousand cars and engines belonging to every five foot gage in the Confederacy accumulated about Charlotte. The change of gage there prevents their going on. Shermans move will probably cause their destruction. All are heavily loaded with stores. The fortifications around Augusta are being rapidly strengthened by a large force. Two regiments were captured at Charleston and a number of heavy guns. The ammunition was cast into the harbor. The city is now jammed with negro troops. A great part of it has been burned by the fleeing refugees.[56] There is a report that Beauregard hopes to form a junction with Early, who has come out from Richmond, and the battle ground will be on the Catawba river just below Charlotte. Gov Brown has disbanded the Melish [militia].[57]

Feb. 28. Tuesday. Cloudy all day. War has been declared between chess and cards, was to the death at that. So there has not been so much playing of either today. Sue Lou came over this afternoon to tell Mrs McP that she could get a piano, and she sent right off for it. Sue Lou came over again after tea and stayed till bed time. I have commenced reading Boswells life of Johnson. Why I have not read it before I cant imagine. When I will finish it is hard to say.

March 1. Wednesday. Raining all day. Played cards, chess and danced most of the day. Have not been quite so blue because I have not given myself time to think.

March 2. Thursday. Drizzling and disagreeable, went over to Mrs Harwells for a little while. Mr McPherson and Capt W[allace] left for Macon. We have news today that Sherman has been defeated near Charlotte N.C. by Early and Gordon.[58] Today Mary is thirteen.[59] There were a number of girls here this afternoon, dancing, playing &e.

March 3. Friday. Alternate sunshine & clouds all day. Went over to Mrs Harwells for a little while. After dinner Sue Lou sent for us, but we were just going out to see Miss Thomas and Mrs Reid. The Reids and Rogans came over after tea and spent the evening. Soldiers coming in today confirm the news of Shermans defeat. There is nothing of it in the Augusta papers, but we would hear it here as soon as they would there. Every paper confirms there is to be a general exchange of prisoners to take place immediately. Every thing has been arranged between Gen Grant and Col Ould.[60] There is a report that Col Ashby has been killed.[61] Gen Wade Hampton has relieved Gen Wheeler of command, having been appointed Lt Gen and Ch[ief] of Cavly.[62]

Old Fen came in with a mail today. Sherman has almost completely destroyed Columbia, two thirds of the town is in ashes. Thousands of men, women, and children houseless and in a starving condition.[63] The citizens of Augusta are contributing largely for their relief. Three thousand five hundred women & children were killed during the burning of the place. After the town had been burned and sacked, Sherman ordered the pillagers & burners to be shot. I understand that. He had better have issued orders before entering the city against any thing of the kind if he did not intend to allow it. Every article of substance was carried off.

March 4. Saturday. It poured all night, the hardest rain we have had at all. No news of any kind.

March 5. Sunday. Clear and pleasant. Went to church this morning. Mr McDonald preached from the text "Ye that is not with me is against me."[64] After dinner walked out to the grave yard with the Reids. Came home and sat till dark with them. Mr McP & Capt Wallace came back from Macon tonight. They say the Northern papers say Grant has been defeated by Gen Lee. If the Yankees acknowledge it, he must have been badly whipped. Old Mr Reid & Judge Slade came over to hear the news.[65] I thought I would have died, just [to] see the way sister did. I would have given any thing if Fannie Wallace had been here. I know I acted like a fool, but that was natural, so I could not help it.

March 6. Monday. Clear and windy. Mrs McPherson and Mr. Sam Wallace gardening. I went over and asked Mrs Harwell for some seed, then helped to plant a few, but not many. I fell early in the fight. I do wish that I had some patience and perseverance. Mr McPherson says they are exchanging two thousand prisoners a week, which will be continued until all are exchanged. Oh! my dear, dear brothers what happiness it will be to see them again. Almost too much I sometimes fear that I will never realize it. I took a horseback this afternoon with Capt Wallace and enjoyed it very much. I do wish I was a real good rider. I know I am so awkward about it. I am almost ashamed to ride, although there is nothing I like so much. Sue Lou came over after tea and spent the evening.

March 7. Tuesday. Clear and pleasant. Mr McC[lung] and Alice spent the day with us. They think Pleas has the itch, and of course are very much worried about it. This morning we had the greatest fight we have had yet. We wanted to play [chess]. Mrs McP said we should not. We said we would. So we went on the back porch—locked the back door and Capt Wallace put the bucket and cup down by him, so he could throw water on the first person who troubled us. We became so much interested in the game that neither of us saw Mr McP till he had brushed all the men off with a piece of cedar. I picked it [the cedar] up and threw it at him, never thinking it would hurt him, but it did. Unfortunately struck him of a very tender place, his nose, and skinned it, or rather cut it so deep that the blood came. He picked up the bucket and I ran but too late. It all came right on by back. I was soaked through, but it served me exactly right. I ought not to have thrown the cedar.

We all went over to Mr Harwells after tea. There is a Capt Hall staying there for a day or two. I dont think he will ever set the world on fire. He has been wounded and staying out at Mr Little's.[66] We danced, played cards &c, about all we do now. How heartless it seems to pass so much time so when hundreds of our noble men are lying dead and dying on the gory battle field, but what can I do. The only thing I like about it is I never have a moment to think, and that certainly appears to me like a blessing now. Were I to think much I would go crazy.

There are twenty five hundred exchanged prisoners in Richmond now. Oh if Sam or Johnnie are only among them, but I am afraid they are not.

Rumors says in the fight near Charlotte Sherman lost 2,000 men killed and 8,000 prisoners. I am afraid it is not true—Wilmington has gone up. I am really sorry, for although I never doubt the success of our cause in the end it is very sad to have so many of our citys fall one after another into the hands of a ruthless foe.

March 8. Wednesday. Raining in the morning, cloudy in the afternoon. Spent the day as usual, triffled it away. I have been suffering all day from a dreadful headache.

March 9. Thursday. It poured this morning, rained all day. Spent the day as usual, dancing, cards &e. We have good news. Grants defeat has been confirmed, and a rumor that Schofield has been whipped on the Weldon road. Sherman's defeat also confirmed. Report says he surrendered thirty thousand prisoners and that the exchange of prisoners is certainly going on.[67]

This house hold is certainly a merry one. It is fortunate we do not live in a more closely built part of the town we make so much noise. Last night we even had Mr Sam Wallace on the floor dancing. I enjoy the fun while it is going on but the first quiet moment I have to think I feel bluer than ever, and Oh! so homesick—and I have no home—what a thought. Will I ever see my dear, dear parents again. If my life is so spared to see them I will do every thing in my power to contribute to their happiness. They shall know that my love for them is not a name, but a loving reality, the ruling passion of my life.

I fear that I am hoping against hope in regard to Sam and Johnnie being exchanged soon, and yet I hope on. I often wonder if many girls have such parents and brothers as I have. I doubt it.

March 10. Friday. Fast day. Went to church in the morning and found it too cold for comfort. In the afternoon Sister, Sue Lou and I took a walk, went to see Alice. The news of Shermans surrender and Grants defeat confirmed. Sherman himself with the remainder of his men retreating towards Charleston.

March 11. Saturday. Bright and beautiful. No news. Today we played our last game of chess, as Capt Wallace leaves Monday morning. I am sorry because I have become very much fascinated with the game, and would like to play a good game. The Reids and Sue Lou were invited over to spend the evening. Had a very pleasant time though we came very near desecrating the Sabbath. It was quarter to twelve when they left. We had just enough to dance, a foreshadowing of future events, seven ladies & one gentleman.

March 12. Sunday. Another beautiful day. Mr. McDonald preached a splendid sermon on the subject of the war. I never came so near crying in church as I did at one time this morning. Sue Lou came over and we all took a long walk. Good news. Lee pretended to evacuate Richmond. Grant attacked him & lost 2,000 killed & wounded, & 15,000 prisoners. Sherman reported to have changed his course and gone towards Petersburg. Lincoln consented to exchange prisoners because he could get no more recruits till the Yanks we hold as prisoners are exchanged.

March 13. Monday. Clear and beautiful. Mr Sam W. and Capt Tom left this morning. The house seems dull without them. Took a short walk with Miss Annie. After tea we went over to Reids and had some first rate music. Spent a pleasant evening. I received letters from Fannie Wallace, Emily Howell[68] and Libbie Morrow.[69] Mattie L[uttrell] had gone to Cinncinati to school. I know she hated it. Emily says old Jim died the night before our army evacuated Marietta. Poor old man, I am glad he did. The Yankees would have worried him to death.

March 14. Tuesday. Cloudy and drizzling all day. I commenced taking music lessons this morning from Mrs Pearson.[70] If practice will make perfect, I will improve rapidly. I would like so much to be a real first rate performer. Sue Lou was over after dinner and we were having a good time, in a small way, when who should walk in but Jennie Adams.[71] I never was more surprised in my life. She took off her hat and made herself very much at home. She plays and sings well. We made her play for us to dance. After she left Sue Lou and I took a little walk. She says Jennie told her when Capt W[allace] was here she wished so much she was intimate with sister & I. Emma really seems to be very much interested in my affairs.[72] She asked Sue Lou yesterday if Capt

W and I had come to an understanding! I wish she would not trouble herself quite so much about what does not concern her. I should think she ought to be satisfied making love to Johnnie and let other people go.

Charleston was almost entirely destroyed by fire before the Yankees occupied it. Every shot fired in defense of Columbia was fired by Wheeler's men, who the Carolinias delight in abusing, and every man wounded was a Tennesseean or Kentuckian.[73]

March 15. Wednesday. It poured last night and rained heavily this morning. The rest of the day has been a real April one, alternate tears and smiles. We have commenced reading Joseph 2nd & his Court by Muhlbuch, and like it very much.[74] I have been very much interested in the different characters. How soon poor Isabella was forgotten, how wrong of Christina to tell Joseph after her death that she never loved him. It made him so bitter. How equally wrong for her to prejudice him against poor Joseph.

March 16. Thursday. Raining most of the day. When I returned from taking my music lesson found Sue Reid and Nannie Rogan who sat the morning. Sue Lou came over after dinner and stayed till bed time. We received a letter from Cousin Frank. He is [in] Augusta. How dearly I should love to see him. How provoking he should have passed through Millegeville, and not been able to come to see us. He has the itch. I think sister and I have escaped wonderfully. Gen Lee reports that Bragg has whipped Schofield, taken fifteen hundred prisoners and several pieces of cannon. The people of New York are very much frightened. Think two of our rams are going to take the city. There is a report that France has recognized the Confederacy.

March 18. Saturday. Took dinner at Mrs Harwells yesterday. After the dinner Mrs Dennis sent for Sue Lou and I to go spend the night with her. Of course we went. Today is beautiful. We came in about eleven. Carrie came home this afternoon. Found all the family out at Mr Pearson's.

March 19. Sunday. Clear and pleasant. Went to Church, have had a head ache all day. Sue Lou came over and stayed to supper.

March 20. Monday. Bright and beautiful. In the afternoon sister & I returned some visits. Found every one at home except Miss Rosser, so we saved one card but wasted our time. Good news. Gen Hampton has had a fight with Kilpatrick, defeated him, captured six hundred horses &e.[75]

March 21. Tuesday. Spent last night with Carrie, came home about eleven. Rained all night and most of the day. Carrie came over in the afternoon. Mr McP saw a man from Johnsons Island. Says he left Johnnie well. I would like very much to see him.

March 22. Wednesday. For the last two or three mornings I have been up by sun rise, and intend to continue if I can, but I am so mortal lazy. Carrie & I took a long walk. A report that Gen Johnston has had an engagement with Sherman, and whipped him badly, and that he is seventy miles from the east. So he must be in a eight ball fix.

March 23. Thursday. Clear & pleasant. Confirmation of yesterday's report.

March 24. Friday. Bright and beautiful. We received three letters from mother (she gave us a lot of Knoxville news, among others the engagement of Cluss to Miller Baxter's son-in-law.[76] She's do a big business) and one from each of the boys. All have been sick, but are well again.

March 25. Saturday. Clear and pleasant. Some one proposes that the Southern women sell their hair to pay the war debt. Glorious, I only wish I had some. How I dislike short hair. I hope mine will be long some time. This afternoon, sister, Sue Lou and I walked out to see Alice. When we came home I went over and spent the evening with Carrie.

March 26. Sunday. Clear, but very dusty. Wrote Mother, Sam & Fannie Wallace, in the afternoon Mrs Morrow. Then Carrie & I went to see Alice.

March 27. Monday. Clear and dusty. Sister received a letter from Emily. She says our house was burnt down, all except the dining room, which the pickets occupied, and burnt when they left. There is a fort where the carriage house stood.[77] The papers say that in his late fight, Bragg gave the enemy time to receive reinforcements, and in the second days fight lost all he had gained in the first. That seems to be his way of doing things. Carrie and I took a long walk. Wrote mother with onion juice, but am afraid it will show.[78]

March 28. Tuesday. Drizzling this morning but cleared off by afternoon. Carrie & I took a long walk, & I spent the day with her. In the afternoon Miss Kate and Miss Annie Thomas called with Capt Robinson and Lt Cooper.[79] The former is just from Johnsons Island. He left dear Johnnie well. Sue Lou and Mary Rogan were here to supper. Mrs Rogan came tonight.

March 30. Thursday. Late this afternoon Carrie came over for us to take a walk. Coming back we stopped at her house. We had only been there a few minutes when Wallie came running over [to say] that cousin Sam had come. The way I came through the fields flying. When I got to the back steps Mr McP said "I'll declare Ellen it was a shame to fool you so." I felt like I would drop. Wallie said I am not fooling you, so with one desperate effort I mounted the steps, and there in the sitting room was my own dear brother, who thank God has at last been exchanged. What unexpected happiness to us.

He looks old, and is very much sunburnt. He was very sick in Richmond, and part of the way coming on. Some one stold his hat, so he was bareheaded for two days, till some kind soul took pity on him and gave him one. He had to walk over a hundred miles, and his feet are all blistered. He says the Yankees treat our poor fellows who are unfortunate enough to fall into their hands as prisoners shamefully. He was sick for thirteen days. No one came near him, thought he had the Small pox. After that they found that he had Pneumonia. What a blessing he did not die.[80]

In Baltimore the Yankees bayonetted thirteen ladies for speaking to rebel prisoners. He says he saw a soldier take a young lady by the throat and throw her in the house and lock the door. No one was allowed to realize a relation among them in the slightest manner.[81] Oh! how much they will have to answer for, and a day of retribution must come. Thomas is said to be coming towards Knoxville.

April 1. Saturday. Just about sun rise this morning Mamie came running into our room. Oh! cousin Ellen, cousin Sam is very sick, and says please bring him some laudanum. I jumped out of bed, threw on my wrapper, put my feet into a pair of shoes and ran. Opened his door, found him nearly dressed, but still I thought that he might be sick. "How much do you want" I asked. "What" said he. "Laudanum" I replied. "Good gracious do you want to kill me" said he.[82] Just then Mrs McP, who had her room door open to see the fun, called out "1st of April." I never was so completely sold in my life. She enjoyed it so much, I never heard any one laugh as she did. She just opened her mouth and it rolled out. Sister was the only person who was not caught.

Carrie and I took a long walk. As we were coming back met Sister, Sam, Kate and Mamie. We joined them and took another. Went over to Harwells in the afternoon. Sue Lou came home with us and spent the evening. Some Ala Cavalry came in today, on their way to join Wheeler.

April 2. Sunday. As Sam did not feel like going to church this morning, sister and I stayed at home with him. I feel that I do not want to loose sight of him.

April 9. Sunday. The last week has been a merry one. Tom Wallace and Bob Armstrong came over on Wednesday and left this morning. We had a dance every night while they were here. Of course Carrie and Sue Lou were over, and we all enjoyed it very much. Mr McP and Russ left for Athens today too. Capt John S. Reid[83] who came yesterday afternoon says he left Johnnie well. How I wish he would be exchanged while Sam is here. If he is not 'tis hard to tell when they will see each other again, as Sam expects to join Forrest.

April 10. Monday. Rained several times today. I went over and took tea with Carrie. Sue Lou has gone out to Maj Lytles for a few days. After tea sister and Sam came over. Capt Alex Reid was there to see Mary Rogan. He is very attentive.[84]

April 11. Tuesday. After I took my music lesson, Carrie, Mary Rogan, Tom Branch and I went after sweet shrubs. Tom was to show us the way, and such a way as he did take us, through fields, woods, briers, over fences, across creeks. I do not remember ever to have taken such another. We must have walked at least four miles. I was slightly tired when I reached home. After dinner Sister, Sam and I walked out to see Alice. Mr McClung and her sang for us. We enjoyed it very much, but as usual Mr Pleas had to tune up.

April 13. Thursday. Sam says that Grant is reported to have lost 6000 men in his attack on Petersburg, our loss including sick and wounded left in hospitals in Richmond fifteen thousand.[85] There is a rumor that Montgomery has fallen.[86] I hope not. The fall of Richmond does not make me blue. I have been expecting it since Sherman cut the rail roads in Carolina.

Sue Lou spent the evening & took tea. In the afternoon Mary R and Miss Lizzie Reid called. I was so much amused with the latter, she almost over powered me. She had been so anxious to make our acquaintance, was so glad to know us, had so often been prevented from calling &e. We have only been here seven months and a half. After tea we all went over and spent the evening at Mr Harwells very pleasantly. Sam leaves tomorrow. How I hate to see him go. He says he will try and see us again. God grant he may, my dear, dear brother.

April 14. Friday. Pleasant & cloudy. Dear Sam left this morning for Milledgeville. As he had to walk, Carrie, Sue Lou, sister and I walked three miles with him, carried his knapsack, haversack &e as far as we went. I feel as if he had taken all laughter and hope with him. It was almost twelve when we finished our six mile walk. How my feet did ache. But I soon rested and went out to see Alice this afternoon. Carrie has come for me, and I am going to spend the night with her. There is a report that the Blue D——s have Opelika.[87]

April 18. Tuesday. Columbus has gone up. Old Joe Brown has ordered out the "Melish." Some leave today, some not till late Friday. These people here are not fit to have a country, poor miserable creatures that some of them are. Wrote Mrs Robinson. Sue Lou and I went to walk & she spent the evening with us.

April 19. Wednesday. Clear and warm. Sister and I went to see the Miss Thomas &e. There are a number of grape vine reports this evening. Macon, West Point and Eufula are taken. Augusta threatened and Gen Lee's provision train captured, and the fools—lady like—believe it here. I'd like to murder such mean spirited animials. Mr Harwell is the oldest man I have seen lately. I wish we could hear something of dear Sam. I hardly think he could have started for Columbus, and yet I feel very uneasy. I wish that he were here.

April 20. Thursday. Clear and Pleasant. We have a thousand rumors to-day. The Yankees are in Jasper, Hancock, Bibb, Morgan, and Gen Lee killed. Mr McP has brought all his tobacco to the house. If they do come we will loose every thing. I think though he is right. Mrs McP had Wallie hiding her silver. She says it is a constant source of anxiety to her. The Yankees have been reported within eight miles of here twice today. I went over to Mrs Harwells as usual, came home for dinner. Sue Lou came with me. Mr. McP went off today with Mr Rogan and Capts Jno and Will Reid.[88] I dislike the idea of the Yankees coming now more than I have ever done. Some times I almost wish I had never left home. For me might almost as well be in the lines, as to be expecting them all the time. Mrs Lawson came over and sat some time.

April 21. Friday. Sam came this morning from Milledgeville. He says the Yankees certainly have Macon, and that they have flanked him on all sides. When he reached the river coming here, he was told they were in town, but he said he was determined to come on. He left this afternoon for Madison, says he will try to get to Marietta. Mrs McP said she thought he had better stay and hide if they came, but sister and I thought we would feel much better satisfied to have him go.

This morning we heard that Gen Lee had issued a congratulory order to his men.[89] He had fought two battles since leaving Richmond in both of which Grant had been defeated, having lost over sixty thousand men. There was a rumor here yesterday that Gen Lee's provision train had been cap-tured, but I dont believe it. Mr. Lawson came from Milledgeville late this afternoon. He says Gen Lee has capitulated to Grant, which I wont believe. That's the reason Lees congratulory order was issued was to prevent a pause when the truth was known. A strange reason to me. Joe Brown told the Melish we were whipped, the war was over, they might go home. I think he has done the South more harm than any one I know.

April 22. Saturday. One thing is settled today—beyond a doubt, and that is that there is an armistice, but for how long is unknown. The Yankees are staying very quietly at Macon. The report of Gen Lee's surrender is contradicted today. He is said to have capitulated on the 10th and there is a Col Migg here, who left the army on the 11th. Says Gen Lee and his army were in fine spirits, plenty to eat &e. He expects soon to form a junction with Gen Johnston, that the Virginans are sending him in quantities of provisions.

I was over at Mr Harwells today when several gentlemen there, all except a Capt Smith from Montgomery, said we were whipped, that Gen Lee had capitulated. We are not whipped, and never will be if the people of the South are true to themselves. One of them came over to see Mrs McPherson. He told her the war was over, not another gun would be fired, there would soon be a peace concluded, very humilating to us of course. We both gave it to him. We were not whipped we said.

Sister has been sick in bed all day. Went for Dr. Nisbett this evening. He says she is bilious, thinks she will be well in a day or two.

April 23. Sunday. There is no help for it. I must believe now that Gen Lee has capitulated. Oh! how sad it makes me feel, not that I for one moment think that we are whipped. I believe as firmly we will be free as I do there is a God in Heaven. Gen Lee was compelled to surrender. His trains were captured and his men had had nothing to eat for three days. Report says he surrendered only eleven thousand men. Twenty thousand Va troops laid down their arms and refused to leave the State.[90] Lee requested Longstreet to surrender the army but he refused. Oh what a glorious name he might have made for himself had he done so. He is no true patriot or he would not have refused. Gen Lee surrendered his sword to Grant, but Grant refused to take it. He said he was too brave a man, he had not been whipped—he had been overpowered. That Gen Lee is a prisoner I deeply regret, although he is a paroled one. We need all our men, particularly our

Commander-in-Chief. But we have depended too much on Gen Lee too little on God, & I believe God has suffered his surrender to show us he can use other means than Gen Lee to affect his ends. The report we heard yesterday of Old Abe's being killed in Washington is true, and the best of it is that his murderer has escaped. Seward's son was killed the same night in attemping to defend his father. What a pity the father escaped.[91]

We received a letter from father today, dated March 5th. All well. Oh! how much I wish to see them all. Dear Johnnie was well. They have not heard of Sam's exchange. Sams two letters came today. In one he says Henry Cooke was killed in front of Richmond, poor boy.[92] Dr Will Morrow is in Milledgeville, his wife in Griffin. He is cut off from her.[93] There has been the greatest excitement here for the last few days. Thursday and Friday they were running stock off—and a great many people running with them.

April 24. Monday. The weather still continues too cool. Last night I was afraid I would have a chill. Sister was very sick all night. Of course I was up several times and slept but little. The Dr said this morning he feared she was taking jaundice and gave her a powerful dose yesterday to prevent it. He hopes now she will not have it.

Miss Annie came over after breakfast, said there was a report in town last night that the Yankees were in Clinton, and there was considerable excitement in town.[94] Mamie came home from school full of something good Mrs Cross had told them. France had recognized the South, and there had been a naval engagement between the Yankees and French. Capt Will Reid came over after dinner and I asked him what he thought of it. He said he believed France had recognized the South, but did not know about the other. I asked him if he was whipped, he said no nor never would be.

This afternoon Sue Lou went to ride horseback. When she came back she told us she had met Sam out by Mr. Dennis. Carrie was here, and I wanted her to go with me to meet him, but she would not, and went home. So Mary and I started. Met Miss Annie and Sue Reid at the corner, and they went with us. He looked real tired, said he had not been farther than Madison. Stayed with the Lattas there.

Lincoln was assassinated at the Theatre, Seward at his house. Sam says the general belief is that the United States will recognize us. That there has been a treaty between France and the Confederate States, which was to be kept secret till we were in extremity. Spain and Sardinia too have recognized us. They are redeeming Confederate money in Augusta, $1.00 in Gold for $100.00 in Confederate. Pres Davis is expected there today. Many hope for an honorable peace. God grant it may soon come. Sam says at one time he thought he would not come back here, but but then there was no knowing how the armistice would end, and he might never see us again. I am so glad he came.

May 2. Tuesday. I have been in such a state for the last week I could not write. We have heard a thousand rumors. First that we would be recognized, then that we were going back into the Union. I would not believe the last for a long time, but I am obliged to. Oh! how humilating. Gen Johnston has surrendered, or rather Gen Sherman and himself have had a conference in which it was agreed that Gen Johnston's men should be marched to their respective states and disbanded. We to go back into the Union with all our former rights &e.[95] Gen Johnston was so completely surrounded that [he] was compelled to succumb. We have heard so many reports. First that the French have taken New Orleans. That we are to have armed intervention. That Kirby Smith has been reenforced by one hundred thousand French. That there is a French fleet off New York, and I dont know what else.

Lieut Thomas and Capt Robinson called this afternoon, both very blue. How can a true Southerner be any thing else. Yesterday there was a large picnic at Jenkins Mill, neither of us went. I do not think this is any time for picnics &e. Tonight there is to be a dance at Mr Buddins—a Union man.[96] What the young men and girls can be thinking of to go there at such a time I cannot imagine. Almost all the young men have returned. I never saw so many in as small a place.

May 3. Wednesday. Clear and Cool. Oh! I have been so miserably blue today. The Yanks have taken possession of the arsenal at Augusta. It is almost the only one of the Southern cities that they have not occupied during the war, and so has not been injured. I feel as if I never want to see Knoxville again, but I have made up my mind to do whatever will [be] most conducive to the happiness of my parents, even if it is to live there. I will take tea and spend the night with Carrie.

May 4. Thursday. Today is the pleasantest day we have had for some time. Report says there are Yankees in Milledgeville, and there will probably be some here tomorrow. Pres Davis is reported to have left for the Trans Miss. Sam intended joining Forrest, but now he does not know what to do. The negros are all to be put to work on the rail-road, so I hope the state road will be finished before very long. Then H[ome] for Tennessee. I want to take them all by surprise.

Dear Johnnie will reach home before us. How much I wish he could have been exchanged before Lee's surrender. He would have been saved some little humiliation. But I will see him soon, hear his dear voice, and feel his kisses warm upon my lips. My own dear brother. I do not believe there is any love as pure and unselfish as that between brother and sister. I know I am better when I am with him. One glance of his loving eyes is worth more to me than the undivided love of any one else would be. God bless and keep thee my precious, noble brother.

May 5. Friday. Clear and warm. Alice and Mr McClung spent the day here. Sue Lou and Mary Rogan came over after dinner. Late in the afternoon we all walked out to Mr Dennis's. I came back with Miss Kate Thomas. She says she hears the rail-road will be finished as far as Dalton in three weeks. They are going home as soon as they can, though they feel with us that it is hard. Carrie came over after tea, and I am going home with her to spend the night.

May 6. Saturday. Clear and pleasant. Sue Lou came home with me this morning. I have been reading all day Violet, or the Cross and the Crown.[97] After tea, Sam, Carrie, Sue Lou, sister and I walked out to Mr Dennis, and had some music. Some Yanks passed through town today, some Confederates with them, going to Macon to be paroled. The more I think of the present state of things the more I hate it, and the Yankees. How I wish I had the will of them. They are going about the country stealing horses and every thing they can lay their hands on. Some say they are hunting for Pres Davis. His Escort was at Washington [Ga.] three days ago, but he was not with them. I cannot think he will be captured. I believe there is a kind Providence watching over him, and until he is captured I will not think our cause hopeless.

May 7. Sunday. The first thing I heard this morning was "Look at the Yankees." Of course I looked, and there were about a dozen of the devils making a bee line for Mr Reids stable, where they helped themselves to Mr McPhersons buggy horse. They said it was branded U.S. Some one must have told them for the letters were very indistinct. There are two or three hundred here. They say they are not taking private property, only government stores. If they hear of a citizen having forage of any kind they know it is government and go and take it. They are camped in the grove, just in front of the church. I know they will ruin it.

May 25. Thursday. I have felt so badly for some time past I could not write. Our last hope is gone, Pres Davis is a prisoner. He was captured more than two weeks ago with all his family. Gen Smith has surrendered, and the people of the South are slaves—to the vilest race that ever disgraced humanity.[98] It is a humiliating fact, but so it is. All our sacrifices, all the blood shed has been for nothing, worse than nothing, and the Southern people have no one but themselves to thank for it. They do not deserve their freedom or they would have gained it. We will return to Knoxville as soon as possible, but I am very glad that while we had a country, I was not in the Yankee lines. I shall always remember my refugee life as very pleasant, and never forget the kind friends I have here.

Sam went to Macon Tuesday morning with Tom Pearson to get his parole.[99] They came back last night just in time to go to Emma Adams wedding.[100] Capt Wallace & Alex Hazen who are here went too. The rooms were crowded, the supper was fine. We helped make wreaths for the cakes &c. Carrie and Tom P and Tom Branch & Hattie came by for us all to go together, and we had a delightful little dance. I believe we all came to the conclusion we would rather stay at home than go to the wedding. I made a speech to Capt Rich Reid that he must have thought me slightly fast or else wanting in sense.[101] I wish I could learn to think before I speak. Tom W. and Sue Lou are having a grand flirtation. She denies them being engaged. I have my own opinion nevertheless.

Carrie, Hattie & Sue Lou came over and spent the morning. We want to get up a private picnic this week—out at the river, weather permitting.

Sam, Tom W. Alex H. and Tom Branch have just started out to a mill pond, all gone in their shirt sleeves—right through town. I expect the people here will say they are on a spree. They never would have dreamt of such a thing before the war. I taught the children for two weeks, liked it & did not like it. I have stopped since Capt Wallace came, as Mrs McP says it would be perfectly useless to attempt it while he is here. They say now the rail road will not be finished for six weeks. I dont know what we will do. I am anxious to get home, Nights. Well, I expect the people here think the whole family was drunk tonight. I never saw such a looking set as the boys were when they came home. Sam with a red-silk pocket handkerchief tied around his neck and his undershirt in his hand. Tonight we had a grand play of Hurley burley. Made so much noise Capt Reid, Mr Lawson and Mr Adams all started over to see what was the matter. We alarmed the neighborhood.

May 26. Friday. Went over to Mrs Harwell's and sat an hour or two, then came home and sister, Sam and I went to call on the bride. She looked very sweetly. From there went to Reids and spent the rest of the morning. After dinner Carrie and I walked out to see Mrs Clayborne. She was out. We had a real pleasant dance tonight. Carrie, Sue Lou and Hattie, Fannie Morgan and Eliza Beck, Dr Mitchell,[102] Capt Mill, Tom Pearson and Tom Branch, besides home folks. I enjoyed it very much. Mr McClung and Alice spent the day with us. We expect to leave Wednesday or Thursday. Mr Lee Dennis is going to give us a dance Monday night.

May 27. Saturday. This has been a real April day, almost too cool. This afternoon Carrie, Hattie and I walked out to Mr Dennis'. Sam went home with Tom Pearson. It is eleven years today since my little brother Frank died.[103] He was too bright and beautiful for earth, and God took him to himself. I often wonder which one of us will follow him first. May I be ready when my summons comes.

May 28. Sunday. Well, I just know our dance for tomorrow night is knocked in the head. Such a lecture as Mr McDonald gave his church members about dancing. It is perfectly ridiculous. Mr Dennis says if it were not the very next night after he would not care, but as he has been turned out the church twice for dancing, he thinks it would not do. I wish Mr McD had waited till next Sunday for his lecture. Then it would not have interfered with us, or our dance.

May 29. Monday. Sister had a chill today. I am really worried about it. It is so bad as we were about to start for home. It would never do for her to [be] sick on the road with a chill or fever. Tonight we had a very pleasant little dance at home, the Harwells, and Tom Pearson & Capt Lawrence. We will not leave till Thursday. Mr McClung will not go when we do, but we may go on from Marietta together. Of course we will stop there a few days.

May 31. Wednesday. I was too sleepy and tired last night to write. I packed every thing yesterday, and was over at Mrs H[arwell's] half a dozen times. Besides that with the dancing at night came pretty near using me up. This morning I went over to tell Mrs Reid good bye. When I came home found Sue Lou had come for me to spend the day with her. Of course I went, but before dinner time Miss Kate and Miss Annie Thomas came to see us, and Mrs McP sent for me. When I came home found sister had another chill. I wish she could get rid of them.

After dinner Hattie and I started to take a walk, said we were going plum hunting. Did not have to hunt far as we met Tom P[earson] coming in town with a basket full. Of course we turned back with him, as he would have felt very badly if we had not eaten them after his bringing them in. Sister and I took tea over at Mr. H[arwell]'s and the gentlemen came afterwards. Old Mr Fen Epps came in with them. I thought of course he had just happened to meet them, as he was on his way to see Carrie and Sue Lou. After sitting in parlour a little while Carrie and I left and went out in the front yard, to have our last talk. (Dear Carrie how I hate to leave her. I never had a friend to love me as well as she does, and it is very sad to think we may never meet again.)

I suppose we had been out there an hour or more when Mr McP came out after poor me to go in the parlour. Mr Fen Epps had started over here and found we were out so went over there to see us and say goodbye and I had very politely left him. Well I do not think it makes any difference as Mrs McP does. I saw enough of the old goose as it was. He thinks himself as young as either of his sons. I have not got one bit of use for widowers any how, they are so frisky. It was twelve oclock when Sam and I got home. The others went some time before.

We leave here at seven in the morning in an open wagon. We may stop a day in Madison at Mr Latta's, but it is uncertain. I dislike leaving Eatonton very much. I have not many friends, but those I have are warm ones, and seem to really love me. I do not know why any one should love me. I am not beautiful by any means, and I most certainly am not amiable. I wish I was. I do not suppose there ever was any one who wanted to be loved by those around them more than I do, and yet I am constantly doing things that I know will keep them from it, but seem unable to do other wise. Then my tongue is everlastingly saying something that it ought not—and that I regret the very next minute. Poor unfortunate me.

It will be nine months tomorrow since sister and I came to Eatonton, at the repeated invitation of Mr & Mrs McP to make their home our home, while we were cut off from Knoxville. I can never never forget their kindness to us, and I know it is fully appreciated by every member of the family. I hope it may some day be in our power to return it in a measure. I never can fully.

Chapter 6.
I Thought My Heart Would Burst

Knoxville Tennessee. July 18th. Tuesday. Aunt Becky came today and brought me this poor journal of mine that I left—I cannot imagine how—in Eatonton.[1] I was so much worried about it when I found I had left it—but to begin where I left off. [On] Thursday morning, the first day of June, Sam, sister and I started from Eatonton to Madison in an open wagon. Carrie, Hattie and Sue Lou rode with us as far out as Mr Lee Dennis. The day was very warm, and we not particularly comfortable, as we had to sit on our trunks. I laid down some time with my head to the horses, but on starting down a hill, I resumed my upright posish [position], as I had no desire to dance a jig on my head on the back of the horses. We reached Madison about two oclock and drove out to Mr Latta's intending to leave on the three oclock train. The whole family came down to the gate to meet us, and gave us a most cordial welcome. They would none of them hear to our leaving that week any how, so we stayed there till Monday. Had a most delightful time.[2]

The afternoon we got there, several gentlemen who had seen our Grand Entry into town. They came back at night and we had a delightful little dance. Mary has grown very much, she will soon be a young lady. The boys have improved wonderfully. They are really handsome young men, particularly George. He was always my favorite of the two. He is more open and manly than Will. Mrs L. is the same jolly good soul, always in a good humor, and making every one round enjoy themselves. Mr L looks very well and is as pleasant as ever. His house is a delightful one to visit. The family seem to be very popular particularly Mary & George.

Friday [June 2] Miss Laura Ashby—a sister of Col Henry Ashby's—came out to see us, and spent the day. Sister was threatened with another chill, but Mrs Latta dosed her up and she has not had one since. In the afternoon Capt Pense from Sav[annah] called. He is the funniest little ducked leg man I ever saw, though very entertaining. He gave me a lot of Sav. news of old friends there. I liked Miss Ashby very much. She is an innocent little creature. She spent some time in Knoxville summer before last at Mrs Cockes, right near us, but dear Johnnie was sick, and we never called on her. That night Capt and Mrs Harris—her [Laura's] sister—[and] a Mr Post and her came out again and we had another pleasant little dance. There was a Mr and Mrs Davis boarding there—refugees from Nashville—who are very pleasant people, particularly Mrs D, who is very stylish and likes attention and he [Mr D] is rather jealous, so I think. He will not let her dance the fancy dances with gentlemen. I think he is right about that.

Saturday [June 3] we had company all the morning. In the afternoon went to see Mrs Harris & Miss Ashby. Had a dance that night. Mr Beckworth a Tenneseean, two sons of Judge Hawks and a Mr ———. I do not like the latter at all. The others all like him very much. Sam says he is a very clever fellow, but some how I did not fancy him. He was very attentive too.

Sunday [June 4] we went to church and in the afternoon took two long walks, one with Will, the other with George. Madison is a beautiful place. The people are mostly wealthy and bestow great care on their houses and grounds. The house Mr Latta has is an old one, but a very pleasant one. The old couple that own it board with him. They are a strange couple—at least the old woman is. Mr Cary seems to be a very pleasant old Gentlemen.

Monday [June 5] we left much against the wishes of the family, or our own either for that matter, but we thought we ought to. Five or six gentlemen were down at the depot to see us off. That night we reached Atlanta, of all desolate looking places the most. Nothing but walls and chimneys as far as the eye could reach. Such wanton destruction of property was outrageous. The Masonic building and the Gate City hotel the only houses standing. The next morning we saw Mr Howell who had come down for a load of something. We left about 8 1/2 oclock in a covered wagon with six trunks, a man, his cross wife and baby. The day was oppressively warm, the woman's tongue going all the time, fussing at her husband and child, and I just about melting. How thankful I was to reach Marietta. I never received such a welcome in my life & it [was] worth while to take Emily by surprise, for you can see so plainly how glad she is to see you. She seems to love us more than she loves her own family. Priss Charlton[3] is married, done very well, but her husband is younger than she is. I dont fancy that style. We saw the Trenholmes.[4] The old lady looks badly, they have lost every thing. Annie is staying with them now. She has lost almost every thing. Her little boy is very much like Mr Young—dreadfully spoiled. Rennie is married, looks better that I have ever seen her. Mrs Hansell the same old two and six pence, careless as ever. Julia a perfect mountain, the other children overgrown and awkward. Willie's wife is a right sweet young thing. Mrs Wilder looks like a Irish washwoman. Mrs Glover is very frisky. Annie looks as old as she does. Lize is a widow.[5] The Frazers & Hunts are as ugly as ever—they are the ugliest people I ever saw.[6] There is a little Episcopal preacher there, Mr Grant— a fancy little fellow.[7] He took a great fancy to Sister, and Emily. Sam and I teased her almost to death about him. Mr Cooke looks very well.[8]

Marietta is as much destroyed for its size as Atlanta is. The only block on the Square is the one the Masonic building belongs to and the hotel opposite. Thirty-six private dwellings were burnt, ours among the number. I never saw such destruction at one place. You would not think a house had been there for twenty years. It made my heart ache. There is a fort where our carriage house stood, not a fruit tree left in the orchard. Wilders place is uninjured.

We left Marietta Tuesday the 20th of June at eight oclock. Mr Howell came with us in the wagon, Mrs Hansell, Willie and his child and servant & the Gen in another.[9] We had to come as far as Cartersville.[10] I was almost tired to death. A Mrs Wilson took pity on us that night and let us stay there. When we got to Etowah[11] we found that one of the boats were leaking and we had to wait about two hours for them to put another in. While we were waiting a number of Rebel prisoners passed. I stopped one and asked him if he was from Johnson Island. He said yes. I then asked him if Johnnie was released. He said yes. Oh! how glad I was to hear it.

We met Mr McPherson too, who had started to Knoxville, been arrested at Chattanooga, and kept there two weeks. He was on his way home. He said he had received a letter from father saying that Sam must not come home, it was not safe. Sister and I tried to get him to go back with Mr. H, but Willie Cooke would not let him, said that he must come as far as Chattanooga with us.

Wednesday morning [June 21] we left Cartersville and reached C—almost one oclock. Came in a box car—miserable. I think it was the longest afternoon I ever spent. At night we saw Will Ingles just from Knoxville.[12] He said it would be perfectly safe for Sam to go there, so S determined to come on with us. We got to Knoxville five oclock Thursday afternoon. Took them all by surprise. Dear Johnnie was in Nashville, father did not think it safe for him to come home yet. All the Southern boys had been arrested and indicted for treason as soon as they came in. My own darling brother came just two weeks afterwards. He looked badly, had grown a good deal since we last saw him, but he is the same dear, good, noble hearted boy that loves me dearly—and who I love better than any one in the world.[13]

Oh! it is happiness indeed to be with parents and brothers once again. Father and mother both look better than I expected to see them. Will looks badly, Jeanie very well, and little Fannie—my little black eyed bird—a perfect little beauty. She is very shy, has hardly made friends with sister and I yet, though Sam and her have been on the best of terms for some time. It is nearly two years since we have all been together. If the boys could only stay here, but I fear they cannot. Johnnie says Lila Johnston met him at the depot in the carriage and took him to her home. He only stayed a day. She was anxious for him to stay longer, but he wanted to get home. He did not know he would have to stop in M[arietta]. He says that she is a splendid girl. If they both live I expect it will be a match.

In Nashville he had a splendid time. He says he is going back there. He stayed a week out at Cousin Annie's. They were very attentive to him. Auntie named him, and I think he was always her favorite of all father's children, and most certainly he deserves to be. If he lives he will make a great man, and far better than that I believe he will make a good man. He says the girls he has seen most of in Nashville, cousins of Lt. Cahals, have not received visitors since the fall of Fort Donelson. They make a great fuss over the returned Rebels. Johnnie says he received several notes from young ladies, that they would be pleased to have Lt House escort them to different places, and they insist on footing the bills. It is the style in Nashville at present. They know poor rebel prisoners have not more money than they know what to do with.

I was real glad to see our Knoxville boys again, but the ones I knew & liked the best were missing. Their lives have been given up in vain, John Rogers[14] and Hugh McClung. They were the first young men who came to see me after we moved to Knoxville, and I saw more of them than any others till duty called them to defend this country from the foot of the invaders. Poor boys, both went so cheerfully—so confident of success. Hughs short life was soon ended at Fort Donelson. John Rogers was missing after the fight at Murfreesboro, the last day of Dec 1862. I never could believe him dead till since the close of the war. I thought I surely would see him again. I remember so well the last time I saw him. So full of life, he said he would not see me again for full six weeks. His mother still thinks he is alive.

Will [Rogers] is married to Cynthia Brooks. He has grown very stout. He still treats me as if I were a child—I wonder if I ever will be a grown young lady to some people. If I am not old enough to be now, I never will. Jim King is said to have been killed by one of the guards at Point Lookout.[15] I expect though that he will turn up some time, he has been reported killed so often.

Capt May came to see us a few days ago.[16] He promised to let me know where Lt Buchanan is. I hope he will not forget, I would like so much to know. I am afraid he—Lt B—thinks I slighted him, when it was not my fault. I would like so much to see him if only for an hour. There is some thing I want him to explain to me that I cannot exactly understand. I might have continued to write him after I went South, and I think now I ought to have done it. I am afraid I did not do all that I might have done for our poor fellows who were here in prison. I thought at the time I did, but since I went South I have thought of so many things I might have done but now unfortunately it is too late.

When Aunt Becky came today I was in the parlour with Johnnie and an old army friend of his, Mr. Luck from Lewisburg who was here to dinner with him. He must have thought me crazy the way I grabbed at this old Journal, but I was glad to get it. He had the impudence to ask me to let him, a perfect stranger, see it. I like him sorter. I made an engagement to walk out to Temperance Hill with him this afternoon, and after he went I was sorry—and certainly would not have kept it my head ached so badly—had he not been a friend of Johnnies. So we went—the view is beautiful—I have never been there before. He seemed very much surprised when I told him so. He asked me if the Yankees had not pestered me a great deal. I told him yes, they pestered me mightly. I think he seemed to have some doubts of my having any sense. That does not make any difference. I do not suppose I will ever see him again. One thing I do like about him, and that is he seems to think so much of Johnnie. I must like any one who likes him—I cannot help it.

Mother says "Johnnie" is my weak point. A better subject for a weak point I could not have, my own noble brother. He has never caused me one moments pain, and I know—intentionally—he never will. He always loved me better than anyone else did, and I believe he always will.

July 19. Wednesday. Very warm and drizzling off and on all day. A south-ern man named —— was murdered out by Armstrong's today by a union man.

July 20. Thursday. Clear and very warm. This afternoon went to see Mrs French.[17] Took tea with her, so did Dr. & Mrs Murfree, who were over at Col Luttrells.[18] They left tonight for Murfreesboro, [with?] Mr & Mrs Francisco. Hugh French[19] says Marg White is going to unite all the Rebs in town. I met Jim King on the street. I certainly should not have believed my own eyes had not Sam told me this morning that he was here. He certainly has as many lives as a cat. Libbie Morrow is very ill. I am so sorry. I think she is one of the loveliest women I ever knew.

July 21. Friday. Clear and warm. Mr Jim King & Charles Coffin called this morning. It is the first time I have ever met the latter. Like him very much, and think him real good looking. Mrs Fleming, Mrs Rayl, Mary & Kate all came in this afternoon.[20] Mrs Rayal and Kate went out again this afternoon. A negro regiment came in today. The blackest set I ever saw. They say they intend guarding the town with them.

July 22. Saturday. Very warm. The invitations to the wedding are out. Jeanie is not invited. I am sorry for she seems to be so much disappointed. They intended going to New York on a bridal trip.[21] This afternoon Mary Hazen & I went round to the Jail to see Capt Kain, who is there under the charge of murder, the most absurd thing in the world, but I am afraid he will have a right hard time. We asked to see Capt Reynolds too, who has been confined in one of the cages for fourteen months.[22] They both seem to be in pretty good spirits, much better that any one would expect. Libbie Morrow is much better this afternoon, the Dr says he thinks out of danger. After going to see how she was we went around to Rach Rogers for a little while. Coming home met Mrs Eliza McClung who has been here today to see us. I am sorry I missed her.

July 23. Sunday. Another very warm day. I do not remember ever to have suffered with heat as I have the last month. Sunday is such a long tiresome day when there is no church to go to. Mrs French and Mary Hill[23] came down and sat the morning. Mrs Baxter died yesterday and was buried this afternoon.[24] Mrs Fleming and Mary went out to the Brook again this evening. Mary amuses me. She courts Sam & Johnnies society so, and seems perfectly satisfied with them. She received a love letter today from a fellow named Brazrir, who she met two years ago at Mont Vale Springs.[25] It is one of the richest I ever read. She read it aloud for the benefit of the [writing runs off page].

July 24. Monday. Clear and very warm. Sam saw Phi[llip] Reader who has just returned from Athens. He says Sue Lou and Tom are to be married very soon. Tom wanted him to stay and wait on him.

July 25. Tuesday. Very warm. A thunder storm after dinner made it pleasanter by night. Jeanie went up to Dr Strongs to spend the day with her mother. Mrs Fleming and Mrs Rayl, Sister, Sam and Johnnie and I all went to the wedding. Mary looked beautifully. There were a great many there. A Yankee officer or two came quite early in the evening to know what so many people were there for. I suppose they were in hopes they would be invited in. The supper was splendid, and I did full justice to chicken salad and ice cream.

I met Alice for the first time since we came home. She says either Pleas or herself have been sick ever since they have been here. They are going back to Macon to live. She says Sue Lou told her she was engaged to Tom and she thought had been for some time. Bob Armstrong says they were engaged when he was there, and that Tom wanted to go back to Va because he thought then he could get out of it. He ought not to have acted so.

July 26. Wednesday. Today has been abominably warm. We went to call on the bride. She looked beautifully, but very tired. After that we went round to see Libbie Morrow. She is still very sick. She is very weak and does not notice anything. Dr. M says he is going to Ga as soon as she is well enough for him to leave her. There was a fight on the street today between Yanks and negro soldiers. I am real glad. I want them to keep on. The negro regiment here now think they are to have their own way about every thing. They were organized in Chattanooga run-a-ways from upper Ga.[26] Two of them made Gov Brownlow get off the side walk a few days ago. I like that. Mrs Fleming went out to the Brook this afternoon.

July 27. Thursday. It has been the hottest day I ever knew. I have scarcely been comfortable one moment all day. This afternoon Aunt Becky came for me to write her a letter to Mrs McP, which I did, eight pages at that.

July 28. Friday. Today is fathers seventy-first birthday. He is an old man, and I am afraid failing. God grant he may be spared to us for a long long time. He has ever been the kindest and most indulgent of parents. May I be able to contribute to his happiness through the rest of his life is my earnest prayer.

July 29. Saturday. Very warm still. Lizzie Weltker came to see us this morning. I think she is one of the sweetest, prettiest girls in town. Madam rumor says she is engaged to Charlie Coffin. I think it would be a first rate match. He is handsome and very pleasant, and a perfect gentleman.

July 30. Sunday. It has rained a greater part of today. Have enjoyed it so much, the first pleasant day we have had for several. Jeanie and Fannie went out to the Brook this morning, will not return till tomorrow morning. I miss Fannie so much when she is away. She is the smartest, sweetest, prettiest little creature I ever saw. If she is not spoiled and ruined it will be a wonder with so many to pet her.

July 31. Monday. Rained heavily this morning, and about dinner time, Jeanie came in from the Brook and three or four with her. Maj Henderson and Tom Van Gilder called tonight. Mary gave master Tommy a raking down, but he did not seem to mind it at all.

August 1. Tuesday. Pleasant. Sam received a letter from Aunt Mary. She intends going to Pensacola in the fall. I really do believe the boys letters are taken out of the office, for neither have received any except from Ladies since they have been here.

August 2. Wednesday. As it was rather cloudy this morning, sister and I thought we would return some visits we have been intending to ever since our return, but we found it was very warm after we started, warmer as it has been any time this summer. We went to Mrs McClannahans, Cowans, McClungs—Mrs Frank [McClung] has just returned from St. Louis—Mrs Mabry's and Mrs Frenches. Found all at home except Mrs Mabry.[27]

August 3. Thursday. Very Warm.

August 4. Friday. Dear Mothers birthday, she is sixty years old today. I cannot realize it. She does not seem to be near as old, though she has grown old since we left Knoxville last year. I am distressed so at her stooping. She is so beautiful and always had such a beautiful figure till lately. She has contracted a stoop, which worries me so much.

August 5. Saturday. Clear and warm., Sister & I went up to the stores after breakfast to do a little shopping. The only objection I have to the business now is that I have so little money to spend. It is decidedly scarce with us at present, and I dont fancy that state of affairs in the least, for I do love to spend it. But I can make a virtue of necessity and do without very willingly. The dearest wish of my heart at present is to get a house. I am almost crazy to get to house keeping, and so are all the rest, but houses are very difficult things to get. There are so many Yankees here, that every place is filled with them. I am just tired of staying here at Wills. Heaven preserve me from a son's and brother's wife if they are all like Will's.

Mrs Fleming came in yesterday & went out again this morning. She is going home Monday night. I am real sorry, for she is a lady & I like her very much, which is more than I can say for the rest of the tribe. Mary Hill [Alexander] and Fannie Alexander,[28] and Ella Cocke were to see us this morning, and invited the boys and ourselves, Mrs F, Mary, Jeanie & Kate to spend the evening. Jeanie says she cannot go because Sam is going. She spent the last evening at Mrs Frenches and Sam amused Fannie who would not look at any one else.

We all went except Mrs Fleming & Jeanie. Mary and Kate as usual on such occasions, over dressed. They were dressed enough for a large party and there was not another lady there, except Mrs Charles Alexander. The gentlemen were Cols John and Will Reese (the former has just returned from Europe. I think his trip has improved him very much),[29] Mr Jim Cocke, who is over head and ears in love with Fannie Alexander, Hugh French, Jimmie Craighead[30] and Charlie McClung.[31] The last named is rather fine looking, many think that he is very hand some. I think he has a bad face. We spent a very pleasant evening, stayed till eleven oclock.

August 6. Sunday. Very warm. Jeanie went out to the Brook this morning with Mary & Kate. I was very much amused at the breakfast table in speaking of last evening. Mary said Lucy Alexander apologized to her for her not having dressed more.[32] She said she considered her insulting. Lucy told her that the girls told her not to dress, there would not be any one there much dressed. I thought myself it was pretty good. Mr Hilsman preached this morning, in the Baptist church. Most of the rebel girls went to hear him. I wish I had gone too, but did not feel much like it. It rains heavily tonight. There is a gentleman here who has made Sam a splendid offer, but we all think it dangerous for more reasons than one. My greatest objection is that he cannot stand being in the sun, since he was wounded in the head.

August 7. Monday. Clear and warm. Sam this morning commenced acting as private secretary for a Yankee Quarter Master.[33] Poor fellow, it was a bitter pill for him to swallow, and I think he deserves so much credit for taking the place. He has to have a beginning, and this may do for one. Better than we think for Will sent Jeanie a box of peaches which came today, some of them are splendid. I went to see Libbie Morrow this afternoon and took her some. She is much better, able to walk all about the house. Dr. Morrow leaves tonight. Met Lizzie Lewis there.[34] She is going to start for Cincinatti tonight. After tea sister & I helped Jeanie peal peaches to preserve tomorrow.

August 8. Tuesday. Mother, sister and I walked out to see Mrs Crozier this morning. She was out, but Mrs Scott and Alice were at home.[35] Mr [C. A.] McClung is going to Ga this week, he may go to Eatonton. I would write by him, but he is so uncertain, he might forget to deliver the letter. As we came home stopped to see Miss O'Conner. She gave us some peaches & ice water, which was very acceptable. Her mother has gone to Va. There is a party tonight at Charles McClungs. Nan came in to go. She wanted to have her hair frizzed, and sent for a barber to come do it. He worked an hour at it, made it look a sight, and charged $1.00. We told her it made her look beautifully and she was delighted. Mrs Fleming left tonight. Ed Trigg came down for Sam to go up town with him.[36] He is the first Federal officer I have spoken to since my return to K, and I merely said good evening to him.

August 9. Wednesday. Sister and I went up town this morning. After I came home went up again with father to take a set of shells for Cooke Danner to fix for me. In the afternoon went to see Kitty King and Cluss.[37] Today has been delightful.

August 10. Thursday. Very warm. Received a short note from Mrs McPherson, enclosing a letter for Aunt Becky. She never received the long one I wrote her by Will Hazan. It must have been some carelessness on his part that she did not. There is to be a storm party tonight somewhere, Mrs Frenches I expect. Sister is going with Charles King. Johnnie asked Mary Hill but she declined (I did not think she would go) and then he had the impudence to write a note to a girl he had never seen and she accepted. Sam goes with Cluss and I with Mr Charles Coffin. We are to meet at Gen Brook's and go from there. Mrs Crozier called this afternoon. I dont know what I would have done if it had been any one else, begged to be excused I expect, for I had my braids off—braiding it for tonight and my head looked a sight.

August 11. Friday. Well, last night we stormed Mr McNutt. They seemed very much pleased, though entirely taken by surprise. Almost all were disappointed that we did not dance. Spent quite a pleasant evening. Johnnie was bored to death. Fannie King would not talk, and no one would relieve him.

Blannie McClung was there, came down Wednesday night. She is beautiful. We raised more of a storm than we expected for we were caught in the rain.

Mrs Charles [McClung] and Mrs Frank McClung called this morning.[38] The latter I admire very much and always have. She expects to get her house next week. Gen Alexander is moving into Mr Martins.[39] Mrs Charles is the silliest little goose I ever heard talk. I do not think I ever met her she did not make some mistake. She said this morning that Gen Stoneman, the Yankee in command here, Gens Kirby Smith, Stonewall Jackson and Hardee were class mates.[40] The idea of Smith & Hardee being class mates, more like father and son. Then she was describing a cribbage board to Jeanie. She said it looked just like it came from the West Indies, she meant Japan. I know I would have laughed if I had caught either sisters or Jeanie's eye.

Capt May called this afternoon. He has been released only a short time. He says when he hears any thing of Buchanan he will let me know. He expected to hear soon. I would like so much to hear from him. After tea, Mother, sister, Johnnie and I went over to Mrs Mitchells. Lizzie is beautiful and wild. I think Johnnie and her are a good match.[41]

August 12. Saturday. I have had a real bad head ache all day. Finished that everlasting wicked body. I am so glad. I made me sick to look at it.

August 13. Sunday. Very warm. Jeanie and Johnnie went out to the Brook to spend the day. I wrote to Mrs McPherson, Emily and Cousin Annie.

August 14. Monday. When Sister, Jeanie and I went to the stores this afternoon there was quite an excitement on Gay St. (A man named Bergar attacked Capt Claybe Plumlee C.S.A, fired at him and then commenced beating him with a stick.[42] When Capt Plumlee drew his pistol B ran but not soon enough to escape a shot in his shoulder.) There were two black companies besides a number of white soldiers in front of Plumlees store. They said for P. safety. While they were standing there waiting for him to come out, or rather be brought out, they had found him in a flour b[arre]ll. Put a suit of Federal uniform on him and [have] taken him round to the jail. Went to see Blannie McC[lung]. Found her out.

August 15. Tuesday. Father says he hears they intend taking Capt Plumlee down to Chattanooga under guard and releasing him there. He would not be safe here.

August 16. Wednesday. Another man shot. This morning a man (southern) named Cox was in Tooles store when a Lincolnite named Foster came in shook hands with him, inquired after his health & just as Cox turned round shot him in the back first then in three other places. It is said to have been entirely un-provoked. Cox was immediately arrested, and bail refused him. The authorities here say it was a cold blooded murder. Mother heard a negro soldier tell a white man about it and add that had Cox had a dozen lives Foster ought to have taken them all he was such a rebel. Brownlow's teaching. After tea Johnnie and I went round to the Alexanders. There has been only four men killed here today. There certainly is a dreadful state of things. No mans life is safe.[43]

August 17. Thursday. Today has been very pleasant. There is a party round at Mrs Frenches tonight. Sister, Johnnie & Sam have gone. I did not feel like it.

August 18. Friday. Sister surprised us last night when she came home by telling us Cluss & Jim King were married last night and left on the train. I never was more surprised at any thing in my life. This afternoon, Jeanie, sister and I went round to see Mrs McC. She said she had been crying all day. Cluss wanted to put it off another week, but Jim would not hear to it. I do think Cluss and her [him?] are the funniest pair I ever met. I wish I had known she was to be married. I would not have missed it for any thing.[44]

August 19. Saturday. There liked to have been some more shooting in town today between Rebs and Union men. Jim Luttrell snapped a pistol in a mans face who told him he could not stay here. His name was Pasham. Bob Armstrong came near shooting him too. The people here will find rebel boys are not to be fooled with.

August 20. Sunday. Today is my birthday. Just to think of it. I have just this minute found it out. Will Hazen returned from Ga today. Will [House] will be here in a day or two. He says Mr Sam Wallace is dead, was well at supper and died a short time after. How very sudden. I am very glad his wife was with him. How unfortunate that family has been. Tom Wallace has left the firm of McPherson & Co.[45] He cant think or talk or any thing but Sue Lou. They are to be married in Nov, at least that is what they expect now. There is no telling how soon she may change her mind.

August 21. Monday. Today has been oppressively warm. Aunt Becky came for me to write a letter to Liz for her, also one to Cammie Wallace.

August 22. Tuesday. As I did not like the tone of Aunt Becky's letter, I wrote Fannie today and included it to her. Brownlow is making quite a number of threats about what he intends to do to Maj Wallace. He is just near enough to give him a great deal of trouble.[46] He sent to Nashville and had Crow Ramsey arrested on the charge of murder, brought here and is in one of the cages.[47] I hear that Sophie Kennedy is very ill and has been ever since Mrs Frenches party. She is better though today. There is to be a party (storm) out at Mr Ben Stephensons. I am going with Jim White, sister with Lt. Newman. It is to be a dance. Mr. White called this afternoon.

August 23. Wednesday. Disenpating [Dissipating] does not seem to agree with me at all. My head and eyes ache so this morning. We did not get home till after two oclock. Had a right pleasant evening. I dont know why it is, but I cant enjoy any thing of the kind as I used to. I feel really out of place, and the first part of last evening felt as dull and stupid as possible. I am so provoked at myself. I am almost tempted to vow I'll never go to another if I cant do better.

Several of the boys had been drinking. Mr White went out and took a bottle of liquor from a negro boy. They had sent to town for it. I think it is perfectly outrageous, the idea of any one who pretends to be a gentleman acting so. If they want to drink they might to stay at home and do it. They have no business going where ladies are. Tom Van Gilder was there, the first of the Rebel parties he has been to. He seemed to feel himself very much out of place, and did not stay very long, left before supper.

August 27. Sunday. There has been nothing worth writing since Wednesday. Friday afternoon sister and I went to see Libbie Morrow, and the Alexanders. Blannie McClungs sister Mrs Cobb is dead.[48] At night Sister, Johnnie and I went to see Mrs French. On the same day I received a letter from Mr Baird who had been here a prisoner of war before I went South. He was a friend of Mr Dodds who was hung here. It was written on the 7th and send by a Lt Bruwell who came here after the body of Mr Martin who was supposed to have died here in the hospital. I answered it today, and wrote to Cousin Frank too.

This afternoon there was a soldier killed. One of the 8th Tenn. who has been sent here to be payed off was drunk, [went] round by the ordinance office, and one of the negro guards started to arrest him. A friend of the drunken man told the guard not to take him to the guard house, he would take him to camp, but he did not take him soon enough to suit the negro who ran his bayonet through him—the sober man. The 8th Tenn vow they will kill every negro soldier in the street tonight.[49]

August 30. Wednesday. Well I did it this afternoon, in style at that. Aunt Becky came to get me to write a letter for her. I had not felt well all day and was not dressed. Well when I finished I started into mothers room to get an envelope. When I opened my door there sat some one in the boys bed. I thought it did not look like either of them, and took a second look—and he looked at me, a stranger. I seemed rooted to the spot, and when I did move instead of coming in and shutting the door I ran down the entry into Mothers room. Such a sight as I know I looked, only one garment under my wrapper, and such a head. I never hated any thing as badly in my life. It proved to be Jimmie Hatcher, son of Maj Hatcher, a very particular friend of Johnnies, and one who was very kind to us while we were South, although I had never seen him, and the idea of a son of his seeing me in such a plight distresses me beyond measure. It is the first time in my life I was ever caught so, and I truly hope twill be the last. I felt ashamed to look at him the whole evening.

Last night there was a storm party out at Mrs Jim Boyds.[50] None of us went. I would have gone had I not been afraid Mr Luttrell, who asked me to go, would be under the influence of liquor as usual, and I never want to go any where with a man who has been drinking. They say they had a delightful time. I knew they would out there. It was very well I did not go for I was real sick almost all night. I believe some thing is the matter with my heart. I felt so cold and numb, I though for a little while I might be dying. Mother says I need something for my nerves.

There was a negro guard found down the river this morning drowned. Some one had tied his musket down his back & and thrown him into the river head foremost. Yesterday I received a long letter from Carrie. I was very happy to hear from her. She is in deep distress. Dr Andrews has taken Ellie from her.[51] I think it is cruel. She writes me old Judge Pearson is to be married to a young lady 47 years younger than himself. They are two fools. I should not think his children would like it. She did not say one word about Sue Lou or Hattie.

Sept. 1. Friday. Two years today since the Yanks took possession of Knoxville. Oh! how things have changed since that time. It sickens me to think of it. Then we were free, now we are slaves—slaves to the vilest race that ever disgraced humanity. Mr Hatcher left this morning. He seems to be a very clever young man, not at all diffident and at the same time not forward. I would dearly love to see his father.

Sept. 5. Tuesday. Today has been a sad, sad day for us all. I am sick heart sick. Within the last forty-eight hours the most horrible tragedy has been enacted. Right next to us lived a brother and sister with an uncle. Their father was brutally murdered by the Yankees during Sanders raid into E. Tenn more than two years ago.[52] The bro a boy of nineteen was one of Ashby's men, one who had no enemies, a good, quiet, noble little fellow. Yesterday morning a man (union) named Hall, cousin of Judge Hall, went into a barroom and after taking a drink, said, "Now I'll go and knock some damned Rebel down." The first one he met chanced to be Ab Baker. He struck him three times with a stick, broke his stick, when Ab finding that he would not stop drew his pistol and shot him dead. He was arrested and put in jail.[53]

The Union men said they would take him out and hang him. I did not for a moment suppose it would be allowed. But the first thing we heard this morning was that over a hundred of the 13th Tenn went to the jail last night about ten oclock, tied the jailer and took the poor boy out.[54] They told him they were going to hang him. He told them if there was only one he could hold his own, but against so many he could do nothing, but he added I will show you how a brave man can die, and he did. He never flinched. They left him hanging four or five hours then threw his body over in the jail yard.

Will went up to Dr Bakers that morning just after they brought him home.[55] They threw him in an ambulance on some shavings [?], with not even a sheet and drove him [into] town. Whenever the ambulance would jolt he would roll from side to side. His family are very much distressed that they did not go to see him yesterday. They started but friends advised them to wait till today.

I have just come from the funeral. He is buried in the Old Church yard, and I can see his grave from where I sit writing. His sisters wail "My poor brother" is still ringing in my ears. Poor girl, he was her all. There was a Yankee at the funeral. He looked at all the boys there as if he could kill them, and they returned [his look]. I am so sorry there were so few of them out, only Jim White, Lt. Newman, Hector Coffin & Johnnie. Sam could not leave his office, but most of the boys had nothing to keep them from going except fear that there would be some trouble.[56]

No notice has been taken of the affair by the authorities. They cursed at it. The guard was withdrawn instead of being increased as it should have been. When they brought his coffin there were some Yankee officers standing near, and they were laughing and going on about putting a d——d rebel in such a fine one. The officers of the men were with them when they hung him. They say they intend to hang nine more. After they had finished their fiendish act of murdering an innocent boy, they went to a negro Ball and shot into the windows. Killed four men and one woman, and one woman jumped out of the window and broke her neck.

Sept. 8. Friday. Almost all the boys have gone. Johnnie left last night. He said he did not like the idea of leaving now, although he wanted to leave before the murder. But all thought best for him to go. He belonged to the old Nineteenth that was organized right here, and hated so by the Union men, and had been in the Post Head Quarters here at one time.[57] Then it is so hard to keep him from talking. Sam is different, besides having something to do here.

We certainly live in horrible times. Scarcely a day passes some one is not killed. Yesterday two were. This afternoon a man passed here under two guards with a cut in the back of his head and almost covered with blood. A little way behind came a lame soldier who had been shot and was bleeding, and a woman. Will asked them what was the matter. The woman said "She did that work, that [the] man came in and tried to kill her man. He was lame & could not help himself so she picked up an axe and cut him. She would have killed him if the sergeant had not stopped her."

Brownlow as usual gives a false account altogether of the killing of Hall.[58] He says that Baker and himself had a difficulty from years ago. That is simply absurd, the boy was not twenty when he was hung, and [had only] met Hall that morning when Hall commenced abusing him and when he turned to leave shot him in the back of the head. The more I think of it all the more awful it seems. While they were hanging poor Ab, about fifty men blk & white, went to Mrs Frank McClungs, Mrs Frenches &e, serenading. Said they were paid to serenade the Southern families that night. Who ever heard of such fiends. Kate has gone to Va, left this morning. I received a letter from Cousin Annie and also one from Mrs Churchwell.

Sept. 10. Sunday. Today has been the hottest of the summer. Will moves this week to Capt Latta's house, and we keep this.[59] They even threatened to burn Dr Bakers house, and told a Yankee named Ellis who was boarding there he had better leave. Mr Joe Mabry[60] and Mr Sam Atkins have been warned to leave the place. Mr. Davenport, an old friend of father & mothers, came and spent the afternoon and evening.[61] He made himself very pleasant, and I enjoyed his society very much. He took dinner here Thursday, when he really bored me. I think now that perhaps it was my fault. I wanted him to leave because Johnnie was going that night, and I wanted him all to our selves. Will, Jeanie and the baby are in the country.

Sept. 24. Sunday. What a scrubbing and cleaning and fussing round generally we have had since I last wrote. Will moved Thursday week to Capt Latta's house and we have taken his, or rather the one he was living in. Both houses were very dirty. Though I expect his was much the worst as the military have been occupying it ever since the occupation. Will says it was

the filthiest place he ever saw. Capt Chamberlain—a Yankee Quarter master—now a partner of Tom Van Gilders at the drug store, had rented it, and
they had to take him to board to get the house.[62]

The other night Sam, sister and I walked round there. They were eating supper, so we went into the parlour. After a little while Capt Chamberlain walked in—of course we did not speak as he was a stranger—as far as
the centre table when Jessie Rayl who was in sisters lap says "You had better
go out of here." He turned to leave the room and said "I think I will." I just
wanted to laugh so I could hardly keep from it. What a creature a Yankee is.

The baby seems better satisfied here than she does there, a great deal.
When she comes down she never wants to go, and when she has to wants
us all to go with her. We have heard twice from Johnnie. He has not been
able to get a situation yet. Dear boy I hope he will soon succeed in getting
one. Sister has received two letters from Emily lately. They says Essie and
Lila Trenholm are flying round with Yankees Officers extensively, riding
horseback day and night. She says they are engaged to two of Judah's Staff.[63]
I am really very much surprised at them. How southern girls can receive
attentions from Yankees I cant see for the life of me. I hate and despise them
more every day I live.

Dr Baker died Wednesday night. He was in a dying condition for several days. His nephews untimely end no doubt hastened his death. Capt
Wish the leader of that diabolical affair is still here, cursing at Rebels and
copperheads. Gen Stoneman came and went and took no notice at all of it.
But there will, there must be a day of retribution in store for them. Such
devils cannot prosper. God will not allow it. Sometimes I almost feel convinced that we will yet be free.

Marg McDermott was to see us yesterday.[64] She says they have given up
the idea of going to Ga and are going to live on his farm at Tellico plains.[65]
Mary Hazen left for New York yesterday morning with her father. Quite a sudden thing, wont she splurge. Jeanie told me in confidence that she [Mary Hazen]
and Tom Cummings were to be married the last of Oct. I have my doubts on
the subject. I am sorry for any man she marries. She will lead him a dance.

Sister wants to go to Marietta on a visit. I think the reason she has not
gone is because money is so scarce, although she does not say so but keeps
putting it off. Dear father has lost every thing like many others, and he is

too old to do any thing. I do not like the idea of living on Sam as we are at present. He seems to think it all right, but I dont. It is too much for him to have to spend all he makes on the family, but he is such a dear, good, unselfish boy he wont think so. We would be dull enough if it were not for him. He is always so cheerful, and I know it must be a trial and a sore one at that to stay here, almost the only southern boy in the place, all his friends gone, nothing to interest, nothing to amuse him.

Some Quarter masters clerks and their wives are in Dr. Morrow's house. They are a funny sort of people. All this afternoon they have been singing songs, and it was the same last Sunday. I wrote Johnnie. If he stays in N[ashville] I want to go there in Jany—that is if I can get the needful. I have a strange disposition. I am satisfied any where, and still I love change dearly, and am one of the most restless beings in the world.

Oct. Sunday. Today they say is delightful. I cannot judge for I have been in bed. I have not been well for a week since but not obliged to keep my bed till today. I am certainly the most useless creature in existence. As long as I am very careful and do nothing I am very well, but if I exert myself in the least for a few weeks at time, to bed I have to go. Since we have been keeping house, I have been getting up very early superintending breakfast and been pretty busy all day long . . . as we have only one servant & . . . when all of a sudden it came to an end, as all my efforts to be useful generally do.

It has been a long time since I have written in this silly journal. There has been nothing worth writing. Every thing seems so tame now since the close of the war that since I have in a measure become used to our humiliation every thing seems perfectly indifferent. The only strong feeling I have is hatred to the Yankees—oh! how I do hate them. But I have grown so used to hating them that it seems to have been a principle implanted in my breast in infancy, to have grown with my growth and strengthened with my strength, instead of a thing of recent date. Johnnie has a very good situation in Nashville though he hopes to get a better one. Sam is still in Capt Wainwrights office. He appears to get along very well. One of the clerks there, a Mr Fletcher from Nashville, who has been eating over at Davis's is coming here to morrow to board.[66] He took dinner with Sam today, has been over here a good deal ever since we have been keeping house. I like him, because he is no Yankee.

Oct. 29. Sunday. How rapidly the weeks roll around. Today has been delightful. How much I wish for a church. This living week after week, and month after month without entering the house of God is dreadful, particularly when there is no telling how long it may last. I wrote Johnnie a long letter, and Cousin Annie too. Fannie has not been down today, the first day she has missed for a long time. I do think she is the smartest sweetest little creature in the land. Jeanie says if she does not start her down every morning, she will bring her her bonnet and cloak, and give her no peace till she tells her she may come see grand mother. Then she dances, and laughs and starts off. I dont know what we would do without her.

Will is still out of employment. He is getting very restless at leading the life he does. He says he intends going South, and getting into some kind of business and then coming for Jeanie and the baby. I think it is the most sensible thing he can do. How [I] will miss Fan. Jeanie is just recovering the use of her hand, which has been in a dreadful state from her spilling some boiling grape Jelly on it. I was fearful it would be months before she could use it.

Mary [Hazen] has returned from New York, where she has been several weeks with her father. She has seen nothing of the city—or any thing worth seeing. All she seems to have thought of was dry goods. She did not even go to the theatre or up Trinity church steeple. What a girl she is.[67] I hear nothing of her marriage now. Jeanie told me last Aug that Tom Cummings and her were to be married the last of this month. She used to be always telling Sam about him, but he says she has not mentioned his name since her return. We are inclined to think Mr T has given her the slip. He would not be the first who had done so.[68]

Nov. 1. Wednesday. Today has been charming, and the moon is out in all her glory tonight. Sister has been very sick since Sunday, but is very much better today. She says she is going to Marietta next week. I never knew her to talk as much about going away before. She generally makes up her mind about three days before she starts. I'll have a dull old time when she is away. Tis dull enough now to suit any one. Father is working up at Capt W's too, has been for a week or more. I dislike the idea so much, but 'tis far better than doing nothing, and he is so much better satisfied now that he is employed. But the idea of such a man as father being clerk to a Yankee QM is by no means pleasant. I suppose though we ought to be thankful he has any thing to do. So many who were wealthy before the war are now reduced to poverty, and all for nothing, for worse than nothing, to be made the slaves of Northern despotism.

I am glad Lincoln was killed. We were at least saved the humiliation of being under his rule. He would have completed the ruin the war had so fearfully begun. The Southern people would have had their chains riveted with iron. Andy Johnson is more inclined to be just, not that I believe that a true sense of Justice or love for the South has any influence with him, it is his ambition. He thinks that to be reelected he must have Southern votes, and all that he may do will only be to gain his own selfish end.

Nov. 19. Sunday. Clear and pleasant. This morning Mr Fletcher and I went to the Roman Catholic Church.[69] Of course all the services were hum-bug to me, but I was very much pleased with the remarks of father Price—I think his name is—and intend going again. Coming home we had a talk on the subject of drinking &e. which ended very satisfactorily. We agreed per-fectly on the subject. I like him now for more reasons than his not being a Yankee. He is young and boyish, but that makes him like my own darling Jno in some things. He is not going to drink at all. I think him very sensible, for then he will be safe, and only then. There is a Mr. Swain boarding here, another clerk at the office. He seems to be a right smart young man, and no one who was ever in his company five minutes would ever doubt his having a tongue. It goes all the time. There has been a Mr Woodruff boarding here too.[70] He has been a Capt in the Yankee Army who has gone to Ky to be married. We have speculated no little on what kind of a some body she is. Our curiosity will be satisfied soon for he expects to be back again by the first of Dec.

Sister has gone down to Marietta on a visit to Emily. She went down with Will last week. He expects to move down to Atlanta to live this win-ter. What I will do if she does—before sister comes home. Fan is down al-most every day. Sam stays there at night while Will is away. So I have a right lonely time. Mr Fletcher stays here at night now in Sams room. We play chess sometimes after tea, but I do not seem to take as much interest in it as I used to. But I am determined I will like it more, instead of less.

I wrote Jno last night, and Carrie Harwell. I have had a long letter from her [about] Fannie Wallace & Frank M[atthews?]. Frank is teaching school at Mount Sterling, Ky. at fifty dollars a month. Of course he is in love. I never knew the time when he was not. I would really like to know how often he has been desperately in love with some fair young creature, Beautiful, accomplished and wealthy. The last is by no means the least attraction, or at least so I suspect. Fannie Wallace has gone over to Eatonton to stay till Jany with Mrs McPherson, who goes to Atlanta then. Mr McP has bought a house there and gets possession of it at that time. I am afraid he will go down hill very fast—from all I hear. Strange how a man will love liquor, more than wife, family, honour, or even his own soul.

Maj Wallace moves to Pumpkin Vine, a beautiful name, about twenty miles from Marietta. The engagement between Tom and Sue Lou is either broken off or postponed for some time. They would make a hopeful couple. Alice McClung has gone to Macon. All my friends are leaving. Rach Rogers has a daughter, red headed. If it is any thing like her blessed darling I know it is a real beauty. I cannot see how she could have married him, but many men of many minds—and I suppose many women too. The strangest part of it is that she seems to think she has done wonders in the matrimonial line. Tom Cummings has been here on a visit to Mary. From appearances I should say they would be married soon, probably some time about Christmas. His purse strings will suffer with her for a wife, but that is none of my business.

Nov. 23. Thursday. The weather has been charming, till this afternoon when it blew up quite cold. Father thinks that we will have ice tonight. I have not been out today, the first time I have missed for more than a week. Mr Rayal has come, so Sam does not have to stay up at Jeanies at night, which is a blessing as Mr Sam Miller would say. Christmas is scarcely a month off. I wish it were passed, and yet I do not want it to come, rather contradicting any one would think. After that time I will feel free. What a relief it will be. Now some times I am so blue. Why did I ever—but no I will not write it here, or any thing about it. I have kept it out of this journal. Why I should have been so averse to mentioning it I cannot imagine, unless it was that I knew I had no right to triffle with any one, as I have done, but never, never will again. So now it ends here for the present any how.

Mr Swain is quite pleasant—and yet I do not know whether I like him or not. He watches me more closely that I like. Why I cannot imagine. He is engaged to be married to a young lady in Philadephia, and is constantly speaking of her. I wonder what they are waiting for, but that is none of my business. This afternoon I was so disappointed. Father told me when he came home Sam had a letter for me, which proved to be by no means what I expected—one from Jennie Wallace to Aunt Becky enclosed to me. Jeanie says Mary is to be married in Feb. I wish she would not put it off so long, for I may not be here then. When Sister returns from Marietta, I expect to go to Nashville on a visit. I know I will enjoy it. Being with my darling brother Jno will be happiness enough for me.

Dec. 3. Sunday. I little thought when I last wrote how dark a cloud was hanging over us, so soon to burst in all its fury, and leave our hearts, blackened and scathed. I cannot realize the dreadful truth now. My precious brother Johnnie is dead. Oh! that awful word seems burned into my brain with letters of fire. So young, so good, every thing that the fondest heart could wish. My darling, darling brother. My heart feels as if it were breaking, such a dreary, longing, aching void—that nothing can ever fill. God help me to say "Thy will be done." Last night was a week ago we received a telegram from Mr. Thompson[71] saying he [Johnnie] had been dangerously wounded the night before by robbers, for father to come on immediately. Half an hour after came another. He was better, but required nursing, send mother and I. Oh! how I thanked God for that. Father and I left that night. I thought the train would never start, that I would never get to him. At last it started, but oh! how slowly it went. After we passed the Nashville train at Decherd, I heard some one say John House had been shot. I told father, he said there was a very exaggerated account of it in the Nashville papers. I could not rest till I saw one.

He—our darling—was on his way to a wedding party on the Franklin Pike, two miles and a half from town. The report of a musket was heard, and the ball went past. Johnnie raised in the buggy to see if he could see who shot when another was fired which struck the iron of the buggy and glanced— entered his thigh and passed through his lungs and liver, lodged in his right breast. He said to Mr Ewing who was in the buggy with him, "Ewing I'm shot you take the pistol and fire."[72] He was carried to the house of Mr Thompson where he lie dying the night before. So the paper said, but father would not let me think for one moment that it was so. But how miserable it made me.[73]

The cars seemed to move so slowly. Would they never reach Nashville. After we got to Murfreesboro some men got on the train, and they commenced jesting about my darling's being shot. One went so far as to say "he was only a Reb." I thought my heart would burst, but I was so thankful mother had not gone instead of me. It would have killed her. When at last the cars reach N, my heart stood still. I thought in a few minutes, I would be with him, and tried to calm myself—so fearful I was I might injure him. I imagined I could see his smile, and feel his arm around my neck, and hear his dear voice say "Sister Ellen." But minute after minute passed and Cousin William did not come.[74] At last he came, his only words, My poor poor Ellen. I knew then that he was gone. He died the night before at eleven oclock, calmly as an infant. Cousin William said as soon as he heard he had been shot he went to him, and never left him. He was perfectly conscious. When Cousin William told him he could not live, he asked him if he was afraid to die. My darling told him he was not afraid to die, but it was hard to die so. Oh! I would have given worlds to have been with him if only for five minutes, just to hear his dear, dear voice again. Almost the only request he made was that Cousin William would telegraph to Lila Johnston if he died, and that he would telegraph for mother and I.

Cousin William had had him brought in from Mr Thompsons where he died that afternoon, and taken to the undertakers, and there I went to see him, who I have always loved better than any one on earth, better even than my maker. Oh! it seemed so hard to leave him there, but father said we ought to. They were all so kind to me, but I felt if I could only die too— it would be such a blessing. When I went back to Cousin Williams, I went into his room to pack his trunk to bring home with me. Every thing there was just as he had left it expecting to return in a few hours, his clothes lying where he had thrown them when he dressed. It seemed like sacrilege to touch them, and yet I had to do it. Could I have waited a few days it might not have been so hard, so I thought then, but I think differently now. They all seemed to love him dearly. My poor murdered brother, they could not help it. There were a Mr & Mrs Neederbecker there, who were very kind. He had the coffin opened and cut me some hair.

Before we left next morning I asked Cousin William to tell me every thing he said. He asked to see an Episcopal minister. Bishop Quintard[75] was absent, and Cousin Wm took Mr B——, a Presbyterian clergyman out to see him. He prayed with him, and Johnnie prayed himself. Oh! how thankful I am he was not afraid to die. Dear father stood it better than I expected, but it has aged him so. Monday morning we left Nashville with all that remains to us of our idolized brother, and reached home the next morning. Sam telegraphed to Will and sister, who came Wednesday. Will said the first he heard of it was the last dispatch sent. "Come home at once Johnnie will be buried tomorrow afternoon." It was sudden for us all, but far more sudden to him.

We laid our darling in the grave Wednesday afternoon. We could not bury him here where he could not live. Put him in the Sneeds vault, so we can move him when we move from here. Oh! how dreadful I felt at his funeral. Father and mother were together, Will and Jeanie, Sister and Sam and I with a comparative stranger—Mr. Fletcher. He who I was always with, lying there cold and still in death, I alone—alone. Then I knelt to pray and though I had no brother John to pray for, and now that Sunday has come and no Johnnie to write to, it is hard to say "Thy will oh, Lord, not mine be done. Teach me Father to bow in humble submission to thy will." Mr Martin buried him. I was so thankful a Southern minister was here, and Southern boys for pallbearers. Jim White, Joe McLain,[76] Charlie Coffin, Hugh French, Willie Bearden and I think Bob Armstrong.[77]

Mr. Fletcher and Mr Swain have been very kind, the latter just as kind as he knew how to be. But Mr Fletcher has been like a brother, so thoughtful. He has a noble heart. He told me he would "try and fill my darlings place," and I believe he will. But Oh! my precious, precious brother, no one can ever fill your place. Father received a tribute of respect from the Employees at the Nashville and Chattanooga store house, where Johnnie stayed for a month. Mr Woodruff and his wife came Friday. Ours is a sad house to bring a bride to.

Dec. 10. Sunday. I had hoped today would be clear so that I could go to Church. I think I had much better go to the Catholic than stay at home Sunday, after Sunday. I cannot bear to spend the Sabbath day so. It will not fit me to join my bro where he now lives in one eternal Sabbath. I believe I feel his death more every day, not a moment in the day but some thing makes me realize more fully my darling is gone. I try to be cheerful on father and mothers account, but it is so hard. The aching at my heart grows worse. But it is God's will he took my brother to himself. I must learn to love him more, for only through his love and mercy can I hope to see my angel brother again.

Wednesday I wrote to Lila Johnston, asking her if I should return her letters and Photographs. Father received a beautiful letter from Maj Thompson, an old army friend of Johnnies, and a note from Capt Kain. He knew and loved him, and can appreciate our loss. Will intends leaving Knoxville and going to Atlanta to live, will probably go this week. How we will miss him. He says there are so few of us left he does not want to go, but it is his duty, and he must. We may all be together again some time—but I fear not. If Sam can only stay at home I will be satisfied. We could not let him leave us. I feel as if I never want him out of my sight, least some harm might happen to him. God protect him, and keep him from harm, is my constant prayer.

One of the Police were killed last night, named Haynes, by a man named Dzrir. Some say it was an accident. Dzrir is in jail, the murdered man has left a wife and three children, the oldest can scarcely talk. It is a sad thing. The Devil seems to be walking at large in East Tenn.

I received a short letter from Mrs McPherson last week, in which she said she expected to be here by the twelfth. I will be very glad to see her. Her kindness to sister and myself I can never forget. Will came down this afternoon, brought Fannie with him. Jeanie is suffering from a very violent head ache and did not come. Sam went with Kate and Mary Hazen round to the jail to see Capt Kain. They saw both he and Dick McCann.[78] The latter was a prisoner at Johnsons Island the same time dear Johnnie was. Gen Hazen is intruding himself for them, and they hope he may soon be able to effect their release.

Dec. 17. Sunday. I was so much disappointed this morning when I woke the ground was covered with snow. I wanted so much to go to church. Yesterday I received a beautiful letter from Lila Johnson. She loved our darling as a brother. I love her for it—and hope some day we may meet. She was a true friend for my noble brother from the time of his capture till he was called away from earth to heaven. There is not a moment in the day that I do not see him, looking at me with those loving blue eyes, or lying cold and lifeless in his coffin. Oh! the weary, weary aching at my heart. If I could have reached him before he died, felt his arms about my neck—his kisses on my lips, if only for a moment, I would give worlds did I possess them, my dear, dear brother. Twas hard to die away from home, and all who loved him best. Oh! that I could have died for him. God help me not to murmer. I love my other brothers dearly, but not like I do my angel brother. I never can love any one as I did him. My high soul, noble, precious Johnnie. I feel your loss more today than I did when we laid you to rest in the cold, cold grave.

Mrs McPherson did not come last week, but we expect her this. Mr McP has been quite sick and I suppose that detained her. Will, Jeanie and Kate spent the day with us. They break up tomorrow and Jeanie goes out to the Brook for the present. I love her better than I ever did before. She has put on mourning for our darling. It is a mark of respect I did not expect from her. I know it was not at Will's suggestion for he was absent when she did so. She never loved Johnnie as much as she did Sam, but Will idolized him, as all the rest of us did. The baby has been very sweet today. I love her dearly, but not as much as I did Jeanies first child. She was such a gentle little creature. When Johnnie was so ill she seemed perfectly satisfied to be on the bed beside him for hours at a time. When her short life was ended, and her little form long cold in death, I little thought the next we would be called to give up to God would be the Uncle she loved so well, and that in so short a time he too would be sleeping his last dreamless sleep. I am afraid Mr Ford or Cousin Annie must be sick, we have not heard from either of them.

Dec. 24. Sunday. Yesterday afternoon sister & I went up to the stores. When we came who should we find but Uncle Frank.[79] We expected him last week, but had given him up. He looks very well. He had not heard of dear Johnnies death till he got here. Anderson told him. He says that all the way he was thinking of Johnnie, how he looked, how he had grown, and how much he was going to make him tell him. He feels his death deeply. He was Johnnies God-father and always loved him very much, every one did that knew him. He was so noble so true and high spirited no one could help loving him. Oh! my brother, my brother will I never see your dear face again.

Uncle Frank has been north to see Pres Johnson and get his pardon, but did not succeed in getting it. He says he is sorry that he asked for one. He had never done any thing that he is sorry for.[80] He did not stop in Washington at all—said that after what he had heard in regard to his pardon, made him think it would be more prudent to come directly through (Capt Simms has been arrested).[81] Capt Shuttlesworth, his brother-in-law, almost turned him out of his house. He was so much [afraid] a rebel being there might be injurious to him, said he would be court martialed for it. The truth is he was afraid Uncle Frank might ask him to lend him some money. The poor miserable creature.

Will broke up house keeping Thursd and came down here, and stayed till Friday when Jeanie, he & the baby went out to the Brook. Sam and Mr Fletcher went out in an ambulance for them this evening and brought them in. Fannie has made friends with Uncle Frank already, something very wonderful for her. She is such a shy little creature. I received a very kind letter today from Fannie Wallace. She had just heard of my dear brother's death. They were warm friends.

Christmas Day 1865. Monday. Oh! how different from what I expected one little month ago. I looked forward to it so eagerly. Sister was coming home, and I was going to Nashville to [see] Johnnie. Tonight is just one month since his pure spirit took its flight, to the God who gave it. This has been a sad, sad day to me.

Sam invited Capt Wainwright and several of the clerks at the office down to drink egg nogg with him, and they nearly all drank a little too much. I did not see any except those staying here. Sam drank just enough to make his tongue go, and it went. Will went right at dinner time, Mr Woodruff enough to make him stupid. His eyes looked just ready to pop out. Thank fortune Christmas comes but once a year. I took a good cry. I could not help it—although sister said I was a fool. Mr Swain who I expected to see tight was not—he says because Capt W. drank too much and he stayed sober to take care of him. Mr Fletcher was perfectly sober. I had not the least fear of his taking too much.

Uncle Frank was decidedly happy. He says he is going tomorrow. I think it is ridiculous, his staying such a short time when we have not seen him for five years. The weather has been miserable ever since he came. It is the second time he has been here, and he has seen nothing of Knoxville either time. There is not much to see, but what little there is would perhaps have given him a little better opinion of the place.

I have received some very pretty presents but the one I always valued the most was missing, and the hand that gave it cold in death. Mr. Fletcher gave sister & I each a toilet set, almost exactly alike, but I think mine de-cidedly the prettiest. Mr Swain gave us each a box of perfumery, and Jeanie gave a set of it. Fan has made friend with Mr Fletcher at last over a paper of candy he gave her. She calls him "Jim" as saucy as you please.

Dec. 26. Tuesday. Uncle Frank went this morning in spite of all we could do. He said every time he heard any one at the front door he thought some one has come to arrest him, and he was very uneasy, beside being so anxious to get home to his wife and children. He has taken a foolish idea into his head that I am very sorry for—and that is that Mr Fletcher and I are engaged, or at least in love. I tried my best to talk him out of it but might as well have talked to the moon. I told him him he was younger than I am—he said he did not believe it, I did not look a day over eighteen. I dont see why I cannot have a friend with out some kind person—who had much better attend to their own business and let mine alone—must say he is courting me or we are engaged. I am sick of it. I wish there was no such thing as love and all that. Then I might enjoy having a friend. Uncle Frank never did have any sense about some things. He says he likes Mr Fletcher and Mr Swain both, particularly the latter, I suppose because he too has been all over the world—almost.

The weather has been miserable—rain all the time. I have wanted so much to go and see Capt Kain. I have not been to see him for so long. I think of him very often and sincerely wish I could do something to relieve the monotony of prison life. We lived right next to each other for three years—and I always liked him so much. His wife is a very lovely woman. They had two little girls, the eldest eight years old. She was perfectly de-voted to Johnnie. She died about a year ago at Wytheville where Capt Kain was stationed at the time, and now my idol has gone too.

Help me Father to say, "Even so, for so it seems good in thy sight. Give me strength to stand this trial as a christian should, and not to murmer against thy will. Make me better, help me to live so here on earth, that when I am called I may join him in his happy home beyond the sky." I am afraid instead of being better I am worse each day. If I only had a church I would be very, very thankful. Will I ever learn to keep my temper and my tongue.

Sister says that Emily told her when Gen Judah was boarding with her

Gen Carters brother, Col C, took dinner with him one day. She asked him if his brother had sent me South. He said yes that I had given some very valuable information to the enemy. I only wish I had had it in my power to do so. I never knew how much importance [sic] I was.

Dec. 31. Sunday. The last day of the year. I thought the beginning sad enough. It is one I could not have seen the end. I thought I mourned over my country when it fell. I did not know what sorrow was then. I had not lost my brother. He is my first thought in the morning, my last at night. I used to think this world so bright and beautiful and that everyone was as happy as they seemed. Now I know differently—know the lips may smile when the heart is well nigh broken. When another year has passed perhaps I too will be sleeping my last dreamless sleep—beside my two angel brothers. May I be ready. There will be none to mourn for me as I mourn for my lost one. I have never given my family the reason to love me as they all did him, and yet it is very sweet to be loved, to feel that when away from home we are missed, that there are eyes there that watch our coming, and grow brighter when we come.

Today I wrote to Lila Johnston. It was always my day for writing Johnnie. Now when it comes round I feel more than ever I've no brother to write to. I never ask for a letter, but there seems a chocking in my thoughts, a weary pain in my heart as I think the ones I so eagerly watched for—and prized more than all others—will never come again, and the heart that prompted them is stilled forever.

> "No more shall lifes shade or sorrow
> Bow or lift his dear young head
> Tender memory now will whisper
> to our risen heart his dead."

Oh! the anguish of that one word—dead. No he is not dead. He lives in heaven. Mother has two children there, saved forever.

It is well Uncle Frank went when he did. Several bridges have been washed away between here and Atlanta. He just left in time. He says he will return next summer, but I think it was only to tease me. I am afraid it will be some time before we see him again.

Today finishes my journal. I do not think I will keep another. I have no reason for keeping one. This I commenced for Johnnie. I thought he would like to know what was passing while he was far away from me in Prison. I have no brother Johnnie to keep one for now. Perhaps he watches over me from his bright and happy home. That thought alone ought to make me better. I must try to live as I ought to and never grieve his spirit. Then when the angel of death comes to me, his spirit may meet me and we may dwell together—where there is no more death, no more sorrow, and where the angels of God praise him from everlasting to everlasting.

Epilogue:
Patriotism Will Not Save the Soul

The shooting death of Johnnie capped the violence of the war for the House family. Unlike the little girl who confronted the Confederate officer at her father's door, John House never had a chance to ask his assailant, "are you a Reb, or a Yank, or a bushwhack?" His killer was likely none of those, probably only a highway robber. The political principles that had channeled, if not always constrained, the violence of wartime East Tennessee disintegrated after the war. Killings and lynchings in Knoxville were repeated in most Tennessee communities, and along a lonely stretch of the Franklin Pike.

House patriarch Samuel Crawford House could not bear the combined strain of the war and the murder of his youngest surviving child. He felt severe pains in his chest, arms, and head one June night in 1866. "He says he feels as well as usual," wrote Ellen a few days later, "but I can see that he is failing. . . . Dear Johnnie's death has done the work of years for him and some times I think it is even harder for him perhaps than for us." He died that same day. His adoring wife Frances survived until 1892.[1]

Ellen's surviving brothers, Sam and Will, prospered in postwar Knoxville. Sam married Julia Addie Hoss in 1872. They had eight children before Sam died in 1890. William's marriage to Jeanie Hazen produced six children. He died in 1884.

Fannie, Ellen's sister, married former Confederate major Thomas O'Conner in 1870. They resided at Melrose, an extensive estate that became part of the University of Tennessee campus after passing out of family hands in the early twentieth century. The house is now gone, but Henson Hall occupies a portion of the estate's former grounds. O'Conner, who became a powerful industrialist and president of the Mechanics' National Bank, gained some degree of immortality when Mark Twain described his death in a shooting incident in *Life on the Mississippi* (chap. 40). Fannie survived him by forty-one years, until 1923.[2]

Much of the rest of Ellen's life was haunted by the war and Johnnie's death. She leaned heavily on James Washington Fletcher, the Nashville-born clerk who came to board with the House family in October 1865. He comforted Ellen in the weeks following Johnnie's murder by telling her that he would try to fill his place in her life. She called him "brother" and allowed him to call her Nellie, a name she preferred to Ellen but which she permitted only a select few to use when addressing her. She poured out her remaining anger, grief, frustration, and guilt to him in the two years immediately following the war.[3]

But the anger would not recede completely within this very violent Rebel, and the aftermath of war enveloped her. Personal violence and political bullying continued to rock Knoxville and East Tennessee. In April 1866, the father of Tom Cummings committed suicide. "He had put a pistol to his mouth and blown his brains out," Ellen reported in her regular correspondence with James Fletcher, who had moved to Chattanooga in search of employment. "His mind has been affected at times for the last year or two—ever since his eldest son died at Johnson's Island." On the same day as Cummings's suicide, Ellen reported, "Yesterday there was considerable excitement in town speaking &e on the subject of making a state of East Tenn." She did not like the idea of being "cut off from the rest of the State," left to the mercy of "Brownlow and his disciples."[4]

"I'll tell you James," she pronounced a fortnight later, "I hate the Yankees more every day I live, if it is possible, and everybody who takes their part against the South. I do not mind talking over the last years with a rebel, but when it comes to hearing any one else on the subject, I want to leave [the room]." And she hated no Yankee or unionist (she made no distinction) more than she did her neighbor and nemesis Parson Brownlow. She rejoiced at rumors in July 1866 that President Johnson would soon appoint a military governor to Tennessee to oversee Governor Brownlow. "I certainly think it is time that something was done," she decided. "Dont you think old Brownlow is the greatest old villain in the country? That is saying a good deal when there are so many."[5]

Ellen chastised herself at times, just as she did during the war, for hating her foes so vehemently. "But I ought not feel so," she once repented of her rage. "Perhaps this time next year some kind hand may plant a rose upon my grave. And hating even my enemies will not fit me for the change." And with the eloquence that so often graced her diary and letters, Ellen considered that "patriotism will not save the soul. . . . It is not a religion, as many seem to think."[6]

The rage and anguish passed slowly, as Ellen came to concentrate her energy and centered her affection on James Fletcher. They settled in Knoxville, and Ellen transferred her love for Johnnie to her new "brother," whom she married in November 1867. She bore in time four children. She named her first born, a girl, Johnnie. The family prospered with the success of James Fletcher's mercantile establishment until a bad investment nearly bankrupted him. The family lost its house, and Ellen complained bitterly thereafter about having to reside in a boardinghouse. Ellen died on May 19, 1907, while visiting a son in South Carolina, just one month before her younger daughter, Ellen, was to be married. She and James, who died in 1914, are buried in the Old Gray Cemetery, Knoxville.

Notes

INTRODUCTION

1. Gary W. Gallagher, ed., *Fighting for the Confederacy: The Personal Recollections of General Edward Porter Alexander* (Chapel Hill, 1989), 313–15.

2. James W. Patton, *Union and Reconstruction in Tennessee, 1860–1869* (Chapel Hill, 1934), 58.

3. Biographical information about the House family is taken from genealogical notes and correspondence in the House Family Papers, in the possession of Ellen Allran and Victoria Guthrie (hereafter cited as House Family Papers). See also U.S. Bureau of the Census, *Population Schedule of the Seventh United States Census, 1850, Cobb County, Georgia*, National Archives Microcopy No. 432 (cited hereafter as 1850 Census [Cobb]), Roll 66, p. 102; *Population Schedule of the Seventh Census [Slave], 1850, Cobb County, Georgia*, National Archives Microcopy No. 432, Roll 89, p. 593. Samuel House had owned only three slaves in 1840 while residing in Savannah. *Population Schedule of Sixth Census, 1840, Chatham County, Georgia*, National Archives Microcopy No. 704, Roll 38, p. 132.

4. C. S. Williams, *Knoxville Directory, City Guide, and Business Mirror for 1859–60* (Knoxville, 1859), 57; Samuel House to father, Aug. 22, 1859, House Family Papers; U.S. Bureau of the Census, *Population Schedule of the Eighth Census, 1860, Knox County, Tennessee*, National Archives Microcopy No. 653, Roll 1259, p. 96 (1st District) (hereafter cited as 1860 Census; district cited by number only). Ellen House never reveals her precise address, but judging from comments she makes about neighbors, the most likely location of the family's residence in 1863 is Cumberland Street.

5. Thomas A. Wigginton et al., *Tennesseans in the Civil War* (Nashville, 1965), 1:119–22, 2:212; Samuel House to father, Dec. 1, 1862, United Confederate Veterans, Florida Division, Records, Florida Dept. of State, Tallahassee (hereafter cited as UCV Records); Samuel House to mother, June 11, 1861, House Family Papers.

6. Wigginton et al., *Tennesseans in the Civil War* 1:214–16, 2:212; Samuel House to mother, June 11, Sept. 24, 1861, House Family Papers; Samuel House to father, Dec. 1, 1862, UCV Records; *Knoxville Daily Tribune*, June 10, 1890.

7. Sam House to Ellen House, Sept. 8, 1862, Sam House Letter, Special Collections, Univ. of Tennessee, Knoxville.

8. Edward W. Callahan, ed., *List of Officers of the Navy of the United States and of the Marine Corps from 1775 to 1900* (New York, 1901), 458; George F. Pearce, *The U.S. Navy in Pensacola: From Sailing Ships to Naval Aviation (1825–1930)* (Pensacola, 1980), 67–69; U.S. War Dept., *Official Records of the Union and Confederate Navies in the War of the Rebellion*, 30 vols. and index (Washington, D.C., 1894–1922), ser. 1, vol. 4, pp. 60–61; Frank B. Renshaw to brother and sister, Feb. 17, Mar. 17, 1861, House Family Papers. For a detailed description of the surrender of Pensacola, see Charles L. Lufkin, "War Council in Pensacola, January 17, 1861," *Gulf State Historical Review* 9 (Fall 1993): 47–64.

9. *War of the Rebellion: A Compilation of the Official Records of the Union and Confederate Armies*, 70 vols. in 128 books and index (Washington, D.C., 1880–1901), ser. 1, vol. 32, pt. 3:226 (cited hereafter as OR; all references are to series 1 unless noted otherwise).

10. Patton, *Union and Reconstruction*, 4–9.

11. The best works on secession and the war in East Tennessee, on which this introduction is largely based, include Charles F. Bryan Jr., "The Civil War in East Tennessee: A Social, Political, and Economic Study" (Ph.D. diss., Univ. of Tennessee, 1978); Noel Charles Fisher, "'War at every man's door': The Struggle for East Tennessee, 1860–1869" (Ph.D. diss., Ohio State Univ., 1993); W. Todd Groce, "Mountain Rebels: East Tennessee Confederates and the Civil War, 1860–70" (Ph.D. diss., Univ. of Tennessee, 1992); Digby G. Seymour, *Divided Loyalties: Fort Sanders and the Civil War in East Tennessee*, rev. ed. (Knoxville, 1982). Good summaries may also be found in Patton, *Union and Reconstruction*, 51–74; and Mary U. Rothrock, *The French Broad–Holston Country: A History of Knox County, Tennessee* (Knoxville, 1946), 127–47.

12. Patton, *Union and Reconstruction*, 14–25; Thomas W. Humes, *The Loyal Mountaineers of Tennessee* (Knoxville, 1888), 105; Richard N. Current, ed., *Encyclopedia of the Confederacy* (New York, 1993), 4:1575; Charles L. Lufkin, "Secession and Coercion in Tennessee, the Spring of 1861," *Tennessee Historical Quarterly* 50 (Summer 1991): 98–109; Charles F. Bryan Jr., "A Gathering of Tories: The East Tennessee Convention of 1861," *Tennessee Historical Quarterly* 39 (Spring 1980): 27–48. For East Tennessee's role in the secession of the upper South, see Daniel W. Crofts, *Reluctant Confederates: Upper South Unionists in the Secession Crisis* (Chapel Hill, 1989).

13. Groce, "Mountain Rebels," 81–82; Charles F. Bryan Jr., "'Tories' Amidst Rebels: Confederate Occupation of East Tennessee, 1861–63," *East Tennessee Historical Society's Publications* 60 (1988): 5–7.

14. Patton, *Union and Reconstruction*, 63; Bryan, "Tories Amidst Rebels," 8–9 and "Civil War in East Tennessee," 85–91.

15. Groce, "Mountain Rebels," 153–60; Fisher, "War at every man's door," 114–20. Noel Fisher summarizes the interpretation of the Confederate occupation presented in his dissertation in an article, "'The Leniency Shown Them Has Been Unavailing': The Confederate Occupation of East Tennessee," *Civil War History* 40 (Dec. 1994): 275–91.

16. Bryan, "Tories Amidst Rebels," 10–17.

17. *OR*, vol. 33, pt. 1:384–93; D. Sullins, *Recollections of an Old Man: Seventy Years in Dixie, 1827–1897* (Bristol, Tenn., 1910), 256–59. For a satirical unionist view of the skirmish, see Leroy P. Graf et al., eds., *The Papers of Andrew Johnson*, 12 vols. (Knoxville, 1967–96), 2:294–96.

18. *OR*, vol. 30, pt. 4:554.

CHAPTER 1. THE YANKEES ARE HERE

1. William Toole, a farmer, and his brother Barcklay W. Toole, a physician, were the only Tooles in Knox County in 1860. The store possibly belonged to their father William, of Blount County, who left an estate of thirty thousand dollars, but no Toole appears in the 1859–60 city directory for Knoxville. 1860 Census, 114–15 (11th); C. S. Williams, *Knoxville Directory, City Guide, and Business Mirror for 1859–60* (Knoxville, 1859). Toole's will gave these two brothers and another son, John E. Toole, all of his lands in Knox County (952 acres), situated on the Holston River at Toole's Bend. "Last will and testament of William Toole," November 7, 1860, Brabson Family Papers, Special Collections, Univ. of Tennessee, Knoxville. John E. Toole also served as provost marshal for the Confederate Department of East Tennessee. *OR*, ser. 1, vol. 23, pt. 2:731; ser. 2, vol. 1, p. 878.

2. Cluss is Mary McClusky, twenty-one-year-old daughter of the widowed Mary McClusky. 1860 Census, 95 (1st).

3. Dr. Francis Alexander Ramsey (1821–84) was born in Knox County. In 1861 he received commissions as surgeon of state forces and as medical director of Gen. Felix K. Zollicoffer's command. Rothrock, *French Broad–Holston Country*, 469–70.

4. Kate White was the twenty-seven-year-old daughter of Mary White. 1860 Census, 104 (1st). Her sister Mary and brother Hugh are mentioned later.

5. William C. Kain (born in 1826) and his family lived next door to the House family. Known in Knoxville as Calib Kain, he organized Kain's Light Artillery Company in the spring of 1862. Wigginton et al., *Tennesseans in the Civil War* 1:133–34.

6. Gen. Braxton Bragg (1817–76) ultimately lost the battle of Murfreesboro, or Stones River (Dec. 31, 1862–Jan. 2, 1863), although early reports accurately reflect a victory on the first day by the Army of Tennessee. The report quoted by House from a Knoxville newspaper was actually addressed to Gen. Samuel Cooper, adjutant and inspector general of the CSA, but the newspaper states that Bragg sent the message to Gen. Edmund Kirby Smith, who commanded the Department of East Tennessee. *OR*, vol. 20, pt. 1:662.

7. Frank Matthews was a cousin of Ellen by John D. and Anne (Renshaw) Matthews, on her mother's side of the family. Gen. John C. Breckinridge commanded the First Division of Gen. William J. Hardee's corps in the battle.

8. Johnnie is one of Ellen's brothers, John Moore House.

9. Mary A. Kain, thirty-six-year-old wife of lawyer William C. Kain, had two children: Lizzie, age eight, and Laura, age five. 1860 Census, 91 (1st).

10. Mary F. McClung, twenty-five-year-old daughter of Hugh L. McClung, married W. B. Francisco in January 1862. Her sister, twenty-two-year-old Rachael, married M. L. Rogers in January 1863. 1860 Census, 65 (1st); Roscoe C. d'Armand and Virginia C. d'Armand, comps., *Knox County, Tennessee, Marriage Records, 1792–1900* (Knoxville, 1970), 668.

11. Miss Massell (possibly Morrell or Marrell) does not appear in the census.

12. Adaline Russell, age thirty, was the eldest of six children of widower Moses Russell, a grocer. 1860 Census, 70 (1st).

13. Martha E. Churchwell was the thirty-three-year-old wife of lawyer William M. Churchwell, noted secessionist who organized the Fourth Tennessee Infantry (later, Thirty-fourth Tennessee Infantry) in August 1861. Churchwell served as colonel of the regiment. Laura E. Luttrell, comp., *United States Census 1850 for Knox County, Tennessee* (Knoxville, 1949), 47; Wigginton et al., *Tennesseans in the Civil War* 1:246–47.

14. Elizabeth Charlton, thirty-three-year-old wife of C. W. Charlton, the thirty-eight-year-old postmaster of Knoxville and a strong secessionist. 1860 Census, 91 (1st).

15. W. L. Latta, a fifty-six-year-old tanner from North Carolina, lived with his wife Mary, age thirty-seven, and three children. 1860 Census, 71 (1st).

16. Victoria Vaux was the daughter of William Vaux, rector of St. John's Protestant Episcopal Church.

17. Gen. Simon B. Buckner (1823–1914), who abandoned Knoxville on August 25, 1863. *OR*, vol. 30, pt. 4:554.

18. John W. Foster, Sixty-fifth Indiana (Mounted) Infantry, commanded Second Brigade, Fourth Division, IX Corps.

19. The house of William H. Sneed, a prominent secessionist who had fled the city, stood on the corner of Prince (now Market) and Cumberland Streets. It served as Federal general headquarters for the rest of the war. Seymour, *Divided Loyalties*, 84.

20. Not all Knoxville soldiers were as lucky as Ellen's brother, Samuel House. Two sons of David A. Deaderick were at home when the Federals entered the city, and one of them was captured. Samuel C. Williams, ed., "Journal of Events (1825–73) of David Anderson Deaderick," *East Tennessee Historical Society's Publication* 9 (1937): 99.

21. Mary W. McPherson, age twenty-nine, was the wife of thirty-eight-year-old merchant R. M. W. McPherson, worth nearly thirty thousand dollars in 1860. They had four children. 1860 Census, 39 (1st).

22. Ellen refers sarcastically to William G. Brownlow (1805–77), one of the first unionists to return to Knoxville. A preacher, politician, and editor, Brownlow moved to Knoxville in 1849 to publish the *Knoxville Whig and Independent Journal*. He defended slavery but decried secession. E. Merton Coulter, *William G. Brownlow: Fighting Parson of the Southern Highlands* (Chapel Hill, 1937).

23. Ambrose E. Burnside (1824–81) commanded the Army of the Ohio. His headquarters belonged to John H. Crozier (1812–89), located on the corner of Clinch and Gay Streets and "set well back from the street in a shady lawn." When William T. Sherman met there with Burnside in December, he described the house as "a large, fine mansion" with a lavish interior. After the war, the house was converted into the Hotel Farragut. Seymour, *Divided Loyalties*, 85–86; William T. Sherman, *Memoirs of General William T. Sherman*, 2 vols. (1875; reprint, New York, 1984), 2:367, 368; Lucile Deaderick, ed., *Heart of the Valley: A History of Knoxville, Tennessee* (Knoxville, 1976), 31.

24. Gen. Samuel P. Carter (1819–91), a native of East Tennessee, served as Federal provost marshal in Knoxville until January 1865. He made his headquarters in the home of Landon C. Haynes (1816–75), a Confederate senator and one of the most influential Tennesseans in the Confederate government. Establishing a provost marshal office for East Tennessee was one of Burnside's first acts during Federal occupation. Current, *Encyclopedia of the Confederacy* 2:752–53; Fisher, "War at every man's door," 270. Carter made a notable raid into East Tennessee in late 1862 in an effort to support unionists in that part of the state. See William G. Piston, "Carter's Raid, Part I," *East Tennessee Historical Society's Publications* 49 (1977): 61–76, and "Carter's Raid, Part II," *East Tennessee Historical Society's Publications* 50 (1978): 31–57. As provost marshal, he could please no one. He tried to protect Rebel property from lawless unionists while also punishing Rebels for deprivations by the Confederate army. Parson Brownlow eventually called him a copperhead. Bryan, "Civil War in East Tennessee," 124–26.

25. Alexander P. Stewart (1821–1908).

26. Unknown to the House family, Burnside was planning to make a loyalty oath the linchpin of Union occupation in East Tennessee. Fisher, "War at every man's door," 285–86.

27. Sophronia Strong was the forty-seven-year-old wife of Dr. Joseph Churchill Strong Jr. (1808–78), son of a well-known Knoxville physician of the same name who died in 1844. 1860 Census, 225 (18th); Rothrock, *French Broad–Holston Country*, 492–93.

28. James Campbell, a veteran of the War of 1812, had fled the city. William B. Hesseltine, ed., *Dr. J. G. M. Ramsey: Autobiography and Letters* (Nashville, 1954), 120.

29. "When Burnside's army came in to occupy Knoxville," recalled one resident, "his officers selected the largest homes for their headquarters, the owners getting out entirely or living in the ells of the houses." Ellen's family eventually was forced from its home, too. Mrs. M. D. Plant, "Recollections of War as a Child, 1861–65," *Confederate Veteran* 36 (Apr. 1928): 129.

30. Martha was one of two family servants, both of them apparently slaves, even though the House family does not appear in the slave census for 1860.

31. Nancy Newton Scott was born in Knox County in 1824. Well-educated, including attendance at the Knoxville Female Institute, she was an active Confederate sympathizer. Ellen sometimes refers to her as Nannie. Rothrock, *French Broad–Holston Country*, 482.

32. David H. Cummings, a prominent Knoxville secessionist who helped to organize the Nineteenth Tennessee Infantry in May–June 1861. He was soon released from prison. One prominent unionist complained by mid-November, "David H. Cummings walks the streets as impudent as the devil himself." Rothrock, *French Broad–Holston Country*, 131; Wigginton et al., *Tennesseans in the Civil War* 1:214–16; Edward Maynard to Washburn Maynard, Nov. 17, 1863, Horace Maynard Papers, Special Collections, Univ. of Tennessee, Knoxville (hereafter cited as Maynard Papers).

33. Mary Hazen was the nineteen-year-old daughter of Gideon M. and Mary Strong Hazen, farmers worth sixty-two thousand dollars in 1860. 1860 Census, 25 (12th). Her older sister Jane married Ellen's brother William McLean House in September 1860.

34. Gideon M. Hazen Jr. was Mary's younger brother, age eighteen. He would become a lieutenant in Company D, Ninth Tennessee Cavalry. Wigginton et al., *Tennesseans in the Civil War* 2:198.

35. Dr. John Jackson and Susan Jackson, both in their mid-thirties, had been born in England. Dr. Jackson was a druggist. 1860 Census, 60 (1st).

36. The unpopular Confederate Conscription Act, passed in April 1862, ordered men between eighteen and thirty-five into the army.

37. Thomas W. Humes (1815–92) was rector of St. John's Protestant Episcopal Church until 1861, when he resigned because of his sympathy for the Union. Burnside requested that Humes resume his post when the Federals entered Knoxville. Rothrock, *French Broad–Holston Country*, 431–32.

38. William Vaux, a Confederate sympathizer, replaced Humes as rector of St. John's for 1861–63. Rothrock, *French Broad–Holston Country*, 294–95.

39. Jane (Jeanie) Hazen House was Ellen's sister-in-law, the wife of Will.

40. Rev. Dr. Joseph H. Martin (listed as James in the 1860 Census, 90 [1st]) served as pastor of Knoxville's Second Presbyterian Church (founded in 1818), 1851–63. The First Presbyterian had been converted to a hospital. It would be returned to the elders briefly in July 1864 only to be taken back by the Federal army as a barracks. Rothrock, *French Broad–Holston Country*, 129, 142, 282.

41. Both Cherokee Indians and whites served in Col. William H. Thomas's "Legion of Indians and Highlanders," known officially as the Sixty-ninth North Carolina Infantry. Organized in September 1862 at Knoxville, the regiment in September 1863 was the only Confederate unit seriously harassing Burnside's forces. The Federals accused the Rebels of using "Indian savages" to hunt down Tennessee loyalists. When a Cherokee lieutenant was killed in September, the Indians responded by scalping several Union soldiers who had been killed and wounded. Walter Clark, ed., *Histories of the Several Regiments and Battalions from North Carolina in the Great War 1861–'65*, 5 vols. (Raleigh, N.C., 1901), 3:729–46; John R. Finger, *The Eastern Band of Cherokees, 1819–1900* (Knoxville, 1984), 82–100; Graf et al., *Papers of Andrew Johnson* 6:244 n. 3, 331, 332 n. 3, 679 n. 10; *OR*, vol. 33, pt. 2:711, 946. See also Vernon H. Crow, *Storm in the Mountains: Thomas' Confederate Legion of Cherokee Indians and Mountaineers* (Cherokee, N.C., 1982); and E. Stanley Godbold Jr. and Mattie V. Russell, *Confederate Colonel and Cherokee Chief: The Life of William Holland Thomas* (Knoxville, 1990).

42. Sidney was the family's other servant.

43. Isabella R. Boyd, thirty-one-year-old wife of Sam B. Boyd, a Virginia-born merchant worth forty-six thousand dollars in 1860. 1860 Census, 73 (1st).

44. Three days after taking Knoxville, Burnside led a third of his force toward Cumberland Gap, controlled by the Confederates. Gen. James Longstreet (1821–1904) would be detached from the Army of Northern Virginia to serve under Bragg, but he did not receive his orders until September 9.

45. Mrs. S. Levenia Cocke, thirty-seven-year-old widow of John Cocke Jr., had two children at home, seventeen-year-old Ella and six-year-old John. Another daughter, twenty-one-year-old Laura, had married Henry C. Gillespie in December 1861. Willene B. Clark, ed., *Valleys of the Shadow: The Memoir of Confederate Captain Reuben G. Clark, Company I, 59th Tennessee Mounted Infantry* (Knoxville, 1994), 136–37 n. 35; 1860 Census, 201 (3d); d'Armand and d'Armand, *Marriage Records*, 209. Mary Morgan was a North Carolina–born sixty-three-year-old widow. Luttrell, *Census 1850 for Knox County*, 97.

46. Hugh Lawson McClung helped organize the Tennessee Light Artillery Company (the Caswell Artillery) at Knoxville in the fall of 1861. It was consolidated in May 1862 with Captain Rutledge's Tennessee Battery. On September 7, McClung checked a Federal advance at Watauga Bridge on the East Tennessee and Virginia Railroad. Wigginton et al., *Tennesseans in the Civil War* 1:139–40; *OR*, vol. 30, pt. 2:604, pt. 4:624.

47. Old Buchanan, or Buck, was a servant of Mrs. Kain.

48. Gen. John W. Frazer surrendered twenty-five hundred men and fourteen guns to Burnside at Cumberland Gap the next day, September 9, after having been essentially surrounded two days earlier with no hope of reenforcements. Most importantly, Frazer had forfeited the main thoroughfare between Kentucky and Tennessee. However, the Second Tennessee Infantry (U.S.), which consisted of unionist refugees, was not "cut to pieces." *OR*, vol. 33, pt. 2:548–49, 612–24; Vernon H. Crow, "Justice for General Frazer," *Civil War Times* 9 (Dec. 1970): 20–27.

49. Mr. and Mrs. Sam Wallace were probably Confederate refugees in Knoxville.

50. Bragg had not fallen back as far as Dalton, Georgia, but on September 7 he did evacuate Chattanooga with most of his army and moved into northwest Georgia. Peter Cozzens, *This Terrible Sound: The Battle of Chickamauga* (Urbana, 1992), 56–57.

51. Columbus Powell was a thirty-three-year-old Knoxville merchant worth $45,700 in 1860. He and his wife Sarah had three children. Hesseltine, *Ramsey Autobiography*, 103; 1860 Census, 48 (1st).

52. For the fight at Limestone, see *OR*, vol. 30, pt. 2:92, 590, 643.

53. Capt. James Pike, Fourth Ohio Cavalry. I cannot further identify Catherine and Joanne.

54. Probably D. A. Wilkins, Company H, Nineteenth Tennessee Infantry, which was organized at Knoxville in the spring of 1861. Wigginton et al., *Tennesseans in the Civil War* 1:215, 2:432.

55. Archibald Gracie Jr. (1832–64) led a brigade in Gen. William Preston's division of Buckner's corps.

56. Alfred Hendricks, fifty-eight years old, was a Virginia-born carpenter with a wife and seven children. 1860 Census, 4 (16th).

57. William G. Swan and William M. Churchwell received a franchise for installing gas lighting in Knoxville and supplying the city with water in 1854. Deaderick, *Heart of the Valley*, 20.

58. Nonnie is one of the Kains' daughters, probably six-year-old Laura. 1860 Census, 91 (1st).

59. George Washington Mabry (1823–1912), farmer and state legislator (1851–55), was born in Knox County. In 1851 he built a brick house on three thousand acres. Soldiers camped on the land because of its excellent spring. The house stands today on Kingston Pike near the intersection of Mabry and Hood Roads. Deaderick, *Heart of the Valley*, 563–64.

60. James G. M. Ramsey (1797–1884), born in Knox County, built "Mecklenburg" at the junction of the French Broad and Holston Rivers. He lived there until the Federals burned it, along with many valuable manuscripts. Rothrock, *French Broad–Holston Country*, 470–71; Hesseltine, *Ramsey Autobiography*, 171–74. F. A. R. McNutt, a forty-year-old farmer worth forty-five hundred dollars in 1860, was a widower with seven children. 1860 Census, 1 (2d).

61. John Williams was a moderate unionist who opposed the radicalism of men like Brownlow and "did a great deal to ameliorate the hardships" of Confederate prisoners in Knoxville. Clark, *Valleys of the Shadow*, 63, 135. He was also known as Colonel Williams. Paul W. Prindle, comp., *Ancestry of William Sperry Beinecke* (North Haven, Conn., 1974), 249.

62. Frank Wolford, First Kentucky Cavalry, commanded an independent cavalry brigade attached to XXIII Corps at Knoxville. Hambleton Tapp, "Incidents in the Life of Frank Wolford, Colonel of the First Kentucky Union Cavalry," *Filson Club History Quarterly* 10 (Jan. 1936): 82–99; E. Tarrant, *The Wild Riders of the First Kentucky Cavalry: A History of the Regiment in the Great War of the Rebellion, 1861–1865* (Louisville, 1894), 201–2. He was described in one Kentucky newspaper as a "unique, peculiar, original, energetic, fighting commander" who was "the universal favorite of the officers, the army, and the people everywhere." *Louisville Journal*, Jan. 14, 1864, p. 1.

63. Wallie, or Wallace, was the thirteen-year-old son of the McPhersons. 1860 Census, 39 (1st).

64. Thomas O'Conner, senior lieutenant in Kain's company. His unit surrendered at Cumberland Gap, and he was sent to Johnson's Island, Ohio. In 1870, he married Fannie House, Ellen's sister. Deaderick, *Heart of the Valley*, 588–90; *Confederate Veteran* 4 (Dec. 1896): 437.

65. W. Cooke Danner Jr. was a second lieutenant, Charles S. King a first sergeant, and Elijah Green McClanihand a private in Kain's company. Wigginton et al., *Tennesseans in the Civil War* 2:118, 236, 270.

66. Camp Chase was a Federal military prison camp in Columbus, Ohio.

67. Col. Robert K. Byrd organized the First Tennessee Volunteer Infantry (U.S.) from among Tennessee refugees at Camp Dick Robinson, Kentucky, in Sep-

tember 1861. Also known as First East Tennessee Infantry and First East Tennessee Mounted Infantry. Wigginton et al., *Tennesseans in the Civil War* 1:375–78; Oliver P. Temple, *Notable Men of Tennessee, from 1833 to 1875* (New York, 1912), 79–80.

68. Lt. Col. James C. Brownlow, a son of Parson Brownlow, led the First Tennessee Cavalry (U.S.) at this time. Lt. Col. Edward Maynard, a Massachusetts-born son of Horace Maynard, had originally enlisted in Byrd's regiment, but in September 1863 he served in the Sixth Tennessee Infantry (U.S.). Rothrock, *French Broad–Holston Country*, 387; Wigginton et al., *Tennesseans in the Civil War* 1:318–20, 375, 387–89, 2:480, 549; 1860 Census, 96 (1st).

69. Greeneville was some seventy miles east of Knoxville by rail.

70. Longstreet's corps was en route to Georgia, where it would arrive September 17, from Virginia. Gen. Richard S. Ewell (1817–72) remained with his corps in Virginia.

71. Concord was located about twelve miles southwest of Knoxville, just below Campbell's Station on the East Tennessee and Georgia Railroad. The only action at Jonesboro came on September 21 and 28.

72. She was the wife of Col. James Burch Cooke, who helped to organize the Fifty-ninth Tennessee Mounted Infantry. Clark, *Valleys of the Shadow*, 87.

73. Burnside was executor of the estate of his wife's sister, who married Buckner. William Marvel, *Burnside* (Chapel Hill, 1991), 37–38, 248. House misjudges Buckner's actions, however. He was responsible for guarding all East Tennessee with a force far smaller than Burnside's. Marvel, *Burnside*, 271–73.

74. Maria W. McClanihand, age thirty-five, was the wife of miller Elijah G. McClanihand, both born in Virginia. 1860 Census, 60 (1st). Eliza A. McClung, age twenty-six, was the Missouri-born wife of Frank McClung, a merchant worth forty-five thousand dollars in 1860. 1860 Census, 41 (1st).

75. Morristown was forty miles northeast of Knoxville on the East Tennessee and Virginia Railroad.

76. Loudon was nearly thirty miles southwest of Knoxville on the East Tennessee and Georgia Railroad.

77. Gen. Ambrose Powell Hill (1825–65), commanding the 3rd Corps in the Army of Northern Virginia, did not accompany Longstreet to Georgia. However, Gen. Daniel Harvey Hill (1821–89) did command a corps in Bragg's Army of Tennessee.

78. Burnside left Knoxville to join Gen. William S. Rosecrans at Chattanooga.

79. A tory was a Union sympathizer. The term seems to have been used widely in Knoxville. The *Knoxville Register* asserted in May 1861 that those "who would betray Tennessee into the power of the unholy despotism of the North, are tories, and will bear the stigma of tories." Quoted in Bryan, "Civil War in East Tennessee," 49. See also Oliver P. Temple, *East Tennessee and the Civil War* (Cincinnati, 1899), 367.

80. Strawberry Plains was fifteen miles northeast of Knoxville on the East Tennessee and Virginia Railroad.

81. Kingston was thirty miles southwest of Knoxville.

82. Charles McClung McGhee (1828–1907), heir of the founder of Knoxville. Rothrock, *French Broad–Holston Country*, 447–48; Deaderick, *Heart of the Valley*, 24, 42.

83. Possibly Augustus MacHan, Company C, Thirty-ninth Georgia Infantry. Lillian Henderson, ed., *Roster of Confederate Soldiers of Georgia, 1861–1865,* 6 vols. and index (Spartanburg, S.C., 1982), 4:271–72.

84. Lt. Col. John Bell Brownlow, the second son of Parson Brownlow, served in the Ninth Tennessee Cavalry (U.S.). Wigginton et al., *Tennesseans in the Civil War* 1:342–44.

85. Lt. Col. Edward Maynard saw many old friends when he returned to the occupied city, but several Rebels, particularly young women, seemed to scorn him. "I met on the street Blannie McClung and Martha Luttrell," he informed his brother, "passed close enough to brush Blannie's dress but did not make any sign of recognition nor did they and you know we were once intimate." Edward Maynard to Washburn Maynard, Nov. 17, 1863, Maynard Papers.

86. A skirmish at Cleveland, Tennessee, produced a Confederate victory, but no official report of casualties survives. *OR,* vol. 30, pt. 2:579, 586.

87. Kingston, Georgia, was about fifty miles northwest of Atlanta, but there does not seem to have been significant fighting there at this time.

88. *Dollars and Cents* was a novel by Anna Bartlett Warner, published in 1852 by G. P. Putnam, New York.

89. Federals began heavy shelling of the forts in Charleston Harbor, South Carolina, in August 1863.

90. The Lamar House, established in 1817, was Knoxville's leading hotel. Located on Gay and Cumberland Streets, it served as a hospital during Federal occupation. Deaderick, *Heart of the Valley,* 20, 31; Rothrock, *French Broad–Holston Country,* 140; Dean Novelli, "On a Corner of Gay Street: History of the Lamar House–Bijou Theater, Knoxville, Tennessee, 1817–1985," *East Tennessee Historical Society's Publications* 56–57 (1984–85): 17–20.

91. The Second Brigade, Fourth Division, XXIII Corps, commanded by Col. John W. Foster, not Carter, drove seven hundred Confederates out of Bristol, Tennessee,.on September 19. He then proceeded to tear up the railroad and burn the bridges two miles above the town. *OR,* vol. 30, pt. 2:579, 592.

92. Bragg defeated Rosecrans at Chickamauga, in northwest Georgia, September 19–20. In separate action, an engagement took place at Blountsville, Tennessee, on September 22, but neither Blountsville nor Athens, Tennessee, was burned. Skirmishing would follow in a few days, on September 25 and 27, at Athens. *OR,* vol. 30, pt. 2:586–87, 592, 605.

93. William C. Lackey led Company E of the Knoxville Guards, also known as the Grays, Nineteenth Tennessee Infantry. The regiment fought at Chickamauga, where it suffered 94 casualties of 242 men engaged. Wigginton et al., *Tennesseans in the Civil War* 1:214–16, 2:113. Robert C. Crozier, a twenty-five-year-old lieutenant in the Second (Ashby's) Tennessee Cavalry, was killed, but not Jim King. King is James M. King of the Third Tennessee Mounted Infantry, organized at Knoxville in May 1861. King would marry Ellen's friend Cluss McClusky. Wigginton et al., *Tennesseans in the Civil War* I:178, 2:237. For Crozier's obituary see Hesseltine, *Ramsey Autobiography,* 139–41.

94. Maryville was fifteen miles south of Knoxville.

95. Gen. George Gordon Meade (1815–72), commander of the Army of the Potomac.

96. The flight of unionists into Knoxville could also work to the disadvantage of the Confederacy. "We are recruiting our army rapidly since we came here," maintained a Union soldier on September 25. "At least 2,000 Tennesseans have enlisted in our army since Burnside came here. He brought arms and equipments to arm them as fast as they enlist. A large number of rebel prisoners and deserters have taken the oath and enlisted in our army. Everything works well and Burnside's great movement has been a great success so far." William G. Gavin, ed., *Infantryman Pettit: The Civil War Letters of Corporal Frederick Pettit, Late of Company C, 100th Pennsylvania Veteran Volunteer Infantry Regiment, "The Roundheads," 1862–1864* (Shippensburg, Pa., 1990), 118. See also Richard N. Current, *Lincoln's Loyalists: Union Soldiers from the Confederacy* (Boston, 1992), 52–54, 188–89.

97. Houses were searched and goods seized because Union supply lines through the Cumberland Mountains could not support Burnside's troops in Knoxville and the railroad lines had been thoroughly disrupted by this time. Seymour, *Divided Loyalties*, 94. For an interesting effort to provision the army, see Palmer H. Boeger, "General Burnside's Knoxville Packing Project," *East Tennessee Historical Society's Publications* 35 (1963): 76–84.

98. Fifty-three-year-old Sarah was the wife of John Parmers, a North Carolina–born farmer. 1860 Census, 2 (16th).

99. Mrs. Jennings was probably a refugee.

100. Anne Maria Breck was Frank Ramsey's first wife. They married in 1842 and by 1860 had seven children. Rothrock, *French Broad–Holston Country*, 469–70; 1860 Census, 104 (1st).

101. Matthew and Mary E. Gammon were in their early sixties. He was a clerk of court. 1860 Census, 60 (1st). A Pennsylvania soldier reported on September 25, "We live mostly upon the country as there is plenty of grain, mills, and beef cattle here. We drew soft bread this morning baked in Knoxville. There is a large slaughter house near our camp, built for the rebels which in now run for our benefit." Gavin, *Infantryman Pettit*, 117.

102. John D. Matthews, a Presbyterian minister, married Anne Renshaw, a sister of Ellen's mother.

103. A Federal military prison camp was located at Demopolis, Alabama.

104. Edmonia Danner was twenty-four years old. 1860 Census, 60 (1st). Sarah White was a thirty-five-year-old widow and mother of two. 1860 Census, 53 (1st).

105. Burnside had tried to resign on September 10, following the capture of Knoxville and his victory at Cumberland Gap. He would try to resign again in mid-October, but in neither case was his action inspired by political ambition. His health was bad, and he feared he would not be able to hold Knoxville against the Rebels. Marvel, *Burnside*, 279–80, 294–95, 467 n. 63.

106. Samuel Morrow (1816–64) was a Knoxville banker. However, service records show him not to have been a captain but a sergeant in Company H, Fifth Tennessee Cavalry (U.S.). Graf et al., *Papers of Andrew Johnson* 4:280–81.

107. Prof. Strong was probably fifty-five-year-old Dr. Joseph C. Strong, a well-known unionist. Later in the war he became an agent for the United States Sanitary Commission. 1860 Census, 225 (18th); OR, vol. 31, pt. 3:507; Laura Maynard to Washburn Maynard, Jan. 19, 1864, Maynard Papers.

108. Gen James M. Shackleford (1827–1900), of Kentucky, commanded the Third Brigade, Fourth Division, IX Corps. He arrived at Greeneville at 11:00 A.M. and was in action at Blue Springs before the day ended. His photograph does not show him to be physically disgusting. OR, vol. 30, pt. 2:547, 551, pt. 4:274; Ezra J. Warner, Generals in Blue: Lives of the Union Commanders (Baton Rouge, 1964), 433–34. Dr. Ramsey says he made his headquarters at Dr. B. B. Lenoir's office, but this must refer to brigade headquarters, while Ellen refers to his personal quarters. Hesseltine, Ramsey Autobiography, 158.

109. The baby was Mary House, daughter of William McLean House.

110. Lizzie Campbell could be either seventeen-year-old Elizabeth Campbell, who lived with Nancy Music, or Margaret E. A. Campbell, the twenty-two-year-old daughter of John S. Campbell, a wealthy farmer. 1860 Census, 25 (10th), 104 (11th).

111. James Churchwell Luttrell III (1841–1914), son of Knoxville mayor and postmaster James C. Luttrell, served in Capt. William H. Burrough's Tennessee Light Artillery Company, mustered into service at Camp Sneed, Knoxville, in August 1861. He became a merchant and public official after the war. He had a brother who fought in the Union army. Wigginton et al., Tennesseans in the Civil War 1:127–28; Rothrock, French Broad–Holston Country, 441; Seymour, Divided Loyalties, 165.

112. Most of these rumors were true. A skirmish took place at Blue Springs and Bulls Gap on October 10. It was a Union victory, but Nathan B. Forrest and Joseph Wheeler had not taken Nashville. A Confederate regiment established itself near Blountsville, but Gen. Shackleford drove it out of East Tennessee October 14–15. Gavin, Infantryman Pettit, 123; OR, vol. 30, pt. 2:547, 595.

113. Details about the captured wagons are sketchy, but apparently such an episode occurred. OR, vol. 30, pt. 4:742.

114. Rosecrans's losses at Chickamauga were 16,170 of fewer than 60,000 engaged.

115. John E. Helms (b. 1828) published the Knoxville Daily Gazette and Mail beginning in 1866. Clark, Valleys of the Shadow, 138 n. 17.

116. Foster had conducted a fairly successful campaign since September 9, insofar as driving the Rebels away from Knoxville and toward southwestern Virginia. He had not been placed under arrest.

117. Probably either James or William C. Ford, both of whom served in Company C, Second (Ashby's) Tennessee Cavalry. Wigginton et al., Tennesseans in the Civil War 1:52–54, 2:157.

118. Annie was the daughter of John D. and Anne Matthews. Mary Bostwick Renshaw was a sister of Ellen's mother.

119. Possibly N. C. McLean, who had been charged with bushwhacking. OR, ser. 2, vol. 6, p. 1005.

120. Horace Maynard (1814–82), born in Massachusetts, moved to Knoxville in 1838 to teach mathematics at the University of East Tennessee. He was admitted

to the bar in 1844 and served in the U.S. Congress from 1857 to 1863. He served as attorney general of Tennessee under Federal occupation (1863–65). One Knoxville Confederate described him as a "cold blooded Yankee, full of vengeance." Rothrock, *French Broad–Holston Country*, 453–54; Temple, *Notable Men of Tennessee*, 137–42; Clark, *Valleys of the Shadow*, 60–62. His wife Laura, also in the city at this time, explained their residence with the Dickinsons by saying, "Our house is occupied by a Federal officer, Gen. [Samuel A.] Gilbert, & is in a wretched condition." Laura Maynard to Washburn Maynard, Oct. 18, 1863, Maynard Papers.

121. Perez Dickinson (1813–1901) was born in Massachusetts, but moved to Knoxville to be a schoolteacher in 1829. He became a merchant and slave owner, but remained a moderate unionist who tried to relieve the hardships of Confederate prisoners in Knoxville. His house was on Main Street. Betsey B. Creekmore, *Knoxville*, 2d ed. (Knoxville, 1967), 131–47; Deaderick, *Heart of the Valley*, 22–23; Temple, *Notable Men of Tennessee*, 114–15; Clark, *Valleys of the Shadow*, 62; Rothrock, *French Broad–Holston Country*, 411–12.

122. Refers to Captain McLean and Lieutenant Spencer. Mr. Spicer was from Memphis.

123. In fighting on October 10–12, Gen. Robert E. Lee forced Meade out of Culpeper County, Virginia, and north of the Rappahannock River. Many people speculated that someone, if not Gen. Daniel Sickles (1819–1914), would replace Meade as commander of the Army of the Potomac.

124. Rosecrans had not been beaten again, but Gen. George H. Thomas (1816–70) did replace him as commander of the Army of the Cumberland on October 17.

125. Mary French, thirty-eight-year-old wife of Andrew French. Luttrell, *Census 1850 for Knox County*, 160. Elsewhere, Ellen means Isabella French.

126. Eliza P. Coffin was a fifty-one-year-old widow worth seventeen thousand dollars in 1860. 1860 Census, 22 (2d).

127. William Lunt of General Burnside's staff made his headquarters in the home of Joseph A. Mabry Jr. Jack Rentfro, "Remnants of Civil War Knoxville," *Civil War Times* 33 (May–June 1994): 50, 56.

128. Wolford was surprised at Philadelphia on October 20 and driven back to Loudon with the loss of six mountain howitzers and 479 men, mostly missing or captured. But Wolford was not captured, as suggested in the entry of October 22. *OR*, vol. 31, pt. 1:5–14.

129. Shaw was a member of the provost marshal staff.

130. Possibly William M. McLowry, former United States marshal who resided in Greeneville. Williams, *Knoxville Directory*, 30.

131. Aola McCalla, thirty years old, was the wife of merchant James A. McCalla, worth nine thousand dollars in 1860. 1860 Census, 93 (1st).

132. The Gen. Joseph E. Johnston (1807–91) and Gen. John C. Pemberton (1814–81) feud arose from the Vicksburg campaign, but Pemberton never brought charges against Johnston. Michael B. Ballard, *Pemberton: A Biography* (Jackson, Miss., 1991), 181–84, 193–95; Craig L. Symonds, *Joseph E. Johnston: A Civil War Biography* (New York, 1992), 216–26.

133. There was skirmishing around Philadelphia and Sweetwater, below Loudon on the railroad and about thirty miles southwest of Knoxville, on October 25–27.

134. Either P. W. Thomas, First Kentucky Cavalry, captured at Chickamauga, or R. E. Thomas, Second Kentucky Cavalry. "Memorial of the Federal Prison on Johnson's Island, Lake Erie, Ohio, 1862–1864," *Collections of the Virginia Historical Society*, n.s., 6 (Richmond, 1887): 309.

135. Ellen may be referring to one of two men. Israel Garrard commanded the Seventh Ohio Cavalry, Third Brigade of Samuel P. Carter's Fourth Division, IX Corps. Theophilus T. Garrard entered the war as colonel of the Seventh Kentucky Infantry (U.S.) but was promoted to general prior to October 1863. Tarrant, *Wild Riders of the First Kentucky Cavalry*, 8–9; Warner, *Generals in Blue*, 168–69.

136. Carter L. Stevenson (1817–88) had a division and forced the Federals out of Loudon on October 27, but he only made a demonstration against Knoxville, which resulted in fighting at Leiper's Ferry on October 28. *OR*, vol. 31, pt. 1:9.

137. Gen. John Pegram (1832–65) was not operating in the area of Glasgow and Danville, Kentucky, at this time.

138. "Rosey" Rosecrans was no longer in command of the army at Chattanooga. It had not been defeated in any case, although it remained besieged by Bragg's army.

139. Seventeen-year-old Mary R. and fifteen-year-old Jeanie were the daughters of Frank A. Ramsey. They also had a sister named Mary A., who was nineteen years old. Uncle Thomas was Thomas W. Humes, related by marriage to the Ramseys. 1860 Census, 104 (1st); Rothrock, *French Broad–Holston Country*, 431–32, 469–72.

140. James W. Rivers served in Holman's Tennessee Partisan Ranger Battalion. Wigginton et al., *Tennesseans in the Civil War* 1:43–44.

141. A common medical treatment of the time was to blister the skin by applying wrappings soaked in irritants.

142. Sophia Moody Park White, age fifty-three, was the wife of county recorder George McNutt White, former mayor of Knoxville (1852–53). Thirty-nine-year-old Mary McKinny was the wife of Judge Robert J. McKinny. He was born in Ireland, she in Tennessee. 1860 Census, 101, 106 (1st); Rothrock, *French Broad–Holston Country*, 449–50, 500.

143. Possibly Joseph W. Walker, a merchant worth thirty-five thousand dollars in 1860. 1860 Census, 48 (1st).

144. Probably fifty-three-year-old William Rogers, although forty-one-year-old William Rogers and James Rodgers (1818–98) are possible candidates. 1860 Census, 85 (1st), 95 (5th), 145 (13th); Rothrock, *French Broad–Holston Country*, 476.

145. I have not been able to identify the men held as prisoners, but Eliza Crocket was the twenty-nine-year-old wife of Joseph H. Crocket, a cabinetmaker who served on the board of aldermen in the 1850s and 1861–64. Anna McClung was the thirty-eight-year-old wife of Hugh L. McClung, a clerk at the railroad depot. 1860 Census, 65 (1st); Deaderick, *Heart of the Valley*, 637–38.

146. I have not been able to identify Mrs. Drake, but Rev. George Horne, a sixty-six-year-old Methodist minister, lived with his wife Amanda, four children, and two grandchildren. 1860 Census, 20 (2d).

147. John W. Paxton, a thirty-nine-year-old physician, had seen service as a captain of the Knoxville Guards or Knoxville Grays. 1860 Census, 33 (1st); Wigginton et al., *Tennesseans in the Civil War* 2:317.

148. Capt. A. C. Plumlee, Company E, Fourth Tennessee Cavalry Battalion, consolidated with Fourth and Fifth Tennessee Cavalry Battalion into Second (Ashby's) Tennessee Cavalry Regiment in May 1862. Plumlee may have been captured at Chickamauga. Wigginton, et al., *Tennesseans in the Civil War* 1:25–26, 52–54.

149. Neither Gen. Joseph Wheeler, preparing to lead his cavalry toward Knoxville with Longstreet, nor John Pegram was operating in Kentucky at this time. Wheeler had been operating in Tennessee for much of October while disrupting Rosecrans's supply lines into Chattanooga. John P. Dyer, *From Shiloh to San Juan: The Life of "Fightin Joe" Wheeler* (1961; reprint, Baton Rouge, 1989), 98–107, 112–13. Pegram was serving under Gen. Nathan B. Forrest.

150. Bettie was the eleven-year-old and youngest daughter of Frank A. and Anne M. Ramsey. 1860 Census, 104 (1st).

151. Sarah Newman was the twenty-six-year-old wife of James A. Newman, a Virginia-born lawyer. 1860 Census, 24 (2d).

152. Gustave A. Huwald's Howitzer Battery was mustered into service at Knoxville in June 1862. It was later known as D. Breck Ramsey's Tennessee Battery. Wigginton et al., *Tennesseans in the Civil War* 1:145–47.

153. In action at Rogersville, about sixty miles northeast of Knoxville, on November 6, Gen. William E. Jones and Col. Henry L. Giltner captured nearly the entire Second East Tennessee Mounted Infantry (U.S.) and half of the Seventh Ohio Cavalry—nearly eight hundred men and their mounts, plus four pieces of artillery and thirty-two wagons. This marks one of the first actions of the Knoxville campaign (Nov. 4–Dec. 23, 1863). *OR*, vol. 31, pt. 1:550–66; Marvel, *Burnside*, 303–4.

154. Parson Brownlow, who had reestablished his newspaper with the onset of Federal occupation, rejoiced that 250 Rebels, including some political prisoners, were to be sent north. Edward Maynard, noting the arrest of Charles McGhee, Columbus Powell, and other chameleons "of that stripe," said they were bound for Camp Chase, Ohio. *Knoxville Whig and Rebel Ventilator*, Nov. 11, 1863, p. 3; Edward Maynard to Washburn Maynard, Nov. 17, 1863, Maynard Papers.

155. Ellen C. McClung was the twenty-one-year-old daughter of Eliza J. McClung. Luttrell, *Census 1850 for Knox County*, 83.

156. Mary Gaudy Van Gilder was the wife of merchant John Somers Van Gilder. Both were born in New Jersey in 1825; they moved to Knoxville in 1851. 1860 Census, 93 (1st); Rothrock, *French Broad–Holston Country*, 499–500.

157. This was John C. Phillips (even though his report is shown as having been signed by Samuel N.), Battery M, Second Illinois Light Artillery, who lost four guns and thirty-three men. Later reassigned to the Second U.S. Artillery, he served as chief of artillery during the siege of Knoxville. *OR*, vol. 31, pt. 1:288, 341–44, 551.

158. Alice, or Allie, McPherson was the five-year-old daughter of R. M. W. and Mary McPherson. 1860 Census, 39 (1st).

159. There was skirmishing at Maryville, Little River, Rockford, and Huff's Ferry on November 14. At Maryville, Joseph Wheeler scattered a Federal force as he tried to gain the heights south of Knoxville. He failed to take the high ground, but did provide an effective diversion for Longstreet's general advance on November 13–14. *OR*, vol. 31, pt. 1:540–41. Also on the thirteenth, Longstreet tried to move between Burnside and Knoxville, but Burnside eluded him by falling back toward the city from defensive positions around Loudon and Lenoir's Station. "Everything was immediately in confusion and preparation made to leave for Knoxville immediately," reported one Federal soldier on November 14. "Burnside came down early in the day and ordered the troops to face the enemy and the trains to start for Knoxville." Michael E. Haskew, "Icy Assault Routed," *America's Civil War* 4 (May 1991): 25; Gavin, *Infantryman Pettit*, 126.

160. No significant fighting at Chattanooga occurred at this time.

CHAPTER 2. A LEADEN CLOUD HANGS OVER OUR SPIRITS

1. There is no evidence that Knoxville was to be evacuated at this time, even though James Longstreet had crossed the Tennessee River and headed for Knoxville on November 14.

2. Other unionists, including William G. Brownlow, John Baxter, and Oliver P. Temple, were also reported to have "left town for one of the Cumberland mountain gaps." However, many of the refugees—most notably Brownlow—soon returned to Knoxville. Graf et al., *Papers of Andrew Johnson* 6:504.

3. The siege of Knoxville began on November 16 with an engagement at Campbell's Station as Burnside tried to hold the Kingston Road and get his army safely into the city. Longstreet's corps had begun to arrive, detached from Bragg's forces on Missionary Ridge, on November 5. For a synopsis of Longstreet's campaign, see Jeffry D. Wert, *General James Longstreet: The Confederacy's Most Controversial Soldier—A Biography* (New York, 1993), 340–58. Burnside sought to draw Longstreet as close to Knoxville as possible and away from Chattanooga, where Ulysses S. Grant was making plans to assault Bragg's army. Longstreet missed his best chance to defeat Burnside because of less than aggressive action by subordinates, mainly Generals LaFayette McLaws, Micah Jenkins, and Evander McIvor. Several observers believed that if Longstreet had moved more swiftly, he could have taken Knoxville without a siege, a siege that ultimately failed. *OR*, vol. 31, pt. 1:274; Marvel, *Burnside*, 306–15; Haskew, "Icy Assault Routed," 25; Guy R. Swanson and Timothy D. Johnson, "Conflict in East Tennessee: Generals Law, Jenkins, and Longstreet," *Civil War History* 31 (June 1985): 101–10; Seymour, *Divided Loyalties*, 126–32; Hesseltine, *Ramsey Autobiography*, 149–50.

4. Isiah Davenport, an old friend of Ellen's father, was a southern-born man living in Cincinnati. Ellen later described him as "a Southern man with Southern feelings." Ellen House to James Fletcher, May 18, 1866, House Family Papers.

5. Joseph Hooker (1814–79) commanded XI and XII Corps in the Army of the Cumberland.

6. A Federal soldier arriving in Knoxville on November 16 "found everything in greatest confusion. Everybody that could preparing to leave. Brownlow left the day before and his family were packing up. Government officials were all ready to leave at a moments notice. The wagon trains were all collected and prepared to be turned if necessary. The general impression was that everything would be destroyed and the troops fall back to the mountains." Gavin, *Infantryman Pettit*, 128.

7. The rumor that the Federals were arming local blacks may have come from the fact that they used them to dig rifle pits and entrenchments. Gavin, *Infantryman Pettit*, 128.

8. John Baxter (1819–86) moved to Knoxville from North Carolina, where he had been a state representative and speaker of the state house. A Whig in politics and a lawyer by profession, Baxter was a slaveholder who remained a unionist, even though he acquiesced in Confederate rule for part of 1861–62 as a means of seeking a peaceful resolution of the war. Deaderick, *Heart of the Valley*, 21–22; Rothrock, *French Broad–Holston Country*, 376; Temple, *Notable Men of Tennessee*, 66–74.

9. Oliver Perry Temple (1820–1907) was a Whig lawyer who opposed secession and remained in Knoxville to defend unionists tried in Confederate courts, including Andrews's Raiders in June 1862. Rothrock, *French Broad–Holston Country*, 496–97; Joseph W. Needham, "Oliver Perry Temple: Entrepreneur, Agrarian, and Politician" (Ph.D. diss., Univ. of Tennessee, 1990). Many unionists in addition to Baxter and Temple began to flee Knoxville at this time, often headed for Cincinnati. Humes, *Loyal Mountaineers of Tennessee*, 245–46; Graf et al., *Papers of Andrew Johnson* 6:504.

10. Judge William B. Reese Sr. had died in 1859, but he was survived by his wife, Sarah M. Cocke, and four children. Two sons, John J. and William B. Jr., were lawyers. 1860 Census, 30 (12th). Rothrock, *French Broad–Holston Country*, 473–74; William Rule, ed., *Standard History of Knoxville, Tennessee* (Chicago, 1900), 498–99.

11. John L. Moses (1822–87), a Confederate sympathizer born in New Hampshire, moved to Knoxville in the 1840s, where he became a lawyer and merchant. He was listed as a banker in the 1860 census. He and his wife Susan W., age thirty-eight, had five children. His forty-five-year-old brother James C. Moses, a hardware merchant worth forty thousand dollars in 1860, was also married to a Susan W., age fifty-one, and they had six children. 1860 Census, 24 (2d), 92 (1st). Rothrock, *French Broad–Holston Country*, 461–62.

12. Richmond had not been evacuated, and Charleston had not fallen.

13. Gen. William Price Sanders (1833–63), born in Kentucky and graduated from West Point in 1856, was mortally wounded on the Kingston Road, November 18, while he and his men were attempting to establish an advance line of defense. Sanders, a bachelor, did not die until the following day, after he had been removed to the bridal suite of the Lamar House. In June, Sanders had led a raid into East Tennessee in preparation for Burnside's invasion. *OR*, vol. 31, pt. 1:274–75; Marvel, *Burnside*, 315–17; Seymour, *Divided Loyalties*, 77–79, 138–50. Burnside tried to conceal Sanders death for the sake of morale and did not publicly acknowledge his demise until November 24. Seymour, *Divided Loyalties*, 148–49. Gen. Speed Smith

Fry (1817–92), also of Kentucky, was not killed in the war. He is credited with killing Gen. Felix K. Zollicoffer in the battle of Mill Springs, Kentucky, January 1862,
but this is impossible to prove because Zollicoffer died in a volley of shots. Roger
Tate, "The Campaign and Battle of Mill Springs," *Blue & Gray Magazine* 10 (Feb.
1993): 52–53.

14. Robert Houston Armstrong, a thirty-four-year-old lawyer, was a son of
Drury P. and Ann Amelia (Houston) Armstrong. His house, built in 1850 on the
Kingston Road, was called Bleak House. Besides serving as a hospital, it was used by
Confederate sharpshooters during the siege and by James Longstreet as a headquar-
ters. It is now the property of the United Daughters of the Confederacy and serves
as the Confederate Memorial Hall. 1860 Census, 30 (12th); Rothrock, *French
Broad–Holston Country*, 370; Deaderick, *Heart of the Valley*, 417, 562; Seymour, *Di-
vided Loyalties*, 141; Rentfro, "Remnants of Civil War Knoxville," 50–51. Loudon
Hill, like the homes of Armstrong and Reese, was located west of Knoxville.

15. The First Presbyterian Church was located on the northeast corner of
Church and State; the Second was located on the west side of Clinch Street between Prince and Crooked. Williams, *Knoxville Directory*, 22.

16. Jesse A. Rayal was a thirty-seven-year-old bookseller. 1860 Census, 24 (2d).

17. Peter Staub (1827–1904) was a Swiss immigrant and tailor worth twenty-
eight hundred dollars in 1860. He built an opera house on the corner of Gay and
Cumberland in 1872 and served as mayor of Knoxville, 1874–75 and 1881–82. 1860
Census, 48 (1st); Deaderick, *Heart of the Valley*, 38; Rothrock, *French Broad–Holston
Country*, 489–90.

18. Samuel H. Lunt, described by another soldier as "a nice, intelligent gentleman," served as quartermaster for Wolford's cavalry brigade. Tarrant, *Wild Riders of
the First Kentucky Cavalry*, 204.

19. The round house and railroad depot sat on the northern edge of the city.

20. Oliver J. K. Peed, a forty-five-year-old shoemaker, had two daughters,
Anna, age fifteen, and Cornelia, age thirteen. 1860 Census, 55 (1st).

21. John M. Fleming (1832–1900) was the former editor of the Whigish *Knoxville Register* and a staunch unionist in 1864, when he turned against the Lincoln
administration and became a Democrat. Rothrock, *French Broad–Holston Country*,
417–18; Temple, *Notable Men of Tennessee*, 118–22.

22. College Hill, located west of the city and standing 160 feet high, was the
site of East Tennessee University, now the University of Tennessee. Temperance
Hill was east of Knoxville overlooking the railroad tracks and stood 225 feet high.

23. James H. Armstrong was a forty-eight-year-old farmer worth forty-six thousand dollars in 1860. 1860 Census, 1 (12th).

24. With Samuel Morrow, a forty-seven-year-old banker, away, the Morrow
household would have included his wife Melinda and their five children, ages ten
to twenty-one. 1860 Census, 96 (1st).

25. J. M. Borders, assistant surgeon in the Forty-sixth and Fifty-fifth Tennessee
Regiments. Joseph Jones, "Roster of the Medical Officers of the Army of Tennessee," *Southern Historical Society Papers* 22 (1894): 178.

26. James H. Renshaw was a thirty-seven-year-old cabinetmaker worth sixty-five hundred dollars in 1860. 1860 Census, 42 (1st).

27. The Deaf and Dumb Institute, which would later serve as city hall, had been founded in 1844 as the Deaf and Dumb Asylum. It served as a hospital for both sides during the war. Rothrock, *French Broad–Holston Country*, 133, 257. A photograph appears in Seymour, *Divided Loyalties*, 171.

28. Carrick W. Crozier, a fifty-six-year-old physician, lived with his wife Elizabeth and six children, ages nine to twenty-seven. 1860 Census, 106 (1st). He and part of his family had abandoned their house some months earlier when he joined the army. His house was not burned until November 24, when Mrs. Crozier reported that the light from the blaze of it and several other houses "illuminated the city with one grand light." By that time, she and the two youngest children, who had remained behind, fled to the homes of neighbors. Hesseltine, *Ramsey Autobiography*, 160; Elizabeth Baker Crozier Journal, 1863–64, pp. 1–7, Special Collections, Univ. of Tennessee, Knoxville (hereafter cited as Crozier Journal). The journal has been published in Seymour, *Divided Loyalties*, 135–42.

29. The house of David Anderson Deaderick (1797–1873) and his third wife, Elizabeth Jane Crozier, daughter of John Crozier, the merchant (d. 1838). The Deadericks had opposed secession, but once Tennessee joined the Confederacy, they gradually embraced the Cause. Their house had been in the thick of the fighting since November 17. Deaderick left his own account of the destruction of his house. 1860 Census, 27 (12th); Rothrock, *French Broad–Holston Country*, 410–11; Williams, "Journal of Events," 101–2.

30. James Hervey Cowan (1801–71) was a Knoxville-born merchant. With brother-in-law Perez Dickinson, he formed the mercantile firm of Cowan and Dickinson in 1832. A unionist moderate worth nearly $140,000 in 1860, he tried to improve conditions for Confederate prisoners in Knoxville. 1860 Census, 40 (1st); Rothrock, *French Broad–Holston Country*, 401–4, 411; Creekmore, *Knoxville*, 133; Clark, *Valleys of the Shadow*, 62.

31. There were two Rogan families in Knoxville with whom Ellen was probably familiar, but she likely refers here to fifty-year-old L. H. Rogan. Octavius N. Rogan was a forty-eight-year-old bookkeeper and father of eight. 1860 Census, 48, 73 (1st).

32. Margaret Alexander was the widow of Judge Ebenezer Alexander. Luttrell, *Census for 1850 Knox County*, 47; 1860 Census, 90 (1st).

33. David Deaderick recorded on this day, "The wagons occupy the vacant spaces and lots in town, and many of the troops are in the streets with tents in the yards, and under coverings stretched along the sidewalks, leaned against trees." Williams, "Journal of Events," 102.

34. A Pennsylvania soldier wrote on November 27, "Our rations were reduced to one quarter of a pound of bran bread and 1 lb. of meat daily to each man. No more coffee or sugar." The army had begun to receive some food from loyalists in the region. Ironically, many of the supplies were delivered by the same method used to fire the bridge—by water. Gavin, *Infantryman Pettit*, 129; Seymour, *Divided Loyalties*, 164–66.

35. Azro A. Barnes, a Vermont-born lawyer of forty-two, lived with his wife Iris T. Barnes and their two children. 1860 Census, 18 (12th).

36. William A. Branner died in March 1865. Deaderick, *Heart of the Valley*, 147. For Deaderick's efforts to salvage his household goods, see Williams, "Journal of Events," 101. A good many houses were destroyed by both sides, particularly if they obstructed fields of fire or could be used to advantage by the enemy. Gavin, *Infantryman Pettit*, 128–29; Seymour, *Divided Loyalties*, 164–65.

37. Hospitals had been established in several buildings of the university, as well as in the city's churches, the court house, the Female Academy, the principal hotels, and the Deaf and Dumb Institute. Williams, "Journal of Events," 102.

38. Two brigades led by Gen. Bushrod R. Johnson of Gen. Buckner's division did reinforce Longstreet but not until November 26. *OR*, vol. 31, pt. 1:460–61.

39. The Federals had set fire to homes, railroad machine shops, and the roundhouse (which the Confederates had used as an arsenal) north of the railroad. The blaze "roared and crackled with an unearthly sound, casting a broad belt of dazzling light over the fields and into the forests." David Deaderick also identified the railroad round house and Dr. Crozier's house as being in flames, as well as the John McCampbell house. It is strange that Ellen does not mention that the flames ignited a store of condemned ammunition in the roundhouse, thus setting off an explosion "that shock the earth and startled the anxious residents of the city." Williams, "Journal of Events," 102; Seymour, *Divided Loyalties*, 168–69.

40. As Ellen guessed, Shackleford's men did not advance beyond their defenses, although they repulsed a sharp Confederate attack on November 24. *OR*, vol. 31, pt. 1:277.

41. Eliza J. (Morgan) McClung, worth $130,000 in 1860, was the sixty-year-old widow of Matthew McClung. Hugh L. McClung, a twenty-year-old clerk, was her youngest son. Lucy Alexander was the widow of Major Charles Alexander. Luttrell, *Census 1850 for Knox County*, 83; 1860 Census, 41, 90 (1st).

42. Several young men named Glenn served in units mustered at Knoxville. Wigginton et al., *Tennesseans in the Civil War* 2:171.

43. Robert Craighead was a forty-eight-year-old bookkeeper. 1860 Census, 28 (12th).

44. Margaret Sedgwick, wife of merchant George Sedgwick. 1860 Census, 50 (1st). Cornelia White McGhee, wife of Charles McClung McGhee.

45. Blanch, or "Blannie," McClung was the seventeen-year-old daughter of Hugh L. and Anna McClung. 1860 Census, 65 (1st). No Brinkly or Brinkley family appears in the 1850 or 1860 census. Dr. Jackson Buckley had several daughters, but none of them was named Annie. 1860 Census, 73 (7th). The Brinklys are probably refugees from Memphis. See entry of December 9.

46. Cordie Fletcher, mentioned also in the entry for January 1, 1864, was probably a refugee.

47. Bean's Station was a village northeast of Knoxville. One Confederate officer described it as "not upon the railroad, but on the old stage line, & it was a village of a rather large hotel, & perhaps twenty other houses in a well cultivated rolling valley." Gallagher, *Fighting for the Confederacy*, 331.

48. Gen. Orlando B. Willcox reported on November 28: "Negro [who] left rebel camp of Knoxville yesterday morning says fighting has not been very heavy; principally artillery and sharpshooters. Longstreet hoped to reduce Knoxville by starvation." *OR*, vol. 31, pt. 3:266.

49. "The rebels drove in our pickets about 10 o'clock last night," a Union soldier reported on November 29. "We tumbled into the ditches in a hurry." Gavin, *Infantryman Pettit*, 129. This was the beginning of the most famous episode in the siege of Knoxville: the attack on Fort Sanders, which protected the west side of the city. The defenses had been known as Fort Loudon, but following the death of Colonel Sanders, Burnside renamed the fort in his honor. Military men considered the cannonading on the night and early morning of November 28–29, from midnight to 6:30 A.M., to be "slow," at a rate of forty shots per minute. Sometimes heavy skirmishing also occurred during the night. But at 6:30 A.M. a "furious fire" fell upon the fort and the attack began in earnest. Harold S. Fink, "The East Tennessee Campaign and the Battle of Knoxville in 1863," *East Tennessee Historical Society's Publications* 29 (1957): 94–95, 105–9; Seymour, *Divided Loyalties*, 177–204; Orlando M. Poe, "The Defense of Knoxville," in *Battles and Leaders of the Civil War*, ed. Robert U. Johnson and Clarence C. Buel, 4 vols. (New York, 1887), 3:741–45; *OR*, vol. 31, pt. 1:277–78, 298–99; Gallagher, *Fighting for the Confederacy*, 325–29.

50. The Federals admitted that the Confederate attack was gallant and persistent, but in the end it was "handsomely repulsed" with slight loss (4 killed and 11 wounded). In less than thirty minutes, the Confederates lost 3 battle flags, 129 men killed, 458 wounded, and 226 missing, mostly captured. The prisoners came from the Thirteenth and Seventeenth Mississippi, and the Sixteenth Georgia. Within thirty minutes of the conclusion of the fight, Longstreet received word that Bragg had been beaten at Chattanooga and was falling back to Ringgold, Georgia. Later in the day, Burnside learned that three relief columns (25,000 men) were in motion toward Knoxville. Fink, "East Tennessee Campaign," 109–11; Gavin, *Infantryman Pettit*, 130; *OR*, vol. 31, pt. 1:273, 298–99.

51. Capt. Bell does not appear on the roster of Georgia infantry regiments from Baker County.

52. George Duffield Rice Jr., or Duff, was a Marietta friend of Ellen. He was the twenty-one-year-old son of George D. Rice, and he served in Company E, First Confederate Regiment Infantry. U.S. Census Bureau, *Population Schedule of the Eighth United States Census, 1860, Cobb County, Georgia*, National Archives Microcopy No. 653 (cited hereafter as 1860 Census [Cobb]), Roll 117, p. 294; Henderson, *Roster of Confederate Soldiers of Georgia* 1:57.

53. Lt. Col. A. G. O'Brien commanded the Thirteenth Mississippi Infantry. *OR*, vol. 31, pt. 3:890. His sister was Eliza A. Brownlow.

54. Ford is probably an enlisted man and not the Confederate captain referred to elsewhere by Ellen.

55. Lt. Thomas W. Cummings, adjutant of the Sixteenth Georgia Infantry, was captured inside Fort Sanders. When first surrounded, he boldly told his captors that they would soon be his prisoners. He enlisted in Company K, Twentieth Georgia

Infantry, in Richmond County, Georgia, in August 1861, was elected second lieu-
tenant of his company in February 1862, and appointed adjutant of the Sixteenth
Georgia in March 1862. He was later exchanged but recaptured at Deep Bottom,
Virginia, in August 1864. E. Porter Alexander, "Longstreet at Knoxville," in
Johnson and Buel, *Battles and Leaders of the Civil War* 3:749 n.; Henderson, *Roster of
Confederate Soldiers of Georgia* 2:833.

56. Cpl. Thomas M. Bones, Company A, Fifth Georgia Infantry, was wounded
in the leg at Chickamauga. He survived the amputation to be discharged for disability in March 1864. Henderson, *Roster of Confederate Soldiers of Georgia* 1:644.

57. William H. Torr, Fifteenth Indiana Battery, if attached to Gen.
Shackleford's staff, had recently been reassigned, for he had been serving on the
staff of Col. Robert K. Byrd, although the brigades of both Byrd and Shackleford
formed part of Gen. Carter's division. *OR*, vol. 30, pt. 2:555.

58. Mary Hill Alexander, described as "beautiful and charming" by one Confederate soldier, was a twenty-year-old sister of Major Charles Alexander. 1860 Census, 90 (1st); Clark, *Valleys of the Shadow*, 64–65.

59. Carter Cummings was the son of Col. David H. Cummings.

60. Margaret E. Ault, twenty-one years old, was the eldest daughter of merchant Henry Ault, worth fifty thousand dollars in 1860. Her youngest sister was
twelve-year-old Mary E. Ault. 1860 Census, 71 (1st). Miss O'Conner is probably
Rebecca O'Conner, sister of Thomas O'Conner, Ellen's future brother-in-law.

61. Lizzie Kennedy Vanuxum (also spelled Van Uxon and Vanuxem) married
Cuban-born Frederick Vanuxum in 1854. Elizabeth Baker Crozier and her two children, as well as Dr. William Baker and his wife, resided briefly with the Vanuxums
after having been driven from their own homes by the Federals. Luttrell, *Census
1850 for Knox County*, 43; d'Armand and d'Armand, *Marriage Records*, 1046; Crozier Journal, pp. 5–6.

62. Michael Branner is probably G. M. Branner, a thirty-five-year-old banker.
1860 Census, 93 (1st).

63. It is true that Sherman's men met the most resistance and engaged in the
heaviest fighting in the assault on Missionary Ridge. Sherman said the attack "cost
us dear," and a recent biographer admits that Sherman "failed to break through on
the flank as he was supposed to." *OR*, vol. 31, pt. 2:573–74; John F. Marszalek,
Sherman: A Soldier's Passion for Order (New York, 1993), 243–45.

64. Dickinson's corner probably refers to the northeast corner of Gay and Main,
the location of Cowan and Dickinson's store. Rule, *History of Knoxville*, 227. Photograph in Clark, *Valleys of the Shadow*, xxi.

65. G. K. Levine was a thirty-three-year-old physician born in New York. 1860
Census, 102 (1st).

66. Jane McCaffrey was the thirty-six-year-old wife of saddler James McCaffrey.
1860 Census, 57 (1st).

67. Far from receiving cavalry reinforcements at this time, Longstreet was re-
sisting an order to send a portion of his cavalry to Bragg. In fact, Longstreet had
begun his withdrawal from around Knoxville the day previous, December 2, as he

moved back toward Virginia. The siege was lifted on December 4, as his troops settled in around Morristown. From there, Longstreet could threaten the flank of any potential Federal move into Georgia. *OR*, vol. 31, pt. 2:462; Fink, "East Tennessee Campaign," 112; Bruce L. Allardice, "Longstreet's Nightmare in Tennessee," *Civil War* 18 (June 1989): 32.

68. "The Rebel Pickets were withdrawn from our front at one o'clock this morning," reported a jubilant Union soldier. "Their position was reconnoitered and the whole army found gone. I never felt more relieved in my life than when we found the rebel army gone." Gavin, *Infantryman Pettit*, 131.

69. Bragg's defeat refers to the Confederate disaster at Missionary Ridge (November 25), which had, in fact, sent the Army of Tennessee reeling back to Dalton, Georgia. Bragg resigned command of the army on November 29, to be relieved temporarily the following day by Gen. William Hardee. Robert E. Lee, however, was safely encamped for the winter south of the Rapidan River after having defeated the Army of the Potomac under George G. Meade in the Mine Run campaign (Nov. 26–Dec. 1). Longstreet by this date had retired as far as Blaine's Cross Roads.

70. Gen. John Gray Foster (1823–74) was assigned to relieve Burnside in response to Burnside's own request to be relieved. However, Foster did not arrive in Knoxville until December 10. He assumed command the following day. *OR*, vol. 31, pt. 3:384–85; Marvel, *Burnside*, 331.

71. Gen. Edward Ferrero (1831–99) commanded the First Division, IX Corps.

72. Gen. Orlando B. Willcox engaged cavalry of Wheeler's command at Walker's Ford, on the Clinch River, in action on December 2 and skirmishing on December 5. Casualties were not high, and the Federals held the ford. The General Jones identified by Ellen was not Samuel (1819–87) but William E. "Grumble" Jones (1824–64). *OR*, vol. 31, pt. 1:293, 394–99. Gen. William T. Sherman's relief column arrived at Knoxville on this date (December 6) under the command of Gen. John G. Parke.

73. Rosa Mitchell, forty-nine years old, was the wife of saddler Thomas Mitchell. 1860 Census, 41 (1st).

74. Sixteen-year-old Martha McCaffrey was the daughter of James and Jane; Harriet Park, forty-four, lived with her mother, Sophia Park. 1860 Census, 57, 101 (1st).

75. Wheeler's report of the Knoxville campaign does not mention the loss of Major Smith. *OR*, vol. 31, pt. 1:540–44. However, the plight of a Major Smith fitting this description does appear in Humes, *Loyal Mountaineers*, 290, 292.

76. Gen. Francis P. Blair Jr. and his staff would be reassigned the next day, December 7, to Grant at Chattanooga. Command of XV Corps would be handed over to Gen. John A. Logan. *OR*, vol. 31, pt. 3:353–54.

77. S. B. G. Winslow was a forty-three-year-old printer. He and his wife Kate were born in Pennsylvania. They had three children. 1860 Census, 91 (12th).

78. Annie McFarlane was the twenty-two-year-old second daughter of silversmith George McFarlane and his wife Malinda. 1860 Census, 42 (1st).

79. Thirty-eight-year-old James Park was the president of the Deaf and Dumb Institute. 1860 Census, 51 (1st).

80. If Ellen does not here refer to her brothers, Sam and John were probably sons of Joseph Churchill Strong Jr. Rothrock, *French Broad–Holston Country,* 492–93; Luttrell, *Census 1850 for Knox County,* 94.

81. Gen. Gordon Granger (1822–76) did not replace Carter as provost marshal. Granger commanded IV Corps as part of the relief force from Chattanooga. Interestingly, however, on December 10, Carter asked Granger to control his troops more closely as they were guilty of "depredations" against citizens considered loyal to the U.S. government. He sent a similar plea to Gen. Edward E. Potter on December 26. *OR,* vol. 31, pt. 3:358–59, 372, 506–8. Ellen does not mention Sherman's presence in the city. Nor did she know that he was miffed at Burnside for having given the impression that the garrison was in dire straits. "Had I known of this," Sherman recalled, "I should not have hurried my men so fast; but until I reached Knoxville I thought our troops there were actually in danger of starvation." Sherman, *Memoirs* 1:367–68.

82. References to Foster as another Butler here and elsewhere suggest harsh treatment of civilians as evidenced by Gen. Benjamin Butler in the occupation of New Orleans in 1862. On December 9, Foster officially superseded Burnside as commander of the Department of the Ohio.

83. Joseph Wheeler was not with Longstreet, but two of his cavalry divisions, commanded by Gen. Will Martin, and two brigades from Southeast Virginia, commanded by "Grumble" Jones, had been assigned to Longstreet. Longstreet had continued to withdraw northeast from Knoxville to Rutledge (December 6) and Rogersville (December 8). Allardice, "Longstreet's Nightmare," 35.

84. A. P. Russell belonged to Company E (Knoxville Grays), Nineteenth Tennessee Infantry. W. J. Worsham, *The Old Nineteenth Tennessee Regiment, C.S.A.* (Knoxville, 1901), 220–21, gives a complete roster of the company.

85. William J. Dumas, Company K, First Georgia Infantry, was from Monroe County, Georgia. He was captured November 29, 1863, and later sent to Fort Delaware. Henderson, *Roster of Confederate Soldiers of Georgia* 5:611.

86. Andrew White was the thirteen-year-old son of George McNutt and Sophia White. 1860 Census, 101 (1st).

87. These were mostly false rumors, prompted more by hope than accurate information. Longstreet's men had been engaged in skirmishing around Morristown on December 10, but his corps was based at Rogersville, northeast of Morristown. The Army of Tennessee, without Bragg, was still at Dalton, not Ringgold.

88. Lucinda E. Humphreys was the forty-nine-year-old wife of J. S. Humphreys. 1860 Census, 22 (2d).

89. All three women were nineteen and resided in Marietta. Ruth T. Bostwick was the daughter of Elona F. Bostwick; Mary B. Brumby was the daughter of A. V. Brumby, a manufacturer worth twelve thousand dollars in 1860; and Annie Glover was the daughter of J. P. Glover. 1860 Census (Cobb), Roll 117, pp. 236, 253, 256.

90. Gen. Milo Smith Hascall (1829–1904) commanded a Federal division at Knoxville, but he was very much alive.

91. Capt. S. H. Hall, Company A, Eighth Georgia Infantry, from Floyd County, Georgia, was wounded November 29, 1863, but records state that he died on December 1. Henderson, *Roster of Confederate Soldiers of Georgia* 1:917.

92. Wayne W. Wallace was a forty-five-year-old lawyer. 1860 Census, 95 (1st).

93. Ann E. Rayal was the thirty-three-year-old wife of Jessie A. Rayal. They had two children. 1860 Census, 24 (2d).

94. John G. Parke had advanced ten thousand infantry as far as Rutledge, and General Shackleford had moved his cavalry to Bean's Station, eight miles ahead of Parke. Threatening movements and some fierce but uncoordinated fighting on December 14–16 near Bean's Station and Blaine's Cross Roads produced little advantage for either side. The Federals drew back, but without great loss. Allardice, "Longstreet's Nightmare," 34–43; Wert, *General James Longstreet*, 355–57.

95. On December 14, a Federal soldier wrote, "We have seen hard times in East Tenn. Yet we do not complain. We believe it has all been necessary and for that reason we have been willing to endure it. This war is not over yet neither are its hardships. . . . We are willing to do our duty. But month by month disease thins our ranks and every skirmish or battle carries off some of our bravest men." Gavin, *Infantryman Pettit*, 131.

96. Wofford's Brigade helped lead the assault on Fort Sanders. Wofford's Hospital consisted largely of wounded men from that unit and was staffed by some of the brigade's surgeons.

97. Sgt. Joseph X. Beauchamp, Company E, Tenth Georgia Infantry, was from Clayton County, Georgia. His wound, received November 19, 1863, left him permanently disabled. Henderson, *Roster of Confederate Soldiers of Georgia* 2:32.

98. Samuel A. Gilbert, who commanded the First Brigade, Third Division, IX Corps, was made military governor of Knoxville on September 3. He had not been killed. Indeed, he was promoted to general in 1865. *OR*, vol. 30, pt. 2:554; vol. 30, pt. 3:334; Francis B. Heitman, *Historical Register and Dictionary of the United States Army*, 2 vols. (Washington, D.C., 1903), 1:455.

99. Joseph H. Parsons commanded the Ninth Tennessee Cavalry (U.S.), four companies of which had been raised in Knox County. Wigginton et al., *Tennesseans in the Civil War* 1:342–44, 429. For an insight into Parsons's personality see Clark, *Valleys of the Shadow*, 51–52.

100. William M. Piggott was an assistant surgeon in Wofford's Brigade. Henderson, *Roster of Confederate Soldiers of Georgia* 3:1; Jones, "Roster of the Medical Officers," 247.

101. Thomas Van Gilder was the son of John S. Gilder, president of the Knoxville Leather Company. There were several merchants named Nelson in Knoxville, but Ellen probably refers to the store of Matthew Nelson, worth forty-three thousand dollars in 1860. 1860 Census, 96 (1st).

102. The Sixty-ninth North Carolina was in the region at this time, but there is no official report of action at Louisville. Clark, *Histories of the Several Regiments and Battalions* 3:742–43. The Confederates captured two wagon trains on December 14,

one near Bean's Station, the other near Clinch Mountain Gap. *OR*, vol. 31, pt. 1:605–6, pt. 3:837. Thomas's Legion did engage in action at Gatlinburg earlier in the month. Crow, *Storm in the Mountains*, 53–54.

103. Ellen was close friends with several members of the Andrew Hansell family and with Emily Howell, referred to frequently in her 1857–58 diary. Bolan Glover was the twenty-year-old brother of Annie Glover; sixteen-year-old Peter Cox was the son of R. H. Cox; and Judge George D. Rice was the father of Duff Rice.

104. Joseph F. Cotton was an assistant surgeon in the Tenth Georgia Infantry. Jones, "Roster of the Medical Officers," 185.

105. Edmund B. Whitman, Quartermaster Department, Army of the Ohio, was in charge of receiving and issuing clothing and equipage. *OR*, vol. 32, pt. 2:204; *Knoxville Whig and Rebel Ventilator*, Feb. 20, 1864, p. 3

106. Wallie McPherson's report of Longstreet's movement was wrong. Longstreet's men by this date were settling into winter quarters around Russellville, Morristown, and Rogersville. Wert, *General James Longstreet*, 357.

107. No surviving reports place Confederate cavalry at Clinton or Gen. John C. Breckinridge at Sweetwater.

108. With the increased number of soldiers and civilian refugees in Knoxville, sickness and disease of all types spread alarmingly. The army established smallpox hospitals in town but with no effort at quarantine. Consequently, the epidemic ran rampant. Bryan, "Civil War in East Tennessee," 139–40; *Knoxville Whig and Rebel Ventilator*, Feb. 6, 1864, p. 2.

109. A series of operations around Mossy Creek and Dandridge between December 22 and 29, described as "one of the hardest and bitterest cavalry campaigns of the war," resulted in a skirmish at Dandridge on December 22–23, action at Hay's Ferry on December 24, and the battle of Mossy Creek on December 29. The Federals got the better of the fighting. *OR*, vol. 31, pt. 1:632; Stephen Z. Starr, *Union Cavalry in the Civil War*, 3 vols. (Baton Rouge, 1979–85), 3:348–50; John Rowell, "The Battle of Mossy Creek," *Civil War Times* 8 (July 1969): 11–16, and *Yankee Cavalrymen: Through the Civil War with the Ninth Pennsylvania Cavalry* (Knoxville, 1971): 159–65.

110. Nineteen-year-old Elizabeth P. Lyles was the daughter of S. M. Lyles, a Marietta tanner, although the name appears as Pyles in the census. 1860 Census (Cobb), Roll 117, p. 291.

111. Camp Douglass was a military prison camp at Chicago.

112. Park Baker was probably William P. Baker, a clerk for J. A. Rayal. See Williams, *Knoxville Directory*, 35. Benjamin J. Stephenson was a thirty-year-old druggist, married to Isabella and the father of two children. He served on the Knoxville board of aldermen in 1870–71, 1877–79, and 1883–84. 1860 Census, 82 (1st); Deaderick, *Heart of the Valley*, 639, 641–42.

113. James A. Newman was a lieutenant in Kain's Light Artillery. His wife's name was Sarah, but daughter Mattie does not appear in the census. Wigginton et al., *Tennesseans in the Civil War* 2:303; 1860 Census, 118 (21st).

114. Possibly Margaret E. (King) Cocke, who married James R. Cocke in 1839. D'Armand and d'Armand, *Marriage Records*, 209. She was the aunt of Ella Cocke mentioned in entry for December 25.

115. The report concerning John Hunt Morgan north of Chattanooga is false. It is surprising that Ellen does not report that Morgan had only recently escaped from the Ohio State Penitentiary after having been captured in July during his raid through Kentucky. In December, Morgan was still reorganizing his command.

116. Preston J. Lea was a sixty-nine-year-old farmer. Luttrell, *Census 1850 for Knox County*, 69.

117. William B. Rogers and his brother John R. Rogers, twenty-nine and twenty-seven years old, respectively. 1860 Census, 93 (1st). Will worked for Van Gilder.

118. Foster, falling with his horse on "a ledge of rock," reopened an old leg wound. He eventually had to relinquish command. Whatever defects Ellen saw in Foster, Henry Halleck called him "a good officer and a live man," and one historian has judged him "a confident, clear-eyed, level-headed officer with an orderly administrative mind." Starr, *Union Cavalry in the Civil War* 3:343–44.

119. Summit Battery, or Fort Comstock as the Federals dubbed it, was located on Summit Hill near the railroad depot. *OR*, vol. 31, pt. 1:312.

120. Grant reported at 11:00 A.M. on December 31, "Have just arrived at this place [Knoxville], and will go to the front this evening or in the morning." He remained several days and upon inspecting troops at Strawberry Plains found them "in bad condition for clothing." *OR*, vol. 31, pt. 3:542; vol. 32, pt. 2:19.

CHAPTER 3. I AM DETERMINED NOT TO BE BLUE

1. An interesting notice by a Capt. John H. Lester of Deming, New Mexico, appeared in the *Confederate Veteran* 22 (Jan. 1914): 2: "[I] would like to hear from any survivors of the two hundred prisoners who left Knoxville on the 1st of January 1864, under guard of the Twenty-first Massachusetts Infantry, for a Northern prison, or from any member of that regiment, especially Captain Sampson."

2. Capt. George V. Moody commanded Moody's (Louisiana) Battery under Col. Edward Porter Alexander, Longstreet's chief of artillery. As Longstreet withdrew from Tennessee, Alexander reported on January 15, 1864, "One of my most gallant officers (Capt. G. V. Moody) was compelled to be left dangerously ill at a private house near Knoxville, and must have fallen into the hands of the enemy." *OR*, vol. 31, pt. 1:452, 480. Humes, *Loyal Mountaineers of Tennessee*, 290, says Moody suffered from heart disease, and that he and Major Smith were brought in together. Humes maintains that Moody's "really distinguished presence," "remarkable stature and aristocratic physique," and "lordly bearing, combined to embody the idea which the natives entertained of 'Southern chivalry.'"

3. Ephraim Shelby Dodd, a Kentuckian by birth, was a member of Company D, Eighth Texas Cavalry, better known as Terry's Texas Rangers. He was captured December 17, 1863, by unionist Home Guards. Dodd made the following entry in his own diary for January 1, 1864: "Received one pair of drawers from Miss Nannie Scott, two shirts from Mrs. House. One hundred and fifty prisoners start to-day for Strawberry Plains. We go to-morrow." *Louisville Journal*, Feb. 20, 1864, p. 1; Thomas Munnerlyn, ed., *Diary of Ephraim Shelby Dodd, Member of Company D, Terry's Texas Rangers, December 4, 1862–January 1, 1864* (1914; reprint, Austin Texas, 1979), 2, 31, 32.

4. Brownlow was in Cincinnati during the first half of December 1863.

5. Ellen probably refers to First Creek, the easternmost of the three creeks that bisected Knoxville. Seymour, *Divided Loyalties*, 151; OR, vol. 31, pt. 1:313.

6. Gens. Edmund Kirby Smith and Richard Taylor had not yet encountered Nathaniel Banks, although the report anticipates the results of the Red River campaign in the spring.

7. Gen. Davis Tillson (1830–95) supervised Federal defensive works during the siege of Knoxville. In late April 1864 he would be assigned to lead the Second Brigade, Fourth Division, XXIII Corps. Warner, *Generals in Blue*, 506–7; Frank J. Welcher, *The Union Army, 1861–1865: Organization and Operations. Volume II: The Western Theater* (Bloomington, 1993), 214.

8. Citizen's prison, also known as Confederate prison, refers to the Knoxville County Jail, used during Federal occupation to house Confederate prisoners of war and unionist criminals. A picture and description of the jail, also known as Castle Fox for Robert F. Fox, a county constable and the jailer during Confederate occupation, appear in Clark, *Valleys of the Shadow*, xxvi–xxix. Prindle, *Ancestry of William Sperry Beinecke*, 237, 244, 249; 1860 Census, 71 (1st). Prindle, *Ancestry of William Sperry Beinecke*, 244–49, also offers a description of the jail and its inmates. The second principal prison, known as the Federal prison because it housed primarily Union soldiers charged with crimes and misdemeanors, was located in Temperance Hall, East Knoxville. For a description of this prison see Prindle, *Ancestry of William Sperry Beinecke*, 249–59.

9. Melissa E. Gillespie was the wife of Colonel James G. Gillespie, who commanded the Forty-third Tennessee Infantry, organized at Knoxville, December 14, 1861. Wigginton et al., *Tennesseans in the Civil War* 1:268–70.

10. Dodd wrote in his diary on December 19, 1863, "I send a summons to the Lodge for assistance; two members call on me and promise to attend to my case, but I hear no more from them." Munnerlyn, *Diary of Ephraim Shelby Dodd*, 31. See also Humes, *Loyal Mountaineers*, 289.

11. This was Gen. Carter's Order No. 13. Brownlow approved of this and several similar orders aimed at Knoxville Rebels: "The General is firing in the right direction, and is striking some good licks. Hit them again, General, and increase their pains and agonies." *Knoxville Whig and Rebel Ventilator*, Jan. 9, 1864, pp. 2–3; Hesseltine, *Ramsey Autobiography*, 174–75.

12. Ellen's statement confirms a report by Edward Porter Alexander that Longstreet hanged a member of the Eighth Michigan Cavalry and left him dangling as "a warning to spies." Gallagher, *Fighting for the Confederacy*, 330–31. See also Humes, *Loyal Mountaineers*, 292.

13. Sweetwater is about forty miles southwest of Knoxville on the East Tennessee and Georgia Railroad, but no official mention survives of this action. Wheeler was in Georgia with Johnston's army at this time, but two-thirds of his cavalry had been assigned to Longstreet. Reports of Wheeler being in and around Knoxville refer to the men of his command. OR, vol. 32, pt. 2:510.

14. Melancthon C. Cowdery, Second Ohio Cavalry, was assigned to the provost marshal's force. OR, vol. 36, pt. 1:895.

15. Corporal Connerly was Dodd's guard mentioned on January 7. In Dodd's final letter to his father he reported, "I am treated as kindly by the guard as I could be under the circumstances." *Louisville Journal*, Feb. 20, 1864, p. 1.

16. The Texas star was the emblem of many Texas units, including the Texas Rangers.

17. For another contemporary account of the Dodd hanging, see Munnerlyn, *Diary of Ephraim Shelby Dodd*, 33–36.

18. Lt. Col. William E. Riley, Eleventh Kentucky Cavalry.

19. Richard Owen Currey (spelled "Curry" by Ellen), who had operated the Daughter's Collegiate Institute before the war, joined the Confederate army as a surgeon in the Sixty-third Tennessee Infantry and supervised one of the principal hospitals in Knoxville. He died February 1865 while on duty at an army hospital at Salisbury, N.C. Rothrock, *French Broad–Holston Country*, 134; Creekmore, *Knoxville*, 97; Jones, "Roster of the Medical Officers," 189.

20. Mattie (Martha A.) Luttrell, was the fifteen-year-old daughter of James Churchwell Luttrell and Elizabeth Carr Bell Luttrell and sister of Lt. Luttrell. 1860 Census, 73 (1st).

21. P. H. Goodlin was the fifty-four-year-old wife of Dr. C. M. Goodlin. They were refugees from Grainger County, Tennessee. U.S. Bureau of the Census, *Population Schedule of the Eighth United States Census, 1860, Grainger County, Tennessee*, National Archives Microcopy No. 653, Roll 1250, p. 470.

22. Rachel Currey, thirty-nine years old, was the wife of Richard Owen Currey. 1860 Census, 42 (1st).

23. Ulysses S. Grant was in fact trying to repair the railroads in Tennessee and northern Alabama (particularly at Bridgeport) in order to supply the army at Knoxville. While the road was being repaired, he was forced to provision the city by river. *OR*, vol. 32, pt. 2:30, 32, 88–89, 110–11; John Y. Simon, ed., *Papers of Ulysses S. Grant*, 20 vols. (Carbondale, Ill., 1967–95), 10:31–32. There were no U.S Colored Troops at Nashville.

24. Mr. Baird was a Confederate prisoner of war. For a complete look at the Dodd episode, see Daniel E. Sutherland, "Blind Justice," *Civil War Times* 35 (May 1996):28–35.

25. Averell's raid probably refers to the November 1–8, 1863, raid to Lewisburg, West Virginia, by Gen. William W. Averell, although Averell's men also engaged in smaller raids all through December.

26. Sarah J. Hamilton was the twenty-five-year-old wife of William Hamilton, a jeweler. 1860 Census, 92 (1st). Fourteen-year-old Mary Eastin resided with Dr. and Mrs. Currey. 1860 Census, 42 (1st).

27. Horace H. Thomas was Gen. Carter's assistant adjutant general, in charge of issuing passes, oaths of allegiance, and certificates of loyalty. *Knoxville Whig and Rebel Ventilator*, Feb. 20, 1864, p. 3.

28. Gen. William J. Hardee had his headquarters at Dalton, Georgia, at this time.

29. Charleston, Tennessee, was about seventy miles southwest of Knoxville on the railroad.

30. L. T. Shepherd was a forty-year-old sash and blind manufacturer from Connecticut. 1860 Census, 43 (1st).

31. Brownlow published the names of all who took the oath. Claiming that fully half of the oath-takers were insincere, he encouraged true unionists to watch these people and to report their names to the provost marshal should they betray themselves, that they might be "arrested and sent South." Mr. and Mrs. House's names appeared in Brownlow's newspaper two weeks after they took the oath. One unionist thought many Rebels took the oath to escape General Carter's restrictions on purchases at local shops and stores. *Knoxville Whig and Rebel Ventilator*, Jan. 23, 1864, p. 2, Jan. 30, 1864, p. 3; Laura Maynard to Washburn Maynard, Jan. 19, 1864, Maynard Papers.

32. Gen. Robert B. Vance (1828–99), brother of North Carolina governor Vebulon B. Vance, made a raid toward Sevierville with 300 cavalry on January 14. He captured 23 wagons sent out from Knoxville to gather forage, but he was pursued by Colonel William J. Palmer, Fifteenth Pennsylvania Cavalry, who, some two dozen miles from Sevierville, recaptured all lost wagons, drivers, and animals plus 150 saddle horses, 100 stands-of-arms, and a Confederate ambulance filled with medical stores. *OR*, vol. 32, pt. 1:73–77.

33. Brownlow's attack was on William Craig, clerk of the Knoxville County Court.

34. In an editorial of January 9, 1864, Brownlow called Knoxville's "Rebel females" the "most hateful and disgusting rebel women—traitors to the government, and as mean as the men of the same faith." In January he advocated sending them out of the country; by April he wanted them locked up in a "female" prison. *Knoxville Whig and Rebel Ventilator*, Jan. 9, 1864, p. 1; Rothrock, *French Broad–Holston Country*, 142. Provost Marshal Carter found them a trial, too. Fisher, "War at every man's door," 291–93. Brownlow's description of the prisoners' departure on January 10 verifies events described by Ellen: "On Sabbath morning, as the prisoners passed out of Gay street to the Depot, Curry's front portico was filled with *she* rebels, who made a bold, impudent, and *flirting* demonstration—such as it takes a Southern she-rebel to make. The rebel prisoners, as a matter of course, replied with shouts and yells. Every one of the women ought to be sent South, and the Curry house ought to be taken for a hospital." *Knoxville Whig and Rebel Ventilator*, Jan. 16, 1864, p. 2.

35. The New Market fight was actually around Dandridge, a dozen miles southeast of New Market (a station on the railroad about twenty-five miles northeast of Knoxville). The Federals, commanded by Gen. Samuel D. Sturgis, were pushed back by John Bell Hood's division. Longstreet reported, "During the night the enemy retired to New Market and to Strawberry Plains, leaving his dead upon the field." The Federals were indeed "demoralized," but Longstreet's men were in little better shape. "Our infantry was not in condition to pursue, half of our men being without shoes," reasoned Longstreet. "Our cavalry is almost as badly off for want of clothing, and the horses are without shoes, or nearly half of them." Henry Campbell, "Skirmishing in East Tennessee, the Atlanta and Nashville Campaigns, End of the War, and Home: Campbell Diary—Final Installment," *Civil War Times* 3 (Jan. 1965): 36–37; *OR*, vol. 32, pt. 1:45, 78–94.

36. General Foster reported on January 18, "We have a rumor that John Morgan is advancing toward Maryville. I have ordered General Sturgis to meet him at

the crossing of the Little Tennessee." *OR*, vol. 32, pt. 2:127. This was Gen. John T. Morgan (1824–1907), who led a division of Longstreet's cavalry. None of the other rumors about Confederate advances mentioned for this date is true.

37. Foster was desperately short of forage for cavalry horses and draft animals, which were "dying by the hundreds daily." Longstreet's men and horses were faring just as poorly in the "severe" weather of January. *OR*, vol. 32, pt. 1:44–45, 93–94.

38. Mary Polk is not listed in the 1860 census. Her sudden appearance in the diary suggests that she may have been a refugee.

39. George Sedgwick, age forty, was an English-born merchant worth thirty-five hundred dollars in real and personal property in 1860. 1860 Census, 50 (1st).

40. Another Knoxville resident expressed the morbid acceptance that came to characterize the attitude of many local people toward smallpox: "The small pox still exists here, but there is not so much said about it now as when it first appeared." E. T. Hall to Martha, Jan. 16, 1864, Hall-Stakely Papers, Special Collections, Univ. of Tennessee, Knoxville.

41. D. Griffin, Thirteenth Mississippi Infantry. J. C. Rietti, comp. *Military Annals of Mississippi* (Spartanburg, S.C., 1976), 176.

42. Probably Dr. William J. Baker (1800–1865), who had brought "a number of slaves from Kentucky" when he moved to Knoxville in 1825. However, two of his brothers were also doctors. Rothrock, *French Broad–Holston Country*, 373–74. Kate Crozier was the sixteen-year-old daughter of Dr. Crozier.

43. Newton is either Jasper (twenty-five years old) or Alfred (twenty-three years old), sons of J. C. Newton, a small farmer near Marietta. 1860 Census (Cobb), Roll 64, p. 272. Pvt. H. M. Pate would die of smallpox within a few days. Henderson, *Roster of Confederate Soldiers of Georgia* 5:594–95.

44. While frequently discussing the many Confederate prisoners being brought into the city, and the difficulty of feeding them, House never mentions the many civilian refugees who poured into Knoxville, especially from Tennessee's northern counties, beginning in the fall of 1863. The city became a major refugee center and faced all kinds of problems as a result, from shortages of food and housing to increased crime and health hazards. The Union army tried to distribute rations to the refugees, but East Tennessee unionists, led by Nathaniel G. Taylor of Carter County, also organized a massive relief effort. Many of the financial contributions to purchase food for the resulting association came from the Northeast. In Knoxville, the relief effort was coordinated by Gideon M. Hazen. Bryan, "Civil War in East Tennessee," 137–45; William C. Harris, "The East Tennessee Relief Movement of 1864–65," *Tennessee Historical Quarterly* 48 (Summer 1989): 86–96.

45. Gen. Henry L. Benning (1814–75) led a brigade of Georgia infantry in Hood's division. Capt. William H. Bennett, commissary on Benning's staff, was captured with seven other men while seeking forage on January 22. *OR*, vol. 32, pt. 1:110.

46. Gideon Robards belonged to the Seventh Arkansas Infantry, Francis M. Welch to the First South Carolina Infantry, and Pleasant W. Nicholson to the Fifteenth Alabama Infantry. They were sent north to prison camps a couple of weeks later. *Louisville Journal*, Feb. 12, 1864, p. 3.

47. Eliza G. Wilson was the fifty-nine-year-old wife of Rev. James Wilson, and Rebecca Echels was the thirty-eight-year-old wife of house builder W. R. Echels, worth thirty thousand dollars in 1860. 1860 Census, 27 (12th), 96 (1st). Fifty-seven-year-old Dr. C. M. Goodlin, worth nearly fourteen thousand dollars, was the husband of P. H. Goodlin. Mary and Kate Hazen were Jeanie's sisters.

48. Maj. Louis A. Gratz, Sixth Kentucky Cavalry (U.S.), served as provost marshal in the absence of General Carter. Heitman, *Historical Register and Dictionary* 2:105. Rebel citizens of Knoxville considered him petty and rude. For a satire of him, see Hesseltine, *Ramsey Autobiography*, 161–62, 176–78.

49. Sam T. Atkins, one of the earliest manufacturers in Knoxville, was a forty-year-old father of five children who manufactured iron for the Confederacy. He and his wife, Nancy, took in at least one family evicted from their home by Union officers. One of the refugees recalled visiting Atkins in a temporary jail (a private residence) at the corner of Main and Prince (now Market) Streets. Civilian prisoners were housed downstairs with soldiers jailed upstairs. "Each man sat on a cot in a small, stuffy room," she testified, "which, however, was much better than the room above." The soldier prisoners begged her to send them food, but "once a week two armed guards escorted Mr. Atkins home to take dinner with his family. They stood their guns in the hall and sat down to the meal too." She also reported seeing Will Rogers and "several other citizens in the prison." 1860 Census, 109 (1st); Rule, *History of Knoxville*, 200–201; Seymour, *Divided Loyalties*, 16, 34; Plant, "Recollections of War," 129.

50. Lt. Col. Fordyce M. Keith, First Ohio Heavy Artillery.

51. Eight-year-old Lizzie, or Sissie, Kain was the elder daughter of William C. and Mary A. Kain. 1860 Census, 91 (1st).

52. Sixty-year-old Hannah Haire was the wife of James A. Haire, a retired farmer worth ten thousand dollars in 1860. 1860 Census, 32 (1st).

53. Alice C. Helms was the fourteen-year-old daughter of Thomas (a printer) and Mary L. Helms. 1860 Census, 106 (1st).

54. This is probably sixty-one-year-old George McFarlane, a Virginia-born silversmith worth twenty thousand dollars in 1860. 1860 Census, 42 (1st).

55. Brownlow published the names of all who took the oath, and many Confederates, including Joseph A. Mabry and Charles McClung McGhee, switched sides when they saw it was to their advantage. Rothrock, *French Broad–Holston Country*, 141–42; Deaderick, *Heart of the Valley*, 27.

56. Madam Millie was probably slave who had run away.

57. Fort Delaware, located on Pea Patch Island in the Delaware River, housed Confederate prisoners from 1862 to January 1866. Ann L. B. Brown, "Fort Delaware: The Most Dreaded Northern Prison," *Civil War Quarterly* 10 (Sept. 1989): 36–40. At least some of the Philadelphia ladies who cared for the prisoners were southern-born. See Daniel E. Sutherland, "The Rise and Fall of Esther B. Cheesborough: The Battles of a Literary Lady," *South Carolina Historical Magazine* 84 (Jan. 1983): 30–31.

58. A. C. North was an assistant surgeon in the Seventh Georgia Infantry. Paper Mill Hospital was the name given to the Confederate hospital housed in the

paper mill owned by Gideon Morgan Hazen and Marcus D. Bearden. Jones, "Roster of the Medical Officers," 243; Deaderick, *Heart of the Valley*, 532; Rothrock, *French Broad–Holston Country*, 141.

59. J. C. Spinks was an assistant surgeon in the Thirteenth Mississippi Infantry. Jones, "Roster of the Medical Officers," 259.

60. Lt. Col. John W. Barriger was chief commissary of subsistence in Knoxville. His office was on the southwest corner of Gay and Clinch. Ellen first identifies him as "Barrington."

61. Brownlow published the list of names, which included women and children, and applauded the action. It was entirely proper, he said, to send them out of the county, for unionist families had suffered similar fates when the Rebels held sway. *Knoxville Whig and Rebel Ventilator*, Feb. 6, 1864, p. 2.

62. Gen. John M. Schofield (1831–1906) arrived to relieve Foster as commander of the Department and Army of the Ohio on February 9, 1864. He had been appointed to the post on January 28, after Foster had asked to be relieved "on account of disability for service in the field arising from wounds." *OR*, vol. 32, pt. 2:251, 322; James L. McDonough, *Schofield: Union General in the Civil War and Reconstruction* (Tallahassee, 1972), 68–69. McPherson was James B. McPherson.

63. Thomas's Legion engaged the Fourteenth Illinois Cavalry on February 2 near Quallatown, North Carolina. Some 600 Union cavalrymen, with three pieces of artillery, fought about 250 Indian and white Rebels. Confederate reports say 20 to 30 of their men were captured and 2 Indians killed. Federal reports say 54 Confederates were captured, "nearly 200 of them having been killed." Thomas was not captured. *OR*, vol. 32, pt. 1:137–38, 159, pt. 2:749.

64. This could be either J. E. Holbrook, Fourth Battalion Ohio Cavalry, or A. Halleck Holbrook, Second New York Cavalry. U.S. War Dept., *Official Army Register of the Volunteer Force of the United States Army for the Years 1861, '62, '63, '64, '65*, 8 vols. (Washington, D.C., 1865), 2:450, 5:345.

65. I have not been able to further identify Col. Eastin, although he appears to be a Knoxville civilian rather than an army officer.

66. The Federals conducted a reconnaissance from Maryville on February 1–2 and a scout near the same place on February 8, but no heavy fighting occurred in either instance. *OR*, vol. 32, pt. 1:160–61, 391–92.

67. Ellen further identifies Lt. Buchanan on February 20, but I cannot identify the other officers.

68. On January 27, Mabry and Frederick S. Heiskell (1786–1882) sent a letter to General Carter to protest the deprivations of Federal troops encamped on farms like theirs around Knoxville. *OR*, vol. 32, pt. 2:245. For Heiskell, see Rothrock, *French Broad–Holston Country*, 422–24.

69. Schofield and Longstreet engaged in a sparing match, characterized by demonstrations and skirmishes, in mid-February. On February 20, Schofield informed Grant, "[Confederate] Infantry appears to be near Strawberry Plains, on either side of the river, and most of his cavalry south of the French Broad. I am at a loss to interpret his movements, unless he means to attack this place." *OR*, vol. 32, pt. 2:433.

70. The murdered man was Samuel Duncan, and two other men had been whipped. Edward Maynard to Horace Maynard, February 13, 1864, Maynard Papers.

71. M. D. Smallman was adjutant of the Thirteenth Tennessee Cavalry, although that unit was "known in the field, and mustered throughout the war as 8th Tennessee Cavalry Regiment." Wigginton et al., *Tennesseans in the Civil War* 1:83, 2:369.

72. Catherine Hazen was the sixteen-year-old sister of Mary and Gideon Hazen Jr. 1860 Census, 25 (12th). A letter in the House Family Papers from John D. Matthews to Samuel House, dated June 22, 1864, says Kate was in Lexington staying with an aunt and doing "very well."

73. Gideon Morgan Hazen, a unionist, owned and operated the paper mill with his cousin Marcus DeLafayette Bearden two miles from Knoxville on Middlebrook Pike (now Paper Mill Road). The mill operated on a combination of water and steam power until 1866. Hazen was also the Knoxville agent for the East Tennessee Relief Association, which sought to raise money in the Northeast to provide food and other necessities to East Tennessee unionists. Deaderick, *Heart of the Valley*, 532; Rothrock, *French Broad–Holston Country*, 141, 222, 378; Harris, "East Tennessee Relief Movement," 86–96, although Harris errs in calling him George Hazen.

74. P. H. Cardwell was a forty-four-year-old dentist. 1860 Census, 101 (1st).

CHAPTER 4. I AM ORDERED TO LEAVE ON MONDAY

1. Mary E. Currey was the fourteen-year-old daughter of Dr. and Mrs. R. O. Currey. 1860 Census, 42 (1st).

2. Peter Recardi was a thirty-five-year-old confectioner born in Italy and worth twenty-five hundred dollars in 1860. 1860 Census, 42 (1st).

3. Tom Lewis was possibly the twenty-seven-year-old teacher who was the son of Isaac and Ellen Lewis. There were three Jim Joneses and two John Millers in Knox County. 1860 Census, 109 (1st).

4. John Beatty (1828–1914), of Ohio, led the Second Brigade, Second Division, XIV Corps.

5. *Louisville Journal*, Feb. 20, 1864, p. 1.

6. There was a skirmish at Ringgold, Georgia, on February 18 and a Federal demonstration at Dalton on February 22–27. For the latter see OR, vol. 20, pt. 1:417–84.

7. Gordon Granger (1822–76) commanded IV Corps.

8. Robert A. Hatcher, of whom Stewart wrote during the Chickamauga campaign, "There is not a more active or faithful officer in the service." OR, vol. 30, pt. 2:365.

9. Marsh Plumlee was the brother of Capt. A. C. Plumlee.

10. On February 20, the Federals suffered a decisive defeat in the battle of Olustee, or Ocean Pond, the largest battle of the war fought in Florida. The Federals suffered 1,861 casualties in a force of 5,500. The Confederates lost 934 of 5,000 men. William H. Nulty, *Confederate Florida: The Road to Olustee* (Tuscaloosa, 1990), 124–69.

11. Schofield reported to Grant on March 1 that he had taken a force as far as Morristown. Longstreet was still in his front, but Schofield remained uncertain of the Rebel's intentions. *OR*, vol. 32, pt. 3:3.

12. The Meridian expedition, February 3–March 6, was largely a failure for Sherman. *OR*, vol. 32, pt. 1:164–391.

13. Fifty-one-year-old Joseph L. King was a clerk at the railroad depot. He lived with his wife Catherine, age fifty, and their four children. 1860 Census, 43 (1st).

14. Leo was the family dog.

15. This is probably the unionist refugee family from Virginia mentioned in the entry of February 16.

16. Lee and Meade were still in winter camp on opposite sides of the Rapidan River, but the Kilpatrick-Dahlgren raid had been turned back on the outskirts of Richmond March 1. It had been planned by Gen. Judson Kilpatrick.

17. Charles E. McAlister, Engineer Battalion, served on the headquarters staff of Gen. Jacob D. Cox.

18. There had been a skirmish at Panther Spring, Tennessee, on March 5.

19. Probably sixty-four-year-old Thomas McAlister. U.S. Bureau of the Census, *Population Schedule of the Seventh United States Census, 1850, Chatham County, Georgia*, National Archives Microcopy No. 432, Roll 64, p. 285.

20. Pickets may have been run in somewhere along the line, but generally the Federals were preparing to move against Confederate forces near Knoxville.

21. Lusie was apparently a servant.

22. See the introduction for Francis Bostick Renshaw, Ellen's uncle, though he was not an admiral. Gen. Carter is the only American to have achieved the ranks of general in the army and admiral in the navy. He graduated from the United States Naval Academy in 1846.

23. There is no record of Longstreet offering a flag of truce. In fact, Longstreet was in full retreat by March 12 and attempting to sabotage a trestle bridge across Mossy Creek. *OR*, vol. 32, pt. 3:44.

24. Fifty-six-year-old Abner G. Jackson was a Virginia-born farmer and merchant worth nearly sixty thousand dollars in 1860. He and his wife Elizabeth had seven children. 1860 Census, 24 (2d).

25. Grant was promoted to lieutenant general on March 9 and was made commanding general of the Union armies on the following day.

26. A skirmish occurred at Cheek's Cross-Roads, above Morristown, on March 13, but it was not a Federal defeat.

27. Brownlow reported a concert given by a Mrs. Wicks and her pupils three weeks later. *Knoxville Whig and Rebel Ventilator*, Apr. 9, 1864, p. 3.

28. Susan C. Boyd was the nineteen-year-old daughter of unionist Samuel B. Boyd. Luttrell, *Census 1850 for Knox County*, 41.

29. Hannah Haire operated a school for girls that provided "thorough instruction in all the elementary branches of a good English education." Rothrock, *French Broad–Holston Country*, 134, 144.

30. Gen. Simon B. Buckner, but there is no record of a flag of truce.

31. Justice came swiftly for Wolford. He was arrested on March 18 and dishonorably discharged from the army on March 24 for "using disrespectful words against the President of the United States, for disloyalty, and for conduct unbecoming an officer and a gentleman." Tarrant, *Wild Riders of the First Kentucky Cavalry*, 304–9; *OR*, vol. 32, pt. 3:88, 146.

32. Following the failed Kilpatrick-Dahlgren raid on Richmond in February–March, papers were found on the body of Colonel Ulric Dahlgren that described a plan to burn the city and kill Jefferson Davis and other government officials. See Virgil Carrington Jones, *Eight Hours before Richmond* (New York, 1957).

33. There was a Federal prisoner-of-war camp in the Mississippi River between Rock Island, Illinois, and Davenport, Iowa.

34. Gen. John C. Breckinridge commanded the Department of Southwest Virginia, not Longstreet's army.

35. The report of France offering aid was false. The possibility of any European nation intervening on behalf of the Confederacy was a forlorn hope by this stage of the war.

36. Little ape Wilson (referred to later as little fool Wilson) is Mr. Wilson, the clerk in Captain McAlister's office.

37. The *Richmond Enquirer* announced the fast day, to be held Friday, August 8, in its March 15 issue. The *New York Times* reported this on March 18.

38. Rutledge and Mossy Creek were thirty miles northeast of Knoxville. Harriet C. Rogers was a twenty-seven-year-old teacher and the sister of William B. and John R. Rogers. Their mother was fifty-nine-year-old widow H. M. Rogers. 1860 Census, 93 (1st).

39. Economic inflation had nearly crippled the Confederacy by the spring of 1864. In Knoxville, as early as February, flour sold for twenty dollars a barrel, butter for one dollar a pound, potatoes for three dollars a bushel, and salt for seventy cents a pound. Bryan, "Civil War in East Tennessee," 138–39.

40. Cynthia Brooks was the twenty-six-year-old daughter of Joseph A. Brooks, a farmer worth twelve thousand dollars in 1860, and his wife Margaret A. Brooks. 1860 Census, 23–24 (2d).

41. Maud A. Mordic, of Marietta, was the thirty-two-year-old wife of farmer J. A. Mordic. 1860 Census (Cobb), Roll 117, p. 439.

42. Mary McClusky, the mother of Ellen's good friend "Cluss," was fifty-one years old in 1864. 1860 Census, 95 (1st).

43. Fortress Monroe, Virginia, was erected in the 1820s and 1830s for coastal defense. It served as headquarters for the Federal Department of Virginia and was used to house political prisoners.

44. Libby prison, located in Richmond, housed captured Federal officers.

45. The raid on Louisville, Tennessee, occurred on March 27. The Federals reported that "15 to 20 mounted rebels dashed into Louisville yesterday, captured a Union citizen and left in the direction of . . . Maryville." *OR*, vol. 32, pt. 1:628.

46. Parmenian Fatio, a native of Switzerland, married Mary L. Lones in 1850, but there is no record of a second marriage for Mrs. Fatio. D'Armand and d'Armand, *Marriage Records*, 331, 634.

47. Gen. William T. Sherman was named commander of the Military Division of the Mississippi, composed of the Departments of the Ohio, the Cumberland, the Tennessee, and the Arkansas, on March 12. In preparing to take command, he visited Knoxville to confer with Gen. Schofield and inspect the city. Gen. George H. Thomas did not accompany him. *OR*, vol. 32, pt. 1:58, 171, 178.

48. Twelve-year-old John Peed was the son of Oliver Peed, the shoemaker, and his wife Mary, who was a sister of Thomas O'Conner. The Peeds had five other children. 1860 Census, 55 (12th); Deaderick, *Heart of the Valley*, 588.

49. Probably the Wilson who served as McAlister's clerk.

50. Gustave A. Huwald raised an artillery battery that mustered into Confederate service at Knoxville in June 1862. However, a sketch of the battery's history indicates that Huwald never rose above the rank of captain. When Huwald was captured on March 30, Capt. D. Breck Ramsey took command, and the unit was thereafter officially designated Ramsey's Tennessee Battery. Wigginton et al., *Tennesseeans in the Civil War* 1:145–47.

51. For the moment, Longstreet still commanded in East Tennessee, based at Bristol. However, his corps did report to Virginia on April 7. During Nathan Bedford Forrest's expedition into West Tennessee and Kentucky from March 16 to April 14, he attacked Paducah on March 25 and held the city for a day before withdrawing.

52. Don Carlos Buell did not replace Schofield, although rumors to that effect were so widespread that Sherman was forced to reassure Schofield from Nashville, "There is no truth in this. The report seems to have originated in Chattanooga, and I have telegraphed to Thomas to punish the operator." *OR*, vol. 32, pt. 3:226.

53. The Brook refers to Middlebrook, the home of Gideon M. Hazen and his family. *Knoxville Journal*, Nov. 21, 1971.

54. David Pierson (b. 1837) served in the Third Louisiana Infantry. Robert K. Krick, *Lee's Colonels: A Biographical Register of the Field Officers of the Army of Northern Virginia*, 4th rev. ed. (Dayton, Ohio, 1992), 472. There was a skirmish at Cleveland on April 2, but IV Corps was not wiped out.

55. Lt. Col. Gustave Cook (1835–97). Krick, *Lee's Colonels*, 431.

56. Robert Strong was the twenty-nine-year-old son of Dr. Joseph C. and Sophronia Strong. 1860 Census, 225 (18th).

57. If Brownlow was responsible for Ellen's exile, it is not surprising. He was vehement about sending Rebels south, particularly "rebel females" and "she rebels." *Knoxville Whig and Rebel Ventilator*, Jan. 16, 1864, p. 2; Feb. 6, 1864, p. 2.

58. Another young woman exiled at this time was Susan Ramsey, daughter of Dr. J. G. M. Ramsey. She was to have left Knoxville on the same day as Ellen but missed the train. She, like Ellen, was "sent out for disloyal *acts*," but as Susan's brother asked her, "What disloyal act can you, a girl of sixteen, have perpetrated—surrounded as you were by two army corps of the United States?" For her experience, quite similar to Ellen's, see Hesseltine, *Ramsey Autobiography*, 160–63, 165–66, 175–80. See also Margaret B. Crozier Diary, Special Collections, Univ. of Tennessee, Knoxville.

59. As commander of the Trans-Mississippi Department, Gen. Edmund Kirby Smith received credit for a series of victories in March and April that halted the Federal Red River campaign. On April 8, Gen. Richard Taylor defeated Gen.

Nathaniel Banks in the battle of Mansfield, or Sabine Crossroads, in Louisiana. On April 9, Banks suffered a second defeat at Pleasant Hill. The Federals did, indeed, have about 1,500 men captured or missing at Mansfield, with total casualties of 2,235. They lost 1,369 men at Pleasant Hill.

60. Probably William Morrow.

61. Henry M. Ashby commanded the Second (Ashby's) Tennessee Cavalry, organized May 1862. Wigginton et al., *Tennesseans in the Civil War* 1:52; James L. Mohan, "Defending the Confederate Heartland: Company F of Henry Ashby's 2nd Tennessee Cavalry," *Civil War Regiments* 5 (Mar. 1994): 1–43. W. B. Hayes, Twenty-first (Wilson's) Tennessee Cavalry, is the only Captain Hayes in a Tennessee unit, but he "disappeared from the regiment and [remained] unaccounted for." Wigginton et al., *Tennesseans in the Civil War* 1:99.

62. The Confederates captured Plymouth, North Carolina, on April 20. The Federals lost twenty-eight hundred killed, wounded, and captured. For the controversy surrounding that event, see Weymouth T. Jordan and Gerald W. Thomas, "Massacre at Plymouth: April 20, 1864," *North Carolina Historical Review* 72 (Apr. 1995): 125–97.

63. For the controversy concerning the Fort Pillow "massacre," April 12, see Lonnie E. Maness, "The Fort Pillow Massacre: Fact or Fiction," *Tennessee Historical Quarterly* 40 (Spring 1986): 287–315; John Cimprich and Robert C. Mainfort Jr., eds., "Fort Pillow Revisited: New Evidence about an Old Controversy," *Civil War History* 18 (Dec. 1982): 293–306.

64. Federal cavalry conducting a "strong reconnaissance" engaged Gen. Alfred E. Jackson's brigade on April 25 at Carter's Station. *OR*, vol. 32, pt. 3:831.

65. Abingdon, Virginia, is on the railroad about twenty miles north of the Tennessee state line.

66. While serving under Longstreet, Lt. Col. John Floyd King commanded King's Artillery Battalion, or the Thirteenth Virginia Light Artillery Battalion, part of E. P. Alexander's artillery reserve in the Department of East Tennessee. In April, he served under Gen. Simon B. Buckner. Gallagher, *Fighting for the Confederacy*, 412, 600 n. 21, 603 n. 18; Stewart Sifakis, *Compendium of the Confederate Armies: Virginia* (New York, 1992), 16.

67. Zollicoffer, Tennessee (now Bluff City), was located about twenty miles southwest of Abingdon.

68. Jeremiah McGuire, Company G, Fifty-ninth Tennessee Mounted Infantry. Wigginton et al., *Tennesseans in the Civil War* 1:298–300, 2:276.

69. Simon B. Buckner was transferred from command of the Department of East Tennessee to the Trans-Mississippi on April 28, 1864, but Kirby Smith had not been killed. *OR*, vol. 32, pt. 3:838.

70. Saltville, Virginia, is located about twenty-five miles northeast of Abingdon.

71. By early May, the Red River campaign was coming to an end as the Federals retreated toward Alexandria, Louisiana.

72. Thomas and Capt. Charles B. Wallace, ages twenty-three and twenty-seven, respectively, were the sons of Campbell and Susan E. Wallace. Luttrell, *Census 1850 for Knox County*, 46–47.

73. Generals Richard S. Ewell, Ambrose Powell Hill, and Henry Heth formed part of Lee's Army of Northern Virginia as the Wilderness campaign commenced. In fighting on May 5–6, the Confederates had 7,500 casualties, the Federals 17,666.

74. Dublin Station, Virginia, was on the Virginia and Tennessee Railroad less than ten miles south of Cloyd's Mountain.

75. Gen. Bushrod Rust Johnson was not at Spotsylvania. Gen. Edward Johnson was there, but he and most of his command were captured at the Bloody Angle. In any case, Burnside did not perform well at Spotsylvania. William D. Matter, *If It Takes All Summer: The Battle of Spotsylvania* (Chapel Hill, 1988), 226.

76. Probably Capt. Barckley Martin, Nineteenth Tennessee Cavalry. Wigginton et al., *Tennesseans in the Civil War* 2:261.

77. Kingsport, Tennessee, was located about twenty-five miles southwest of Abingdon.

78. The "raid" was an expedition by Gen. George Crook with more than eight thousand men against the Virginia and Tennessee Railroad that culminated in the battle of Cloyd's Mountain on May 9. Crooks's men passed through Dublin, and although there was no engagement there, the Federals destroyed supplies at the depot as well as much track and the New River Bridge. Casualties in fighting at Cloyd's Mountain were 538 for the Confederates (23 percent) and 66 for the Federals (10 percent). See Faust, *Historical Encyclopedia of the Civil War*, 146; *OR*, vol. 37, pt. 1:8–68; Howard R. McManus, *The Battle of Cloyd's Mountain* (Lynchburg, 1989). John Hunt Morgan, in combination with Gen. William E. Jones, moved his command from Saltville to Wytheville, where they defeated Averell's cavalry in an engagement at Crockett's Gap on May 11. James A. Ramage, *Rebel Raider: The Life of John Hunt Morgan* (Lexington, Ky., 1986), 211–12. The "yellow flags" refers to hospital flags.

79. Concerning reports of May 14, the Federals lost nearly eleven thousand men in fighting at Spotsylvania on May 10 and 12. Total Union dead and wounded for the campaign exceeded eighteen thousand, but the number of prisoners is unknown. Gen. James E. B. Stuart was killed in fighting at Yellow Tavern, Virginia, on May 11. Neither Johnston nor Hardee was near Cleveland; the Army of Tennessee was busy fighting Sherman in the Atlanta campaign. The last reported skirmishing around Cleveland had been in mid-April. Taylor, not Gen. Sterling Price, had forced Banks to retreat, but he had no opportunity to demand his surrender.

80. Concerning reports of May 16, Lee lost about ten thousand men killed and wounded at Spotsylvania. Gen. Philip Sheridan was nearing the end of his raid around Richmond, May 9–24. Edward G. Longacre, *Mounted Raids of the Civil War* (New York, 1975), 258–82. Sherman and Joseph Johnston battled at Resaca on May 14–15. In danger of being outflanked, Johnston pulled back on May 15. For the Atlanta campaign see Albert Castel, *Decision in the West: The Atlanta Campaign of 1864* (Lawrence, Kans., 1992).

81. Breckinridge defeated Gen. Franz Sigel, not Averell, in the battle of New Market, Virginia, on May 15. Beauregard forced Butler away from Petersburg in fighting at Drewry's Bluff on May 16, but Federal casualties were only about four thousand. See William Glenn Robertson, *Back Door to Richmond: The Bermuda Hundred Campaign, April–June 1864* (Newark, Del., 1987).

82. Nancy J. Martin was the twenty-three-year-old daughter of Knoxville farmer Samuel Martin. Luttrell, *Census 1850 for Knox County*, 61.

83. Gen. John Crawford Vaughn (1824–75).

84. The reported arrest of Annie Law followed the reconvening of a Federal District Court in Knoxville by Judge Connally F. Trigg on May 17. Bryan, "Civil War in East Tennessee," 127; Rothrock, *French Broad–Holston Country*, 496.

85. William Edmondson "Grumble" Jones was shot dead in the battle of Piedmont, seven miles southwest of Port Republic in the Shenandoah Valley, on June 5. The Confederates lost six hundred killed and wounded and one thousand captured. Johnston and Sherman had engaged in fighting in the area of New Hope Church and Dallas, Georgia, between May 25 and June 2, when Sherman withdrew toward Allatoona Pass.

86. The Federals, under Gen. David Hunter, only occupied Staunton, Virginia, for two days on May 6–7, but they did tremendous damage to the town. Marshall M. Brice, *Conquest of a Valley* (Charlottesville, 1965), 95–102.

87. Grant's destination was the James River, but his army would not move toward the river from Cold Harbor until June 12. It began to cross on June 14. The Sixtieth Virginia Infantry fought valiantly at Piedmont, and it is unfair to say that they lost the battle. Brice, *Conquest of a Valley*, 70–77.

88. Butler attempted an advance once again against Petersburg on June 9, but Beauregard turned back the poorly organized affair.

89. Heavy fighting took place up and down the Shenandoah Valley during June, but Federals held Liberty only briefly later in the month (June 19), after Jubal Early had pushed Hunter out of Lynchburg.

90. David Fry (c. 1826–71), part of the bridge-burning conspiracy of 1861, was originally captain of Company E, Second Tennessee Infantry (U.S.). In July 1863 he attempted to raise his own regiment, hence the title of colonel. He had been captured and treated as a spy earlier in the war but escaped from prison. His recapture raised concern in the North. Gen. George G. Meade received the following report in January 1865: "Our attention is again called to a Colonel Fry, a Union officer, in irons in a cell in Castle Thunder [Richmond] who is greatly emaciated and is living upon very coarse, scanty fare in a damp cell. It is said there is a desire to kill him without a public execution." However, the Confederates were willing to release him for a payment of five thousand dollars. Graf et al., *Papers of Andrew Johnson* 6:257–58, 283; *OR*, vol. 36, pt. 2:171; ser. 2, vol. 1, p. 862–63, 881–82, 889; vol. 4, pp. 509, 723.

91. Forrest won a stunning victory at Brice's Crossroads, Mississippi, on June 10. Morgan had departed Abingdon on May 30 on his last raid into Kentucky. He was very successful until defeated near Cynthiana on June 12 and compelled to retreat. He arrived back in Abingdon, as Ellen states below, on June 19. Gen. Leonidas Polk was struck and killed by a Federal shell on Pine Mountain, Georgia, June 14.

92. Col. (not General) Henry L. Giltner lost hundreds of men from his brigade when Morgan was surprised near Cynthiana. Morgan tried to gloss over the defeat,

but he was roundly criticized in several quarters. Ramage, *Rebel Raider*, 222–25; Cecil F. Holland, *Morgan and His Raiders: A Biography of the Confederate General* (New York, 1943), 326–28. Jubal Early, not Breckinridge, pushed Hunter out of Lynchburg and past Liberty on June 17–19. Brice, *Conquest of a Valley*, 119–21.

93. The Federals had been launching assaults against Petersburg since June 15, but their most recent drive, on June 21, against the Weldon and Petersburg Railroad, would be stopped the following day, as Ellen mentions on the twenty-second. Johnston had won no recent victories against Sherman, but his army had established a formidable position on Kennesaw Mountain.

94. William Ingles, sixty-nine years old, was a Virginia-born miller from Knoxville worth sixteen thousand dollars in 1860. 1860 Census, 65 (1st).

95. Johnston had whipped Sherman on June 27, not the twenty-fifth, in the battle of Kennesaw Mountain. Sheridan's cavalry was turned back on June 23 in raids against the South Side Railroad and the Weldon and Petersburg Railroad. Hunter had been pushed back completely into West Virginia by June 23.

96. There is no report that shows Wheeler captured a wagon train between Dalton and Kingston. He was with Johnston's army at this time, falling back toward Kennesaw Mountain. Dyer, *From Shiloh to San Juan*, 134–35.

97. Probably refers to Kennesaw Mountain, but Sherman had taken the offensive against Johnston. The Federals lost two thousand men.

98. Early drove Sigel back across the Potomac River into Maryland following engagements at more than half a dozen places, including Martinsburg, West Virginia.

99. Refers to Early's raid toward Washington, D.C., July 5–14. See Frank E. Vandiver, *Jubal's Raid: General Early's Famous Attack on Washington in 1864* (New York, 1960) and B. Franklin Cooling, *Jubal Early's Raid on Washington: 1864* (Baltimore, 1989).

100. Alexander Peter Stewart replaced Polk as corps commander to rank as lieutenant general from June 23.

101. Gen. John Bell Hood received command of the Army and Department of Tennessee on July 17.

102. Hunter, defeated by Early in fighting on July 17, had also offered to resign his command on that date, protesting that he was being used as "the scapegoat to cover up the blunders of others" in the Shenandoah campaigns. *OR*, vol. 37, pt. 2:365.

103. Sherman whipped Hood convincingly at Peach Tree Creek on July 20. Hood's men fought more effectively in the battle of Atlanta (July 22), but they were still forced to retreat.

104. The report of the twenty-sixth was not false; Hood was besieged in Atlanta on this date.

105. Gen. Lovell Harrison Rousseau (1818–69) operating along the Southern Railroad between Columbus, Georgia, and Montgomery, Alabama, destroyed a considerable portion of that line July 10–22.

106. Refers to the mine assault of Petersburg, July 30. The Federals actually lost about eight thousand men.

107. Maj. Campbell Wallace (1806–95), president of the East Tennessee and Virginia Railroad, had fled to Georgia in December 1863. James A. Ward, ed., *Southern Railroad Man: Conductor N.J. Bell's Recollections of the Civil War Era* (De Kalb, Ill., 1994), 27. See also William L. Ketchersid, "Major Campbell Wallace: Southern Railroad Leader" (M.A. thesis, Univ. of Tennessee, 1966).

108. Madison, Georgia, is nearly ninety miles west of Augusta and twenty miles south of Atlanta.

109. Eatonton, Georgia, is twenty miles south of Madison.

CHAPTER 5. CUT OFF FROM KNOXVILLE

1. *OR*, vol. 38, pt. 2:929; Joel Chandler Harris, *On the Plantation: The Story of Georgia Boy's Adventures during the War* (New York, 1892); Laurence Huff, "'A Bitter Draught We Have to Quaff': Sherman's March Through the Eyes of Joseph Addison Turner," *Georgia Historical Quarterly* 72 (Summer 1988): 311–26; John C. Inscoe, "The Confederate Home Front Sanitized: Joel Chandler Harris's *On the Plantation* and Sectional Reconciliation," *Georgia Historical Quarterly* 76 (Fall 1992): 664–68.

2. Georgia was a popular destination for many Confederate refugees from East Tennessee. See Groce, "Mountain Rebels," 173–76.

3. Fort Morgan, the last Confederate position guarding the entrance to Mobile Bay, Alabama, fell on Sunday, August 23, 1864. Castle William held Confederate prisoners of war on Governor's Island in New York Harbor. Sam wrote to his father shortly after his arrival there, "I am delighted to know you are all well, tell Mother to cheer up. God orders all things for the best. I hope the day is not far distant when our now scattered family will be gathered under the roof tree." About a month later he wrote, "My health continues very good with the exception of a Cold but I will try and take better care of myself & cure it." Samuel House to Father, Oct. 22, Nov. 27, 1864, UCV Records.

4. The niece was Frances, or Fannie, born to William and Jeanie Strong House.

5. The Federals had been defeated at Fort Fisher, Wilmington, North Carolina, in the last part of December 1864. However, the Yankees were already outfitting a second expedition that would capture the fort on January 15. See Rod Gragg, *Confederate Goliath: The Battle of Fort Fisher* (New York, 1991).

6. Talk of Gen. Joseph E. Johnston assuming command of the Army of Tennessee was just a rumor at this time. Congress passed a resolution to do so January 16, although Richard Taylor had been made temporary head of the army on January 13. Johnston finally received his appointment to command the army and all troops in the Department of South Carolina, Georgia, and Florida, on February 22.

7. There were several Reid families in Putnam County, but Ellen's friends were probably twenty-nine-year-old Annie C. Reid and eighteen-year-old Susan T. Reid, daughters of Edmund and Elizabeth Reid, worth $100,000 in 1860. U.S. Bureau of the Census, *Population Schedule of the Eighth United States Census, 1860, Putnam County, Georgia*, National Archives Microcopy No. 653, Roll 134, p. 12 (cited hereafter as 1860 Census [Putnam]).

8. Margaret Rogan was the forty-four-year-old wife of L. H. Rogan. 1860 Census, 73 (1st).

9. C. S. Dennis was the twenty-six-year-old wife of L. C. Dennis, a farmer worth twenty-five thousand dollars in 1860. 1860 Census (Putnam), 11.

10. Alice Deaderick McClung, twenty-one years old, was the wife of Charles A. McClung. They had married in June 1863. D'Armand and d'Armand, *Marriage Records*, 667. Her son was Pleasant McClung.

11. Elizabeth C. Harwell was the forty-five-year-old wife of merchant Thomas B. Harwell, worth thirty-six thousand dollars in 1860. 1860 Census (Putnam), 7.

12. Terry H. Cahal enlisted in Company K, Forty-fifth Tennessee Infantry. In 1863 he served with John House on Stewart's staff. Wigginton et al., *Tennesseans in the Civil War* 1:273–75, 2:72; *OR*, vol. 30, pt. 2:365; Joseph H. Crute Jr., *Confederate Staff Officers, 1861–1865* (Powhatan, Va., 1982), 185.

13. Sherman sent Lincoln the following message on December 22, the day after his troops marched into the abandoned city: "I beg to present you as a Christmas-gift the city of Savannah, with one hundred and fifty heavy guns and plenty of ammunition, also about twenty-five thousand bales of cotton." Sherman, *Memoirs* 2:231.

14. Rebecca Lawson, seventy years old, lived with her twenty-six-year-old daughter Jane. 1860 Census (Putnam), 35.

15. Susan L. Harwell was the sixteen-year-old daughter of Thomas and Elizabeth Harwell. 1860 Census (Putnam), 7.

16. Fen Epps, who seems to be a refugee in Eatonton.

17. A raid by Gen. George Stoneman's cavalry from East Tennessee into southwestern Virginia in December 1864 resulted in the destruction of salt works in and around Saltville, Virginia, on December 20–21, 1864, and the destruction of lead works seventeen miles from Wytheville on December 17. One of several Confederate units driven back by the Federals was commanded by Gen. John C. Vaughn. *OR*, vol. 45, pt. 1:806–41. A far more controversial battle had been fought at Saltville in October 1864. See William C. Davis, "The Massacre at Saltville," *Civil War Times* 9 (Feb. 1971): 4–11, 43–48; William Marvel, "The Battle of Saltville: Massacre or Myth?" *Blue & Gray Magazine* 8 (Aug. 1991), 1019, 46–54.

18. John E. Mulford was assistant agent for prisoner exchange. Ellen refers to him as "Munford."

19. Fanny Wallace was the nineteen-year-old daughter of Campbell Wallace. 1860 Census, 26 (12th).

20. Carrie Pearson was the sixteen-year-old daughter of Samuel Pearson, a farmer worth nearly $130,000 in 1860. 1860 Census (Putnam), 14.

21. When Sherman entered Savannah, the citizens "drew up resolutions asking the Governor to call a convention to decide whether the war should be continued." T. Conn Bryan, *Confederate Georgia* (Athens, Ga., 1953), 172.

22. Ellen Clapp was the sixteen-year-old daughter of Henderson Clapp, a farmer worth fifty-five hundred dollars in 1860. 1860 Census, 93 (5th).

23. The wartime governor of Georgia was Joseph E. Brown (1821–94).

24. Mary Rogan was the twenty-one-year-old daughter of L. H. and Margaret Rogan. 1860 Census, 73 (1st).

25. Hood's Army of Tennessee was in retreat from Tennessee, headed for Mississippi. Sherman's XVII Corps moved into Millen, about sixty miles northwest of Savannah, on December 3, 1864. Branchville, South Carolina, was never one of Sherman's targets.

26. M. A. Davis was the thirty-nine-year-old wife of attorney R. T. Davis, worth $11,500 in 1860. They had two children. 1860 Census (Putnam), 8.

27. The only Hardins residing in Putnum County were Daniel H. Hardin and his wife Elizabeth. They had no daughter.

28. A week of heavy rain had caused the Savannah River to flood the main part of Augusta with two to five feet of water. The pressure broke rotting canal gates, which compounded the problem. Florence F. Corley, *Confederate City: Augusta, Georgia, 1860–1865* (Columbia, S.C., 1960), 89.

29. Gen. Gustavus W. Smith (1821–96) commanded Georgia's militia.

30. Fort Fisher surrendered on January 15.

31. Francis Preston Blair served as a peace envoy between Richmond and Washington in mid-January.

32. Rebecca Pike, fifty-nine years old and born in North Carolina, lived with fifty-four-year-old Mary Gilmer, also a Tar Heel. 1860 Census (Putnam), 8.

33. L. Claiborne was the twenty-four-year-old wife of forty-year-old grocer T. B. Claiborne. 1860 Census (Putnam), 3. Kate and Annie Thomas were fellow refugees.

34. These could be any of several young ladies residing in Putnam County. James Wingfield, an attorney worth ninety thousand dollars in 1860, had two daughters, age eighteen and twenty. Three families named Adams had daughters that might have befriended Ellen, but she probably refers to the family of D. R. Adams, a farmer worth nearly ninety thousand dollars in 1860. David Rosser, a farmer worth eighty-two thousand dollars in 1860, had three daughters between the ages of fifteen and nineteen. 1860 Census (Putnam), 12, 13, 19, 81, 82.

35. John Adams Dix (1798–1879) commanded the Department of the East.

36. Greensboro, Georgia, is about twenty-five miles northeast of Eatonton.

37. The Hampton Roads Conference was held aboard the U.S. steamer *River Queen* at Hampton Roads, Virginia, on February 3. Stemming from Blair's mission to Richmond, the conference was intended to find a peaceful resolution to the war. The Confederacy was represented by Vice President Alexander H. Stephens, Senator Robert M. T. Hunter of Virginia, and Judge John A. Campbell, an assistant secretary of war. The United States was represented by President Lincoln and Vice President William H. Seward.

38. All the men, including Samuel McKinney and Jacob Austin Sperry, were residents of Knoxville. Dr. J. G. M. Ramsey had two sons with the middle name of Crozier, but Ellen refers here to Lt. John Crozier Ramsey, who was recovering from a wound at Bristol under the care of his uncle, Dr. Frank A. Ramsey, a Confederate surgeon. The raid came on December 13, 1864. Curiously, Dr. Ramsey's autobiogra-

phy does not mention either he or Crow being captured, but Sperry wrote a detailed account of the capture and subsequent imprisonment in his diary. Hesseltine, *Ramsey Autobiography,* 240ff; Prindle, *Ancestry of William Sperry Beinecke,* 233–59.

39. Elizabeth T. Bearden was the twenty-year-old daughter of merchant Marcus D. Bearden. She did, in fact, marry the major on October 10, 1865. Luttrell, *Census 1850 for Knox County,* 43; d'Armand and d'Armand, *Marriage Records,* 64.

40. Reuben B. Clark (1833–1900) was charged with murder while being held as a prisoner of war in Knoxville. This false charge had been brought against him by Parson Brownlow. Clark was, indeed, incarcerated in an "iron cage," November 1864, in the Knoxville County Jail. He remained there until released on bond in June 1865. He was cleared of the murder charge later that year. Clark, *Valleys of the Shadow,* xxiv–xxix, 54–75.

41. The Marietta Hotel had not been destroyed by fire, although as Sherman's soldiers marched through town in mid-November 1864 they set fires that spread to buildings across the street from the hotel. Sarah B. G. Temple, *The First Hundred Years: A Short History of Cobb County in Georgia* (Atlanta, 1935), 354.

42. Probably L. C. Dennis, the thirty-two-year-old husband of C. S. Dennis. 1860 Census (Putnam), 11.

43. If referring to railroads, the Federals had destroyed the tracks around Bamberg, South Carolina, between Aiken and Branchville. *OR,* vol. 47, pt. 1:251.

44. Monticello is less than twenty miles west of Eatonton.

45. Mr. Smith does not appear in the 1860 census, but the biblical verse reads, "As for me, I will behold thy face in righteousness; I shall be satisfied, when I awake, with thy likeness."

46. Adelade Reid was the eighteen-year-old daughter of A. S. Reid, a farmer worth $128,000 in 1860. 1860 Census (Putnam), 11.

47. M. A. Nisbet was the thirty-four-year-old wife of Dr. R. B. Nisbet, worth $32,500 in 1860. They had two children. 1860 Census (Putnam), 8.

48. Louisa E. Dennis was the seventeen-year-old daughter of Howard J. Dennis, a trader worth twenty-five hundred dollars in 1860. 1860 Census (Putnam), 1.

49. Ellen had sent two letters to Sam in January, which he received about a month later. He was feeling "tip top" on February 17, for although the weather in New York had been stormy and cold, he described the 17th as "the first fine day we have had this year." Samuel House to Father, Feb. 12 and 17, 1865, UCV Records.

50. Mamie is identified in entry for April 1, 1865, as a cousin.

51. The Federals captured Columbia, South Carolina, on February 17; they entered Charleston unopposed on February 18.

52. Tennessee congressman Henry S. Foote (1804–80), a former governor of Mississippi, asserted in late 1864 that the Confederacy was doomed. He fled northward but was captured and returned to Virginia. He fled again, was recaptured, and imprisoned January 28, 1865.

53. A day earlier, John House had written to his parents from Johnson's Island to say that he was well and hoped to be exchanged soon. John M. House to Father & Mother, Feb. 24, 1865, UCV Records.

54. Thomas S. Rumbough, Company E, Sixteenth Tennessee Cavalry Battalion, was killed in a skirmish near Morristown about a week after Morgan was killed. Wigginton et al., *Tennesseans in the Civil War* 2:351; James A. Ramage, *The Life of John Hunt Morgan* (Lexington, 1986), 290 n. 43. For the circumstances surrounding Morgan's death on September 4, 1864, and the role of Lucy Williams, Rumbough's sister, see Ramage, *Life of John Hunt Morgan*, 231–40.

55. The burning of Columbia, South Carolina, February 17–19, is shrouded in controversy. The Confederates said Sherman did it; the Federals charged Gen. Wade Hampton's cavalry. Sherman did destroy militarily useful equipment, such as railroads, machine shops, and foundries. See Marion B. Lucas, *Sherman and the Burning of Columbia* (College Station, Tx., 1976) and Walter B. Edgar and Deborah K. Woolley, *Columbia: Portrait of a City* (Norfolk, 1986).

56. The Confederates evacuated Charleston on February 16–17; the Federals marched in on February 18 to find the city ablaze. Some blacks troops marched with the Federal forces. E. Milby Burton, *The Siege of Charleston* (Columbia, S.C., 1970), 318–25.

57. The Georgia Militia had not been disbanded, although its ranks had been seriously depleted by desertion. *OR*, vol. 47, pt. 2:999–1000.

58. Sherman feinted toward Charlotte, North Carolina, on February 22, but this produced no major engagement. Indeed, Gen. Pierre G. T. Beauregard advised Robert E. Lee on February 15 that he could not "concentrate in time sufficient force" to halt Sherman: "I advise removing soon as possible all stores from his line of march." *OR*, vol. 47, pt. 2:1193. Generals Jubal A. Early and John B. Gordon were not in the vicinity of Charlotte.

59. Mary McPherson was the elder daughter of R. M. W. and Mary W. McPherson. 1860 Census, 39 (1st).

60. Robert Ould was the Confederate agent for prisoner exchange, and arrangements for the exchange of equal numbers of prisoners had been worked out in January after many months of noncooperation by the Northern and Southern governments. Ellen's brother John informed the family from Johnson's Island in February, "We hear a General Exchange has been agreed upon. They are taking a few from here about 225 have already gone & 200 more have signed the rolls & will leave in a day or two." James M. McPherson, *Battle Cry of Freedom: The Civil War Era* (New York, 1988), 791–800; John M. House to Parents, Feb. 24, 1865, UCV Records.

61. Col. Henry M. Ashby, Second (Ashby's) Tennessee Cavalry, survived the war, but was shot to death June 10, 1868, in a quarrell in Knoxville at Main and Walnut streets. Wigginton et al., *Tennesseans in the Civil War* 1:52–54; Deaderick, *Heart of the Valley*, 34.

62. Hampton quietly relieved Wheeler, whom Beauregard believed could not "properly control and direct successfully so large a corps of cavalry [the cavalry corps of the Military Division of the West]," on February 17. Dyer, *From Shiloh to San Juan*, 171–72.

63. Very few people died in the burning of Columbia, although seven to eight thousand did receive Federal rations for up to three months. As to the extent of the destruction, no more than a third of the city—mostly the central business district—was destroyed. One historian has concluded, "Enough buildings remained unburned

to house all the citizens who remained in Columbia, and the Union authorities made an effort to provide food for those left in the capital after the fire." Lucus, *Sherman and the Burning of Columbia,* 166.

64. George G. McDonald apparently came to Eatonton as a refugee. As some indication of his time of arrival, he performed his first marriage ceremony in Eatonton in November 1863. Putnam County Marriage Records, Vol. F (1848–68), p. 212, Georgia Dept. of Archives and History, Atlanta (hereafter cited as Putnam County Marriage Records).

65. Daniel Slade was a fifty-eight-year-old Connecticut-born merchant worth nearly $44,000 in 1860. 1860 Census (Putnam), 11.

66. Several Little families resided near Eatonton, but Ellen most likely refers here either to Kinchen Little, a seventy-year-old farmer worth more than $130,000 in 1860, or Lewis Little, a farmer worth nearly $45,000. 1860 Census (Putnam), 70, 77.

67. The whirl of rumors seemed to increase for Ellen in Georgia. None of the reported Federal defeats had occurred. In Schofield's case, he had sent two divisions from Wilmington to Kinston, North Carolina, on March 6. His men met stiff Confederate resistance in fighting near Kinston on March 8–9, but they turned back a Confederate assault on March 10. McDonough, *Schofield,* 156.

68. Emily Howell was a friend from Marietta. She married her sister's husband in 1857, nine months after her sister's death. Diary of Ellen Renshaw House, 1857–58, House Family Papers.

69. Libbie Morrow could be Elizabeth Morrow, the twenty-year-old daughter of Charles Morrow, a Knoxville brick mason, but is probably Mary E. Morrow, the twenty-one-year-old daughter of Sam Morrow, worth twenty thousand dollars in 1860. Luttrell, *Census 1850 for Knox County,* 100; 1860 Census, 96 (1st).

70. Lucinda Pearson was the sixty-two-year-old mother of Carrie. 1860 Census (Putnam), 14.

71. Jennie F. Adams was the twenty-one-year-old daughter of J. F. Adams, a farmer worth more than fifty thousand dollars in 1860. 1860 Census (Putnam), 81.

72. Emma V. Adams was the fifteen-year-old daughter of D. R. Adams. 1860 Census (Putnam), 82.

73. Wheeler's men did, in fact, provide most of the defense for the evacuation of Charleston. Whether he did so exclusively with Tennesseans and Kentuckians is doubtful, for regiments from other states were also engaged in the fighting. Dyer, *From Shiloh to San Juan,* 172–73; John G. Barrett, *Sherman's March Through the Carolinas* (Chapel Hill, 1956), 126–30, 148–58; OR, vol. 47, pt. 2:1071–73.

74. Ellen's edition of *Joseph the Second and His Court; An Historical Romance,* by Luise Muhlbach (pseud. for Clara Müller) was probably the one published at Mobile by S. H. Goetzel in 1864.

75. On March 10, Hampton surprised Kilpatrick in his camp at Monroe's Cross Roads, North Carolina, and momentarily routed his men. Kilpatrick escaped in his nightshirt, but he managed to organize a counterattack and win the day. Kilpatrick's cavalry was also engaged in fighting on March 16–19 around Averasboro and Bentonville, North Carolina. Starr, *Union Cavalry in the Civil War* 3:583–87; Barrett, *Sherman's March,* 117–34, 148–64.

76. Apparently James M. King.

77. Ellen here mourns the destruction of the family's Marietta house.

78. This reference to onion juice—a type of invisible ink—raises yet another question about the persistent rumors that Ellen acted as a spy in Knoxville.

79. Capt. W. J. Robinson, Tenth Tennessee Infantry, had been captured September 17, 1863. "Memorial of the Federal Prison on Johnson's Island," 300.

80. Several weeks later, Ellen's uncle informed her mother from Lexington, Kentucky, concerning Sam's release, "Sam I heard had been sent to Richmond before the surrender and very likely has reached you. Many hundreds have & are coming home, despirited, wrecked, and positionless poor fellows." John D. Matthews to Fanny House, May 19, 1865, House Family Papers.

81. I can find no verification for these reported events in Baltimore.

82. Laudanum, a solution of opium in alcohol, was commonly used for medicinal purposes in the nineteenth century.

83. John S. Reid, Company B, Third Georgia Infantry, had been captured at Gettysburg and sent to Johnson's Island. He was the twenty-four-year-old brother of Sue Reid. Henderson, *Roster of Confederate Soldiers of Georgia* 1:448; 1860 Census (Putnam), 11.

84. Alexander S. Reid, Company G, Twelfth Georgia Infantry, was the twenty-four-year-old son of Andrew Reid, a farmer worth nearly $120,000 in 1860. Henderson, *Roster of Confederate Soldiers of Georgia* 2:214; 1860 Census (Putnam), 11.

85. Grant's losses in the attack on Petersburg are closer to 4,140, of 63,000 engaged. This included 624 killed, 3,189 wounded, 320 missing. E. B. Long, *The Civil War Day by Day: An Almanac 1861–1865* (Garden City, N.Y., 1971), 663.

86. Federal cavalry moved in to occupy Montgomery on April 12.

87. Skirmishing continued at Opelika, Alabama, on April 16.

88. William T. Reid, Company F, Twenty-seventh Battalion Georgia Infantry, was a twenty-seven-year-old farmer worth fifteen hundred dollars in 1860. Henderson, *Roster of Confederate Soldiers of Georgia* 1:448; 1860 Census (Putnam), 82.

89. Ellen refers to Lee's eloquent General Order No. 9, issued April 10 after his surrender at Appomattox on April 9.

90. Lee surrendered about 26,765 men at Appomattox, with another 13,769 captured during the campaign.

91. William H. Seward was severely wounded in an assassination attempt while recovering in bed from a carriage accident. He was saved by a male nurse and a son, Augustus, who was injured but not killed. A second son, Frederick, was also injured by the assassin, Lewis Powell, or Paine. John M. Taylor, *William Henry Seward: Lincoln's Right Hand Man* (New York, 1991), 242–44.

92. Probably Henry P. Cook, twenty-one-year-old son of Marietta tanner Nathaniel Cook. 1850 Census (Cobb), Roll 66, p. 230.

93. Milledgeville is more than sixty miles east of Griffin.

94. Clinton is only about twenty miles southwest of Eatonton.

95. Joseph E. Johnston surrendered to Sherman at Durham Station, North Carolina, on April 26. The controversial surrender terms, based on complex negotiations over several days, were generous, but not so generous as House suggests. Marszalek, *Sherman*, 341–49.

96. B. F. Buddin was a forty-five-year-old farmer worth two thousand dollars in 1860, but his father, who lived with his son, daughter-in-law, and two grandchildren, was worth nearly twelve thousand dollars. 1860 Census (Putnam), 73.

97. *Violet, or the Cross and the Crown,* by Maria J. McIntosh, was published in Boston by John P. Jewett and Company in 1856.

98. Davis was captured at Irwinsville, Georgia, on May 10 with Mrs. Davis, Postmaster General John Reagan, and his private secretary Burton N. Harrison. Gustavus Smith surrendered his remaining Georgia militia at Macon on April 20.

99. Thomas Pearson was the twenty-two-year-old son of Samuel Pearson and a brother of Carrie. 1860 Census (Putnam), 14.

100. Emma V. Adams married John T. Dennis on May 24, 1865. Putnam County Marriage Records, Vol. F, p. 225.

101. Richard A. Reid, thirty-four-year-old brother of Capt. John S. Reid, served in Company G, Twelfth Georgia Infantry and was a regimental quartermaster. 1860 Census (Putnam), 112; Henderson, *Roster of Confederate Soldiers of Georgia* 2:161, 221.

102. F. K. Mitchell was an assistant surgeon in the Twenty-fourth Georgia Infantry. Jones, "Roster of the Medical Officers," 239.

103. Charles Frank House was born in 1848 and died May 27, 1854.

CHAPTER 6. I THOUGHT MY HEART WOULD BURST

1. Aunt Becky is probably forty-five-year-old Elizabeth House of Cobb County. Mary E. Martin, *Cobb County, Georgia, in 1860: A Transcription and Index of the Federal Population Census* (Marietta, 1987), 144–45.

2. The family of fifty-eight-year-old W. L. Latta, a Knoxville tanner, included his wife Mary N., age thirty-nine, and their three children, William (eighteen), George (seventeen), and Mary (fifteen). Each is mentioned in the following paragraph. 1860 Census, 71 (1st).

3. Frances "Priss" Charlton was the twenty-four-year-old daughter of Frances Charlton. 1850 Census (Cobb), Roll 66, p. 94.

4. A. C. Trenholm was a fifty-three-year-old widow worth only $250 in 1860. She had three daughters, age fifteen through twenty-six, who were among Ellen's closest friends when she lived in Marietta. 1860 Census (Cobb), Roll 117, p. 235.

5. J. P. Glover was a forty-three-year-old widow born in South Carolina and worth nearly $130,000 in 1860. Eliza, age twenty-two, was her elder daughter and the sister of Anne. 1860 Census (Cobb), Roll 117, p. 253.

6. R. W. Frazer, a bachelor school teacher, is the only person of that name in the census. John J. Hunt, fifty-four years old, was an Episcopal minister, born in Connecticut. He and his wife had four children. 1860 Census (Cobb), Roll 117, pp. 246, 447.

7. Samuel B. Grant was a thirty-nine-year-old Episcopal minister, born in Connecticut. He and his wife had four children. 1860 Census (Cobb), Roll 117, p. 244.

8. Mr. Cooke was the father of two of Ellen's Marietta friends, Emily and Nellie.

9. The Howell and Hansell families appear in Ellen's diary from the 1850s.

10. Cartersville is about twenty miles northwest of Marietta.

11. Etowah, Tennessee, is about ninety miles north of Cartersville.

12. Thirty-two-year-old William C. Ingles was the youngest son of miller William Ingles and his wife Elizabeth. Their son served in Company B, Fourth Tennessee Cavalry, from Knoxville. 1860 Census, 65 (1st); Wigginton et al., *Tennesseans in the Civil War* 2:219.

13. John House wrote his last surviving letter from Johnson's Island on June 7, 1865. "I have no idea when I will be released," he said, "& think it doubtful if any are *pardoned.*" His uncle had recently sent him five hundred dollars to pay his way home and had advised him to take the oath. "I see no reason why he should hesitate taking the oath," Mr. Matthews told John's mother, "as his people are a vanquished people." John was convinced the family did not receive half his letters. His only remaining correspondents at this time were his parents, his aunt and uncle, and Lila Johnston, in Louisville. John D. Matthews to Fanny House, May 19, 1865, John M. House to Anne B. Matthews, June 7, 1865, UCV Records.

14. John R. Rogers, the twenty-five-year-old son of H. M. Rogers when he enlisted, served either as captain in Company B, Second Tennessee Cavalry, or as lieutenant in Company C, Fifth Tennessee Cavalry Battalion. 1860 Census, 93 (1st); Wigginton et al., *Tennesseans in the Civil War* 2:348.

15. William B. Rogers married Cynthia A. Brooks on February 9, 1865. D'Armand and d'Armand, *Marriage Records,* 887. Pt. Lookout, Maryland, was the North's largest military prison.

16. Possibly either Lambert May, who served on the staff of Gen. James P. Anderson, or John R. May, Eighteenth Tennessee Infantry, who served on the staff of Gen. Joseph P. Palmer. Crute, *Confederate Staff Officers,* 4, 145.

17. Isabella L. French was the forty-five-year-old wife of lawyer William B. French. Luttrell, *Census 1850 for Knox County,* 63.

18. I cannot identify Dr. and Mrs. Murfree, but Richard Luttrell was a seventy-five-year-old farmer worth fifteen hundred dollars before the war. 1860 Census, 234 (18th).

19. Hugh L. W. French was the twenty-seven-year-old son of William and Isabella French. Luttrell, *Census 1850 for Knox Country* 63; Margaret C. White, thirty-five years old, owned a farm and slaves worth $11,500 before the war. 1860 Census, 27 (12th).

20. Charles Coffin was the twenty-three-year-old son of Eliza Coffin. Anna Howard Boyd Fleming was the wife of John M. Fleming. Rothrock, *French Broad–Holston Country,* 401, 418; 1860 Census, 22 (2nd).

21. Ellen fails to identify the wedding couple.

22. John T. Reynolds, Sixty-fourth North Carolina Infantry, was captured in April 1864 at Greeneville. "He was taken to Knoxville and confined in a cage eight feet square. He was allowed to be out of his cage during daylight," stated a report of November 1864. Several attempts were made to exchange him. OR, ser. 2, vol. 7, pp. 561, 1112; vol. 8, pp. 208, 389–90.

23. Probably Mary Hill Alexander.

24. Orra Alexander Baxter was the second wife of John Baxter. They married in 1842. Rothrock, *French Broad–Holston Country,* 376.

25. Montvale Springs, located near Maryville, was a popular watering place.

26. If organized at Chattanooga, this black regiment could be the Forty-fourth U.S. Colored Infantry. However, two other black regiments organized elsewhere in Tennessee—the Fourteenth and Fortieth U.S. Colored Infantry—were based at nearby Greeneville. Wigginton et al., *Tennesseans in the Civil War* 1:399–401, 404, 405, 405–6.

27. Mrs. Mabry could be either Laura E. Mabry, wife of Joseph A. Mabry, a financier, or her sister-in-law Jenett S. Mabry, the wife of George W. Mabry, a farmer worth fifty-six thousand dollars when the war started. 1860 Census, 23 (1st), 20 (10th).

28. Eighteen-year-old Fannie Alexander, sister of Mary Hill Alexander and Charles Alexander. 1860 Census, 90 (1st).

29. Lt. Col. John J. Reese, forty-one years old, served in the Third (Vaughn's) Tennessee Infantry, organized at Knoxville on May 29, 1861, and later designated the Third (Lillard's) Tennessee Mounted Infantry. William B. Reese Jr., a thirty-six-year-old lawyer, was his brother, and the son of Judge William Brown Reese, worth $100,000 when the war started. 1860 Census, 30 (12th); Wigginton et al., *Tennesseans in the Civil War* 1:178–80; Rothrock, *French Broad–Holston Country*, 474.

30. James P. Craighead was the twenty-one-year-old son of bookkeeper Robert Craighead. Luttrell, *Census 1850 for Knox County*, 44; 1860 Census, 28 (12th).

31. Charles A. McClung was the twenty-two-year-old son of Hugh L. McClung. Luttrell, *Census 1850 for Knox County*, 52. He was the husband of Alice.

32. Lucy Alexander, sixteen years old, was a sister of Fannie, Charles, and Mary Hill Alexander. 1860 Census, 90 (1st).

33. The Yankee quartermaster was Captain Hiram S. Chamberlain, mentioned in entry of October 1865.

34. Lizzie Lewis was possibly the thirty-one-year-old daughter of Henry H. Lewis. Luttrell, *Census 1850 for Knox County*, 30.

35. Margaretta F. Scott was the twenty-nine-year-old wife of F. A. R. Scott, a manufacturer worth sixteen thousand dollars before the war. Alice Deaderick McClung was Margaretta's sister, and they were the daughters of D. A. and Elizabeth J. Deaderick. 1860 Census, 61 (1st), 27 (12th); d'Armand and d'Armand, *Marriage Records*, 917.

36. Ed Trigg was the U.S. marshall in Knoxville, described by some as a "little 'swell German major' and 'petty tyrant.'" Clark, *Valleys of the Shadow*, 59.

37. Amanda E. King was the twenty-two-year-old daughter of Joshua H. and Miranda O. King, farmers worth seven thousand dollars in 1860. 1860 Census, 38 (9th).

38. Margaret Cowan McClung was the thirty-one-year-old wife of merchant Charles J. McClung. 1860 Census, 41 (1st); d'Armand and d'Armand, *Marriage Records*, 667.

39. Andrew J. Alexander (d. 1887).

40. George Stoneman (1822–94) and Thomas J. "Stonewall" Jackson both graduated in 1846 from West Point, but Edmund Kirby Smith was a year ahead of them, and William J. Hardee graduated in 1838.

41. Sophia Elizabeth Mitchell was the seventeen-year-old daughter of Thomas and Rosa Mitchell. Lizzie eventually married David Smith in 1868. 1860 Census, 41–42 (1st); d'Armand and d'Armand, *Marriage Records*, 738.

42. A. C. Plumlee. Several Barger (but not Bergar) families resided in Knox County. 1860 Census, 101–4 (11th).

43. *Knoxville Whig and Rebel Ventilator*, Sept. 13, 1865, p. 2, comments on the shooting of D. Foster by W. M. Cox. There is no mention of the three other attacks, but this was clearly a time of violence and reprisals in the first few months after the war. See Thomas B. Alexander, "Neither Peace nor War: Conditions in Tennessee in 1865," *East Tennessee Historical Society's Publications* 21 (1949): 42–29; Fisher, "War at every man's door," 403–9; Groce, "Mountain Rebels," 180–93; Bryan, "Civil War in East Tennessee," 166–84; *Knoxville Whig and Rebel Ventilator*, Aug. 30, 1865, p. 2, Sept. 6, 1865, p. 2, Sept. 13, 1865, p. 2. One Knoxville woman recalled, "When the boys who wore the gray came home . . . [they] were told by a leader of a gang that no Rebel could stay in this town. After daily visits from this leader and his tribe, warning them to leave or be shot, they finally left, . . . some going to Nashville and some to Atlanta." Plant, "Recollections of War," 129–30.

44. James M. King and Mary McClusky were married by James Park on Aug. 17, 1865. D'Armand and d'Armand, *Marriage Records*, 587.

45. Thomas Wallace was the twenty-three-year-old son of Campbell and Susan Wallace. 1860 Census, 26 (12th).

46. Such threats imply a form of legal harassment of former Confederates. Brownlow, who had been elected governor of Tennessee in March 1865, was a leader in seeking this sort of vengeance. He even undertook a private lawsuit against William Sneed. Fisher, "War at every man's door," 410–16; Groce, "Mountain Rebels," 193–99; Coulter, *William G. Brownlow*, 262–93.

47. Crow Ramsey was acquitted at his trial in June 1866. Hesseltine, *Ramsey Autobiography*, 243–45; Ellen House to James Fletcher, June 19, 22, 1866, House Family Papers.

48. This is probably Eveline Cobb, thirty-three-year-old wife of Benjamin Cobb, a farmer worth forty thousand dollars before the war. 1860 Census, Roll 1259, p. 224 (18th).

49. *Knoxville Whig and Rebel Ventilator*, Aug. 30, 1865, p. 2, reports that the murder of Allen Hendricks of the Ninth Tennessee Cavalry (U.S.) was one of several instances of violence against citizens by black troops. The Hendricks incident produced "intense feeling among the Tennessee troops." The community wanted no war against the blacks, insisted Brownlow, but even he stated his opposition to "the freedom with which they use their bayonets and level their muskets at white men."

50. Ivanona Boyd was the twenty-six-year-old wife of fifty-one-year-old James Boyd, a farmer worth forty-three thousand dollars before the war. 1860 Census, 30 (2d).

51. Jonathan Andrews was a thirty-year-old Eatonton doctor, but the connection between Carrie Pearson, Ellie, and him is unclear. 1860 Census (Putnam), 6.

52. Gen. William P. Sanders led a raid through East Tennessee June 14–23, 1863 to disrupt Confederate communications prior to Burnside's advance against Knoxville. Welcher, *Union Army, 1861–1865*, 568.

53. Abner Baker had been a private in Company E, Fourth Tennessee Cavalry Battalion. The man he killed was William Hall, son of M. L. Hall, a clerk of the Federal court in Knoxville. The incident is described very much as House relates it in Rothrock, *French Broad–Holston Country*, 145. See also Williams, "Journal of Events," 107.

54. The Thirteenth Tennessee Cavalry (U.S.) had been organized on authority of General Burnside and mustered in at Strawberry Plains in October–November 1863. The regiment was mustered out at Knoxville, September 5, 1865. Wigginton et al., *Tennesseans in the Civil War* 1:351.

55. Dr. William J. Baker was Abner's uncle. Rothrock, *French Broad–Holston Country*, 373–74.

56. The Baker lynching caused Laura Maynard to declare, "We have had wild times here with rebels." Returning unionist soldiers had "no fondness for 'sesesh,'" and several former Confederate soldiers, sobered by the Baker affair, left town. "You know they used to say that the Union men & 'Southern' men could not live here together," reflected Laura Maynard, "& the former now take them at their word, & send them away." Laura Maynard to Washburn Maynard, September 26, 1865, Maynard Papers. Today a stone marker stands in front of the old Baker home at 9000 Kingston Pike as a memorial to Abner Baker. See Seymour, *Divided Loyalties*, 236, for a photograph of the marker. Hector Coffin was a brother of Charles.

57. The Nineteenth Tennessee Infantry was organized June 11, 1861, at Knoxville. John House was a private in Company E. Wigginton et al., *Tennesseans in the Civil War* 1:214–16, 2:212.

58. Brownlow's account of the Hall shooting in *Knoxville Whig and Rebel Ventilator*, Sept. 6, 1865, p. 2.

59. This is either Samuel R. Latta, Thirteenth Tennessee Infantry, or William S. Latta, Sixteenth Tennessee Cavalry. Wigginton et al., *Tennesseans in the Civil War* 2:244.

60. Joseph A. Mabry (1826–82), a Knoxville financier and brother of George W. Mabry, acted in the development of the Knoxville and Kentucky Railroad. He supported the Confederacy early in the war, but changed sides when Burnside entered Knoxville. Deaderick, *Heart of the Valley*, 564–65; Rothrock, *French Broad–Holston Country*, 76, 111, 130–31, 134, 146, 200, 228–29, 493; Jerome G. Taylor Jr., "The Extraordinary Life and Death of Joseph A. Mabry," *East Tennessee Historical Society's Publications* 44 (1972): 41-70.

61. Isiah Davenport (see diary entry of Nov. 16, 1863), visiting the House family from Cincinnati, seems to have been a garrulous fellow who proved to be more a bore than welcome guest in Ellen's eyes. In a letter of May 13, 1866, she called him "the greatest blow you ever heard talk."

62. Hiram S. Chamberlain, from Ohio, helped to create the Knoxville Iron Company. He had been chief quartermaster at Knoxville during the war. He went on to direct the Roane Iron Company at Rockwood and Chattanooga. Deaderick, *Heart of the Valley*, 32-33. For his wartime memoirs, see "Reminiscences of Knoxville in the Campaign of '63," *Knoxville Journal*, May 7, 1893.

63. Gen. Henry Moses Judah (1821–66).

64. Margaret McDermotte was formally Margaret P. White. She married S. A. McDermotte on July 25, 1865. D'Armand and d'Armand, *Marriage Records,* 673.

65. Tellico Plains, in Monroe County, was located nearly fifty miles southwest of Knoxville.

66. James Washington Fletcher was Ellen's future husband.

67. For the influx of Southerners to northern cities as visitors and emigrants after the war, see Daniel E. Sutherland, *The Confederate Carpetbaggers* (Baton Rouge, 1988).

68. In fact, Mary M. Hazen did capture Thomas W. Cummings. They were married in June 1866. D'Armand and d'Armand, *Marriage Records,* 462.

69. The Church of the Immaculate Conception was erected in 1852. Rothrock, *French Broad–Holston Country,* 296.

70. William Wallace Woodruff, a Federal captain from Kentucky, opened a hardware store on Gay Street in 1865. In time, he became one of Knoxville's leading merchants and citizens. Deaderick, *Heart of the Valley,* 33–34, 96, 350, 411, 418, 653. He married Ella Connelly of Frankfort, Kentucky. *Knoxville Whig and Rebel Ventilator,* Dec. 3, 1865, p. 3.

71. Former Confederate major John C. Thompson lived about seven miles from Nashville on the Franklin Pike. He served with John House on A. P. Stewart's staff as assistant inspector general. Crute, *Confederate Staff Officers,* 186.

72. William Ewing was the gentlemen with whom John had entered a draying business in Nashville.

73. This is the story as it appeared in the *Nashville Daily Press,* Nov. 26, 1865, p. 3. Different versions were published by the *Nashville Dispatch,* Nov. 26, 1865, p. 5, and the *Nashville Republican Banner,* Nov. 26, 1865, p. 2, Dec. 1, 1865, p. 3.

74. William Ford, with whom John had been living in Nashville.

75. Charles T. Quintard had been made the new bishop of the Tennessee diocese on November 24, 1865, the very day John was shot.

76. Joseph McLain was the twenty-two-year-old son of James A. and Martha McLain. Luttrell, *Census 1850 for Knox County,* 111.

77. Several of these former soldiers—Armstrong, White, and French—had reportedly fled town, fearing for their lives, following the lynching of Abner Baker. Laura Maynard to Washburn Maynard, Sept. 26, 1865, Maynard Papers.

78. J. Richard McCann, Reuben Roddie, J. Crozier Ramsey, and William C. Kain were accused of murder because of their role in the trial and execution of bridge-burner A. C. Hawn in 1861. Their case was dismissed by the district court. See Brownlow's criticism in *Knoxville Whig and Rebel Ventilator,* Dec. 20, 1865, p. 1; Groce, "Mountain Rebels," 197.

79. Francis B. Renshaw.

80. Renshaw must have said or done something to offend Andrew Johnson, or he was just unlucky. Johnson's pardon policy was extremely lenient by the end of 1865. While at first giving pardons to former Confederate leaders and wealthy planters on an individual and very limited basis, by September 1865 he was issuing them "wholesale." Eric Foner, *Reconstruction: America's Unfinished Revolution, 1863–1877* (New York, 1988), 190–91.

81. Raphael Semmes, the Confederate admiral, was arrested on December 15 at Mobile and taken to prison in Washington. He was released four months later. For a biography see John M. Taylor, *Confederate Raider: Raphael Semmes of the Alabama* (New York, 1995).

EPILOGUE: PATRIOTISM WILL NOT SAVE THE SOUL

1. *Knoxville Daily Commercial*, June 26, 1866; Ellen House to James Fletcher, June 22, 1866, House Family Papers.

2. For a biography of O'Conner, see Rebecca Hunt Moulder, *May the Sod Rest Lightly: Thomas O'Conner, Halifax Court House, 1836, Knoxville, Tennessee, 1882* (Tucson, Ariz., 1977). For another version of the shooting incident, which involved Joseph Mabry and his son, Joseph Mabry, Jr., see Taylor, "Life and Death of Mabry," 65–69.

3. Ellen House to James Fletcher, June 5, 13, 1866, House Family Papers.

4. Ellen House to James Fletcher, Apr. 29, 1866, House Family Papers.

5. Ellen House to James Fletcher, May 13, July 24, 1866, House Family Papers.

6. Ellen House to James Fletcher, May 23, Aug. 2, 1866, House Family Papers.

Bibliography

PRIMARY SOURCES

Manuscripts

Brabson Family Papers. Special Collections, Univ. of Tennessee, Knoxville.

Elizabeth Baker Crozier Journal. Special Collections, Univ. of Tennessee, Knoxville.

Margaret B. Crozier Diary. Special Collections, Univ. of Tennessee, Knoxville.

D. A. and Inslee Deaderick Papers. McClung Historical Collection, Knox County Public Library, Knoxville.

Hall-Stakely Papers. McClung Historical Collection, Knox County Public Library, Knoxville.

House Family Papers. Possession of Ellen Allran and Victoria Guthrie.

Sam House Letter. Special Collections, Univ. of Tennessee, Knoxville.

Knox County Court House Minute Books, Vol. 22 (1860–64). Knox County Public Library, Knoxville.

Eliza Morgan McClung Diary. Special Collections, Univ. of Tennessee, Knoxville.

Horace Maynard Papers. Special Collections, Univ. of Tennessee, Knoxville.

T. A. R. Nelson Papers. McClung Historical Collection, Knox County Public Library, Knoxville.

Putnam County Confederate Roster, Superior Court Records. Georgia Dept. of Archives and History, Atlanta.

Putnam County Marriage Records, Vol. F, 1848–68. Georgia Dept. of Archives and History, Atlanta.

Putnam County Ordinary County Court Minutes Book, Vol. C, 1864–69. Georgia Dept. of Archives and History, Atlanta.

Mrs. J. G. M. Ramsey Journal. McClung Historical Collection, Knox County Public Library, Knoxville.

O. P. Temple Papers. Special Collections, Univ. of Tennessee, Knoxville.

United Confederate Veterans, Florida Division, Records. Florida Dept. of State, Tallahassee.

Published Records

Callahan, Edward W., ed. *List of Officers of the Navy of the United States and of the Marine Corps from 1775 to 1900.* New York: L. R. Hamersly, 1901.

D'Armand, Roscoe C., and Virginia C. d'Armand, comps. *Knox County, Tennessee, Marriage Records, 1792–1900.* Knoxville: Family Records Society, 1970.

Luttrell, Laura E., comp. *United States Census 1850 for Knox County, Tennessee.* Knoxville: East Tennessee Historical Society, 1949.

Martin, Mary E. *Cobb County, Georgia, in 1860: A Transcription and Index of the Federal Population Census.* Marietta, Ga.: Mary E. Martin, 1987.

Otto, Rhea Cumming, comp. *1850 Census of Georgia: Putnam County.* Savannah, Ga.: Walter W. Otto, 1979.

Sistler, Byron, and Barbara Sistler, eds. *1860 Census—Tennessee.* 5 vols. Nashville: Byron Sistler, 1981.

U.S. Bureau of the Census. *Population Schedule of the Eighth Census of the United States, 1860.* National Archives Microcopy No. 653.

U.S. Navy Dept. *Register of Officers of the Confederate States Navy 1861–1865.* New ed. Mattituck, N.Y.: J. M. Carroll, 1983.

U.S. War Dept. *Official Army Register of the Volunteer Force of the United States Army for the Years 1861, '62, '63, '64, '65.* 8 vols. Washington, D.C.: Government Printing Office, 1865.

———. *War of the Rebellion: A Compilation of the Official Records of the Union and Confederate Armies.* 70 vols. in 128 books and index. Washington, D.C.: Government Printing Office, 1880–1901.

Williams, C. S. *Knoxville Directory, City Guide, and Business Mirror for 1859–60.* Knoxville: C. S. Williams, 1859.

Newspapers

Brownlow's Knoxville Whig and Rebel Ventilator
Knoxville Register
Louisville Journal
Nashville Daily Press
Nashville Dispatch
Nashville Republican Banner

Correspondence, Diaries, and Memoirs

Barber, Flavel C. *Holding the Line: The Third Tennessee Infantry, 1861–1864.* Edited by Robert H. Ferrell. Kent, Ohio: Kent State Univ. Press, 1994.

Brownlow, William G. *Sketches of the Rise, Progress, and Decline of Secession; with a Narrative of Personal Adventures Among the Rebels.* Philadelphia: George W. Childs, 1862.

Campbell, Henry. "Lilly's Battery Nearly Destroyed at Mossy Creek: Campbell Diary—Part V." *Civil War Times Illustrated* 3 (Oct. 1964): 46–48.

———. "Skirmishing in East Tennessee, the Atlanta and Nashville Campaigns, End of the War, and Home: Campbell Diary—Final Installment." *Civil War Times Illustrated* 3 (Dec. 1965): 36–39.

Clark, Walter, ed. *Histories of the Several Regiments and Battalions from North Carolina in the Great War 1861–'65.* 5 vols. Raleigh: E. M. Uzzell, 1901.

Clark, Willene B., ed. *Valleys of the Shadow: The Memoir of Confederate Captain Reuben G. Clark, Company I, 59th Tennessee Mounted Infantry.* Knoxville: Univ. of Tennessee Press, 1994.

Crow, Vernon H., ed. "The Justness of Our Cause: The Civil War Diaries of William W. Stringfield." *East Tennessee Historical Society's Publications* 56–57 (1984–85): 71–101.

Dyer, Gustavus W., and John T. Moore, comps. *The Tennessee Civil War Veterans Questionnaires.* 5 vols. Easley, S.C.: Southern Historical Press, 1985.

Gallagher, Gary W., ed. *Fighting for the Confederacy: The Personal Recollections of General Edward Porter Alexander.* Chapel Hill: Univ. of North Carolina Press, 1989.

Gavin, William G., ed. *Infantryman Pettit: The Civil War Letters of Corporal Frederick Pettit, Late of Company C, 100th Pennsylvania Veteran Volunteer Infantry Regiment, "The Roundheads," 1861–1864.* Shippensburg, Pa.: White Mane, 1990.

Graf, Le Roy P., Ralph W. Haskins, and Paul H. Bergeron, eds. *The Papers of Andrew Johnson.* 12 vols. Knoxville: Univ. of Tennessee Press, 1967–96.

Hesseltine, William B., ed. *Dr. J. G. M. Ramsey: Autobiography and Letters.* Nashville: Tennessee Historical Commission, 1954.

Horn, Stanley F., ed. *Tennessee's War, 1861–1865, Described by Participants.* Nashville: Tennessee Civil War Centennial Commission, 1965.

Humes, Thomas W. *The Loyal Mountaineers of Tennessee.* Knoxville: Ogden Brothers, 1888.

Johnson, Robert Underwood, and Clarence Clough Buel, eds. *Battles and Leaders of the Civil War.* 4 vols. New York: Century, 1887.

Munnerlyn, Tom, ed. *Diary of E. S. Dodd, Co. D, Terry's Texas Rangers & An Account of his Hanging as a Confederate Spy.* Austin: Ranger Press, 1979.

Plant, Mrs. D. A. "Recollections of War as a Child, 1861–65." *Confederate Veteran* 36 (Apr. 1928): 129–30.

Prindle, Paul W., comp. *Ancestry of William Sperry Beinecke.* North Haven, Conn.: Van Dyck, 1974.

Scott, Samuel W., and Samuel P. Angel. *History of the Thirteenth Regiment Tennessee Volunteer Cavalry, U.S.A.* Philadelphia: P. W. Ziegler, 1903.

Sherman, William T. *Memoirs of William T. Sherman.* New York: D. Appleton, 1875.

Simon, John Y., ed. *The Papers of Ulysses S. Grant.* 20 vols. Carbondale: Southern Illinois Univ. Press, 1967–95.

Sullins, D. *Recollections of an Old Man: Seventy Years in Dixie, 1827–1897.* Bristol, Tenn.: King, 1910.

Tarrant, E. *The Wild Riders of the First Kentucky Cavalry: A History of the Regiment in the Great War of the Rebellion, 1861–1865.* Louisville: R. H. Carathers, 1894.

Temple, Oliver P. *East Tennessee and the Civil War.* Cincinnati: Robert Clarke, 1899.

———. *Notable Men of Tennessee, from 1833 to 1875.* New York: Cosmopolitan, 1912.

Ward, James A., ed. *Southern Railroad Man: Conductor N. J. Bell's Recollections of the Civil War Era.* De Kalb: Northern Illinois Univ. Press, 1994.

Williams, Samuel C., ed. "Journal of Events (1825–73) of David Anderson Deaderick." *East Tennessee Historical Society's Publications* 9 (1937): 93–110.

Worsham, W. J. *The Old Nineteenth Tennessee Regiment, C.S.A.* Knoxville: Paragon, 1902.

SECONDARY SOURCES

Alexander, Thomas B. "Is Civil War History Polarized?—A Question Suggested by the Career of Thomas A. R. Nelson." *East Tennessee Historical Society's Publications* 29 (1957): 10–39.

———. "Neither Peace nor War: Conditions in Tennessee in 1865." *East Tennessee Historical Society's Publications* 21 (1949): 33–51.

———. *Thomas A. R. Nelson of East Tennessee.* Nashville: Tennessee Historical Society, 1956.

Allardice, Bruce L. "Longstreet's Nightmare in Tennessee." *Civil War Magazine* 18 (June 1989): 31–43.

Barrett, John C. *Sherman's March Through the Carolinas.* Chapel Hill: Univ. of North Carolina Press, 1956.

Boatner, Mark M., III. *The Civil War Dictionary.* Rev. ed. New York: David McKay, 1988.

Boeger, Palmer H. "General Burnside's Knoxville Packing Project." *East Tennessee Historical Society's Publications* 35 (1963): 76–84.

Brown, Ann L. B. "Fort Delaware: The Most Dreaded Northern Prison." *Civil War Quarterly* 10 (Sept. 1987): 36–40.

Bryan, Charles F., Jr. "The Civil War in East Tennessee: A Social, Political, and Economic Study." Ph.D. diss., Univ. of Tennessee, 1978.

———. "A Gathering of Tories: The East Tennessee Convention of 1861." *Tennessee Historical Quarterly* 39 (Spring 1980): 27–48.

———. "'Tories' Amidst the Rebels: Confederate Occupation of East Tennessee, 1861–63." *East Tennessee Historical Society's Publications* 60 (1988): 3–22.

Bryan, T. Conn. *Confederate Georgia.* Athens: Univ. of Georgia Press, 1953.

Burton, E. Milby. *The Siege of Charleston, 1861–1865.* Columbia: Univ. of South Carolina Press, 1970.

Campbell, Mary E. R. *The Attitude of Tennesseans Toward the Union, 1847–1861.* New York: Vantage Press, 1961.

Corley, Florence F. *Confederate City: Augusta, Georgia, 1860–1865.* Columbia: Univ. of South Carolina Press, 1960.

Coulter, E. Merton. *William G. Brownlow: Fighting Parson of the Southern Highlands.* Chapel Hill: Univ. of North Carolina Press, 1937.

Creekmore, Betsey B. *Knoxville.* 2d ed. Knoxville: Univ. of Tennessee Press, 1967.

Crofts, Daniel W. *Reluctant Confederates: Upper South Unionists in the Secession Crisis.* Chapel Hill: Univ. of North Carolina Press, 1989.

Crow, Vernon H. "Justice for General Frazer." *Civil War Times Illustrated* 9 (Dec. 1970): 20–27.

———. *Storm in the Mountains: Thomas' Confederate Legion of Cherokee Indians and Mountaineers.* Cherokee, N.C.: Museum of the Cherokee Indian, 1982.

Crute, Joseph H., Jr. *Confederate Staff Officers, 1861–1865*. Powhatan, Va.: Derwent Books, 1982.

Current, Richard N. *Lincoln's Loyalists: Union Soldiers from the Confederacy*. Boston: Northeastern Univ. Press, 1992.

Current, Richard N., ed. *Encyclopedia of the Confederacy*. 4 vols. New York: Simon & Schuster, 1993.

Davidson, James F. "Michigan and the Defense of Knoxville, Tennessee, 1863." *East Tennessee Historical Society's Publications* 35 (1963): 21–53.

Davis, William C. "Massacre at Saltville." *Civil War Times Illustrated* 9 (Feb. 1971): 4–11, 43–48.

Davis, William C., ed. *The Confederate General*. 6 vols. New York: National Historical Society, 1991.

Deaderick, Lucile, ed. *Heart of the Valley: A History of Knoxville, Tennessee*. Knoxville: East Tennessee Historical Society, 1976.

Faust, Patricia L., ed. *Historical Times Illustrated Encyclopedia of the Civil War*. New York: Harper & Row, 1986.

Finger, John R. *The Eastern Band of Cherokees, 1819–1900*. Knoxville: Univ. of Tennessee Press, 1984.

Fink, Harold S. "The East Tennessee Campaign and the Battle of Knoxville in 1863." *East Tennessee Historical Society's Publications* 29 (1957): 79–117.

Fisher, Noel. "'The Leniency Shown Them Has Been Unavailing': The Confederate Occupation of East Tennessee." *Civil War History* 40 (Dec. 1994): 275–91.

————. "'War at every man's door': The Struggle for East Tennessee, 1860–1869." Ph.D. diss., Ohio State Univ., 1993.

Garrett, Franklin M. *Atlanta and Environs: A Chronicle of Its People and Events*. 3 vols. Athens: Univ. of Georgia Press, 1969–87.

Godbold, E. Stanley, Jr., and Mattie Russell. *Confederate Colonel and Cherokee Chief: The Life of William Holland Thomas*. Knoxville: Univ. of Tennessee Press, 1990.

Groce, W. Todd. "Mountain Rebels: East Tennessee Confederates and the Civil War." Ph.D. diss., Univ. of Tennessee, 1992.

Harris, William C. "The East Tennessee Relief Movement of 1864–1865." *Tennessee Historical Quarterly* 48 (Summer 1989): 86–96.

————. "East Tennessee's Civil War Refugees and the Impact of the Civil War on Civilians." *Journal of East Tennessee History* 64 (1992): 3–19.

Haskew, Michael E. "Icy Assault Routed." *America's Civil War* 4 (May 1991): 23–28.

Heitman, Francis B. *Historical Register and Dictionary of the United States Army, From Its Organization, September 19, 1789, to March 2, 1903*. 2 vols. Washington, D.C.: Government Printing Office, 1903.

Henderson, Lillian, ed. *Roster of Confederate Soldiers of Georgia, 1861–1865*. 6 vols. and index. Spartanburg, S.C., 1982.

Hesseltine, William B. *Civil War Prisons: A Study in War Psychology*. New York: Frederick Unger, 1964.

Holland, Cecil F. *Morgan and His Raiders*. New York: Macmillan, 1943.

Holmes, Clay W. *The Elmira Prison Camp: A History of the Military Prison at Elmira, N.Y., July 6, 1864, to July 10, 1865*. New York: G. P. Putnam's Sons, 1912.

Huff, Lawrence. "'A Bitter Draught We Have Had to Quaff': Sherman's March Through the Eyes of Joseph Addison Turner." *Georgia Historical Quarterly* 72 (Summer 1988): 306–26.

Inscoe, John C. "The Confederate Home Front Sanitized: Joel Chandler Harris' *On the Plantation* and Sectional Reconciliation." *Georgia Historical Quarterly* 76 (Fall 1992): 652–74.

Jones, Joseph. "Roster of the Medical Officers of the Army of Tennessee." *Southern Historical Society Papers* 22 (1894): 165–280.

Klein, Maury. "The Knoxville Campaign." *Civil War Times Illustrated* 10 (Oct. 1971): 4–10, 40–45.

Krick, Robert K. *Lee's Colonels: A Biographical Register of the Field Officers of the Army of Northern Virginia*. 4th ed. Dayton, Ohio: Morningside Press, 1992.

Lindsley, John B., ed. *The Military Annals of Tennessee, Confederate*. Nashville: J. M. Lindsley, 1886.

Lucas, Marion B. *Sherman and the Burning of Columbia*. College Station: Texas A&M Univ. Press, 1976.

Lufkin, Charles L. "Secession and Coercion in Tennessee, the Spring of 1861." *Tennessee Historical Quarterly* 50 (Summer 1991): 98–109.

MacArthur, William J. "The Early Career of Charles McClung McGhee." *East Tennessee Historical Society's Publications* 45 (1973): 3–13.

Marvel, William. *Burnside*. Chapel Hill: Univ. of North Carolina Press, 1991.

"Memorial of the Federal Prison on Johnson's Island, Lake Erie, Ohio, 1862–1864, Containing a List of Prisoners of War from the Confederate States Army." *Collections of the Virginia Historical Society*, n.s., 6 (Richmond: W. M. Ellis Jones, 1887).

Mohon, James L. "Defending the Confederate Heartland: Company F of Henry Ashby's 2nd Tennessee Cavalry." *Civil War Regiments* 5 (Mar. 1994): 1–43.

Moulder, Rebecca Hunt. *May the Sod Rest Lightly: Thomas O'Conner, Halifax Court House, 1836, Knoxville, Tennessee, 1882*. Tucson, Ariz.: Skyline Printing, 1977.

Needham, Joseph W. "Oliver Perry Temple: Entrepreneur, Agrarian, and Politician." Ph.D. diss., Univ. of Tennessee, 1990.

Novelli, Dean. "On a Corner of Gay Street: History of the Lamar House–Bijou Theater, Knoxville, Tennessee, 1817–1985." *East Tennessee Historical Society's Publications* 56–57 (1984–85): 3–45.

Partin, Robert. "The Wartime Experiences of Margaret McCalla: Confederate Refugee from East Tennessee." *Tennessee Historical Quarterly* 24 (Spring 1965): 39–53.

Partin, Winfred. "Contesting Cumberland Gap." *America's Civil War* 4 (July 1991): 27–32.

Patton, James W. *Union and Reconstruction in Tennessee, 1860–1869*. Chapel Hill: Univ. of North Carolina Press, 1934.

Piston, William G. "Carter's Raid, Part I." *East Tennessee Historical Society's Publications* 49 (1977): 61–76.

———. "Carter's Raid, Part II." *East Tennessee Historical Society's Publications* 50 (1978): 31–57.

Rentfro, Jack. "Remnants of Civil War Knoxville." *Civil War Times Illustrated* 33 (May–June 1994): 50–60.

Rietti, J. C., comp. *Military Annals of Mississippi*. Spartanburg, S.C.: Reprint Company, 1976.

Rothrock, Mary U., ed. *The French Broad–Holston Country: A History of Knox County, Tennessee*. Knoxville: East Tennessee Historical Society, 1946.

Rowell, John W. "The Battle of Mossy Creek." *Civil War Times Illustrated* 8 (July 1969): 10–16.

———. *Yankee Cavalrymen: Through the War with the Ninth Pennsylvania Cavalry*. Knoxville: Univ. of Tennessee Press, 1971.

Rule, William, ed. *Standard History of Knoxville, Tennessee*. Chicago: Lewis Publishing, 1900.

Seymour, Digby G. *Divided Loyalties: Fort Sanders and the Civil War in East Tennessee*. Rev. ed. Knoxville: East Tennessee Historical Society, 1982.

Sutherland, Daniel E. "Blind Justice." *Civil War Times Illustrated* 35 (May 1996): 28–35.

Swanson, Guy, and Timothy D. Johnson. "Conflict in East Tennessee: Generals Law, Jenkins, and Longstreet." *Civil War History* 31 (June 1985): 101–10.

Symonds, Craig L. *Joseph E. Johnston: A Civil War Biography*. New York: W. W. Norton, 1992.

Tapp, Hambleton. "Incidents in the Life of Frank Wolford, Colonel of the First Kentucky Union Cavalry." *Filson Club History Quarterly* 10 (Jan. 1936): 82–99.

Taylor, Jerome G., Jr. "The Extraordinary Life and Death of Joseph A. Mabry." *East Tennessee Historical Society's Publications* 44 (1972): 41–70.

Temple, Sarah B. G. *The First Hundred Years: A Short History of Cobb County in Georgia*. Atlanta: Walter W. Brown, 1935.

Wallenstein, Peter. "Which Side Are You On? The Social Origins of White Union Troops from Civil War Tennessee." *Journal of East Tennessee History* 63 (1991): 72–103.

Warner, Ezra J. *Generals in Blue: Lives of the Union Commanders*. Baton Rouge: Louisiana State Univ. Press, 1964.

———. *Generals in Gray: Lives of the Confederate Commanders*. Baton Rouge: Louisiana State Univ. Press, 1959.

Wert, Jeffry D. *General James Longstreet: The Confederacy's Most Controversial Soldier—a Biography*. New York: Simon & Schuster, 1993.

Wigginton, Thomas A., et al. *Tennesseans in the Civil War: A Military History of Confederate and Union Units with Available Rosters of Personnel*. 2 vols. Nashville: Civil War Centennial Commission, 1964–65.

Wilson, Sandra S., and Dennis L. Snapp, eds. *Broken Hearts, Broken Lives: Jefferson County, Tennessee, 1860–1868: Civilian Life in the Civil War*. Jefferson City, Tenn.: Jefferson City Printing, 1986.

Index